Psychology AS

The Complete Companion

Mike Cardwell

•

Cara Flanagan

Published in 2005 by:

Nelson Thornes Ltd
Delta Place
27 Bath Road
CHELTENHAM
GL53 7TH
United Kingdom

06 07 08 09 / 10 9 8 7 6 5 4 3

A catalogue record for this book is available from the British Library

ISBN 0 7487 9463 8

Illustrations by Angela Lumley, Ed McLachlan, Mick Stubbs

Page make-up by Patricia Briggs and GreenGate Publishing Services

Printed in Croatia by Zrinski

Acknowledgements

Action Plus Sports Images (p. 95); Associated Press / Stuart Ramson (p. 144 [top]); BBC Photograph Library (p. 103); John Birdsall Photography (p. 104); Bridgeman Art Library (pp. 134/135 [top]); British Film Institute (p. 170); Bubbles / Denise Hager (pp. 65, 192); Bubbles / Jennie Woodcock (p. 71); Bubbles / Loisjoy Thurston (p. 55); Corbis / Bettman (pp. 136, 141, 163 [both]); Corbis / Russ Ressmeyer (p. 6 [both]); Digital Vision 17 (NT) (p. 151); Families & Work Institute, New York, USA (p. 69); Family Life Picture Library / Angela Hampton (p. 57); The Far Side ® by Gary Larsen © 1984 Far Works Inc, All Rights Reserved (p. 166); Getty Images (p. 26); Grantland Cartoons (p. 113); Harlow Primate Laboratory, University of Wisconsin, Madison, USA (p. 54); Holt Studios (p. 45); Hulton Getty Archive (pp. 3, 174, 175 [bottom]); Jorvik Viking Centre (p. 20); Nick D Kim (p. 127); Kobal Collection (p. 67); Elizabeth Loftus (pp. 32, 33); Mary Evans Picture Library (p. 175 [top]); Mirror Syndication (p. 145); NON SEQUITUR © 2001 Wiley Miller, distributed by Universal Press Syndicate (p. 180); NY Newsletter / Sands / Corbis Sygma (p. 181); Obedience © 1965 by Stanley Milgram, courtesy of Alexandra Milgram (pp. 176, 179); PAWS, INC. © 2001 distributed by Universal Press Syndicate (p. 87); Popperfoto / Alamy (p. 171); Popperfoto / Rick Wilking / Reuters (p. 188); Retna / Andrew Kent (p. 173); Rex Features Limited (p. 59 [bottom]); Rex Features Limited / Timepix (p. 56); Joyce Robertson (pp. 59 [top], 62); The Ronald Grant Archive (p. 134 [bottom]); Nick Rose (p. 12); Shout Picture Library (p. 30); Robert Thompson (p. 74); © Transport for London (p. 8); Wellcome Trust Medical Photographic Library (pp. 90, 132 [all], 133, 144 [bottom]); Wellcome Trust Medical Photographic Library / Anthes Sieveking (p. 110); Philip Zimbardo, Psychology Department, Stanford University (p. 186 [both])

Contents

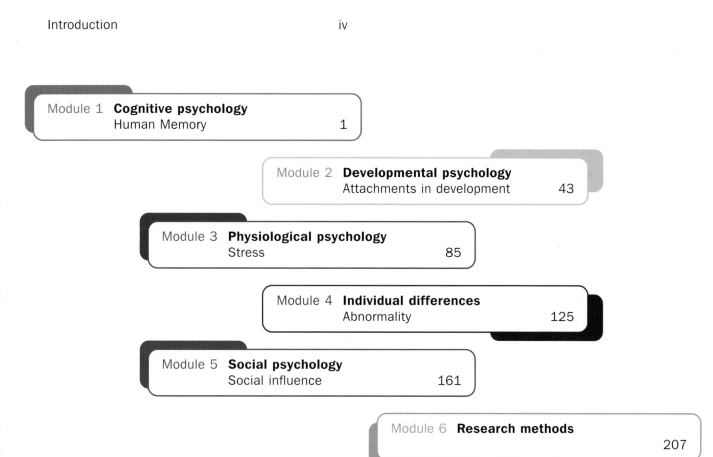

Introduction

How to use this book

We have divided the book into six modules, and each module into three sections – reflecting the structure of the AQA A AS specification. Each section starts with an introduction and consists of about five double-page spreads (some sections are longer than others). Each of these spreads is intended to be equivalent to one hour of studying time. You may find that you want to spend more time on some spreads, but we think they are 'one hour's worth of work'.

Each module ends with summaries and multiple-choice questions for every section, and a list of research terms covered in the module. There is also a list of revision topics for the module, plus sample examination questions, with two sets of student answers and examiner's comments, and a question to try yourself.

The final module, on research methods, is a bit different because this material is actually discussed throughout the book. Module 6 is a summary of research methods and related issues plus some sample questions. Throughout the book there are also ideas for research activities.

In total, there are 65 double-page spreads (65 hours, though some are optional), 15 introductions, 15 summaries, 150 MCQs, 10 sets of exam-style questions and answers plus the research methods section (with more questions). We have also included the occasional website, but remember that websites come and go, so don't be disappointed if such links turn out to be nonexistent.

We hope we have written a book that is (like the authors) fun, attractive, highly informative and above all will help you pass your exam!

Note about this revised edition

This edition has been updated to match the revised AQA A AS specification for teaching from September 2005. The new specification can be found at www.aqa.org.uk/qual/pdf/AQA-5181-6181-W-SP-06.pdf.

Dedication

To Denise: my 'complete companion' (MC)

To Rob: my 'fixt foot ... thy firmness makes my circle just' – John Donne (CF)

Acknowledgements

The authors would like to thank Rick Jackman and Peter Oates at Nelson Thornes for having the commendable lack of good sense to agree to this project in the first place and thereafter arguing our corner at every turn. We would also like to extend our gratitude to Louise Watson for the exacting work that goes on behind every book, Nigel Harriss for the brilliant cover and, especially, to Patricia Briggs for making it all look so good on the page. Mike would also like to apologise to his colleagues in the psychology department at Bath Spa – Dr Alison Lee and Dr Nigel Holt – for using their names so flippantly throughout the student answers and for reminding him that, even after all these years, psychology can still be good fun.

Mike Cardwell

Cara Flanagan

Cognitive psychology is one area of psychology. Cognitive psychologists believe that human behaviour can be best explained if we first understand the mental processes that underlie behaviour. It is, therefore, the study of how people learn, structure, store and use knowledge – essentially, how people think about the world around them.

Cognitive psychology

Human memory

Short-term memory and long-term memory

We all have jokes about failing memory, as well as numerous experiences where our own memories have let us down in some way. But what is memory, and how does it work? These are questions that psychologists have been trying to provide answers to for over a century. The Oxford English Dictionary defines memory as 'the ability to keep things in one's mind and recall them at will'. This would have been especially important to our ancestors, as they would have been able to remember the best places to hunt and gather food, potential dangers, and effective avoidance strategies. Memory has undoubted significance for our survival, but probably never evolved as an efficient system for

specification breakdown

Specification content	Comment
Research into the nature of short-term memory (STM) and long-term memory (LTM) (e.g. encoding, capacity and duration).	One way to consider human memory is to look at the characteristics of **short-** and **long-term memory**. One way to distinguish between these memory stores is in terms of **encoding** (how the material is stored), **capacity** (how much data can be held in the store) and **duration** (how long the memory lasts).
The multi-store model of memory (Atkinson & Shiffrin) and at least one alternative to this (e.g. working memory: Baddeley & Hitch; levels of processing: Craik & Lockhart).	One model of memory is named in the specification: the **multi-store model**. This means that you must study this model. In addition you are required to study **one alternative model**, such as working memory or levels of processing. For each of the two models that you study you must be able to describe them and demonstrate your understanding, be familiar with appropriate research evidence, and also with the criticisms of the model.

remembering vast numbers of facts for examinations or accurate representations of childhood events. The famous Swiss psychologist, Jean Piaget, once reported a vivid memory of nearly being kidnapped when he was 2. He recalled watching his nurse bravely fighting off the kidnapper, the scratches she received in the process, and a policeman with a short cloak and white baton who finally chased the kidnapper away. All of these were real memories for Piaget yet, in a letter to his parents when he was 15, his nurse admitted that she had, in fact, made up the whole story. Piaget had somehow heard it when he was very young and created a visual memory that, although recalled as if it were real, was actually false.

The first memory that Cara can recall is when her cat had four kittens, which were born on her fourth birthday. What does this tell us about memory?

Mike says he can still remember the names of all the players in the 1965–66 Liverpool team. What does this tell us about memory?

We may have similar false memories from our childhood, but usually experience memory failures on more familiar grounds. If we try to remember our own mobile telephone number, the contents of a book we have just read, or even a round of drinks, our memory might let us down. Yet in other areas we might demonstrate an astounding ability to recall events that happened years ago on holiday, the exact route to where we live, the 1965 Liverpool cup-winning team, even the precise details of what we were doing when we first heard of the death of Princess Diana or the attack on the World Trade Centre on 11 September 2001.

The fallibility of human memory also has important implications for the legal system, particularly when people are called to give their 'eyewitness testimony' connected with a crime. Human memory does not function like a video recorder, so is not particularly suitable for the accurate recall of crime events. The testimony of a witness can mean the difference between a guilty person being prosecuted or a culprit getting away with a crime. Memory, then, has both personal and institutional significance. This first section of the book gets close up to one of the most fallible yet fantastic aspects of human ability.

Try this: Below is a string of digits, each in a separate box. Cover all the boxes except the first and say the digit, then shut your eyes and recall it. Were you right? Now try it with two digits: look at the two digits, cover them up, recall them and check to see if you were correct. Keep going until you don't get them right.

| 2 | 4 | 3 | 7 | 5 | 9 | 4 | 6 | 2 | 1 | 5 | 3 | 2 | 8 | 0 |

How many digits could you recall correctly? This is the capacity of your immediate or short-term memory.

What is meant by memory, STM and LTM?

The term **memory** has a number of meanings in psychology, but the essential definition is that it refers to the process by which we *retain information about events that have happened in the past*. Note that 'the past' does not simply refer to things that happened *years* ago, but things in our immediate past. Your memory for events in the present or immediate past is referred to as your **short-term memory** (or STM for short). Your memory for events that have happened in the more distant past is referred to as your **long-term memory** (or LTM for short).

LTM refers to memories that last anywhere from 2 minutes to 100 years or more, i.e. anything that isn't short-term. LTM is like having a library with virtually unlimited storage capacity. We might think about STM as resembling a notepad where we mentally scribble down things that we need to remember for just a short period of time. The trouble with this 'notepad' is that it can't hold much information and the 'ink' fades very quickly. An example of STM in action would be trying to remember a 7-digit phone number you have just been given. This is maintained in STM by repetition until the number is dialed, and then fades once the conversation starts.

The way most people keep information in their STM for more than a few seconds is to *rehearse* it. So rehearsal – saying something to yourself over and over to keep re-presenting it to the STM – is one way of keeping a memory active.

The process of memory has three stages: *encoding*, *storage* and *retrieval*.

Encoding	This stage is where we actually *create* a memory trace, i.e. a representation of an event in our memory.
Storage	Once encoded, we need to store the memory trace somewhere within the memory system.
Retrieval	Storing a memory isn't enough – we also need to be able to *recall* or *remember* it.

How are STM and LTM different?

STM and LTM differ in three important ways: **duration**, **capacity** and **encoding**.

Duration	STM has a very limited duration (a memory in STM doesn't last long), whereas LTM has potentially unlimited duration. A memory in LTM could, theoretically, last for the whole of a person's life.
Capacity	This is a measure of how much can be held in memory. STM has a very limited capacity (7-plus-or-minus-2 'chunks' of information), whereas LTM has potentially unlimited capacity.
Encoding	Information in STM tends to be encoded *acoustically* (i.e. information is represented as *sounds*), whereas information in LTM tends to be encoded *semantically* (i.e. information is represented by its *meaning*).

starSTUDY

The nature of STM
(PETERSON & PETERSON, 1959)

Some people who suffer from poor memories develop techniques to improve their memory. One is to repeat something over and over again. This is called *verbal rehearsal*. The result of such rehearsal is that short-term memories are held in the short-term memory store and eventually become long-term, i.e. the item will be remembered.

Aims

Lloyd and Margaret Peterson set out to investigate the duration of short-term memories, i.e. how long it is before such memories disappear. All psychology studies have an **aim**. This is a statement of what the researcher(s) intend to find out. Peterson and Peterson aimed to systematically study how long information is retained in memory when there is no verbal rehearsal. In other words, they had three aims: to conduct a systematic and controlled study; to look at the duration of immediate or short-term memory; and to do this when verbal rehearsal is prevented.

Star studies

In the AQA specification you need to know a lot of detail about a selected group of 16 studies, which we've called 'star studies'. You may be asked to describe the aims, procedures, findings, conclusions and criticisms (*apfcc*) of these studies. You need to know about many studies conducted by psychologists, but you only need to know *apfcc* details for the star studies.

KEY TERMS

Memory: The process by which we retain information about events that have happened in the past. This includes fleeting (short-term) memories as well as memories that last for a few hours or days (long-term), and those memories that last a lifetime (also long-term).

Short-term memory: Your memory for immediate events. Short-term memories last for a very short time and disappear unless they are rehearsed. The short-term memory store has limited duration and limited capacity.

Long-term memory: Your memory for events that have happened in the past. This lasts anywhere from 2 minutes to 100 years. The long-term memory store has potentially unlimited duration and capacity.

What is the difference between a finding and a conclusion?

A finding is what was found out. It consists of pieces of factual information such as percentage of correct answers. A conclusion is an interpretation of the facts – your opinion, based on the facts.

There is more than one kind of long-term memory

A criticism that is made about many memory experiments is that they relate to one *particular* kind of memory. We actually have lots of different kinds of memory: memory for words (**semantic memory**), memory for what you did yesterday or a film you saw last week (**episodic memory**), and memory for riding a bicycle (**procedural memory**). Most memory experiments are concerned with semantic memory and the findings don't necessarily apply to other kinds of memory.

Procedures

Peterson and Peterson enlisted the help of 24 students attending their university (a very common way to find willing participants in psychology). Recall was tested as follows: the experimenter said a *nonsense trigram* to the participant (e.g. WRT), and then said a 3-digit number. The participant had to count backwards from this number in 3s or 4s until told to stop. Then the participant was asked to recall the nonsense trigram. Each participant was given 2 practice trials followed by 8 trials. On each trial the *retention interval* (time spent counting backwards) was different: 3, 6, 9, 12, 15 or 18 seconds.

Findings

Participants remembered more words accurately when they only had a 3-second retention interval and recalled far fewer words when the retention interval was 18 seconds. They remembered about 90% when there was only a 3-second interval and about 2% when there was an 18-second interval. The findings are shown in the line graph.

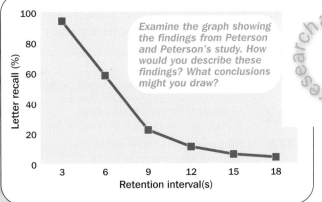

Examine the graph showing the findings from Peterson and Peterson's study. How would you describe these findings? What conclusions might you draw?

Conclusions

The point of any research study is to *draw conclusions*, i.e. to make some statement about what the findings show. We can conclude from this study that information remains in STM for less than 18 seconds if verbal rehearsal is prevented. In fact, much information has disappeared within a few seconds. This allows us to assess the duration of STM.

Why was it necessary to count backwards during the retention interval?

Do you think that Peterson and Peterson's findings are right? Use the standardised instructions from this study (see below) and try them out on some participants. (You need *naive* participants who don't know the experimental aims. This is called a **single blind design**, because the experimenter knows the aim but the participants don't.)

Whenever conducting research you must behave as a proper psychologist and make sure that you treat participants with respect. You must inform them of your aims beforehand, if possible, or tell them afterwards what the aims were. Do not bring psychology into disrepute!

Criticisms

What does this study actually tell us about real life?

A major problem for a lot of psychological research into memory is that tests using strings of consonants (nonsense trigrams) in a **laboratory** are not much like what we do in real life. What was the last thing that you remembered? It might have been something related to schoolwork or a new skill (e.g. riding a bicycle). An important criticism of memory research is that it relates to one aspect of memory and may not apply to all memory.

Students are not like everyone else

A great deal of research in psychology is based on the behaviour of students. It is quite likely that people aged 18–21 have rather different memories than people of other age groups, and students may be more than averagely intelligent! Psychology students are also likely to try to guess what the experiment is about and this may affect their behaviour (and the findings). This is called **participant reactivity** – the fact that participants react to cues in an experimental situation. The single blind technique can be used to reduce this 'reactivity'. In addition, the **double blind design** can be used, where the investigator is also unaware of the purpose of the experiment and therefore cannot communicate any cues.

Research methods
What is research?

Anyone can have an opinion about human behaviour. You probably have lots of them, such as believing that if you eat less you will lose weight, or that girls have a better sense of humour than boys. But how do you know? Scientists aim to produce answers that are better than *common sense*. They do this by conducting *well-controlled* studies. Throughout this book we will look at how they do this.

Research methods
Standardised instructions

Peterson and Peterson read the following standardised instructions to each participant: 'Please sit against the back of your chair so that you are comfortable. You will not be shocked during this experiment. In front of you is a little black box. The top or green light is on now. The green light means we are ready to begin a trial. I will speak some letters and then a number. You are to repeat the number immediately after I say it and begin counting backwards by 3s (4s) from that number in time with the clock ticking that you hear. I might say ABC 309. Then you say, 309, 306, 303, etc. until the bottom or red light comes on. When you see this red light you stop counting immediately and say the letters that were given at the beginning of the trial. Remember to keep your eyes on the black box at all times. There will be a short rest period and then the green light will come on again and we will start a new trial.'

Such standardised instructions ensure that each participant hears exactly the same unambiguous instructions. If this were not the case, the participants' performance might vary because of receiving different instructions – which would threaten the meaningfulness of the findings.

The nature of STM and LTM

I n the first spread, you examined an experiment on memory in detail. On this spread we will look at various other studies related to duration, capacity and encoding. Such research supports the view that short- and long-term memory are different.

Gerald J. Bricca
Gerry gave generously of his time and talents during his four years to the swimming team, the 'Sanc.', the Sodality, the Inside SI and the IRC.

Gerald L. Brown
Gerald was a four-year basketball player with the lightweights, a member of the 'Sanc.', Sodality, Block Club and the IRC Dance Committee.

▲ Photographs from a high-school yearbook. Forty years on, would participants still remember the names of their classmates?

starSTUDY

The nature of LTM

(BAHRICK *ET AL.*, 1975)

What is your earliest memory? Whatever it was, it must have been quite a long time ago. Does this demonstrate that memory is long-lasting?

Aims

Some studies have looked at the duration of memory over time but have found that memories fade. It is possible that memories actually last much longer than was found in these studies. The problem is that the information people were asked to remember was not very interesting, which is why it was forgotten. In real life people have many things they remember over a long time, but these tend to be personally important things. This study aimed to investigate VLTM in a natural setting where the things to be remembered were of personal significance. The study also aimed to compare verbal and visual LTM.

Procedures

Nearly 400 participants aged 17–74 were tested. There were various tests, including:

1 A free-recall test where participants were asked to list all the names they could remember of individuals in their graduating class.

2 A photo-recognition test consisting of 50 photos, some of which were from the participant's high school yearbook.
3 A name-recognition test for ex-school friends.

There was also a photo-matching test, a name-matching test and a photo-cueing test.

Findings

Participants who were tested within 15 years of graduation were about 90% accurate in identifying faces and names (i.e. visual and verbal recognition).

After 48 years, this declined to about 80% for name recognition and 70% for photo recognition.

Free recall was less good. After 15 years this was about 60% accurate, dropping to 30% after 48 years.

Conclusions

There is evidence of very long-term memories up to 57 years after graduation, though there is some loss of memory over time. People remembered the names (verbal recall) almost as well as the faces (visual recall). Recognition was better than recall. This suggests that in real life our memories contain a vast amount of information but we are not always able to recall it. When given a recognition test this jogs our memory and we can remember it (VLTM). Therefore our vast store of memory is there but not always easily accessed.

Criticisms

This is a good way to test memory

Studies carried out in the laboratory have found much poorer retention over long periods than were found in this study. This is probably because such studies involve rather trivial information and people have little motivation to remember it. This means that psychologists build up theories based on data which are not true to real life.

Were there some things that weren't controlled?

It is possible that the reason for better recall in this study than when memories are tested in laboratory settings was because the participants regularly rehearsed this knowledge. They might have even seen ex-classmates regularly. The researchers tried to control for this by asking participants how often the participants met up with past classmates and looked at their yearbooks. They found that recent graduates saw classmates and looked in their yearbooks a lot, but this tailed off the longer it was since they left school.

Research methods
Experiments

Baddeley's study is an **experiment**. An experiment is a particular kind of study where there is an **independent variable** (**IV**) and a **dependent variable** (**DV**). In Baddeley's experiment the IV was the kind of list (acoustic or semantic, similar or dissimilar). The experimenter *manipulates* the IV – i.e. he or she determines when and how the IV is given to someone. The DV in Baddeley's experiment was recall – how many words a participant correctly recalled. The DV is something that is *measured* by the experimenter. The DV *depends* in some way on the IV.

Baddeley's study is called a **laboratory experiment** because it took place in a room set aside especially for conducting the study – an *artificial* environment.

The study by Bahrick *et al.* (see page 6) is called a **natural experiment**. There was an IV (length of time since initial learning) and a DV (recall), but in this case the IV was not directly controlled by the experimenter – it varied naturally and the experimenters were able to make use of this natural IV.

The need for controls

It could be that some of the participants in Baddeley's experiment couldn't hear very well and this would explain their poor performance, rather than being acoustically confused. To check for this Baddeley gave all participants a listening test, where they listened to words on a tape recorder and wrote them down. Any participants who didn't score perfectly on this test were not used. Poor hearing could be an **extraneous variable** that might affect the dependent variable (recall) and potentially spoil the findings.

Research into the nature of STM

Duration of STM

The study by Peterson and Peterson (on the previous spread) demonstrated that STM has a very short duration. This is supported in a study by Sebrechts *et al.* (1989) where the duration of STM was tested by showing participants 3 words. Then the participants were asked to recall the words (they didn't expect this and therefore shouldn't have been rehearsing them). They did quite well if they were tested immediately but if the researcher waited even 4 seconds, recall was almost zero. This supports the notion that STM has a very limited duration when data is not rehearsed or processed.

Capacity of STM

A very ancient study by Jacobs (1887) demonstrated the capacity of STM using the serial digit span technique. A participant is presented with a sequence of digits and required to repeat them back in the original order. They are first given 1 digit to repeat and this is gradually increased adding 1 digit at a time to the sequence. The point at which a participant is correct 50% of the time is said to be his or her digit span. Jacobs found that the average span for digits was 9.3 items and 7.3 for letters. This span increased steadily with age.

Why does it increase with age? This may be because people learn **chunking**, where items are chunked together into bigger units. Chunking makes it possible to, for example, remember phone numbers – it is easier to remember 3 chunks than 11 separate digits.

Seven plus or minus two

George Miller (1956) wrote a memorable article called 'The magic number seven plus or minus two'. Why do so many things come in sevens? There are seven notes on the musical scale, seven days of the week, seven deadly sins and so on. Could it be that we cope rather well with registering seven things at once (the span of immediate memory)? A number of studies have investigated this. People can cope reasonably well with counting seven dots flashed onto a screen but not many more than this. The same is true if you are asked to recall musical notes, digits, letters and even words.

It also seems to be true that people can recall 5 *letters* as well as they can recall 5 *words* – we chunk things together and then can remember more, at least that was what Miller thought. He concluded that chunking is a vital activity to reduce the load on memory and enable us to remember more things at one time.

The size of the chunk

Simon (1974) demonstrated that the number of chunks did have some effect on memory. People had a shorter span for larger chunks, such as 8-word phrases, than smaller chunks, such as one-syllable words.

Encoding in STM

Conrad (1964) found that if you presented participants with a list of words that were acoustically similar (e.g. cat, cat, cab) and asked them to recall them immediately, they made errors in their recall. This suggests that data in STM is stored in an acoustic manner.

STM may not **always** use an acoustic code

In general STM appears to rely on an acoustic code for storing information – but some experiments have shown that visual codes are also used in STM. Brandimote *et al.* (1992) found that participants used visual encoding in STM if they were given a *visual* task (pictures) and prevented from doing any *verbal* rehearsal (they had to say 'la la la') in the retention interval before performing a *visual* recall task. Normally we 'translate' visual images into verbal codes in STM but since verbal rehearsal was prevented they were only able to use visual codes.

Research into the nature of long-term memory

Duration of LTM

Experimental research on the study of memory has suggested that people don't retain information over a long period of time – but we all know that we do remember things. Perhaps the problem is that experiments require participants to remember things that are not very interesting.

Bahrick *et al.* (1975) set out to study very long-term memories in a natural context. This study is described in the star study on page 6 opposite.

Waganaar and Groeneweg (1990) interviewed people who had been imprisoned in concentration camps during the Second World War. Thirty years on their recall was still good for certain details, such as the name of the camp commandant, but they had forgotten many other details. This supports the idea that some long-term memories are enduring. The question is why are some memories enduring while others aren't? We will consider some possible answers in the section on forgetting in LTM.

Encoding in LTM

Baddeley (1966) adapted Conrad's study on encoding in STM and investigated the effects of acoustic and semantic similarity on LTM recall. The experiment involved 4 word lists, as shown below.

List A	man, cab, can, cad, cap, mad, max, mat, map	*acoustically similar*
List B	pit, few, cow, pen, sup, bar, day, hot, rig, bun	*acoustically dissimilar*
List C	great, large, big, huge, broad, long, tall, fat, wide, high	*semantically similar*
List D	good, huge, hot, safe, thin, deep, strong, foul, old, late	*semantically dissimilar*

There were 4 groups of participants; each one was given one list of words to learn, followed by a 20-minute retention interval during which the participants performed another task. Then they were asked to recall the list in the order presented. For LTM recall those participants with List C (semantic similarity) did worst. This suggests that information is stored (encoded) semantically in LTM.

CORNER

All your examination questions (with the exception of Research Methods) are divided up in the same way. The first two parts of each question are called the **AO1** questions, and the last part is the **AO1 + AO2** question. Up to now, all the material in this section has been *descriptive*, i.e. it is for answering **AO1** type questions. **AO1** stands for assessment objective 1 and the objective is to assess your ability to *describe* psychological information.

In the final part of each question you are also required to demonstrate your **AO2** skills (i.e. your ability to *analyse* and *evaluate* material). Essentially, the **AO1 + AO2** question is your chance to show that you can *think* about the specification content in such a way as to answer a slightly more challenging question about the topic. This final part is assigned 18 of the 30 marks available for the total question. Of those 18 marks, 6 are given for the **AO1** (i.e. descriptive) content, and 12 are given for the **AO2** (i.e. analysis and evaluative) content.

For example:

Give a brief account of the differences between STM and LTM, and consider the extent to which research supports the distinction between them.

In this question, a brief account of the main differences between STM and LTM would be worth 6 marks, and the rest 12 marks. 'The rest' is, of course, your ability to construct an argument that shows either that research does or does not support a distinction between STM and LTM. There is a knack to this, and we will use a variety of techniques in these Commentary Corners to show you how to get it.

What are models of memory?

In psychology, a 'model' of something should never be taken as an exact copy of the thing being described, but rather as a representation of it. A map of the London Underground, for example, is a representation of the Underground layout that helps us appreciate how it works and where it goes. Of course direction, scale, etc. must be distorted somewhat to make it all fit neatly on the page. A model of memory is also a representation. Based on the evidence available, a model provides us with an analogy of how memory works. Describing memory in terms of 'stores' or 'levels' or 'loops' makes our understanding more concrete, and simply conveys to a reader an approximate idea of how a particular psychologist has attempted to understand and explain the available evidence. These models change as the available evidence changes, so should not be seen as permanent fixtures. In this section we look at three models, each offering a slightly different perspective on the organisation and function of memory.

The multi-store model

The multi-store model of memory is an explanation of how memory processes work. You hear and see and feel many things, but only a small number are remembered. Why are some things remembered and others not?

The multi-store model was first described by Atkinson and Shiffrin in 1968. It is illustrated in the diagram. You should by now be quite familiar with the idea of a short-term store (STM) and a long-term store (LTM).

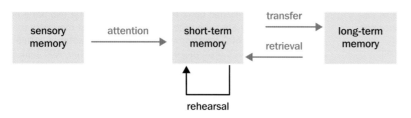

There is a third store in this model: the sensory store (or sensory memory). Sensory memory (SM) is the information collected by your senses – eyes, ears, nose, fingers and so on. The sensory stores constantly receive information but most of it receives no attention. These incoming data remain in the sensory store for a very brief period. If a person's attention is focused on the sensory store (for whatever reason), the data are then transferred to STM. This explains the first step in remembering something – attention.

The second step is moving information from STM to LTM. Atkinson and Shiffrin said that this happens through rehearsal. They proposed a direct relationship between rehearsal in STM and the strength of the long-term memory – the more the information is rehearsed, the better it is remembered.

So the multi-store model is what it says – a description of how memory works in terms of three 'stores': the senses (sensory memory), STM (limited capacity, short duration) and LTM (potentially unlimited capacity and duration). Attention and rehearsal explain how data are transferred. Sounds good – or does it?

Have you ever had the experience of vaguely hearing your mother say something and then hearing her say 'DID YOU HEAR ME???' At which point you say 'What?' but simultaneously 'hear' what she said. This is because her words are still in your sensory store.

Criticisms

There are several criticisms of the multi-store model but we will focus on only a few.

It's right

Many research studies show that there are three distinctly different memory stores. We have looked at these studies and seen how they show differences in terms of duration, capacity and encoding. These differences are further supported by the studies described on the next page. Therefore the model makes good sense. The idea of STM and LTM continues to provide a framework that psychologists find useful for describing and understanding memory.

It's wrong

The multi-store model is probably an oversimplification of memory processes. As we have seen, there are different kinds of LTM (e.g. episodic memory, procedural memory) and this model doesn't include them. The multi-store model proposes just one *long-term* store rather than separate stores for episodic and procedural memory. This model also proposes just one *short-term* store and, as we will see on page 10, there are probably more of these. Finally, the multi-store model proposes one mechanism for how data are stored in LTM – rehearsal. Yet there are many situations when we remember things without having rehearsed the information (e.g. **flashbulb memory**, another topic coming up soon).

Other research that supports the multi-store model of memory

The sensory store

Stimulus material used by Sperling
7	1	V	F	high tone
X	L	5	3	medium tone
B	4	W	7	low tone

Evidence to indicate the duration of the sensory store was collected in a study by Sperling (1960). Participants saw a grid of digits and letters (as in the diagram) for 50 milliseconds (a blink of an eye). They were either asked to write down all 12 items, or they were told they would hear a tone immediately after the exposure and they should just write down that row. When asked to report the whole thing their recall was poorer (5 items recalled, about 42%) than when asked to give one row only (3 items recalled, 75%). This shows that information decays rapidly in the sensory store.

The serial position effect

Glanzer and Cunitz (1966) showed that if participants are given a list of about 20 words, presented one at a time, and then asked to recall any words they can remember, an interesting effect can be observed. They tend to remember the words from the start of the list (a **primacy effect**) and from the end of the list (a **recency effect**), but are less good at recalling words in the middle. The primacy effect occurs because the first words are best rehearsed and transferred to LTM. The recency effect occurs because these words are in STM when they start recalling the list.

Areas of the brain associated with STM and LTM

One way to demonstrate the existence of separate stores in memory is to link STM and LTM to specific areas of the brain. Modern techniques of scanning the brain can be used (such as PET scans and fMRI, which are used to detect brain tumours). These take images of the active brain and enable us to see what region is active when a person is doing particular tasks. Research has found that the prefrontal cortex is active when individuals are working on a task in immediate (i.e. short-term) memory (Beardsley, 1997), whereas the hippocampus is active when long-term memory is engaged (Squire et al., 1992).

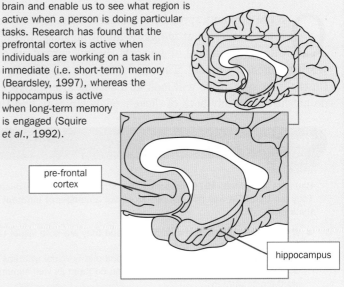

pre-frontal cortex

hippocampus

Models of memory
(continued)

On the previous spread we considered the multi-store model of memory. This model is one way of representing what we know about memory. In the AQA specification you are required to study one alternative model of memory. On this spread we consider one of the possible alternatives: the **working memory model**. This model focuses specifically on how short-term or immediate memory works. On the next spread we will look at a second alternative model: the **levels of processing approach**. You do not have to study both of these models but may find them useful for evaluation of the multi-store model.

The working memory model

Baddeley and Hitch (1974) proposed an alternative model to explain short-term memory. They felt that STM was not just one store but a number of different stores. Why did they think this?

- If you do two things at the same time and they are both visual tasks, you perform them less well than if you do them separately.
- If you do two things at the same time and one is visual whereas the other involves sound, then there is no interference. You do them as well simultaneously as you would do them separately.

This suggests that there is one store for visual processing and one store for processing sounds, which is shown on the right in the diagram.

Baddeley and Hitch used the term 'working memory' to refer to that bit of memory you are using when you are working on something. For example, if you are calculating sums, reading a sentence, or playing chess, there is part of your mind that holds the information you are currently engaged with – your working memory.

Central executive: When you pay attention to something you focus your resources on it. The central executive acts like attention and draws on the phonological loop or the visuo-spatial sketchpad as 'slave systems'. The central executive has a very limited capacity; in other words, it can't attend to too many things at once.

Phonological loop: This too has a limited capacity. The phonological loop deals with auditory information and preserves the *order* of information. It is called a loop because information goes round and round in a loop. Baddeley (1986) further subdivided this loop into the *phonological* store and an *articulatory process*. The phonological store simply holds the words you hear. It is like an inner ear. The articulatory process is used for words that are heard or seen. These words are silently repeated (looped). It is like an inner voice.

It appears that the phonological loop is used when learning new words. The phonological store 'simply' holds auditory data.

Visuo-spatial sketchpad: Visual and/or spatial information is temporarily stored here. Visual information is what things look like. Spatial information is the relationship between things. The visuo-spatial sketchpad is used when you have to plan a spatial task (like getting from one room to another, or hammering a nail into a wall). It is also used if you are engaged in a visual task, such as working out how many windows there are in your house. To do this most people create a visual image of their house in working memory and this enables them to 'count' the windows.

Criticisms

On the positive side

The model explains many observations. For example, it is easier to do two tasks that are different (verbal and visual) than doing two tasks that are similar (and use the same slave system). The model also explains the word-length effect. Such support means that the model may accurately describe what is going on in your head.

On the negative side

There is some concern about the central executive. What exactly is it? The working memory model does little more than say that the central executive allocates resources and is essentially the same as 'attention'. Some psychologists feel this is too vague and doesn't really *explain* anything. Other psychologists feel that the notion of a single central executive is wrong and that there are probably several components. In summary, the account offered of the central executive is unsatisfactory.

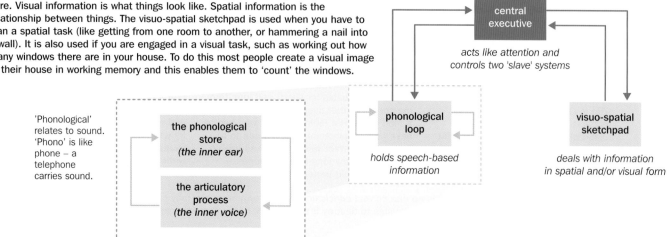

'Phonological' relates to sound. 'Phono' is like phone – a telephone carries sound.

the phonological store
(the inner ear)

the articulatory process
(the inner voice)

central executive

acts like attention and controls two 'slave' systems

phonological loop

holds speech-based information

visuo-spatial sketchpad

deals with information in spatial and/or visual form

Research that supports the working memory model

Doing two tasks using the same or different components

Hitch and Baddeley (1976) gave participants two tasks to do simultaneously. Task 1 occupied the central executive (e.g. participants were given a statement 'B is followed by A' and then asked to say true or false when shown 'AB'). Task 2 either involved the articulatory loop (e.g. asked to say 'the the the' repeatedly), or the central executive plus the articulatory loop (saying random digits), or no additional task. Task 1 was slower when participants were given a task involving both the central executive and the articulatory loop. Speed on task 1 was the same whether using the articulatory loop or no extra task. This shows that doing two tasks that involve the same component causes difficulty. It also suggests that when different components are used, performance is not affected.

The phonological loop and articulatory process

The **word-length effect** has been used to support the working memory model. The word-length effect describes the fact that people cope better with short words in working memory (STM) than long words. It seems that the phonological loop holds the amount of information that you can say in 2 seconds (Baddeley et al., 1975a). This makes it hard to remember a list of long words such as 'association' and 'representative' compared to shorter words like 'harm' and 'twice'. The longer words can't be rehearsed on the phonological loop because they don't fit.

But the word-length effect disappears if a person is given an articulatory suppression task, for example you are asked to say 'the the the' while reading the words. This repetitive task ties up the articulatory process and means you can't rehearse the shorter words more quickly than the longer ones, so the word-length effect disappears. This is evidence of the articulatory process.

The visuo-spatial sketchpad

Baddeley et al. (1975b) demonstrated the existence of the visuo-spatial sketchpad. Participants were given a visual tracking task (they had to track a moving light with a pointer). At the same time they were given one of two other tasks: task 1 was to describe all the angles on the letter F, task 2 was to perform a verbal task. Task 1 was very difficult but not task 2, presumably because the second task involved two different components (or 'slave' systems). This finding is evidence for the existence of a visuo-spatial sketchpad. It also shows that doing two tasks involving the same systems (i.e. both visual) caused problems, and doing two tasks involving different systems (i.e. one visual and one verbal) did not cause problems.

Evidence from studies of brain-damaged patients

Studies of individuals with brain damage also support the working memory model. One such individual, SC, had generally good learning abilities with the exception of being unable to learn word pairs that were presented out loud. This suggests damage to the phonological loop (Trojano and Grossi, 1995). Another patient, LH, who had been involved in a road accident performed better on spatial tasks than those involving visual imagery (Farah et al., 1988). This supports the view that there are separate visual and spatial systems.

COMMENTARY CORNER

In the last Commentary Corner, we showed you *one* way to tackle the **AO1 + AO2** question. Remember that this was only a suggestion, and you may well choose a totally different route or different material to express *your* view of the topic being assessed. A second technique is to decide in advance what your conclusion is going to be, and then construct an argument based on research evidence or alternative viewpoints that support that conclusion. This is rather like a barrister trying to convince a jury of her client's innocence by presenting an argument that will help them reach that conclusion. Of course, this is only a partially suitable analogy, as your 'conclusion' may simply be that there are good *and* bad points about the theory or model being discussed. While this refreshing honesty is quite appropriate in an academic discussion, a barrister who offers an argument based on 'Well...he might be innocent, but then again he might be guilty' would not get much work!

Taking the following question as your starting point, what material would you use to reach a conclusion that (a) the working memory model is very worthwhile, (b) the working memory model is not so hot, and (c) the working memory model has both strengths and weaknesses?

Give a brief account of and evaluate the working memory model of human memory.

As with all these types of question, you are given 6 marks for the **AO1** content (in this case for a brief account of the working memory model) and 12 for the **AO2** content. Remember, you have to use material *effectively* for it to count as **AO2**. So don't just write:

'In a study of brain-damaged patients, LH, who had been involved in a road accident, performed better on spatial tasks than on those involving visual imagery.'

Instead, an effective use of this same material might be:

'In a study of brain-damaged patients, LH, who had been involved in a road accident, performed better on spatial tasks than on those involving visual imagery. This supports the working memory model because it suggests separate visual and spatial systems.'

You might try to do something like this yourself. Write a brief description of one of the studies given on this page. Then add a sentence that turns the description (AO1) into AO2 by making effective use of the material (stating what it shows).

Models of memory

(continued)

We will now examine a second alternative model to the multi-store model: the **levels of processing model**. This representation of memory moves away from the idea of separate stores for different kinds of memory and instead suggests that... well, read on and you will see how it is different.

Processed peas

Why are processed peas called 'processed'? Because they are peas that have been put through some process. Things have been done to them to change them slightly (for better or worse). Processing information is the same.

The levels of processing model

Craik and Lockhart (1972) proposed a different kind of model to explain lasting memories. They suggested that enduring memories are created by the *processing* that is done rather than through rehearsal. Experiences are processed in different ways when information is encoded. Some information is processed more deeply than others. Craik and Lockhart suggested that things that are processed more deeply are more memorable just because of the way they are processed. Memory is an automatic *by-product* of processing.

This model does not propose that the idea of separate stores (the multi-store model) should be scrapped, but that the focus should be on the effect of different *encoding operations*. In the levels of processing model, there are two ways that information can be retained: (1) through deep encoding processes enduring memories are formed; (2) information can be 'recirculated' (or rehearsed) at a lower level of processing in *primary memory* (i.e. like STM) (Craik and Lockhart, 1972, p. 676). The difference between this primary memory and STM is that primary memory is a *flexible processing activity* rather than a limited store.

The key is the 'meaningfulness extracted from the stimulus' (Craik, 1973). In all of the experiments described below, information is being processed in such a way that makes it *automatically* more memorable. No rehearsal is needed. The more you 'work over' or process the information, the more it becomes memorable. This is the core of the levels of processing model.

Criticisms

Recall depends on what you are required to recall

Morris *et al.* (1977) conducted a similar experiment to the one by Craik and Tulving (below), but they gave their participants a *rhyming recognition test*. In other words, the participants weren't asked to simply recall the words but to recall words that rhymed with words on the original list. This time the words that were best remembered were not those that had been deeply processed but those that had been phonemically processed. This is called *transfer-appropriate processing*. This shows that there are other explanations for memory, not just depth of processing. Lockhart and Craik (1990) have recognised this problem and suggest that depth refers to greater processing *within the relevant domain*.

The definition is circular

Many psychologists question the idea of 'depth'. Something is remembered if it is deeply processed. Deep processing leads to better memory. This is a *circular definition*. It is like saying: 'I like ice cream because it is tasty. What is a tasty thing? It is something like ice cream.' This criticism may not be entirely fair as subsequent research has, in fact, tried to extend what is meant by 'depth' to include organisation, distinctiveness, elaboration and effort. 'Depth', then, can be seen to be an increasingly complex interaction with information to be remembered.

Research that supports the levels of processing model

Depth

Craik and Tulving (1975) gave participants a list of common nouns such as 'shark' and asked a question about the word. There were three kinds of question:

1 An analysis of the physical structure (shallow processing): a participant might be asked 'Is the word printed in capital letters?'
2 An analysis of sound (phonemic processing), for example: 'Does the word rhyme with "train"?'
3 An analysis of meaning (deeper processing), such as: 'Is the word a type of fruit?'

There were 60 sentences altogether. Afterwards the participants were shown 180 words and asked to identify any of the original words. Participants remembered most words from condition 3 and least from condition 1. This suggests that deeper processing leads to enhanced memory.

Organisation

Mandler (1967) asked participants to sort a pack of 52 word cards into up to 7 piles, based on any system of categories they wanted to use. When each participant had finished the cards were collected and the participant was asked to repeat the task. This continued until the participant was 95% consistent in their sort. After this they were asked to recall as many words as they could. Recall was best for those who had used the most categories. This suggests that the act of organising information makes it memorable without any conscious effort or rehearsal.

Distinctiveness

Eysenck and Eysenck (1980) found that distinctiveness was important. Some participants were asked to say words in a distinctive way, e.g. saying all the letters of 'c-o-m-b'. Other participants just read the word lists in the normal way. Recall was better for the distinctive condition.

Elaboration

Palmere *et al.* (1983) gave participants a description of a fictitious African nation – a description that was 32 paragraphs long! Some paragraphs were short, whereas others had several extra sentences that elaborated the main idea. When tested later, recall was higher for the ideas that had been expressed in the elaborated paragraphs.

Effort

Tyler *et al.* (1979) conducted an experiment where participants had to solve anagrams. Some were easy (e.g. FAMIYL) while others were more difficult (e.g. YMALFI). When recall was later tested (unexpectedly), participants remembered more of the difficult anagrams. Since all words were processed at the same depth, it must be effort that made some words more memorable.

Research methods
Experimental design

The study by Craik and Tulving is called a **repeated measures design**. This is because the same person does all three kinds of task. Each person is measured several times. The alternative would be to have one group of participants for each kind of task. A third possibility is **matched participants design**, where the participants in each group are not the same (i.e. they are independent) but they are *matched* on key variables such as similar age, intelligence and memory ability (which makes it *almost* as if they were the same person in each group, i.e. almost repeated measures). Participants are matched on **participant variables** – the characteristics of individuals that might be important in the study – such as age, intelligence, social class, and relevant experiences.

Type of experimental design	Advantages	Disadvantages
Repeated measures design	Good control for participant variables. Needs fewer participants.	**Order effects**: participants may become bored because they have to do the same (or a similar) task twice. They may also get better because of practice.
Matched participants design	No order effects. Participant variables partly controlled.	Participants may guess the purpose of the experiment and alter their behaviour, which would spoil the experiment. Matching is difficult and expensive in terms of time and money. Matching is never totally successful.
Independent groups design	No order effects. Avoids participants guessing the purpose of the experiment.	Needs more participants. Lacks control of participant variables.

research activity

You could replicate the study by Craik and Tulving, conducting it as a repeated measures design (as they did) or as an independent measures design.

Repeated measures design: Each participant completes the whole task (10 'shallow', 10 phonemic and 10 semantic questions). These questions should be **randomly** distributed on the questionnaire and there should be a balance of questions that have 'yes' and 'no' answers.

One way to construct the questionnaire is to write the three conditions (shallow, phonemic, semantic) on 30 slips of paper (10 of each) and place them in one pile. In another pile have 30 slips of paper, 15 that say 'yes' and 15 that say 'no'. Write a list of 30 words and for each word draw two slips of paper, one from each pile, and then write the appropriate question. This ensures random distribution of types of question across 30 questions.

Independent groups design: Compose one list of rhyming questions only (list A) and one of semantic questions only (list B). Give list A to half of the participants and list B to the other participants. You can allocate participants to conditions systematically (by giving list A to the first 10 participants, and list B to the second 10 participants) or use **random allocation** (by shuffling up the 10 list A and 10 list B questionnaires and handing them out). Random allocation ensures that there is no pattern in who becomes a member of each group.

COMMENTARY CORNER

We can now consider a third technique for tackling the **AO1** + **AO2** question. It is a little more sophisticated than the previous two, but with practice becomes just as easy. It takes the form of a 'debate' on paper, where one point of view is put forward, only to be challenged by the next point, with each side of the debate trying to gain the ascendancy. Imagine a tennis match, where each player must pay careful attention to her opponent's last shot and put over a shot of her own that will create difficulties for her opponent to return. Let's see how this might be applied in our **AO1** + **AO2** question.

Consider the levels of processing model as an explanation of human memory.

To prepare for your 'debate', you can begin by marshalling all the material you feel is appropriate for a two-sided discussion of this topic. Remember that every time you *describe* something (a piece of research or some assumption of the model), this counts as **AO1**, and when you *comment* on this material, this counts as **AO2**. For example, the debate may begin like this:

Craik and Lockhart (1972) suggested that things that are processed more deeply are more memorable just because of the way they are processed. This was supported in research by Craik and Tulving (1975), who found that participants remembered most words from a list that had been processed for meaning and least from those that had simply been processed for their structure. This showed that deeper processing led to enhanced memory, a key assumption of the model.

However, many psychologists question the idea of 'depth'. To say that something is remembered if it is deeply processed and that deep processing leads to better memory is a circular definition. This criticism may not be entirely fair as subsequent research extended what is meant by 'depth' to include organisation, distinctiveness, elaboration and effort. Research by Eysenck and Eysenck (1980), for example, provided evidence for the importance of elaboration as an aspect of deeper processing, showing that this led to enhanced later recall of material that had been elaborated during initial presentation.

Note how the answer moves between the two positions. This technique is similar to the previous technique, in that you may decide on your conclusion (in this case, that the levels of processing model is a truly worthy contribution to our understanding of memory) and then proceed to demolish arguments along the way, rather like the tennis rally described earlier. You might like to continue the debate that has been started here, and then edit your overall response to make sure that **AO1** and **AO2** are represented in the required 1:2 ratio.

Remembering and forgetting

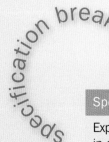

specification breakdown

Specification content	Comment
Explanations of forgetting in short-term memory (e.g. decay and displacement). Explanations of forgetting in long-term memory (e.g. retrieval failure and interference).	**Forgetting in short-term memory** (STM) can be explained rather differently from forgetting in **long-term memory** (LTM) because STM is a limited-capacity store and therefore information may disappear because of space restrictions. The specification provides examples of suitable explanations, but you may use any examples you choose as long as you are familiar with more than one explanation for both STM and LTM. You should also be familiar with relevant research evidence to support your explanations, and any potential weaknesses in the studies and/or explanations.
The role of emotional factors in memory, including flashbulb memories and repression (e.g. Freud).	Emotion may enhance (**flashbulb memory**) or reduce (**repression**) recall of events. Your study of repression can, but need not necessarily, refer to Freud's ideas on this topic. Again you are required to explain the concepts (flashbulb memory and repression) and have a critical awareness of appropriate research evidence.

We all have stories about forgetting – perhaps rather more than we care to remember! It is a perplexing and annoying behaviour. Why do we forget some things and not others?

Forgetting in STM and LTM can be explained differently. Cara suffers from the name-forgetting problem. She is introduced to someone new and, seconds later, realises she can't remember their name. How and why do some people manage to remember the names of everyone they meet while others forget them instantly? We might explain this forgetting in terms of the *decay* of the memory trace, whereas rehearsal might prevent such forgetting. Or maybe one 'forgets' because other information is heard immediately afterwards and this *displaces* the first information.

Psychologists actually have rather few explanations for forgetting in STM, but they have proposed many more explanations of forgetting in LTM. It is possible, of course, that we lose information from LTM simply because it deteriorates over time (i.e. *decays*) so is no longer accessible. This idea of 'if you don't use it you'll lose it' may well explain Mike's inability to recall more than a few words from his five years of learning Latin at school or Cara's inability to remember anything but the first line of the hundreds of songs she grew up with in the 1960s. Trying to prevent decay of such complex material may involve constant refreshing, whereas our memory for physical activities (such as riding a bike) clearly does not.

You may well have experienced the effects of interference when trying to retrieve information from memory. Calling your current partner by the name of your previous partner or getting off at the wrong station because you *used* to live there are both examples of interference at work. Interference may work *forwards* (known as *proactive* interference), where you find it difficult to learn and recall new information because something similar already exists in your memory. For years Mike worked with another psychologist by the name of Alan Finer, then sometime later had a new colleague called Anthony Feiler. Anthony was called Alan on more than one occasion! Interference may also work *backwards* (known as *retroactive* interference), where new information interferes with existing information. Presumably, if Mike met up with Alan Finer again, he would call him Anthony!

Many psychologists believe that all forgetting can be explained simply in terms of our inability to *retrieve* information because of the absence of suitable cues. We have already seen that our memory is not infallible so needs all the help we can give it to successfully retrieve information when we want it. When we commit information to memory, we also commit various context cues (e.g. where we learned it, peculiar sounds, smells or other aspects of the environment) and internal cues (e.g. whether we were happy, sad, anxious). Being able to retrieve successfully means being able, as far as possible, to recreate the circumstances of the initial encoding. This should tell you something about effective revision strategies – don't revise in front of the TV, listening to loud rock music, when you are drunk or overly anxious if you want to recall information in the quiet (and sober) atmosphere of an examination hall!

What is meant by forgetting?

To *forget* has several meanings in psychology but is generally taken to refer to a person's loss of the ability to recall or recognise something that they have previously learned. Forgetting from short-term memory (STM) is usually explained in terms of the information simply being lost from a limited-capacity and limited-duration store. But what about forgetting from long-term memory (LTM)? In the previous section you read that the capacity and duration of LTM are effectively unlimited, so why do we appear to lose information once we have submitted it to LTM? Not being able to retrieve information from LTM may be due to its no longer being available (i.e. it is no longer there) or because over time it has become inaccessible (for whatever reason). Forgetting, therefore, has a simple definition, but its explanation may be rather more complicated.

If you are asked in an examination to 'Outline two factors that explain forgetting in STM', you can use decay and displacement. These are 'factors' in STM forgetting.

What's the difference between remembering and forgetting?

If you *remember* something that you have previously committed to memory, it means you have successfully retrieved it from wherever it was stored in your brain and can now reproduce it in the present time (handy in examinations). Forgetting is the *inability* to retrieve a memory. Don't forget, though, that not everything we retrieve from our memory is *accurate* (remember Jean Piaget?), so remembering something wrongly may be every bit as useless as forgetting it completely.

What is meant by decay and displacement?

Decay is a gradual deterioration or fading away. When used in connection with memory, there is an assumption that a memory trace in our brain disintegrates over time and so is lost.

In the context of memory, **displacement** refers to existing information being displaced out of memory by newer information. Imagine a shelf full of books. Push a new one on at one end and a book drops off the other end. The number of books stays the same but the books themselves are now different.

Factors that influence forgetting in STM

The two most popular explanations of forgetting in STM stress the role of **decay**, where a memory simply fades away over time, and **displacement**, where information currently in STM is 'displaced' by new information. Each of these counts as a 'factor' in forgetting (time, in the case of decay, and new information, in the case of displacement) in STM. These are explained in more detail below. Remember that forgetting in STM is different from forgetting in LTM largely because of the very limited capacity of the STM store. We know that memories in this store are lost rapidly, and these two explanations provide us with the reason why.

KEY TERM

Forgetting: The inability to recall or recognise something that has previously been learned. This may be due either to a lack of availability, as in the case of decay when the information has disappeared, or to a lack of accessibility, as in the case of cue-dependent forgetting when the memory is stored somewhere but can't be found at that time.

Explanation 1: Decay theory

One way to think about memory is in terms of a *memory trace* (or engram). This refers to the physical representation of information in the brain. It is suggested that this trace simply disappears or decays if it is not rehearsed (see page 8). This would explain the findings from the Peterson and Peterson experiment (1959), described on page 4. No rehearsal was permitted and the information had disappeared from STM after 18 seconds at the most.

Criticisms

There is one problem with this explanation. How can we be sure that decay took place? It could be that the first information was simply pushed out or overwritten (as proposed by the displacement theory, described below). In Peterson and Peterson's experiment (described on page 4), the digits that the participants were counting might have *displaced* the original nonsense trigrams. It is difficult to prevent rehearsal without introducing information that will overwrite the original information. So the numbers could have replaced the trigrams.

Reitman (1974) tried to overcome this problem of overwriting by giving participants a different task in the retention interval. She asked participants to listen for a tone. This meant that their attention was diverted elsewhere, which should prevent rehearsal of data. In a 15-second interval participants' recall for 5 words dropped by 24%, which is evidence for decay – except that we can't be *entirely* certain that new information had not entered STM.

The second, obvious explanation for forgetting in STM is that a new set of information physically overwrites an older set. This happens because STM is a limited-capacity store. When it is full and more information is presented, all that can happen then is displacement – by overwriting.

Criticisms

Waugh and Norman (1965) used the **serial probe technique** to investigate forgetting in STM. They presented 16 numbers to participants. If the probe was early in the list, recall was poor (less than 20%). If the probe came near the end of the list, recall was good (over 80%). This supports displacement theory because forgetting must be due to the fact that subsequent numbers increasingly displaced earlier numbers.

It could be decay *and* displacement

Waugh and Norman (1965) designed a further experiment to compare the relative effects of decay and displacement. They used the serial probe technique and this time read the digits out at different speeds: at a rate of 4 per second (faster) or 1 per second (slower). If displacement is the key factor, speed of presentation shouldn't matter (because there are still the same number of digits between the probe and when recall is required, whereas if the faster speed results in better recall this suggests that the information has not decayed).

Waugh and Norman found that presentation speed had only a small effect on recall. However, Shallice (1967) found that recall was better if the numbers were presented faster, although the effect was stronger when position of the probe was moved. This suggests that displacement and decay explain forgetting in STM, but that displacement is more important.

The serial probe technique

A series of numbers is presented. Afterwards one of the numbers (*the probe*) is read out and participants have to recall the number that came after the probe in the list. For example: 11, 23, 45, 31, 56, 32, 19, 23, 16, 12. Then the experimenter says the probe is 45.

CORNER

To what extent does research on forgetting give us an insight into the nature of short-term memory?

As you might imagine, it is difficult to separate what we mean by research on *forgetting* from research on *memory* in general. Research on forgetting is extremely valuable as a way of testing assumptions about the way that memory works and the assumptions of different types of memory. This is a challenging question, but one that can be answered by a careful examination of the material so far. Start by looking at some of the things you know about STM and LTM.

- STM has a very limited capacity, LTM a potentially unlimited capacity.
- STM has very limited duration, LTM potentially unlimited duration.
- Information in STM is encoded acoustically, in LTM information tends to be coded semantically.

The next thing to do is to look through the text for research into forgetting that throws some light on these distinctions between STM and LTM. You might, for example, include the following:

- Waugh and Norman (1965) used the *serial probe technique* and found that if the probe was early in a list of numbers, recall was poor, but if the probe came near the end of the list, recall was good.
- Glanzer and Cunitz (1966) found evidence of a *primacy effect* and a *recency effect* when people had to recall a list of words.
- Bahrick *et al.* (1975) found evidence for very long-term memories in high-school graduates, although findings were better for recognition than they were for recall.

Describing the findings of these studies would count as **AO1**, but there is obviously a lot more work to be done to tease out the **AO2** content. You need to include some commentary that makes it obvious what particular insights these studies gave us about the nature of memory, and particularly the distinctions between STM and LTM. These might include the following:

- Waugh and Norman's study supports the claim that STM has a limited capacity as forgetting was caused by subsequent numbers displacing earlier numbers.
- Glanzer and Cunitz's study supports a distinction between STM and LTM because the first words on the list were best rehearsed and therefore transferred to LTM. The recency effect occurred because these words were still in STM when recall began.
- Bahrick *et al.*'s study supports the claim that LTM duration is virtually unlimited. This also demonstrated that as recognition was superior to recall, forgetting from LTM is largely a matter of not having the right cues available during retrieval.

You can finish by offering a few choice reservations about the conclusions above. For example, you might say that the conclusions drawn from any of the above studies are not all that useful because they all took place in a laboratory. To make this *effective*, you need to add a comment about *why* this detracts from the value of the conclusion drawn:

- This means that psychologists build up theories of memory based on data which are often trivial and not very true to the way our memory works in real life.

Factors that influence forgetting in LTM

We now move on from short-term to long-term memory. Explanations for forgetting in LTM are different from those for STM because LTM has unlimited capacity and duration; therefore insufficient space is not an issue. The main explanations proposed are interference and retrieval failure (cue-dependent forgetting).

At the same time there are also similarities – decay is used to explain forgetting in both STM and LTM.

What is meant by interference, retrieval failure and cue-dependent forgetting?

Interference: When something gets in the way of something else. When used in the study of forgetting it refers to the tendency for one memory to 'interfere with' the accurate retrieval of another (similar) memory.

Retrieval failure: When a person fails to successfully recover from memory failure something that was previously learned. This may not be lost completely but cannot be retrieved at that particular time.

Cue-dependent forgetting: Occurs when information may be stored in memory but may be inaccessible unless there is a specific cue to help retrieve it (e.g. a smell may trigger a memory from childhood).

If you are asked in an examination to 'Outline two factors that explain forgetting in LTM', you can use any two of the three explanations offered here. These are 'factors' in LTM forgetting.

Explanation 1: Decay theory

Do we forget things from years ago because the memory trace simply disappears? The 'decay' explanation was suggested for short-term forgetting. It could apply to long-term forgetting. Individuals who suffer brain damage where parts of their brain no longer function experience forgetting. In this case it is the loss of a memory trace that causes forgetting.

Lashley (1931) conducted some famous experiments on rats. He trained them to learn mazes and then removed sections of their brains. He found that there was a relationship between the amount of material removed and the amount of forgetting that happened. This again supports the view that LTM forgetting may be related to physical decay.

Research methods
Confounding variable

In order to conduct well-controlled experiments, psychologists aim to eliminate **extraneous variables**. These are variables which act like an **independent variable** (IV) because they affect the **dependent variable** (DV). This means they may mask the effect of the IV on the DV and therefore create invalid findings. Any extraneous variable that does this is called a **confounding variable** because it *confounds the findings* of the experiment.

Criticisms

Research evidence

In a classic study Jenkins and Dallenbach (1924) gave participants nonsense syllables and asked them to recall these 8 hours later. The participants were either awake or asleep during the retention interval. Recall was better if they had been asleep, when little information was entering their heads and there was nothing to cause displacement. At night there was no displacement and little forgetting – so forgetting in the day must be due to displacement by new information and not explained by decay theory.

However, there was a major methodological flaw in the study by Jenkins and Dallenbach. In the sleep condition the participants' memory was tested in the morning, whereas, in the awake-for-8-hours condition, it was tested late in the day. This introduced a **confounding variable**.

- Independent variable: sleep or no sleep during the retention interval
- Confounding variable: tested in the morning or tested in the evening
- Dependent variable: amount of information recalled

As the independent variable and the confounding variable occurred together, it is impossible to tell whether better recall was due to sleep in the retention interval or to the time of day when recall took place.

Hockey et al. (1972) found that recall was better in the morning. This means that the original finding can be explained in terms of the time when testing took place rather than lack of displacement while asleep.

If decay was the major explanation of forgetting, why do we have so many long-term memories?

Other evidence indicates that memories *can* be very long-lasting (e.g. Bahrick et al. and flashbulb memories). This means that decay is an unlikely explanation for most long-term forgetting.

Decay or interference?

If you recall, it was hard to distinguish between the effects of decay and displacement in STM. The same problem occurs with decay and interference in LTM. If something disappears from memory, has it decayed or has displacement/interference from other information been the cause? Baddeley and Hitch (1977) conducted a **natural experiment** to investigate this. The dependent variable was recall of rugby fixtures played over a season. Some players played in all of the games in the season, whereas others missed some games because of injury. The time interval from start to end of the season was the same for all players, but the number of intervening games was different for each player. If decay theory is correct, all players should recall a similar percentage of the games played because time alone should cause forgetting. If interference theory is correct, those players who played most games should forget proportionately more because of interference. Baddeley and Hitch found that the more games the players had played, the more they forgot (proportionately). This supports interference theory.

In the 1950s interference theory was the theory of forgetting. Consider the following: you are used to opening a particular drawer to get a knife. Your mother reorganises the kitchen and puts the knives in a different drawer. However, every time you go to get a knife you go to the old drawer. An old memory is continuing to *interfere* with new learning. After many months you have got used to the new arrangement. Then your mother decides to change back to the original scheme. Now what happens? You continue to go to the second location. The newer memory interferes with past learning.

Proactive interference (PI)	Past learning interferes with current attempts to learn something.
Retroactive interference (RI)	Current attempts to learn something interfere with past learning.

Psychologists have found evidence of both proactive and retroactive interference. A typical study on interference uses the **paired-associate technique** and two word lists (e.g. Underwood, 1957). Learning one list *interferes* with learning the other list. Try the research activity to see for yourself.

Criticisms

Interference effects require special conditions

Interference does cause forgetting but only when a similar stimulus is paired with two different responses. These conditions are rare in everyday life and therefore interference explains only a limited range of forgetting.

It is possible to recover from interference

Tulving and Pstoka (1971) conducted an experiment on forgetting. Participants were given six different word lists to learn, each with 24 words. Each list was divided into six different categories (such as kinds of tree and names of precious stones). After each list was presented participants were asked to write down as many words as they could remember (*free recall*). After all the lists were presented there was a final free recall and then the participants were given the category names and again asked to recall all the words from all the lists (*cued recall*).

Some participants only learned one list, others learned two, and so on. According to interference theory, the more lists a participant had to learn, the worse their performance would become. This was what Tulving and Pstoka found. Those who were given only one or two lists remembered a higher percentage of their words than those given more lists. This is evidence of retroactive interference.

But when participants were given cued recall the effects of interference disappeared. With cued recall participants remembered about 70% of the words, regardless of how many lists they had been given. This shows that interference effects may mask what is actually stored in memory. The information is there (available) but cannot be retrieved. This is called cue-dependent forgetting. This means that forgetting happens at the retrieval stage (i.e. retrieval failure).

The paired-associate technique

Participants are shown a list of word pairs, e.g. apple–train, time–chair. Later they are given the first word and asked to recall its partner.

Pstoka? How do I remember his name?

With difficulty. You won't be penalised in an exam if you spell it wrong or you forget it altogether. We can't remember every psychologist's name! But we can remember the details of the studies and that's the most important thing. Names do help, though. They make it clear what study you are talking about and they actually help remember the whole study, because they act as 'cues'.

Research activity

Proactive and retroactive interference

To demonstrate *proactive interference* you give participants a list of word pairs using list A and list B (e.g. 'cat' from list A and 'tree' from list B: the word pair is cat–tree). The participants then have to learn a second list consisting of word pairs from list A and list C (e.g. cat–stone). Finally, participants are asked to recall the list C words when given the list A words. How well do they do?

In order to assess recall it is necessary to use a **control group**. This is a second group of participants who are given no interference task so that you are able to see how people would normally cope with this task. The control group learns another list (of completely different words), then learns A–C and recalls A–C.

Retroactive interference is stronger. In other words, participants in group 3 do less well recalling the words from the first list (A–B) learned than those in group 1 do recalling words from the second list (A–C).

Proactive interference is shown by the fact that participants in group 1 who learned A–B and then A–C have more difficulty recalling A–C than those participants in group 2 whose first word list was entirely different.

To demonstrate *proactive interference*

Group 1 (experimental group)
- Learns A–B, then A–C
- Test by giving list A words and ask to recall list C words

Group 2 (control group)
- Learns another list of word pairs, then A–C
- Same test as above

To demonstrate *retroactive interference*

Group 3
- Learns A–B, then A–C
- Test by giving list A words and ask to recall list B words
- Compare performance with experimental group 1

List A	List B	List C
Cat	Tree	Stone
Candle	Whale	Cloth
Book	Fork	Jail
Plant	Tank	Claw
Water	Market	Gold
Track	Lemon	Kettle
Dish	Cane	Swamp
Flask	Picture	Mast
Cigar	Jelly	Nail
Animal	Nurse	Pencil

Factors that influence forgetting in LTM (continued)

On this spread we consider the third factor, or explanation, for forgetting in long-term memory. The decay and interference explanations suggest that forgetting happens because a memory trace is no longer there. It is no longer *available*. Therefore this is *trace-dependent forgetting*. *Cue-dependent forgetting* means that the memory trace is there, only you can't *access* it. Forgetting in this case is due to retrieval failure.

Availability and accessibility

Some memories are not available, others are simply not accessible.

Explanation 3: Retrieval failure and cue-dependent forgetting

Forgetting in LTM is mainly due to retrieval failure. This is the failure to find an item of information because you have insufficient clues or cues. If someone gave you a hint then the memory might pop into your head but, in the meantime, you are faced with a blank. It is possible that you have a vast store of memories and could access them – if only someone could provide the right cues.

There are several different kinds of cue. The context where initial learning takes place or the mood you were in may act as a cue later.

External cues: Context-dependent learning (or forgetting)

Abernethy (1940) arranged for a group of students to be tested before a certain course began. They were then tested each week. Some students were tested in their teaching room by their usual instructor. Some were tested by a different instructor. Others were tested in a different room either by their usual instructor or by a different one. Those tested by the same instructor in the same room performed best. Presumably familiar things (room and instructor) acted as memory cues. Look at the wall in front of you. Does it trigger a memory? That's a cue.

Internal cues: State-dependent learning (or forgetting)

Goodwin *et al.* (1969) found that people who drank a lot often forgot where they had put things when they were sober but recalled the locations when they were drunk again! Miles and Hardman (1998) found that people who learned a list of words while exercising on a static bicycle remembered them better when exercising again than while at rest.

Criticisms

This is a powerful explanation for forgetting

Some psychologists believe that all forgetting is cue-dependent forgetting. Michael Eysenck (1998) says 'It is probable that this is the main reason for forgetting in LTM'. There is a considerable amount of research to show the importance of cues and how they trigger memory. As we have seen, retrieval is best when conditions during recall match those during original learning. The *encoding specificity principle* further states that a cue doesn't have to be exactly right, but the closer the cue is to the thing you're looking for, the more useful it will be.

Everyday memory and procedural memory

Many of the studies used to support cue-dependent forgetting are laboratory-based and not very like everyday memory. Therefore, cue-dependent recall *may* not apply to some aspects of everyday memory. For example, procedural knowledge (knowing how) is not related to cue-dependent recall. Examples of this kind of memory include remembering how to play ping pong or to play the recorder. Such memories are rather resistant to forgetting, but not totally immune. If you haven't played ping pong in years, there is some re-learning to do, but even so cues don't really explain this.

How might you design a study with the same aims as Abernethy's? State your hypothesis and describe the procedures for your experiment. Write a set of standardised instructions.

A Viking couple preparing dinner, at the Jorvik Viking Centre in York. Aggleton and Waskett (1999) showed that smell acted as an effective retrieval cue when testing recall in visitors at the Jorvik Viking Centre, where smells are very much a feature of the display.

Research methods *Aims and hypotheses*

All research studies have to start out with an aim. The researcher intends to study something. In Abernethy's case the intention was to study memory – more specifically, to study the effects of context on recall. This is called the **aim** or aims of the study. The aims lead on to a **hypothesis**. This is a clear statement of what the researcher believes to be true and is what he or she aims to demonstrate.

A hypothesis states the expected relationship between the IV and DV. In Abernethy's study this might be:

Participants do better on a test when tested in the same room where they were taught rather than tested in a different room.

The DV was performance on the test, the IV was where participants were tested (same or different room). This hypothesis is described as being **directional** because it states whether participants will do better or worse.

Participants perform differently depending on whether they are tested in the same room where they were taught rather than tested in a different room.

This is a **non-directional** hypothesis because it just proposes that there will be a difference between the two groups of participants.

> A **directional hypothesis** predicts the kind of difference or relationship between two groups of participants.
>
> A **non-directional hypothesis** predicts simply that there will be a difference between the two groups of participants.

Researchers select a directional hypothesis because past research or experience suggests this is the likely direction of the findings. For example, on the basis of cue-dependent recall theory, participants tested in the same room would be expected to do better and therefore the hypothesis should be directional.

However, what happens if the participants in the different rooms do better? Then you have found a difference between the two groups, but not in the expected direction! You can't accept your hypothesis because it doesn't describe what happens. You have to state that the hypothesis is wrong and leave it at that. *But*, if you had used a non-directional hypothesis, it would cope with findings in either direction. Therefore it is *safer* to use a non-directional hypothesis in case the findings go in the opposite direction.

Re-learning savings

Memory research has many useful applications. One of these is to offer advice to students revising for examinations. You have probably had the experience of revising a topic one night and then finding that you could remember virtually nothing the next day. 'What was the point of all that work?', you ask yourself.

Ebbinghaus (1885) investigated memory using himself as the subject. He set himself the task of learning nonsense syllables and then, later, seeing how many he could remember. He would then re-learn the list. He noticed that he gradually forgot less and less. This means that he initially *appeared* to forget a lot but in fact he must have stored some of the material because the next time he learned the same material he did better. He called this **re-learning savings**.

So don't despair about wasted time. You are learning things all the time, even though you might not think you are.

Examine the following hypotheses. Which is directional and which is non-directional?

- Girls are better than boys at spelling.
- Older people have different sleep habits than younger people.

COMMENTARY

Give a brief account of and evaluate attempts to explain forgetting in long-term memory.

Now it's time for you to go solo on one of these questions. Which technique appears to be the most suitable? You might try the straightforward three paragraphs technique, so let's look at what might go where.

Paragraph 1

Remember – you don't need to cover all the explanations, but you do have to cover at least two. You could begin with a brief description of at least two explanations of forgetting in LTM, e.g.

- Interference
- Cue-dependent forgetting

How much you write in this first paragraph depends largely on how much you feel you could write in the time available in the exam. If you allow yourself 15 minutes for this part of a question, this first paragraph would amount to 5 minutes' writing or about 100 words. Keep your account focused on the main claims and assumptions of each explanation rather

than filling the paragraph with examples or anecdotes. Précising (i.e. making an account more compact) is best mastered *before* you arrive in the examination hall!

Paragraphs 2 & 3

If you have chosen to write about two explanations, the simplest route through the rest of the answer is to evaluate each in turn. That means that the second paragraph can be dedicated to interference theory and the third to cue-dependent forgetting. Each of these paragraphs would also be about 100 words long, so maintaining the 1:2 (AO1:AO2) ratio required by this sort of question. By using clever linking phrases such as the following, you can structure these last two paragraphs so that they really are *evaluative*:

This explanation is supported by...

This view of forgetting is challenged by the finding that...

However, a problem with this explanation is...

A particular strength of this explanation is...

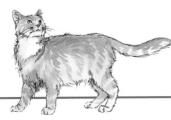

What emotional factors affect memory?

The extent to which we remember (or forget) things is strongly affected by emotional factors. Emotional states may lead to better memories (less forgetting) or worse memory (more forgetting). Flashbulb memories are an example of enhanced recall as a consequence of being emotionally aroused at the time an event takes place. Repression occurs because certain memories create anxiety and this makes such memories inaccessible (forgotten).

What is meant by flashbulb memory?

Flashbulb memories (FBs) are detailed recollections of the context in which people first heard about an important event. FBs tend to be memories of events (i.e. *episodic* memories) rather than memory for facts (i.e. *semantic* memories). The analogy of a *flashbulb* describes the way we can often remember where we were, what we were doing and who we were with, as if the whole scene had been illuminated by a giant flashbulb. This analogy appears to suggest that such memories really are like photographs in their accuracy, but several studies of schoolchildren after the Challenger space shuttle disaster in 1988 showed that even FBs can contain significant inaccuracies. The definitive example of an FB quoted in textbooks is the assassination of President John F. Kennedy in 1963. More recent examples might be the announcement of Princess Diana's death or the terrorist attacks on the World Trade Center towers in New York in 2001. Of course, we have FBs not only associated with important public events but also associated with significant personal events. The key ingredient that all FBs have in common is a high level of emotional arousal at the time the event was committed to memory.

research activity

Flashbulb memory questionnaire

You might try to construct your own flashbulb memory questionnaire, to collect information about people's FBs.

What kind of factors influence flashbulb memories?

The emotional nature of the original event and the extent to which it is rehearsed.

KEY TERM

Flashbulb memory: A memory where an individual has a detailed and enduring recollection of the context in which they first heard about a personally important event.

FBs are claimed to differ from 'ordinary memories' because they involve an enduring imprint of events surrounding an important incident. The imprint is both lasting and unchanging. It is not like a photograph because it does not record every part of the scene.

Research on the role of flashbulb memory

Evidence for flashbulb memory

Brown and Kulik (1977) coined the term 'flashbulb memory' and sought to identify what kind of events did generate FBs. They suspected that national events were likely to generate FBs but that there might be differences between white and black Americans in what events triggered FBs. They asked 40 white and 40 black Americans to fill out a questionnaire. The questionnaire consisted of a list of 10 events. For each event the participants were asked 'Do you recall the circumstances in which you first heard that …?' If the answer was 'no', they were asked to move on to the next event. If the answer was 'yes', the participant was asked to free recall the circumstances in any form or order.

White people had greater recall for events concerning white individuals, and the same was true for blacks. This 'race effect' supports the view that 'consequentiality' is important. In other words, people have FBs for events that are of personal consequence because they are more emotionally important.

Conway et al. (1994) felt that the reason some studies do not find support for FBs is because the event has not been particularly important to the participants and that's why they hadn't formed accurate and enduring flashbulb memories. They

were not really flashbulb memories. Conway et al. looked at personal memories surrounding Mrs. Thatcher's resignation. They tested participants shortly after the resignation and re-interviewed them 11 months later. Eighty-six per cent of the UK participants interviewed still had memories surrounding the event compared with 29% in other countries. This supports the idea that the UK participants had some kind of flashbulb memory for the event.

Evidence against flashbulb memory
Flashbulb memories are not accurate

Schmolck et al. (2000) investigated the events surrounding the announcement of the verdict in the O.J. Simpson murder trial. They interviewed students 3 days after the verdict and again 15 or 32 months later. The quality of the recollections after 32 months was strikingly different from the quality of the recollections after 15 months. After 15 months, 50% of the recollections were highly accurate, and only 11% contained major errors or distortions. After 32 months, only 29% of the recollections were highly accurate, and more than 40% contained major distortions. This suggests that flashbulb memories do decay and are not enduringly accurate – if one accepts that recall for the O.J. Simpson trial constitutes a flashbulb memory.

Flashbulb memories are the same as other kinds of memory

Wright (1993) claimed that FBs were subject to the same processes as all memories, and this suggests that there is no special mechanism involved. Wright interviewed people about their recall of events related to the Hillsborough football disaster where 96 Liverpool supporters were crushed to death. After 5 months most people had rather vague memories and remembered little. Wright concluded that most people reconstructed their memories blending real experiences with accounts by other people and things they had read about. In other words the theory of **reconstructive memory** (discussed on pages 26–29) could explain the behaviour observed.

Research methods
The confederate

In many psychology experiments it is necessary to have someone who appears to be an ordinary person or another participant, but who in fact is working with the experimenter and has been told carefully how to behave. This person is called a **confederate**.

What is meant by repression?

The idea of repression was proposed by Freud over a century ago. In Freud's theory of repression the mind automatically banishes traumatic events from memory to prevent the overwhelming anxiety that they might cause. A repressed memory, therefore, is the memory of a traumatic event placed beyond conscious awareness into the *unconscious mind*. This displacement makes one feel better, at least temporarily. Freud further theorised that these repressed memories continue to affect conscious thought, desire and action, even though there is no conscious memory of the traumatic event.

Most psychologists accept as fact that it is quite common *consciously* to repress unpleasant experiences, even sexual abuse, and then later to remember spontaneously such events. However, most of the controversy centres around memories recovered during 'repressed memory therapy' (RMT). Critics of RMT maintain that many therapists are not helping patients recover repressed memories, but are (often unwittingly) suggesting and implanting 'false memories' of sexual abuse, alien abduction or even satanic rituals.

Doing a bit of research yourself (in books, the Internet and so on) makes you feel more like a real psychologist. Some of the debates around this subject can be extremely complicated and searching, but fascinating nevertheless. It shouldn't take long to come up with a table of evidence for and against, and then you are well prepared to answer questions such as the one at the top of this section.

What kind of factors influence repression?

The emotionally threatening nature of the material to be remembered and the extent to which the individual can cope with such anxiety (non-repressors cope better).

KEY TERM

Repression: A way of dealing with memories for traumatic events so that the anxiety created by the memory does not have to be experienced. The memory for the event is placed beyond conscious awareness.

Research on the role of repression

Evidence for repression

Evidence from Williams (1994) showed that a high proportion of women who had been sexually abused as children did not show any recall of the abuse when interviewed 20 years later. The study used hospital emergency room records of children who had been admitted; details of the abuse were recorded at the time. Of those who did recall the abuse, 16% reported that they had, at one time, been unable to recall these incidents but had 'recovered' the memory.

It is possible that some of the initial reports of abuse in this study were fictitious. However, most children were subjected to physical examination at the time of the initial report, and those rated most credible actually showed the highest levels of forgetting.

Studies of World War II veterans showed that many who experienced battlefield trauma appeared to repress the memories. The resulting mental illness was only relieved when the memories were 'recovered' in therapy (Karon and Widener, 1997).

Response to emotionally charged words

One way to investigate repression has been to study participants' reactions to emotionally charged words. For example, Bradley and Baddeley (1990) read out a list of words.

Participants were asked to respond by saying any word that came into their head (a *word association* task). Some of the trigger words were neutral (e.g. tree or cow) whereas others were negative and emotional (e.g. angry and fear). Later, participants were given the trigger word and asked to recall their own response. They had more difficulty recalling the emotionally charged words. However, the findings were different if there was a longer delay before testing. Some participants were tested after 28 days and they remembered the emotional associations better than those tested quite soon after initial learning. It is possible that anxiety and arousal depresses short-term recall but enhances long-term recall. Alternatively it may be that anxiety/arousal initially causes repression but this disappears over time.

Evidence against repression

A review of 60 years of experimental tests of repression (Holmes, 1990) led to the conclusion that there is no evidence that unequivocally supports the role of repression in forgetting.

The syndrome of post-traumatic stress disorder (PTSD) shows that verifiable traumatic events, rather than being repressed into the unconscious mind, leave trauma victims haunted by intrusive memories in which the victim relives the trauma.

Research methods
Experiments and causal relationships

We have seen that experiments involve manipulating an IV to observe the effect on the DV. In essence this enables us to observe the *effect* that one thing has on another. We can only claim that one thing *causes* another if we have actually manipulated the IV. In a natural experiment (such as the study by Myers and Brewin) the IV is not manipulated – it varies naturally. Therefore, natural experiments are called **quasi-experiments** – they aren't *truly* an experiment because the IV is not directly manipulated and so we cannot claim to investigate cause-and-effect relationships. But they are *almost* an experiment because there is an IV and a DV.

A number of studies, including one where children were interviewed after a sniper had attacked their school, showed that even children who were not present at the time of the attack still had vivid memories of the event. These 'false' memories were apparently created through exposure to the stories of others who were there.

CRITICAL ISSUE:
Eyewitness testimony

Q   Did you blow your horn or anything?
A   After the accident?
Q   Before the accident.
A   Sure, I played for ten years. I even went to school for it.

specification breakdown

Specification content	Comment
Research into reconstructive memory (e.g. Bartlett).	The models of memory discussed so far regard it as a largely passive process. The **reconstructive approach** suggests that memory is an active process. The term 'research' incorporates theories and studies, so we will look at the theory of reconstructive memory and studies supporting this theory.
Memory research into eyewitness testimony, including the role of leading questions.	Our knowledge of memory, and forgetting, can be applied to a real-world example – **eyewitness testimony**. The main issue concerns the accuracy/reliability (or unreliability) of recall. The use of **leading questions** is one explanation for why eyewitnesses sometimes provide inaccurate information.

On 9 February 1995, 66-year-old Margaret Wilson was brutally murdered by a 'large, clean-shaven' yet unidentified man. In what appeared to have been a completely motiveless murder, the defenceless victim's throat had been slashed from ear to ear as she walked home on a country road near to her home. A number of eyewitnesses claimed to have seen a man near to where the murder took place. Most described him as 'clean-shaven', and driving a 'large white car'. One witness referred to a 'dirty estate car, probably white'. A tractor driver described the car as a 'white Montego'. The man's description was used as a basis for a Photofit image, which was to be crucial in the investigation that followed. Three days after the murder, as part of routine enquiries, two police officers visited the house of Derek Christian, a 31-year-old married man. Mr Christian was described by the police who interviewed him as having a 'pronounced goatee beard' and as being the owner of a 'silver estate car'. The same police officers later stated in court that the car had looked white when they had first seen it in the drive of Christian's house.

One year later, one of the police officers told the court that he had not seen a silver car in the drive at all, let alone one that looked white. Nevertheless, Christian was arrested in March 1996 and subsequently sent to prison for 17 years. His family continue to try to overturn this conviction, arguing that the eyewitness testimony, as well as many other areas of circumstantial evidence, fail to provide compelling proof of Derek Christian's guilt.

Eyewitnesses frequently play a critical role in criminal investigations such as the one above, yet the psychological study of the accuracy of eyewitness memory suggests that it is actually far less reliable than we might imagine. The importance of this issue was highlighted in the Devlin Report of 1976, which found that in a large proportion of criminal cases in England and Wales, eyewitness testimony was the only evidence offered in court, and in approximately 75% of these cases the suspect was found guilty. In fact, research in the US has shown that inaccurate eyewitness memory is the main factor leading to false convictions. One study estimated that there may be about 10,000 wrong convictions a year in the US through eyewitness testimony. In those cases, an innocent person is imprisoned, and the guilty person is still free.

Although there were no dramatic changes to the legal system as a result of these studies, a precedent was set in Britain in the 1977 Crown versus Turnbull trial, where the Court of Appeal rejected eyewitness testimony that was presented without supportive evidence. Since then, prosecutions are unlikely to be brought on eyewitness evidence alone, and much greater use is now made of evidence like DNA and closed-circuit TV recordings. However, eyewitness testimony is still an important part of the evidence in many criminal trials, and presents a number of challenges to psychology.

What is meant by reconstructive memory?

The *reconstruction principle* states that remembering the past occurs in the context of the present. When we try to recover a memory, we begin with information supplied by the retrieval cue, combine this with what we can recover from the memory trace, and then fill in the gaps. This may involve fleshing out the details and doing anything else necessary in order to achieve a coherent narrative. We may make inferences based on our expectations, beliefs and prejudices, or we may simply turn to our fund of general knowledge. Remembering is less like *reading* a book and more like *writing* one from often just a few fragmentary notes.

research activity

If you want to try repeating this study have a look at http://www.slc.edu/~kcunliff/warofghosts.html for ideas about how to score changes to the story.

CRITICAL ISSUE: EYEWITNESS TESTIMONY

KEY TERM

Reconstructive memory: Fragments of stored information are reassembled during recall, and the gaps are filled in by our expectations and beliefs to produce a coherent narrative.

star**STUDY**

Reconstructive memory

(BARTLETT, 1932)

Bartlett conducted a series of experiments to demonstrate reconstructive memory. His hypothesis was that if a person was given something to remember and then asked to recall the story or picture over a period of weeks or years, the recollection will be endlessly *transformed*. In particular, if the information to be remembered is somewhat foreign and/or unusual, people will impose their own familiar (**cultural**) expectations and make the story more familiar over time.

Aims

To investigate how memory is reconstructed when recall is repeated over a period of weeks and months. In particular, to see how cultural expectations affect memory and lead to predictable distortions.

Procedures

Bartlett used a technique he called *repeated reproductions*. This involved showing a story or simple drawing to a participant and asking them to reproduce it shortly after (e.g. 15 minutes later), then repeatedly over weeks, months and years. A key feature of the stimulus material was that it belonged to a culture that was exceedingly different to that of the participants. Bartlett reasoned that such material would change markedly in retelling (or redrawing) because memory was inevitably adjusted in terms of social knowledge.

Bartlett used a number of participants and, for each one, kept a record of successive recall (a *protocol*). None of the participants knew the purpose of the study.

The best-known story used by Bartlett was the *War of the Ghosts*, shown on the left.

The original story

One night two young men from Egulac went down the river to hunt seals, and while they were there it became foggy and calm. Then they heard war-cries, and they thought: 'Maybe this is a war-party.' They escaped to the shore and hid behind a log. Now canoes came up, and they heard the noise of paddles, and saw one canoe coming up to them. There were five men in the canoe, and they said:

'What do you think? We wish to take you along. We are going up the river to make war on the people.'

One of the young men said: 'I have no arrows.'

'Arrows are in the canoe,' they said.

'I will not go along. I might get killed. My relatives do not know where I have gone. But you,' he said, turning to the other, 'may go with them.'

So one of the young men went, but the other returned home.

And the warriors went up on the river to a town on the other side of Kalama. The people came down to the water, and they began to fight, and many were killed. But presently the young man heard one of the warriors say: 'Quick, let us go home: that Indian has been hit.' Now he thought: 'Oh, they are ghosts.' He did not feel sick, but they said he had been shot.

So the canoes went back to Egulac, and the young man went ashore to his house, and made a fire. And he told everybody and said: 'Behold I accompanied the ghosts, and we went to fight, many of our fellows were killed, and many of those who attacked us were killed. They said I was hit, and I did not feel sick.'

He told it all and then became quiet. When the sun rose he fell down. Something black came out of his mouth. His face became contorted. The people jumped up and cried.

He was dead.

Recall after 1 day

Two men from Edulac went fishing. While thus occupied by the river they heard a noise in the distance.

'It sounds like a cry', said one and presently there appeared some men in canoes who invited them to join the party on their adventure. One of the young men refused to go, on the grounds of family ties, but the other offered to go.

'But there are no arrows', he said.

'The arrows are in the boat', was the reply.

He thereupon took his place, while his friend returned home. The party paddled up the river to Kaloma, and began to land on the banks of the river. The enemy came rushing upon them, and some sharp fighting ensued. Presently someone was injured, and the cry was raised that the enemy was ghosts.

The party returned down the stream, and the young man returned home feeling none the worse for his experience. The next morning at dawn he endeavoured to recount his adventures. While he was talking something black issued from his mouth. Suddenly he uttered a cry and fell down. His friends gathered around him.

But he was dead.

Bartlett's theory of reconstructive memory

Sir Frederic Bartlett (1886–1969) is one of the 'great' psychologists. His main work was a book called *Remembering: A Study in Experimental and Social Psychology* (1932), which changed the view psychologists had of memory. Before then memory was viewed as an act of reproduction: when we remember something we store a record of an event and retrieve it later without altering the record in any way. This is a passive model of memory. Bartlett proposed that memory is much more of an active process. We store fragments of information and when we need to recall something we reconstruct these fragments into a meaningful whole. This reconstruction leads to inaccuracy. Most importantly, our past experience, beliefs and expectations shape the way we reconstruct memory.

Consider the following example. There was a supposed UFO crash at Roswell, New Mexico, in 1947. The truth about this event is unclear and, by now, there are so many versions of this truth that we can never hope to know what really happened. *People's memories are shaped by their own beliefs.* There are no accurate memories, according to Bartlett.

Recall of the story after 8 days

Two men from Edulac went fishing. While thus engaged they heard a noise in the distance. 'That sounds like a war-cry,' said one, 'there is going to be some fighting.' Presently there appeared some warriors who invited them to join an expedition up the river.

One of the young men excused himself on the grounds of family ties. 'I cannot come,' he said, 'as I might get killed.' So they returned home. The other man, however, joined the party, and they proceeded on canoes up the river. While landing on the banks the enemy appeared and were running down to meet them. Soon someone was wounded, and the party discovered that they were fighting against ghosts. The young man and his companion returned to the boats, and went back to their homes.

The next morning at dawn he was describing his adventures to his friends, who gathered around him. Suddenly something black issued from his mouth, and he fell down uttering a cry. His friends closed around him, but found that he was dead.

Findings

By analysing the protocols Bartlett found that participants remembered different parts of stories and that they interpreted them within their own frames of reference (cultural expectations), changing the facts to make them fit. Bartlett made several observations of the transformations that occurred.

- The story was shortened, mainly by omissions.
- The phraseology was changed to language and concepts from the participant's own culture. For example, using 'boats' instead of 'canoe'.
- The recalled version soon became very fixed, though each time it was recalled there were slight variations.

Conclusions

All of these transformations had the effect of making the material easier to remember. We don't remember details, we remember fragments and use our knowledge of social situations to reconstruct memory. Individuals remembered the *meaning* and tried to sketch out the story using invented details. This reconstructed version of events is simpler to remember and therefore becomes our memory for the event.

Bartlett concluded that much human memory is influenced by factors that are social in origin and that may be obscured by laboratory methods because of the artificial nature of the material used in such experiments. He called his work 'the social psychology of remembering' and said that memory is a 'triumphant solution' to the problem of dealing with absent objects.

On page 7 we described a study by Waganaar and Groeneweg (1990), who interviewed people who had been imprisoned in concentration camps during World War II. Thirty years later their recall was still good for certain details, such as the name of the camp commandant, but they had forgotten many other details. Suggest at least three explanations for this apparent 'forgetting' or apparent 'remembering'.

Criticisms

There is considerable research support for the effect of schema on memory

Bartlett's studies support this idea of reconstructive memory. More research is examined on the next two pages. These studies show that **schema** do affect memory processes. Bartlett made an important contribution to our understanding of memory as an active and unreliable process.

Memory can be very accurate

On the other hand, other studies have shown that memory can be very accurate. For example, in situations that are personally important or distinctive, we do remember considerable and accurate detail. Memory can in such instances be quite passive, for example when you are required to learn lines for a play.

'Cultural expectations' are the views and beliefs passed to you by the society in which you live.

A **schema** is a packet of information about a thing. It is a store of previous information about previous experiences which is used to generate future experiences.

Criticisms

This was not a very well-controlled study

The participants were not given very specific instructions and therefore some of the distortions may have resulted from conscious guessing rather than gaps in memory. Gauld and Stephenson (1967) found that when accurate recall was stressed at the outset, errors fell by almost half. Control was also lacking in the informal way the reproductions were analysed. Bartlett's own beliefs may have affected the way he interpreted the data.

Is it true to real life?

Wynn and Logie (1998) tested students' recall of real-life events over a 6-month period. Recall was relatively accurate and little transformation took place, suggesting that there was very little use of reconstruction in real-life situations.

Reconstructive memory (continued)

CRITICAL ISSUE: EYEWITNESS TESTIMONY

Bartlett's classic studies offered good support for his theory of reconstructive memory. Many subsequent studies have further supported the theory and helped clarify some of the details. We will look at these other studies now, as well as at the factors that influence reconstructive memory.

Other research related to reconstructive memory

The concept of schema

The core of Bartlett's theory is that our beliefs generate expectations and these expectations reconstruct memory. This can be seen in a classic study by Carmichael *et al.* (1932). Participants were shown a set of drawings (see box). There were two groups of participants. Each group saw the drawings but was given a different set of descriptions. When the participants were asked to recall the drawings, the 'label' they had been given affected the drawing they subsequently produced. This shows that the language used affected their memory. In essence, a word conjures up a set of expectations about an object, and this expectation affects the memory. So, in Carmichael's study, we might say that memory was affected by the *schema* provided.

Do schema alter our initial perceptions or do they alter subsequent recall?

Bartlett assumed that it was the retrieval process that was affected by schema, but subsequent research has shown that initial comprehension and storage are also affected. For example, Bransford and Johnson (1972) asked participants to read the sentences shown below, and later to accurately recall as many as possible. Those participants who were given the title ('Making and flying a kite') did much better at recalling the sentences. Why? Because they had a schema (kites) to aid their initial comprehension and storage of information.

Try to remember these sentences.

1 A newspaper is better than a magazine.	8 A seashore is a better place than a street.
2 At first it is better to run than to walk.	9 You may have to try several times.
3 It takes some skill but it's easy to learn.	10 Even young children can enjoy it.
4 Once successful, complications are minimal.	11 Birds seldom get too close.
5 Rain, however, soaks in very fast.	12 Too many people doing the same thing can cause problems.
6 One needs lots of room.	13 If there are no complications, it can be very peaceful.
7 A rock will serve as an anchor.	14 If things break loose from it, however, you will not get a second chance.

The confirmatory bias

The fact that schema influence memory means that they are self-fulfilling. Consider this study by Cohen (1981). Participants were shown a video of a woman and man talking together while eating dinner. The woman was described beforehand as either a librarian or a waitress. When participants were later asked to recall things about

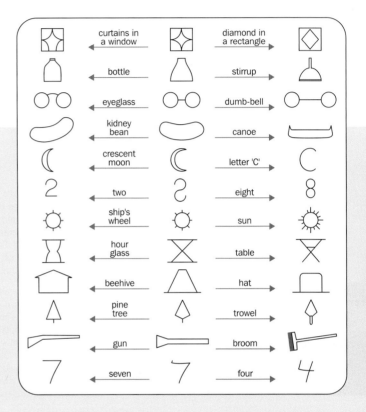

the woman, they tended to recall things in line with the given **stereotype** (schema) of a waitress (e.g. she liked bowling and ate burgers) or a librarian (e.g. she read books and liked roast beef). (You may be asking 'Why is eating roast beef typical of a librarian?' These stereotypes had been established in a previous study.)

The point is that this kind of selective memory then goes on to support your existing stereotype. You don't recall that this waitress liked reading because that is inconsistent with your stereotype, and this helps perpetuate your stereotypes. This has been called a **confirmatory bias**.

Other studies of the effects of schema

Brewer and Treyens (1981) asked participants to wait in an office-like room. In the room were various objects, some that were consistent with the schema of an office (e.g. a desk and a typewriter) and others that were inconsistent (e.g. a skull and a brick). Later, when unexpectedly asked to list the objects, they recalled the consistent items better than the inconsistent ones – except many did recall that there was a skull. Presumably, highly distinctive items are especially memorable (as would be predicted by **levels of processing theory**).

Sulin and Dooling (1974) gave participants a story about a man called Gerald Martin who 'strove to undermine the existing government to satisfy his political ambitions.... He became a ruthless, uncontrollable dictator. The ultimate effect of his rule was the downfall of his country'. Other participants had the same story but the man was called Adolf Hitler. These participants were ... much more likely to indicate that they had read 'He hated the Jews particularly' in the story. Their schema about Adolf Hitler biased their memories.

Factors that influence reconstructive memory

Stereotypes

Stereotypes are (usually) simplistic schema that we have about a particular class or group of people. In order to maintain relative simplicity in our social world, as well as being able to predict the behaviour of those around us, we may resort to commonly held stereotypes when reconstructing a memory. A classic study by Allport and Postman (1947) showed two men (one white and one black) arguing on a subway train. Participants invariably remembered the open razor (the preferred mugging weapon in those days) as being in the hand of the black man, whereas in fact it had been held by the white man.

Interviewing techniques

The way in which a witness is interviewed has been shown to influence *what* they recall – the more leading or suggestive the questions, the lower the accuracy. Interviewers may unintentionally communicate their expectations in various ways (facial expressions, tone of voice). Such expectations are found to affect the reconstruction of a memory and may distort a witness's version of an event.

What is a schema?

Cara visited Naples some years ago and enjoyed it immensely, but she had great difficulty working out the public transport system. She managed to locate the bus stop and found out which bus went to the city centre, but couldn't understand how to get tickets. They were not sold on the bus yet people had them on boarding and inserted them in a machine at the back of the bus. One day she saw someone purchasing a ticket at a kiosk in the street, but she still didn't know how to ask for one in Italian. In short, what Cara lacked was a schema for using buses in Naples, but she was building one up as she gathered experience.

COMMENTARY CORNER

'Memory is more a matter of reconstruction than reproduction.' To what extent has research supported the view that memories are influenced by the retrieval process?

Unlike previous questions in these Commentary Corners, this one is preceded by a quotation. This is designed to help you structure your answer. It implies that memories are 'reconstructed' at retrieval rather than being reproduced in exactly the same form that they had been encoded. By now you should be able to put together a creditworthy response to this question, so you can concentrate on fine-tuning your answer.

The following material has been cut from the preceding text. It is in no particular order so it is your task to structure these statements into a logical response to the question. In addition to the statements you will need a good supply of linking phrases such as 'However…' and 'This is supported by…'. This is quite a relaxing task, particularly if you type out these sentences, 'trim' the excess words, cut them into strips, write your linking words and phrases on smaller pieces of paper and then start piecing the answer together. Remember – you don't need to use *all* the information given here. You be the judge of what is in and what is out.

- A classic study by Allport and Postman (1947) showed two men arguing on a subway train. Participants invariably remembered the open razor as being in the hand of the black man, whereas in fact it had been held by the white man.

- The reconstruction principle states that remembering the past occurs in the context of the present. When we try to recover a memory, we begin with information supplied by the retrieval cue, combine this with what we can recover from the memory trace, and then fill in the gaps.

- It may be that these findings don't hold up under more naturalistic conditions. Wynn and Logie (1998) tested students recall of real-life events over a 6-month period. Recall was relatively accurate and little transformation took place, suggesting that there was very little use of reconstruction in real-life situations.

- Bartlett found that participants remembered different parts of stories and that they interpreted them within their own frames of reference (cultural expectations), changing the facts to make them fit.

- Bartlett concluded that much human memory is influenced by factors that are social in origin and that may be obscured by laboratory methods because of the artificial nature of the material used in such experiments.

- This was not a very well-controlled study. The participants were not given very specific instructions and therefore some of the distortions may have resulted from conscious guessing rather than gaps in memory. Gauld and Stephenson (1967) found that when accurate recall was stressed at the outset, then errors fell by almost half.

- Bartlett conducted a series of experiments to demonstrate reconstructive memory. His hypothesis was that if a person is given something to remember and then asked to recall the story or picture over a period of weeks or years, the recollection will be endlessly transformed.

- Other studies have shown that memory can be very accurate. For example, in situations that are personally important or distinctive we do remember considerable and accurate detail. Memory can in such instances be quite passive, for example when you are required to learn lines for a play.

- Bartlett assumed that it was the retrieval process that was affected by schema, but subsequent research has shown that initial comprehension and storage are also affected.

What is meant by eyewitness testimony?

The term **eyewitness testimony** (EWT) is a legal term that refers to the use of eyewitnesses (or earwitnesses) to give evidence in court concerning the identity of someone suspected of committing a crime. Psychologists tend to use the term 'eyewitness memory' when carrying out research to test the accuracy of EWT.

Eyewitness memory goes through three stages:

- The witness *encodes* into LTM details of the event and the persons involved. Encoding may be only partial and distorted, particularly as most crimes happen very quickly, often at night, and may be accompanied by rapid, complex and often violent action.

- The witness *retains* the information for a period of time. Memories may be lost or modified during retention (most forgetting takes place within the first few minutes of a retention interval), and other activities between encoding and retrieval may *interfere* with the memory itself.

- The witness *retrieves* the memory from storage. What happens during the reconstruction of the memory (e.g. the presence or absence of appropriate retrieval cues or the nature of the questioning) may significantly affect its accuracy.

Prior to the Devlin Report in 1976, it was generally assumed that EWT was sufficiently accurate to be used as sole evidence for prosecution. After considering the evidence for this claim, however, the Devlin committee made the recommendation that no court should convict on the basis of EWT alone. In subsequent research, psychologists found that not only were witnesses often inaccurate in their memory of people and events, but there was little (if any) relationship between the *accuracy* of their recall and their *level of confidence* (i.e. how certain they were about being right). Since then, psychologists have attempted to find the conditions where EWT is fallible, and how it might be improved. After all, it is often the only source of information available about a crime.

http://eyewitnessconsortium.utep.edu/publications.html
Articles on eyewitness testimony.

starSTUDY

A study into the role of leading questions in EWT

(LOFTUS & PALMER, 1974)

Many studies have been conducted on EWT, a number of them by Elizabeth Loftus. Here she worked with John Palmer to look at some of the ways that memory can be distorted.

Aims

The study's general aim was to investigate the accuracy of memory after witnessing a car accident. In particular it was to see if **leading questions** distort the accuracy of an eyewitness's immediate recall. People are notoriously poor at estimating the speed of moving cars and therefore they might be particularly receptive to any hints (leading questions). This experiment aimed to see if this is true.

Procedures

Forty-five students were shown seven films of different traffic accidents. After each film the participants were given a questionnaire which asked them to describe the accident and then answer a series of specific questions about it. There was one *critical question*: 'About how fast were the cars going when they hit each other?' One group of participants was given this question. The other four groups were given the verbs 'smashed', 'collided', 'bumped' or 'contacted' in place of the word 'hit'.

Each group of participants was shown the films in a different order. Why do you think this was done?

'Do you get headaches frequently?'

According to Loftus' research this is a leading question. People asked this question reported an average of 2.2 headaches per week, whereas those who were asked 'Do you get headaches occasionally, and if so, how often?' reported an average of 0.7 headaches! The *way* the question was asked had a significant effect on the answer given.

KEY TERM

Eyewitness testimony: The evidence provided in court by a person who witnessed a crime, with a view to identifying the perpetrator. The accuracy of eyewitness recall may be affected during initial encoding, subsequent storage and eventual retrieval.

Leading question: Loftus and Palmer state that a leading question 'is simply one that, either by its form or content, suggests to the witness what answer is desired or leads him to the desired answer'.

Research methods *What is a 'control group'?*

We mentioned control groups when looking at research into interference. If a **control group** is used in an experiment, it does not receive the IV but its performance is assessed on the DV. We can compare the **experimental groups** (those who receive the IV or experimental 'treatment') with the control group to see if the IV did have an effect. Without the control group we have no record of the baseline. In a repeated measures study there may be a **control condition**.

Findings

The **mean** speed estimate was calculated for each group, as shown in the table. The group given the word 'smashed' estimated a higher speed than the other groups (about 41 m.p.h.). The group given the word 'contacted' estimated the lowest speed (about 32 m.p.h.).

Speed estimates for the verbs used in Experiment 1

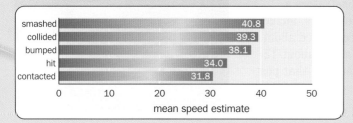

Conclusions

This shows that the form of question can have a significant effect on a witness's answer. In other words, leading questions can affect the accuracy of memory. Such leading questions are an example of what psychologists call **post-event information** – information given after the event which may alter memory. It is possible that such post-event information causes the information to be altered before it is stored so that memory is permanently affected.

A second possible explanation is that the form of the question actually alters the participant's memory representation of the accident, which leads them to produce a higher or lower estimate.

Criticisms

Not very true to life

A laboratory experiment may not represent real life because people don't take the experiment seriously and/or they are not emotionally aroused as they would be in a real accident. Foster *et al.* (1994) found that if participants thought they were watching a real-life robbery and that their responses would influence the trial, their identification of a robber was more accurate.

Emotional arousal may actually enhance the accuracy of memory, as Christianson and Hubinette (1993) found when they interviewed 110 real witnesses to bank robberies. Those witnesses who had been threatened were more accurate in their recall and remembered more details than those who had been onlookers and less emotionally aroused. This continued to be true even 15 months later.

A demand characteristic

In many experiments, the **experimental design** leads to certain inevitable responses from participants. They might feel uncertain about what to do and how to behave, and would look for *cues* about what is expected of them. They would be especially receptive to certain features of the experiment, such as leading questions. These features almost *demand* a particular response and thus these **demand characteristics** might explain the findings of Loftus and Palmer's study.

Try repeating one of the experiments from Loftus and Palmer's study, using a photograph of a car accident and devising a set of questions, one of which will be the *critical question*. Alternatively, you can adapt the design by using a photograph of two footballers colliding. Ask how fast the players were travelling, describing their collision using the verbs 'hit', 'bumped', 'smashed' and so on.

In the experiment by Loftus and Palmer, how might participant reactivity have been a problem? Can you think of a way this might have been overcome?

Star study extra

Loftus and Palmer conducted a second experiment to see if memory was altered by post-event information. A new set of participants was divided into three groups and shown a film of a car accident. Group 1 was given the verb 'smashed', group 2 the verb *hit*, and group 3 (the **control group**) was not given any question about the speed of the vehicles. The participants returned one week later and were asked 10 questions about the accident, including another *critical question*: 'Did you see any broken glass?' There was no broken glass in the film but, presumably, those who thought the car was travelling faster might *expect* that there would be broken glass. The findings are shown in the table. Participants gave higher speed estimates in the 'smashed' condition, as before. They were also more likely to think they saw broken glass. This shows a significant effect of *post-event information* on later recall of events.

'Yes' and 'No' responses to the question about broken glass

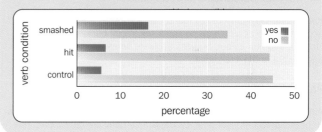

These 'averages' are also described as *measures of central tendency* because they inform us about central values for the group.

Research methods *Calculating an average*

The term 'average' means a typical value for a set of data. Averages are a way of *describing* a set of data. An average can be calculated in different ways:

- The **mean** is calculated by adding up all the scores and dividing by the number of scores. This method makes use of all the values, but it can be misrepresentative if there are extreme values.
- The **median** is the *middle* value in an *ordered* list. This method has the advantage of not being affected by extreme scores, but it is not as 'sensitive' as the mean because not all values are reflected.
- The **mode** is the value that is *most* common. This is useful when the data are in categories (e.g. number of people who like pink). It is not a useful way of describing data when there may be an **experimental** and **control condition**.

Other research on eyewitness testimony

Leading questions

The study by Loftus and Palmer demonstrated how the use of leading questions (or post-event information) may affect subsequent recall. Loftus (1975) showed participants a short video of 8 demonstrators disrupting a lecture. Participants were later given a questionnaire, including the critical question: 'Was the leader of the 4 (or 12) demonstrators a male?' A week later the participants were asked several questions, including one about the number of demonstrators. Those who had been asked about 4 demonstrators gave a mean answer of 6.4, whereas those asked about 12 demonstrators gave a mean of 8.9. This further supports the idea that post-event information effects subsequent recall.

Loftus and Zanni (1975) used a film of a car accident, and then asked a series of questions including the critical question: 'Did you see a broken headlight?' Other participants were asked if they saw 'the' broken headlight. In fact, there was no broken headlight. As expected, participants were more likely to answer 'yes' if they were asked the question with 'the'.

▲ Misleading information? This can affect the accuracy of recall.

Factors that influence the accuracy of EWT

Memory for personal characteristics

Kebbel and Wagstaff (1999) found that witnesses were normally very accurate when describing a person's sex, racial background, style of clothing and hair colour, but less accurate when describing things like age, height and overall build.

Arousal

Although evidence is mixed, many researchers believe that the effects of physiological arousal on eyewitness testimony are *curvilinear*. This means that *small* to *medium* increases in arousal may increase the accuracy of memory, but *high* levels interfere with accuracy. There is also some evidence that in violent crimes, arousal may focus the witness on more central details of the attack (e.g. a **weapons effect**) than the more peripheral details (e.g. what else was going on).

Other factors – ADVOKATE

Other important factors that determine the accuracy of EWT can be remembered using the mnemonic ADVOKATE (Wagstaff, 2002). Accuracy is improved under the following conditions:

A **amount of time** – the longer the time for which the event was observed.

D **distance** – the closer the witness is to the event.

V **visibility** – the clearer the visibility.

O **obstructions** – few obstructions between witness and event.

K **known** – the more familiar the person, the better the identification.

A **any reason to remember** – the more novel or emotionally salient the better.

T **time** – the shorter the time between the event and recall, the better the memory.

E **errors** – the more inaccurate parts of a witness's testimony are shown to be, the less reliable is the rest of their testimony.

Is EWT unreliable?

Buckhout (1980) conducted a study with 2,000 participants. A 13-second film was shown on prime-time TV. Later an identity parade was shown on TV and viewers were invited to phone in their choice of suspect. Only 14% got it right!

Yuille and Cutshall (1986) interviewed 13 people who had witnessed an armed robbery in Canada. The interviews took place more than 4 months after the crime and included two misleading questions. Despite these questions, the witnesses provided accurate recall that matched their initial detailed reports. This suggests that post-event information may not affect memory in real life. This study also shows that EWT can be very reliable.

Acquisition or retrieval: Do leading questions alter the way information is stored or the way it is retrieved?

Loftus et al. (1978) showed slides of events leading up to a car accident. One group was shown a red Datsun stopping at a junction with a 'STOP' sign. The other group was shown a 'YIELD' sign (i.e. 'GIVE WAY'). Later all participants were given a set of questions. Half of each group were asked: 'Did another car pass the red Datsun while it was at the YIELD sign?', and the other half had the question with 'STOP sign'. Finally, they were shown pairs of slides and had to identify which slides were in the original sequence. Seventy-five per cent of participants who had consistent questions picked the correct slide, whereas only 41% who had a misleading question picked the correct slide. In other words, the misleading question affected their recall.

Bekerian and Bowers (1983) replicated the stop sign/yield sign study by Loftus et al. (1978). In the recognition part of the experiment Loftus et al. had presented the slides out of sequence (in a random order). Bekerian and Bowers gave the slides in the original order and found that recall was now the same for the consistent and misleading groups. This shows that the participants' memories were intact in spite of misleading post-event information. Therefore misleading questions (post-event information) would appear to affect the retrieval of memories rather than their storage.

Lindsay (1990) showed a series of slides to participants in which a man steals some things from an office. The participants were then given an account of the crime that contained misleading information. Later they were given a questionnaire and warned not to pay attention to the account of the crime just given but to rely on their own memory. Nevertheless, they were influenced by the misleading information. This suggests that leading questions (post-event information) actually change the way information is stored and it isn't just about retrieval!

People believe EWT

Loftus (1974) described a fictitious case to 50 students. A man and his granddaughter had been murdered during a robbery at a grocery store. On the evidence presented only 9 students thought the suspect was guilty. However, another set of 50 students was told there was a witness who could identify the suspect. Now 36 said that the suspect was guilty. A third group of students was additionally told that the witness had not been wearing his glasses at the time of the crime and therefore was unlikely to have seen the suspect's face clearly. Nevertheless, 34 still said he was guilty. This study underlines why it is so important to find out about the reliability of EWT.

The effects of expectations

See the discussion on schema and stereotypes (pages 28–9).

Insignificant versus significant details

Loftus (1979b) showed participants a series of pictures of a man stealing a red wallet from a woman's bag. Later 98% identified the colour correctly. Furthermore, despite later being given an erroneous description of the wallet as brown, participants persisted in describing the wallet as red. This shows that we may have good recall for important information, and that recall of such information may not be distorted even by misleading information.

Loftus (1979a) identified the **weapon focus**. There were two conditions in this experiment. In both conditions participants heard a discussion in an adjoining room. In condition 1 a man emerged holding a pen and with grease on his hands. In condition 2 the discussion was rather more heated and a man emerged holding a paper-knife covered in blood. When asked to identify the man from 50 photos, participants in condition 1 were 49% accurate compared with 33% accuracy in condition 2. This suggests that the weapon may have distracted attention from the man and might explain why eyewitnesses sometimes have poor recall for certain details of a crime.

Elizabeth Loftus

CORNER

To what extent has research shown eyewitness testimony to be inaccurate?

Psychologists such as Elizabeth Loftus are frequently asked to appear as 'expert witnesses' in US courts. Their role is to testify about whether a particular testimony is likely to be accurate and to comment generally on the reliability (or otherwise) of EWT. Your role in this exercise is to play the part of an expert witness and, using the material in this section, construct *your* response to the above question. Of course Loftus is not usually constrained to 300 words or so, nor does she have to balance her descriptive content (AO1) with her evaluative content (AO2) in that now familiar 1:2 ratio. And yes she does get paid a lot more for her contribution, but does she get the same sense of satisfaction at a job well done?

But wait...

Although much of the research has highlighted the fallibility of EWT, research has also looked at ways in which its accuracy can be improved. Geiselman et al. (1985) reviewed the relevant psychological literature on memory and related this to the way that interviews were carried out by the police in real life. They found, for example, that people remember events better when they are provided with *retrieval cues*. This could be accomplished in the police interview by mentally reinstating the context of the event being recalled. They also found that police interviewers often asked questions out of chronological order and frequently shifted from one modality to another (e.g. going from a question about what someone *said* to a question about their physical *appearance*). Such procedures had the effect of restricting the available retrieval cues for witnesses to accurately recall a person or event. Geiselman et al. developed an interviewing technique, the *cognitive interview*, which was based on proven psychological principles concerning effective memory recall. Although there are some problems with the cognitive interview in use (it is, for example, very time-consuming), it does tend to produce more detailed and accurate information than a standard police interview. Current research is focused on the relative contribution of each of the individual components of the cognitive interview in an attempt to make the technique more streamlined and time-efficient.

SUMMARIES

Short-term and long-term memory

Memory: process by which we retain information about events in the past; short- and long-term.

Short-term memory (STM): memory for immediate events, they last a very short time and disappear unless rehearsed; limited duration and limited capacity.

Long-term memory (LTM): memory for events in the past, from 2 minutes to 100 years; potentially unlimited duration and capacity.

The nature of memory

Short-term memory

Duration: how long memory lasts.

Star Study: Peterson and Peterson trigram recall. Criticisms: laboratory study, student participants.

Duration: Unexpected recall of words after 4 seconds was almost zero (Sebrechts et al.).

Capacity: Serial digit span technique is 9.3 for digits and 7.3 for letters (Jacobs). Increased using chunking (Miller 7±2), but size of chunk may matter (Simon).

Encoding: Acoustic encoding demonstrated (Conrad, Baddeley) but not if given visual task and verbal rehearsal prevented (Brandimote et al.).

Long-term memory

Capacity: amount that can be held in memory.

Duration: Naturalistic studies (e.g. Bahrick et al.) show VLTM. Some but not all memories enduring (Waganaar and Groeneweg).

Capacity: Unlimited – demonstrated by unlimited duration.

Encoding: Semantic encoding (Baddeley), but more than one kind of LTM, e.g. semantic and episodic.

Star study: Bahrick et al. yearbook pictures. Criticisms: good way to test memory, possibly confounding variables.

Models of memory

Multi-store model

Multi-store model: three stores (sensory, STM, LTM); transfer of data by attention (SM to STM) and rehearsal (STM to LTM).

Research: studies of the sensory store (Sperling), serial position effect (Glanzer and Cunitz), PET scans of prefrontal cortex and the hippocampus.

Criticisms: good research support but oversimplifies memory storage and processing.

Working memory model

Working memory model: central executive, phonological loop (phonological store and articulatory process) and visuo-spatial sketchpad.

Research: performance slower when doing two tasks using the same component (Hitch and Baddeley), word-length effect (Baddeley), articulatory suppression task, studies of brain-damaged patients (e.g. SC and LH).

Criticisms: good research support, central executive is sketchy.

Levels of processing model

Levels of processing model: emphasises depth of processing

Research: meaning (Craik and Tulving), organisation (Mandler), distinctiveness (Eysenck and Eysenck), elaboration (Palmere et al.), effort (Tyler et al.).

Criticisms: transfer-appropriate processing, concept of depth may be circular.

— Alternatives to multi-store model. —

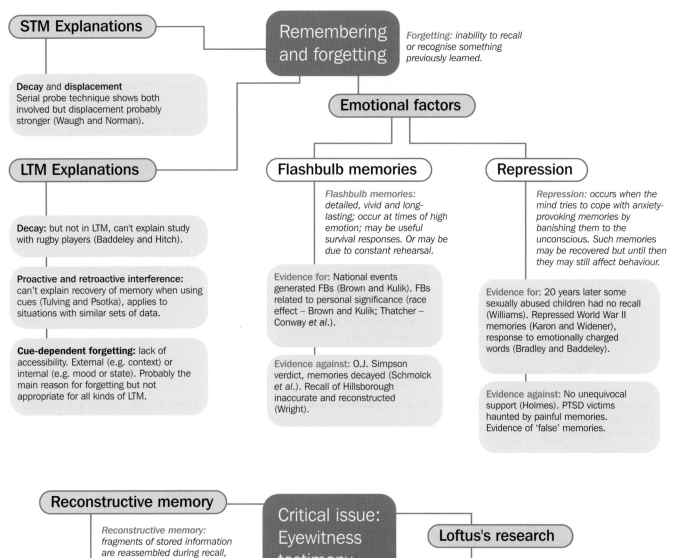

STM Explanations

Decay and **displacement**
Serial probe technique shows both involved but displacement probably stronger (Waugh and Norman).

Remembering and forgetting

Forgetting: inability to recall or recognise something previously learned.

Emotional factors

LTM Explanations

Decay: but not in LTM, can't explain study with rugby players (Baddeley and Hitch).

Proactive and retroactive interference: can't explain recovery of memory when using cues (Tulving and Psotka), applies to situations with similar sets of data.

Cue-dependent forgetting: lack of accessibility. External (e.g. context) or internal (e.g. mood or state). Probably the main reason for forgetting but not appropriate for all kinds of LTM.

Flashbulb memories

Flashbulb memories: detailed, vivid and long-lasting; occur at times of high emotion; may be useful survival responses. Or may be due to constant rehearsal.

Evidence for: National events generated FBs (Brown and Kulik). FBs related to personal significance (race effect – Brown and Kulik; Thatcher – Conway et al.).

Evidence against: O.J. Simpson verdict, memories decayed (Schmolck et al.). Recall of Hillsborough inaccurate and reconstructed (Wright).

Repression

Repression: occurs when the mind tries to cope with anxiety-provoking memories by banishing them to the unconscious. Such memories may be recovered but until then they may still affect behaviour.

Evidence for: 20 years later some sexually abused children had no recall (Williams). Repressed World War II memories (Karon and Widener), response to emotionally charged words (Bradley and Baddeley).

Evidence against: No unequivocal support (Holmes). PTSD victims haunted by painful memories. Evidence of 'false' memories.

Reconstructive memory

Reconstructive memory: fragments of stored information are reassembled during recall, and the gaps are filled in by our expectations and beliefs to produce a coherent narrative.

Star study: Bartlett: recall of *War of the Ghosts* was shortened, made more familiar, coherent and stereotyped. Criticisms: not well controlled; not true to life.

Reconstructive memory Bartlett: memory is an active process, a reconstruction that combines memory fragments with expectations (schema). Schema may affect storage and recall. Criticisms: well-supported by research studies but cannot explain situations where memory *is* very accurate.

Factors that influence reconstructive memory: stereotypes and leading questions.

Critical issue: Eyewitness testimony

EWT is evidence provided in court by a person who witnessed a crime to help identify perpetrator.

Loftus's research

Star study: Loftus and Palmer leading questions (using *smashed* rather than *hit*) alter recall of events. Criticisms: findings not related to 'real-life'; demand characteristics.

Other research: EWT can be reliable (Buckhout), post-event information alters memory (Berkerian and Bowers); EWT believed easily (Loftus); EWT affected by expectations (Bartlett); significant details remembered well (Loftus).

Factors that influence EWT: personal characteristics and arousal; ADVOKATE.

Section 1 Short-term memory and long-term memory

1 **Short-term memory and long-term memory are different in terms of**
   a Capacity
   b Capacity and duration
   c Capacity, duration and encoding
   d Capacity, duration, encoding and location in the brain

2 **In relation to memory, encoding means**
   a Writing something down in code
   b Storing information in memory
   c The way that something is stored in memory
   d The form that something is stored in memory

3 **Short-term memory uses**
   a Mainly an acoustic code
   b Mainly a semantic code
   c Both an acoustic and a semantic code
   d None of the above

4 **Most memory experiments involve**
   a Episodic memory
   b Procedural memory
   c Semantic memory
   d All kinds of memory

5 **The multi-store model suggests that there are**
   a Two kinds of memory store
   b Three kinds of memory store
   c Four kinds of memory store
   d Many kinds of memory store

6 **The working memory model relates to**
   a Short-term memory
   b Long-term memory
   c Short- and long-term memory
   d Memory used by working people

7 **Examples of deep processing include**
   a Depth only
   b Depth and organisation
   c Depth, organisation, distinctiveness and elaboration
   d Any activity that increases meaningfulness

8 **A key characteristic of an experiment is**
   a That everything is very controlled
   b It is artificial
   c Both of the above
   d Neither of the above

9 **The experimenter manipulates**
   a The experiment
   b The dependent variable
   c The independent variable
   d Extraneous variables

10 **Psychology is different from common sense because**
   a Psychologists are very clever
   b Psychologists can tell us about the world
   c Psychologists conduct well-controlled studies
   d Psychology is the same as common sense

Section 2 Remembering and forgetting

1 **The serial probe technique is used to investigate**
   a Forgetting in STM
   b Forgetting in LTM
   c The order that numbers can be remembered
   d The rate of forgetting

2 **If a series of numbers is read out faster but this has no effect on recall of the number after the probe, this is evidence that forgetting in STM is due to**
   a Decay
   b Displacement
   c Decay and displacement
   d Neither decay nor displacement

3 **Decay happens in LTM but is not a major explanation because**
   a It means brain cells have to die
   b We would lose all our memory eventually
   c It can't explain why we do have very long-term memories
   d Interference is a better explanation

4 **Proactive interference is when**
   a An old memory interferes with learning something new
   b A new learning experience affects something learned in the past
   c An old memory resurfaces
   d None of the above

5 **Cue-dependent forgetting is an example of a memory that is**
   a Available but not accessible
   b Accessible but not available
   c Available and accessible
   d Neither available nor accessible

6 **Flashbulb memories are caused by**
   a Being in a state of high emotion
   b Experiencing events of great personal significance
   c Frequently rehearsing the memory
   d All of the above

7 **It is possible that repression affects**
   a Short-term memories but not long-term ones
   b Long-term memories but not short-term ones
   c Both short- and long-term memories
   d Neither short- nor long-term memories

8 **A confounding variable is a variable**
   a That confuses the participants
   b That is not controlled
   c That acts like another independent variable
   d That does not affect the findings of the study

9 **A control group is used in an experiment**
   a To make sure that the experiment is well controlled
   b To act as a means of comparison
   c To test the independent variable
   d None of the above

10 **A natural experiment**
   a Has no IV
   b Has no DV
   c Is not a true experiment
   d Is a true experiment

Section 3 Critical issue: Eyewitness testimony

1 The theory of reconstructive memory suggests that memory is
a A passive process
b An active process
c A flawed process
d A reliable process

2 Schema affect
a The retrieval process
b Initial comprehension
c Both of the above
d Neither of the above

3 Bartlett's study aimed to show that
a People aren't very good at remembering things
b Recall is influenced by cultural schema
c It's difficult to understand some stories
d People remember things for a long time

4 A more real-life study of reconstructive memory (Wynn and Logie) found that
a Recall was inaccurate
b Recall was relatively accurate
c Recall was very accurate
d Students couldn't recall much

5 Post-event information
a May affect memory
b May have no effect on memory
c Neither of the above
d Both a and b

6 EWT may be unreliable because
a Eyewitnesses are questioned a long time afterwards
b Eyewitnesses are questioned by psychologists
c Eyewitnesses are emotionally aroused
d Eyewitnesses are affected by stereotypes

7 A leading question is one which
a Suggests the desired answer
b Confuses the witness
c Tells the witness the right answer
d All of the above

8 Weapon focus refers to the fact that
a Weapons scare people
b Weapons are used in many crimes involving eyewitnesses
c Weapons distract attention from significant details
d Eyewitnesses can reliably report what weapons were used

9 A demand characteristic is
a A feature of an experiment that invites participants to behave in a predictable way
b A design problem that makes the findings hard to interpret
c Any aspect of the experimental situation that prompts participants to interpret the study in a particular way
d All of the above

10 The median is the best method for describing the data
a To obtain a sensitive measure of the average
b When there are extreme values
c When the data are in order
d When there are lots of duplicate scores

Section 3 answers					Section 2 answers					Section 1 answers				
6d	7a	8c	9d	10b	6d	7a	8c	9b	10c	6a	7d	8a	9c	10c
1b	2c	3b	4b	5d	1a	2b	3c	4a	5a	1d	2d	3a	4c	5b

RESEARCH METHODS
terms covered

- Aims
- Conclusions
- Confederate
- Confounding variable
- Control group
- Controls
- Demand characteristics

- Dependent variable (DV)
- Directional hypothesis
- Double blind design
- Experiment
- Experimental design
- Extraneous variable

- Findings
- Hypothesis
- Independent groups design
- Independent variable (IV)
- Laboratory experiment
- Matched pairs design
- Mean

- Median
- Mode
- Natural experiment
- Non-directional hypothesis
- Order effects
- Participant reactivity
- Participant variables

- Procedures
- Quasi-experiment
- Random allocation
- Repeated measures design
- Research
- Single blind design
- Standardised instructions

Revision list

Key terms

You may be asked 'explain what is meant by ...' any of the following. Each explanation may be for 2 or 3 marks (and very rarely 6 marks). Make sure that what you write is related to the number of marks. Use examples to amplify your explanations where appropriate.

✓

☐ Eyewitness testimony	p. 30
☐ Flashbulb memory	p. 22
☐ Forgetting	p. 16
☐ Leading question	p. 30
☐ LTM	p. 4
☐ Memory	p. 4
☐ Reconstructive memory	p. 26
☐ Repression	p. 23
☐ STM	p. 4

Star studies

This is the 'apfcc question'. You need three-minutes worth of writing on aims, procedures, findings and conclusions for each of these. You may also be asked for one or two criticisms of these studies. Criticisms can be positive or negative.

✓

☐ Nature of STM (Peterson and Peterson, 1959)	p. 4–5
☐ Nature of LTM (Bahrick *et al.*, 1975)	pp. 6–7
☐ Reconstructive memory (Bartlett, 1932)	pp. 26–7
☐ The role of leading questions in EWT (Loftus and Palmer, 1974)	pp. 30–1

Research

You need to be able to outline the findings and conclusions of research (theories and/or studies). Such material is sometimes presented in a feature called 'Research on ...' but studies are also described in other places.

✓

☐ STM	pp. 4–5
☐ LTM	pp. 6–7
☐ Related to the multi-store model	p. 9
☐ Related to the working memory model	p. 10
☐ Related to the levels of processing model	p. 12
☐ Forgetting in STM	pp. 16–17
☐ Forgetting in LTM	pp. 18–21
☐ Flashbulb memories	p. 22
☐ Repression	p. 23
☐ Reconstructive memory	pp. 28–9
☐ EWT including the role of leading questions	pp. 30–35

Factors that influence

You should be able to write about at least two factors of the following:

✓

☐ Forgetting in STM	p. 16
☐ Forgetting in LTM	pp. 18–19
☐ Flashbulb memories	p. 22
☐ Repression	p. 23
☐ Reconstructive memory	p. 29
☐ Accuracy of EWT	p. 32

Theories/explanations

You may be asked to describe or outline a theory/explanation for 6 marks. You are also likely to be asked an AO2 question about theories/explanations and discuss their strengths and limitations. When discussing a theory it is useful to refer to other research (theories and/or studies) as a means of evaluation.

✓

☐ Multi-store model of memory	p. 8
☐ Working memory model	p. 10
☐ Levels of processing model	p. 12
☐ Decay theory	pp. 16, 18

✓

☐ Displacement theory	p. 17
☐ Interference	p. 19
☐ Retrieval failure (cue-dependent forgetting)	p. 20
☐ Reconstructive memory	p. 27

Sample memory question with students' answers and examiner's comments

1 (a) Describe **two** differences between short-term memory (STM) and long-term memory (LTM).

(3 marks + 3 marks)

Alison's answer: Short-term memory has a very limited duration (less than 20 seconds without rehearsal), whereas long-term memory is thought to have unlimited duration. A memory in long-term memory could, theoretically, last for the whole of a person's life but retrieval may become more difficult as time goes by.

The capacity of short-term memory is very limited. It is generally thought to be about 7 items, although these 'items' may be, for example, single digits or chunked into groups of digits. Long-term memory, on the other hand, has potentially unlimited capacity for storage.

Nigel's answer: Long-term memory and short-term memory differ in terms of their duration in that short-term is short-term (a very short time) and long-term is long-term (a very long time).

Long-term memory has a very great capacity but short-term memory has a very small capacity (7 plus or minus 2 items).

Examiner's comments: Alison's answer is accurate and she has offered some appropriate elaboration in order to secure all **3 marks** in both. It is important for you to remember that the person marking this question must have a way of discriminating between an answer worth 1, 2 or 3 marks, so make it easy for them! Nigel's answer to the 'duration' question simply recycles the words 'long-term' and 'short-term'. This isn't particularly helpful but does demonstrate some very basic understanding of the difference between them. It would get **1 mark**. His capacity answer is slightly better, and he does at least qualify what is meant by a 'very small capacity'. It would get **2 marks**.

1 (b) (i) Outline **one** explanation of forgetting in short-term memory (STM).   (3 marks)
(ii) Describe **one** criticism of the explanation you outlined in (i).   (3 marks)

Alison's answer: (i) The decay explanation of forgetting proposes that the reason we forget is because the actual physical memory trace disappears over time. It is supposed that if you rehearse information this keeps the memory trace alive. If you don't rehearse the information in STM it decays rapidly, as in Peterson and Peterson's experiment

(ii) One criticism of this explanation is that it difficult to distinguish between decay and displacement. It could just be that the information that isn't rehearsed is displaced.

Nigel's answer: (i) When people can't remember something it may be because of displacement. This means that one piece of information is displaced by another piece of information. This happens because there isn't much room.

(ii) This explanation is supported by research such as a study where a probe was used to see how much people remember. If the probe was early they found that people didn't remember as much.

Examiner's comments: Alison has provided a detailed and accurate description of one explanation; many candidates find it difficult to get beyond saying 'decay is the disappearance of the memory trace'. The first part of Alison's answer is worth the full **3 marks** but her criticism lacks clarity and so is worth **2 marks**. She could have explained that, in Peterson and Peterson's experiment, it could be that the numbers being repeated actually displaced the trigrams and thus it was displacement not decay that caused forgetting. Nigel's explanation is appropriate and described accurately. It requires a little more elaboration and thus gets **2 marks**. For part (ii) Nigel has used supporting research as a positive criticism of his explanation but he should have given some further details for the full 3 marks (such as the name of the study – Waugh and Norman, and saying *why* this is a positive criticism). Thus **2 marks** for part (ii).

1 (c) Consider the extent to which research into memory has helped our understanding of eyewitness testimony.   (18 marks)

Alison's answer: There is a great deal of research into memory that has informed our understanding of eyewitness testimony. During eyewitness testimony, the witness must go through the stages of encoding, storage and retrieval. There are a number of insights into these three stages that might explain why eyewitness testimony is not that reliable. First, during encoding, things may happen very quickly with lots of distracting action, so that encoding may be only partial and distorted. Second, the witness must retain the information for a considerable period of time, during which they are exposed to the effects of decay and interference. Finally, they must attempt to retrieve the memory, often in the absence of appropriate retrieval cues.

Research has also shown that much of the distortion in memories over time can be explained in terms of what happens during reconstruction. Loftus and Palmer (1974) carried out a study to see if leading questions would distort the accuracy of eyewitness recall. Their work supports the idea that post-event information alters the accuracy of a memory. Although research such as that carried out by Loftus and Palmer is important in understanding the processes in eyewitness memory, its relevance can be questioned. Laboratory experiments such as this one may not represent real-life behaviour because participants do not take the experiment that seriously. On the other hand, a study by Foster *et al.* (1994) found that if participants thought they were watching a real robbery, and that their memories would be important later on, their identification of the robber was much more accurate. This claim is supported by research by Yuille and Cutshall (1986), who interviewed people who had witnessed an armed robbery and given evidence 4 months earlier. Despite the interviewers using misleading questions, the witnesses' recall was still remarkably accurate, showing that post-event information may not actually affect memory in real life.

Memory research has highlighted the importance of appropriate retrieval cues. Recall of a memory is influenced by whether some of the cues originally available at encoding are also available at retrieval. Much of the forgetting that takes place in LTM can be explained in terms of the absence of appropriate cues (cue-dependent forgetting). Geiselman and Fisher compared research into memory with the ways in which police interviews of witnesses were carried out. As a result of this, they developed a procedure called the 'cognitive interview', where the context of the event being recalled is mentally reinstated and the witness encouraged to take a number of perspectives during their attempts to recall information. The cognitive interview has been successful in producing more detailed and accurate information than the standard police interview.

continued…

Nigel's answer

We can understand eyewitness testimony best by looking at research into other types of memory. For example, research into retrieval failure has shown that people probably forget more because of problems at retrieval than because of storage or encoding problems. The encoding specificity principle claims that we are more likely to recall things accurately if we have the same cues that were available during encoding. Research on deep-sea divers, for example, showed that recall was better if they recalled material in the same place that they had learned it (either underwater or on the surface).

Research on emotional factors shows that emotion can have two effects on memory. It can make the memory stronger as in flashbulb memories. People remember the context of the situation when they first heard about something. There are studies that suggest this is true, for example, Brown and Kulik's study about flashbulb memories. But other studies have found that flashbulb memories aren't any different than other memories, i.e. they are inaccurate and easily forgotten.

Research on repression suggests that emotional factors can have the opposite effect. Being in an emotional state could lead you to forget what you witnessed because of the anxiety. In fact one real-life study of eyewitness testimony found that people who witnessed a real-life robbery (and therefore must have been in an emotional state) actually remembered more than people in experiments. This shows you that experiments on memory may not apply to eyewitness testimony because there is no emotional involvement.

Examiner's comments: Alison's answer demonstrates excellent use of the time available, and she has taken pains to represent material in the correct 1:2 ratio of AO1 and AO2. Most of the first paragraph is AO1 as Alison sets the scene, but she has consistently used the subsequent research details in a very evaluative way. We are constantly told that such and such a piece of research supports a claim or that another one challenges a conclusion. She has clearly linked together research into memory with our understanding of eyewitness testimony, as required by the question. This is clearly worth **18 marks**.

Nigel has chosen slightly different (albeit quite appropriate) memory research. The first paragraph is entirely AO1 but fails to successfully relate this material to eyewitness testimony, as required by the question. There is a great deal of implicit relevance but Nigel should have taken more effort to make these links explicit. The rest of the answer is pretty much the same – descriptive, and the degree to which this informs our understanding of eyewitness testimony is not made explicit. The final sentence is the only real bit of relevant AO2 content. This would get 4 marks for AO1 and just 2 for AO2, a total of **6 marks**.

> **Total marks: Alison 29/30 (clearly a Grade A) and Nigel 13/30 (probably a Grade C).**

Research methods question with students' answers and examiner's comments

A psychologist wished to investigate whether recall was better at different times of day: in the morning or in the afternoon. To do this she arranged to read a story out to a group of 40 schoolchildren from her local primary school. She divided one class into two groups and read them a story she had written. Group A (20 students) heard the story at 9 a.m. while Group B heard it at 3 p.m.

The students were told that they would later be tested on their recall of the story.

One week later the researcher met with all the students and gave them a test to assess how much they remembered. The test was marked out of 100. The findings are shown in the table on the right.

Findings	
	Mean score on memory test
Group A (morning)	55
Group B (afternoon)	86

(a) Write a suitable directional hypothesis for this experiment. (2 marks)

Alison's answer: Participants will do better in the morning group than the afternoon group.

Nigel's answer: Participants in group A (story in morning) will recall more than participants in group B (story in the afternoon).

Examiner's comments: Alison's hypothesis is clearly directional and expresses the right relationship between the two conditions, but too much is implicit. It reads as a fairly commonsensical statement rather than a testable one. As such, it is worth **1 mark**. Nigel's answer is much better – this time it is both accurate and clear. The addition of the word 'recall' brings the study more into focus. This would receive **2 marks**.

(b) Identify the independent variable and the dependent variable in this study. (2 marks)

Alison's answer: An independent variable is something that is manipulated in an experiment to see the effect it has on a dependent variable. A dependent variable is some change in behaviour that can be measured as a result of the influence of the independent variable.

Nigel's answer: The IV was the time of day when the participants heard the story. The DV was recall performance on the test a week later.

Examiner's comments: Alison gives good definitions of IV and DV, but unfortunately this is not what was asked for. The question asked for an identification of the IV and DV 'in this study', so her answers get **0 marks**. Nigel provides an accurate identification of the IV and DV used 'in this study', so gets the full **2 marks**.

(c) Identify the research design used in this study. (1 mark)

Alison's answer: This is an independent groups design.

Nigel's answer: This is a laboratory experiment design.

Examiner's comments: Alison has worked out that there were different participants in each group, therefore this must be independent groups design. This gets the **1 mark** available. This is indeed a laboratory experiment, but that is not what is meant by an 'experimental design' in this context, so Nigel's answer gets **0 marks**.

(d) Describe **one** advantage and **one** disadvantage of this design in the context of this study. (2 + 2 marks)

Alison's answer: An advantage of this design is that different participants are used, so no order effects are found as a result of taking part in both conditions of an experiment.
A disadvantage is that there is the possibility of individual differences. It is possible that one group had children with better memories and that is why that group performed better.

Nigel's answer: An advantage of the laboratory experiment is that all the different variables that might influence the outcome can be controlled. A disadvantage is that people don't really behave as they would in real life when studied in a laboratory.

Examiner's comments: Both the advantage and disadvantage are accurate and appropriate in the context of this study, but the advantage is expressed only in general terms (rather than being made explicitly relevant to this study). The disadvantage is well explained and Alison has made good use of her time to guarantee maximum marks. This would receive **1 + 2 marks**. Although it is possible that generous interpretation of the marking scheme might bring Nigel some marks for his response, it is best to see it as irrelevant and worth **0 marks**. It isn't linked to a recognisable 'experimental design' and even if it were, it isn't explicitly linked to this study.

(e) Write a suitable set of instructions for participants. (3 marks)

Alison's answer: I am going to read you a story. Please listen carefully to the story. I plan to return to ask you questions about the story later so it is important that you listen and try to remember details of the story.

Nigel's answer: You are about to hear a short story that I have written. I would like you to pay particular attention to the details of the story because I'm going to come back again to visit you in a week's time and then I will see how much you can recall. I will ask you questions about the people in the story and what they were doing, and what happened in the story. I want you to try your best to recall as many details as possible when I return. If anyone does not wish to take part in this study they can say so when I have finished the story. When you do the test, no one will be told how well you did on remembering details. You will not be asked to give your names.

Examiner's comments: Alison's response is fairly limited although generally accurate in that the two stages of the experiment are mentioned and the participants would have a rough idea of their role in the study. It is worth **2 marks**. Nigel offers a good set of instructions. They are informative, and cover everything that will happen and all that is required from the participants, including their right to withdraw. The comment about anonymity is a nice extra touch, so **3 marks**.

(f) State **one** advantage and **one** disadvantage of using the mean. (2 + 2 marks)

Alison's answer: An advantage is that it uses all the data. A disadvantage is that it is difficult to calculate.

Nigel's answer: The mean gives the most information because it uses all the data. However, it is affected by extreme scores which may make the mean unrepresentative of the data as a whole.

Examiner's comments: The advantage is not really explained by Alison. Why is it an advantage to use all the data? Saying that the mean is 'difficult' to calculate is not sufficient (and probably wrong). This would get **1 + 0 marks**. There is enough information in Nigel's answer and it is all accurate, so **2 + 2 marks**. There is no requirement to contextualise this answer.

(g) State the main findings of this study. (3 marks)

Alison's answer: The main finding was that people who heard the story in the afternoon recalled more than those who heard it in the morning.

Nigel's answer: For the afternoon group, the mean recall score was 86, and for the morning group the mean recall score was 55.

Examiner's comments: Alison provides a fairly brief but not muddled statement of the findings of this study. The quantitative data were available but have been ignored here, so just **2 marks**. Nigel's answer has fewer words than Alison's answer, but a lot more information, so **3 marks**.

(h) Describe **one** conclusion that can be drawn from this study. (2 marks)

Alison's answer: A conclusion is that people who listened to the story in the afternoon got a higher score of 86 than those who listened in the morning who got 55.

Nigel's answer: A conclusion to this study is that memory is better when you initially store information in the afternoon.

Examiner's comments: Alison has obviously been saving this information because she was under the impression that it amounts to a conclusion. It doesn't – it is a finding, so **0 marks**. There isn't a lot more that could be said here, although Nigel might have added a little more detail, such as ' ... than when information is first stored in the morning' or 'The difference in recall rates shows that ...'. , so **1 mark**.

(i) Explain **one** way in which the relationship between researcher and participant (e.g. an investigator effect) might have influenced the findings obtained in this study. (3 marks)

Alison's answer: The researcher might have encouraged one group of students more.

Nigel's answer: It is possible that the researcher encouraged the students in the afternoon group to remember more and this motivated them more highly. The researcher might have emphasised certain words when reading the standardised instructions to one of the groups more than to the other group.

Examiner's comments: Alison's answer is correct but she has failed to take account of the available marks and not elaborated the answer further, so **2 marks**. Nigel gets the full **3 marks** available as he has explained the effect rather than just identified it.

(j) The researcher decides to conduct a further study on time of day and memory, but a study with slightly different aims. Describe the aims and procedures of such a study. (6 marks)

Alison's answer: The aims of this new study would be to see if there is a gender difference in recall in the afternoon and the morning. You would have to make sure that there were an equal number of boys and girls in each group of participants and then they could be read the story as before, and tested in the same way. You can then compare boys versus girls, and morning versus afternoon.

Nigel's answer: A study could be carried out to see if time of recall also was a significant factor in memory because it might be that the initial finding was due to attention rather than memory – the children might have been paying better attention in the afternoon. This would mean having four experimental groups. Group A and B hear the story in the morning but one group is subsequently tested in the morning and the other tested in the afternoon. Groups C and D are tested in the same way but initially hear the story in the afternoon. In order to ensure no bias in the experimental groups children would be randomly allocated to each group at the outset. Instructions should be given that prevent participants trying to guess what the experiment is about (for example, saying that the researcher is an author who is trying to find out what kind of story is best remembered by children).

Examiner's comments: Both Alison's aims and procedures are appropriate but described in limited detail. For example, there is no elaboration of where these aims came from and no mention of how she would ensure the same number of boys and girls in each group. This would receive **3 marks**. Nigel provides a fairly lengthy account, and one that gives clear information about both the aims and procedures of the chosen study. The description is detailed and appropriate for the chosen study, so the full **6 marks**.

Total marks: Alison 13/30 (approximately equivalent to a Grade C) and Nigel 21/30 (a fairly sound Grade A).

Memory question to try

1 **(a)** Describe **two** factors that influence forgetting in short-term memory (STM). (3 marks + 3 marks)

(b) Describe the procedures and findings of **one** study that has investigated memory. (6 marks)

(c) Consider the extent to which research into the process of repression enables us to explain forgetting. (18 marks)

Developmental psychology is concerned with how children and adults change as they get older. Developmental psychology looks at various influences on development, such as the influences of parents, peers and other people around you. These are all environmental influences (called **nurture**). Changes also happen as a consequence of **nature**. 'Nature' refers to biological factors such as genes.

Developmental psychology

Attachments in development

Section 1

The development and variety of attachments

Section 2

Deprivation and privation

Section 3

Critical issue: Day care

End of module review

The development and variety of attachments

Farmers often save the lives of motherless lambs by pairing them with a mother sheep whose own infant has died. The farmer takes the fleece from the dead lamb and wraps it round the orphaned lamb. The hope is that the mother will accept it as her own and look after it without question. Within hours of birth the mother knows the smell of her own infant. This is called imprinting. The mother forms an image of the infant and only cares for this one. This is quite a useful characteristic. Imagine if you were a sheep surrounded by hundreds of lambs – it would be important to know your own infant, otherwise you would end up caring for any lamb and not ensuring the survival of your own genes.

specification breakdown

Specification content	Comment
Stages in the formation of attachments (e.g. Schaffer).	Infants become attached to their caregivers and this process follows a sequence of different stages. Schaffer has offered one account of this sequence, but you can equally use others.
Research into individual differences, including secure and insecure attachments (e.g. Ainsworth) and cross-cultural variations.	It is important to recognise that the development of attachments varies between individuals (**individual differences**). For example, some infants are securely attached whereas others are insecurely attached. You are required to study these differences as they are *included* in the specification. The distinction between **secure and insecure attachments** stems from Ainsworth's research using the Strange Situation. In addition to individual differences there are **cultural differences**, or variations in how children are attached to caregivers in different cultures.
Explanations of attachment (e.g. learning theory, Bowlby's theory).	Explanations of attachments offer an account of how and why children become attached to a caregiver. The best-known and most developed explanation is Bowlby's theory, but there are others such as learning theory and also Freud's theory. The specification requires that you are familiar with *at least two* explanations.

Farmers wrap the fleece of a dead lamb around one that is orphaned so that the dead lamb's mother will care for the orphan as her own.

Imprinting works both ways. It is even more important that infants imprint on a parent. Last summer the swans who live near Cara's house in Scotland had five cygnets. For the first few weeks the cygnets clung to their mother's rear end as she swam around the loch. Sometimes they were barely visible because they were tucked right underneath their mother. Being attached like this must have helped these young animals survive. But how did they know that they should follow this particular individual rather than the ducks or the dogs or any of the other animals around the loch? Do they hatch out with an image of their mother in their heads and follow that image?

Konrad Lorenz (1952) famously demonstrated that animals don't hatch with an image of their parents. Lorenz took a clutch of gosling eggs and divided them into two groups. One group was left with the natural mother while the other eggs were placed in an incubator. When the incubator eggs hatched, the first living (moving) thing the chicks saw was Lorenz, and soon they started following him around (see page 56). To test this imprinting, Lorenz marked the two groups to distinguish them and placed them together. The goslings quickly divided themselves up, one group following their natural mother and Lorenz's brood following him. This suggests that the young animal imprints on the first object it sees. Another study (Guiton, 1966) showed that chicks would even imprint on yellow rubber gloves!

Imprinting is important in the short term for protection and being fed. It is also important in the long term for mating. Studies have shown that mate choice is related to early imprinting experiences. The chicks who imprinted on the yellow rubber gloves tried to mate with them when older. Lorenz described how one of the geese who imprinted on him, called Martina, used to sleep on the end of his bed every night. When she reached maturity she became 'betrothed' to a gander (male goose), who Lorenz called Martin. On their first night Martin followed Martina upstairs into the bedroom, though he was not accustomed to being in a house. As the door banged shut he panicked at being enclosed and flew straight up into the chandelier in Lorenz's elegant bedroom, damaging himself considerably in the process.

Attachment in infants is similar to imprinting, as you will see. It is important in the short term for survival, and is also related in the long term to adult relationships – though in a different way to the birds' imprinting. A number of studies have shown that adults are less likely to mate with individuals with whom they were raised. For example, Shepher (1971) found that not one of the 3,000 Israeli marriage records he studied was between individuals who had been raised together on the same communal farms (kibbutzim). This is called the Westermarck effect after Westermarck (1891), who noted that if children spend considerable time together before the age of 6 (a sensitive period), they avoid subsequently forming sexual relationships with one another, a kind of reverse imprinting. This would clearly be useful in avoiding incest, and incest is undesirable because it increases the chance of developing certain types of genetic disorders.

What is meant by attachment?

> An affectional tie that one person or animal forms between himself and another specific one – a tie that binds them together in space and endures over time. The behavioural hallmark of attachment is seeking to gain and to maintain a certain degree of proximity to the object of attachment. Attachment behaviours aim to maintain proximity or contact, e.g. following, clinging and signalling behaviours such as smiling, crying and calling.

This definition, written by the famous attachment researcher Mary Ainsworth (Ainsworth and Bell, 1970, page 50), captures the essence of what attachment is all about. She describes attachment as an *'affectional'* tie that a person or animal forms between him/herself and another. An affectional tie is one that is based on emotions or *feelings* rather than any other need (such as bodily or cognitive needs). The way that a mother and young child cling to each other tells us that this is a bond that must be based on pretty strong emotions. This tie *'binds them together in space and endures over time'*. As we shall see, young children seek the company of their mother (or caregiver) and are disturbed when they are separated from her/him, even for short periods of time. This is not a one-way process, as any parent of a newborn baby will tell you! Even when we get much older and no longer need the security that our parents provided for us when we were young, that special emotional bond between us still exists.

How do we know if an attachment has developed? Ainsworth has that covered in her definition, too. The infant tries to get close to and then maintain that proximity with the caregiver, using a number of 'strategies' to do so. The infant has one particularly powerful weapon in this process – the way they look. Have you noticed that most young mammals have the same distinctive facial features (big eyes, large forehead, squashed-up nose)? These features, adapted over millions of years, act as a trigger for parenting behaviour, so necessary for the young animal's survival.

KEY TERM

Attachment is an emotional bond between two people. It is a two-way process that endures over time. It leads to certain behaviours such as clinging and proximity-seeking, and serves the function of protecting an infant.

The stages in the formation of attachments

Research shows that infants pass through typical stages as they develop their relationships with others.

Stage 1: Pre-attachment (about 0–2 months)	Newborn infants are said to show *indiscriminate social responsiveness*. They are equally happy being picked up by familiar or unfamiliar people, and can be comforted as easily by strangers as by their parents. However, they soon begin to recognise familiar smells, voices and faces (there is even evidence that at birth they recognise voices they heard when in the womb).
Stage 2: Attachment-in-the-making (about 2–7 months)	This phase is characterised by the increasing ability to *recognise familiar people*. An infant is more easily comforted by someone familiar but still does not show anxiety with strangers or less familiar people.
Stage 3: Specific attachments (from about 7 months)	'Attachment-proper' is signalled by the appearance of two new behaviours. The infant displays **separation protest** – the distress when an infant is separated from his/her caregiver. This may happen when the caregiver puts the infant down or when the caregiver leaves the room. Infants also show especial joy at reunion with that person and are most comforted by her/him.
	The second new behaviour is **stranger anxiety** – distress when picked up or approached by someone who is unfamiliar.
Stage 4: Multiple attachments (from about 8 months)	Initially infants show attachments to one **primary caregiver** (as demonstrated by separation protest). But very soon after a first attachment is formed most infants also show attachments to other people. The number of other attachments that are formed depends on how many consistent relationships the infant has. There is some debate about whether these different attachments are equally intense, or whether the infant always has one special attachment figure at the top of a hierarchy of different attachments. The idea of one special attachment is called **monotropy** (which means 'focused on one person').
Stage 5: Reciprocal relationships (from about 8–24 months)	The infant learns to predict the responses of others and this means that it is possible to consciously influence the behaviour of others. This is the beginning of real relationships.

Criticisms

One weakness in any stage account of development is that it suggests a fixed pattern of development. It is the *sequence* that is important – the actual ages are approximate.

Research on the formation of attachments

A study of infant attachment in Glasgow

Schaffer and Emerson (1964) conducted an important study observing the development of attachments in 60 infants who came largely from working-class homes in Glasgow. The infants were observed over a period of a year in their homes.

Most infants first showed signs of separation protest and stranger anxiety at around age 7 months, indicating the onset of specific attachments.

Soon after an infant formed one specific attachment, other attachments were formed – the infants also displayed separation anxiety when separated from other people. Within 1 month of first becoming attached, 29% of the infants had multiple attachments; within 6 months this had risen to 78%. These attachments were to the other parent, to grandparents, siblings, other relatives, friends and/or neighbours.

Despite forming multiple attachments, it appeared that most infants maintained one *principal* object of attachment, in terms of intensity. This was most often the infant's mother, though not infrequently it was the infant's father. The principal or primary attachment object was not always the person who fed or bathed the infant. In fact, Schaffer and Emerson reported that there was little relationship between time spent together and attachment. In 39% of the cases infants were attached to someone other than the person who bathed or fed them. Responsiveness appeared to be the key to attachment. Schaffer and Emerson observed that intensely attached infants had mothers who responded quickly to their demands and who offered the child the most interaction. Infants who were weakly attached had mothers who failed to interact.

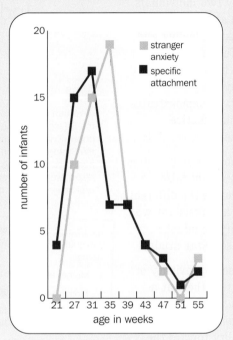

Age of onset of specific attachments (separation protest) and stranger anxiety

Observations of attachment in Baltimore and Uganda

Mary Ainsworth is one of the leading names in attachment research. She spent time in Uganda (1967) and then in Baltimore, USA (1964), observing infants and mothers in their own homes. Her observations led her to conclude that there are two distinctive features of attachment, both of which have **adaptive value**. First, infants seek to be close to their mothers, especially at times when they are threatened by something in the environment. This is called *proximity-seeking behaviour* and you can imagine that it would help an infant survive.

Second, *exploratory behaviour* is also important from an adaptive point of view. Individuals who are interested in exploring novel aspects of their environment will be quicker to learn about their environment. Infants who are close to an attachment (and safety) figure will be more willing to explore in the knowledge that they are safe. They use their caregiver as a **secure base**.

What is 'adaptive value'?

Some inherited behaviours help an individual animal cope better in, or adapt to, the environment in which it lives. Those individuals who can adapt best will be most likely to survive and reproduce. When they reproduce they will pass on the genes for these adaptive behaviours to their offspring. Over time those behaviours which are adaptive persist, and those which are not adaptive disappear without trace. This is the basis of Darwin's theory of **evolution**. He said that some behaviours are **naturally selected**. Any behaviour that promotes successful reproduction (including survival) is selected because that's how the genes survive (i.e. they are naturally selected).

Biologists use the concept of the **environment of evolutionary adaptiveness (EEA)** to describe a time in the past when humans evolved – evolution is a slow process. In the EEA, danger from predators was more of a threat to survival than it is today. But there are still dangers and proximity-seeking behaviour remains adaptive.

'Attachments are not formed by a congenital glue held in limited supply: They are welded in the heat of interactions.' (Maurer and Maurer, 1989)

Factors that influence the formation of attachments

Good mothering

Researchers such as Mary Ainsworth have argued that different styles of mothering have important consequences for the child's development. Certain patterns of behaviour seem to represent 'good mothering' and enable the child to become securely attached. These behaviours appear to be *maternal sensitivity* (being able to respond appropriately to the infant's signals and communications) and *maternal responsiveness* (the proportion of the infant's signals and communications to which the mother responds). The mother of a securely attached child is, therefore, a mother who *notices* what her child is doing, and responds appropriately.

The child's contribution

Attachment grows out of an interaction between two individuals, so the child also has a part to play in this process. Some infants, for whatever reason, may discourage maternal interest in helping them. Maccoby (1980) suggests that certain temperamental characteristics of the infant can shape the mother's responsiveness. 'Normal' infants tend to take the initiative in inviting a maternal response, while other children do not take this initiative. The mother's responsiveness to her infant may be partly a product of her own characteristics, but also an outcome of the characteristics of the child. The fact, therefore, that securely attached infants have responsive mothers may be as much a consequence of the child's characteristics as of the mother's.

What is meant by secure and insecure attachment?

Secure and insecure attachments are examples of a particular type or *style* of attachment bond that may be established between any two individuals (usually the mother and infant). These attachment styles are seen as consistent patterns of thinking, feeling and behaving in interpersonal situations. The fundamental assumption in attachment research on human infants is that consistently *sensitive responding* by the parent to the infant's needs results in an infant who demonstrates secure attachment, while a lack of such sensitive responding results in insecure attachment.

Ainsworth *et al.* (1978) originally proposed two varieties of insecure attachment: *avoidant* and *resistant* (also called *ambivalent*). This distinction between the different attachment styles as secure, avoidant and resistant was originally developed as a way of classifying infant behaviour in the '**Strange Situation**' (see Star Study).

In this situation, *secure* infants either seek proximity or contact with the returning parent or greet them at a distance with a smile or wave. *Avoidant* infants avoid the parent upon her return. *Resistant/ambivalent* infants either passively or actively show hostility toward the parent when she returns.

The **secure attachment** style refers to those who seek and are comfortable with social interaction and intimacy. The securely attached infant is able to function independently because his/her caregiver acts as a secure base.	The **insecure/avoidant** style of attachment characterises those children who tend to avoid social interaction and intimacy with others.	The **insecure/resistant** (ambivalent) style characterises those who both seek and reject intimacy and social interaction.

Because the emphasis here is on 'consistency' of attachment-related behaviour, there are those who argue that there is also a *disorganised* type, which is characterised by a lack of such consistent patterns of social behaviour.

KEY TERMS

Secure attachment: This is a strong and contented attachment of an infant to his/her caregiver, which develops as a result of sensitive responding by the caregiver to the infant's needs. Secure attachment is related to healthy subsequent cognitive and emotional development.

Insecure attachment: This is a form of attachment between infant and caregiver that develops as a result of the caregiver's lack of sensitive responding to the infant's needs. It may be associated with poor subsequent cognitive and emotional development.

star**STUDY**
Individual differences in attachment
(AINSWORTH *ET AL.*, 1978)

Aims

Ainsworth *et al.* devised a method of **controlled observation** called the Strange Situation. The aim was to see how an infant behaves under conditions of mild stress and also novelty. Stress is created in the Strange Situation by the presence of a stranger and by separation from a caregiver. This tests stranger anxiety and separation anxiety, respectively. The Strange Situation is novel and this aims to encourage exploration and test the **secure base** concept.

The Strange Situation consists of 8 episodes, each one lasting about 3 minutes. Three people are involved: a caregiver, her infant and a stranger.

1. Mother and baby enter room.
2. Mother sits quietly on a chair, responding if the infant seeks attention.
3. A stranger enters, talks to the mother then gradually approaches infant with a toy. The mother leaves the room.
4. The stranger leaves the infant playing unless he/she is inactive and then tries to interest the infant in toys. If the infant becomes distressed this episode is ended.
5. Mother enters and waits to see how the infant greets her. The stranger leaves quietly and the mother waits until the baby settles, and then she leaves again.
6. The infant is alone. This episode is curtailed if the infant appears to be distressed.
7. The stranger comes back and repeats episode 3.
8. The mother returns and the stranger goes. Reunion behaviour recorded and then the situation is ended.

This is an example of a **behaviour checklist**.

Procedure

In this study data were combined from several other studies, making a total of 106 middle-class infants observed in the Strange Situation. The experimental room is a *novel environment* (which is important for exploration), a 9 x 9-foot square marked off into 16 squares to help in the recording of the infant's movements.

Observers recorded infant behaviour according to 5 categories: (1) proximity- and contact-seeking behaviours, (2) contact-maintaining behaviours, (3) proximity- and interaction-avoiding behaviours, (4) contact- and interaction-resisting behaviours, (5) search behaviours. Every 15 seconds the observer made a note of which of the above behaviours was being displayed and also scored the behaviour for intensity on a scale of 1 to 7.

*Ainsworth (1967) studied attachment in Uganda and Baltimore using **naturalistic observation** – studying behaviour in a situation where everything has been left as it normally is. Such research is very time-consuming and can also be affected by **observer bias** – the person doing the observing 'sees' what he or she expects to see. Conducting a controlled observation with definite categories and time frames means that such bias can be reduced.*

Research methods
Observation studies and observation techniques

Two of the research methods that you will encounter in psychology are experiments and observation studies. Ainsworth's earlier studies (in Uganda and Baltimore) were naturalistic observations. There are no IVs or DVs. The Strange Situation is an example of a controlled observation, where behaviour is observed under controlled conditions. In the Strange Situation there are IVs (the caregiver goes, the stranger approaches the child, and so on), and the infant's behaviours were observed in response (DV). So, in a way, this is better described as an experiment where observational techniques are used to record the DV. Note the distinction between methods and techniques – you may lose marks in an exam if you fail to notice this distinction.

There are two important observational techniques that are used to collect information when making observations:

- **Sampling technique**. An observer needs some way to decide how often and for how long to make observations. Therefore observational studies use a method of sampling. In the Strange Situation observers made a note of the infant's behaviour every 15 seconds. This is called **time sampling**. An alternative method is **event sampling**. This is where a list of behaviours is drawn up (e.g. crying, smiling, cuddling), and a count is kept of every time each behaviour occurs.

- **Behavioural categories**. You need a means of collecting data. If an observer simply sits and observes it is hard to decide what to record and what not to record. Therefore it is desirable to have an **behaviour checklist** of behaviours to be observed, as was used in the Strange Situation. (There's another example of an observation checklist on page 51.)

Findings

The study found similarities and differences in the way that infants behaved. Similarities noted were that exploratory behaviours declined in all infants from episode 2 onwards, whereas the amount of crying increased. Proximity-seeking and contact-maintaining behaviours intensified during separation and when the stranger appeared. Contact-resisting and proximity-avoiding behaviours occurred rarely towards the caregiver prior to separation.

In terms of differences, 3 main types of children (and 8 subgroups) were found. This classification is shown in the table.

Classification of behaviour in the Strange Situation	Secure attachment (Type B)	Insecure attachment Avoidant (Type A)	Resistant (Type C)
Willingness to explore	High	High	Low
Stranger anxiety	High	Low	High
Separation anxiety	Some, easy to soothe	Indifferent	Distressed
Behaviour at reunion with caregiver	Enthusiastic	Avoid contact	Seeks and rejects
Caregiver's behaviour	Sensitive	May ignore infant	Ambivalent
Percentage of infants in this category	66%	22%	12%

Conclusions

The Strange Situation highlights important behaviours related to attachment: willingness to explore, stranger and separation anxiety, and behaviour at reunion. Infants vary in the way they behave, showing individual differences which may be related to the behaviour of their caregiver. This suggests that an innate tendency (attachment) is affected by life experiences (caregiver's behaviours).

Advantages of a naturalistic observation	Weaknesses
<ul><li>It offers a way to study behaviour where there are objections to manipulating variables, such as arranging for a child to spend time apart from his/her parent.</li><li>Gives a more realistic picture of spontaneous behaviour. It has high ecological validity.</li></ul>	<ul><li>It may not be possible to control extraneous variables.</li><li>The observer may 'see' what he/she expects to see. This is called **observer bias**. This bias may mean that different observers 'see' different things, which leads to low **inter-observer reliability**.</li><li>Possible lack of **informed consent**.</li></ul>

Criticisms

Has proved to be very useful

The Strange Situation procedure has been used widely in attachment research with infants, and has been adapted for studies of children and even adults. This is a positive criticism.

Ethical considerations

The intention of the Strange Situation is to cause mild distress. Is it acceptable to do this to infants? This is an **ethical issue**, and such issues don't have clear-cut answers.

Is the classification valid?

Validity concerns the extent to which something is true. What does the Strange Situation actually measure? Is it something about the infant (that this child is a secure or insecure type), or is it one particular relationship? If infants are tested in the Strange Situation with other caregivers, they respond differently. For example, Main and Weston (1981) found that children behaved differently depending on which parent they were with, which indicates that it is the relationship that determines the response in the Strange Situation rather than attachment being due to the infant's temperament.

This suggests that the classification of an attachment type may not be valid because what is being measured is one relationship rather than something within the individual. On the other hand, if you agree with the concept of **monotropy**, the one relationship the infant has with his/her primary caregiver is all that matters for emotional development. The fact that an infant responds differently with someone other than the primary caregiver tells us something about that relationship, but the attachment *type* is related to the one special relationship.

Differences between secure and insecure attachment

Parenting differences

Secure attachment develops as a result of consistently sensitive responding by the parent to the infant's needs. The notion of 'sensitive responding' is not only that a caregiver reacts to every signal that the infant makes, but is consistent in the kind of response made. Insecure attachment may develop if there is a lack of such consistent sensitive responding.

Later childhood behaviour

Securely attached children seek and are comfortable with social interaction and intimacy. Insecurely attached children tend to avoid social interaction (avoidant type), or both seek and reject contact with others (resistant/ambivalent type).

Adult romantic behaviour

Securely attached adults find it relatively easy to get close to others and are comfortable depending on others and having others depend on them. Insecurely attached adults may find it difficult to trust or depend on others completely (avoidant type), or their desire to merge completely with another person scares others away (resistant type).

Effects of secure and insecure attachment

Behaviour at school

The quality of attachment is related to different patterns of later behaviour. Children who are securely attached explore their environments more thoroughly, are better able to deal with challenging situations, and are better at problem solving. Insecure (avoidant) type children often develop behaviour problems, lack persistence in learning, and are frequently victimisers of other children. Insecure (resistant) type children tend to be overly dependent on teachers for help and attention, may lack confidence and self-esteem, are socially withdrawn from other children, and may be the victims of more aggressive peers.

Adult romantic behaviour

Attachment theory provides not only a way of understanding emotional reactions in infants, but also a framework for understanding love, loneliness and grief in adults. Ainsworth's description of secure and insecure attachment styles has also been used to explain individual differences in *adult* romantic relationships (Hazan and Shaver, 1987).

Secure adults find it relatively easy to get close to others, and are comfortable depending on others and having others depend on them. Secure adults don't often worry about being abandoned or about someone getting too close to them.

Insecure/avoidant adults are somewhat uncomfortable being close to others; they find it difficult to trust others completely, and to allow themselves to depend on others. Avoidant adults are nervous when anyone gets too close, and often love partners want them to be more intimate than they feel comfortable being.

Insecure/resistant adults find that others are reluctant to get as close as they would like. Resistant adults often worry that their partner doesn't really love them or won't want to stay with them. Resistant adults want to merge completely with another person, and this desire sometimes scares people away.

THE DEVELOPMENT AND VARIETY OF ATTACHMENTS

Secure attachments in pets

A group of psychologists in Hungary (Topal *et al.*, 1998) used the Strange Situation to explore the attachments between dogs and their owners. For 10,000 years dogs have been *artificially selected* for certain traits, among them their willingness to become attached to their owners. (Artificial selection is like natural selection except that someone is actually doing the selection rather than leaving it to the forces of nature.) This makes it quite likely that dogs and owners will behave like infants and caregivers. Anxiety is reduced through proximity to an attachment figure and exploration is increased in the presence of a caregiver.

Dogs were placed in the Strange Situation and their behaviours recorded using the checklist. A tick could be entered at regular intervals (e.g. every 15 seconds). Owners were not informed of the purpose of the study.

In this study the findings were that dogs too were securely or insecurely attached.

Behaviour checklist for the Strange Situation

EXPO	exploration when with owner
EXPS	exploration when with stranger
PLYO	playing when with owner
PLYS	playing when with stranger
PASO	passive behaviours when with owner
PASS	passive behaviours when with stranger
CONTO	physical contact with the owner
CONTS	physical contact with the stranger
SBYO	standing by the door when with owner
SBYS	standing by the door when with stranger

Ways to explain individual differences in attachment

Temperament hypothesis

Children are born with innate temperamental differences. Thomas and Chess (1977), in their classic study of innate temperament, identified three basic infant personality types: easy, difficult and slow-to-warm-up. It is quite possible that children form more secure relationships simply because they have an 'easy' temperament, whereas difficult children are likely to form insecure relationships. Jerome Kagan (1984) proposed the **temperament hypothesis**, which focused on the role played by the infant's **temperament** or personality in determining the child's attachment to the mother. Evidence that the infant's temperament may be important was reported by Belsky and Rovine (1987). Newborns who showed signs of behavioural instability (e.g. tremors or shaking) were less likely to become securely attached to their mother than were newborns who did not.

Maternal depression

Numerous studies have demonstrated that the quality of infant attachment to the mother is influenced by maternal sensitivity to the infant during interactions. More recently, researchers have begun to explore factors such as maternal psychological functioning. Research by Teti *et al.* (1995) showed a significant association between maternal depression and infant attachment insecurity. They found that children without coherent attachment strategies tended to have more chronically impaired mothers than did securely attached children.

COMMENTARY CORNER

To what extent has research on individual differences in attachments shown these to impact on later development?

In this section we have been examining the role of individual differences in attachment. The fact that such differences exist is only half the story. We might ask whether research supports the claim that these differences in attachment style somehow affect the subsequent development of the child.

Here is an answer to that question:

Attachment theorists believe that children learn a repertoire of behaviours as a direct result of how their caregivers nurture them. According to this viewpoint, the type of bond that develops between infant and caregiver affects the child's later relationships. Attachment theory describes four bonding types: secure, insecure/avoidant, insecure/resistant and disoriented/disorganised. Secure attachment patterns are thought to develop from a consistent and responsive caregiver, whereas insecure attachments are seen as the result of inconsistent, emotionally neglectful or abusive caregiving. Attachment theory suggests that children who have been abused may be more distrustful, have lower self-esteem and develop more maladaptive relationships in later life than those who are more securely attached in childhood. This suggestion is supported by findings that as many as 80% of abused infants and children exhibit insecure attachment behaviour patterns.

A related problem is the possibility that neglect and abuse in childhood do not only impact on attachment behaviours in childhood, but may carry over to adulthood through an 'internal working model' of relationships, i.e. the caregiving we receive in childhood shapes our expectations of our relationships in adulthood. For example, children raised by neglectful parents develop insecure attachments that may become recreated in their relationships with their own children when they become parents. Research suggests that these attachments can be adaptive and help buffer us from stress (as in securely attached children), or they can be maladaptive and lead to impaired interpersonal relationships. This is demonstrated in Hazan and Shaver's use of attachment theory to provide a framework for understanding love, loneliness and grief in adults (Hazan and Shaver, 1987).

Some attachment theorists believe that the attachment styles we develop in infancy cannot be altered without intensive therapy or through a supportive loving relationship. Recently, however, some theorists have modified this perspective to suggest that it is experiences throughout life that influence our expectations of and behaviour in later relationships. Michael Rutter's (1981) discovery that psychiatric disorders can develop as a result of disruptive events in middle childhood despite secure and adaptive development up to that point suggests that early adjustment patterns are not set forever and may be transformed throughout life.

What is meant by cross-cultural variations?

Culture in this context refers to the rules, customs, morals and ways of interacting that bind together members of a society or some other collection of people. We learn these rules, customs, etc. through the process of *socialisation*, which enables us to interact appropriately with other members of our culture. 'Culture' doesn't necessarily equate to 'country' or even 'society', as many different groups, each with their own rules and customs, may coexist within a country like the UK. 'Subculture' is usually used to refer to a group within a society that, although it shares many of the dominant cultural characteristics of that society, may also have some distinctive characteristics of its own. **Sociologists** tell us that different social classes have different attitudes to, among other things, childrearing, and therefore might be regarded as different 'subcultures'.

Factors related to cross-cultural variations in attachment

The role of the mother

In some cultures, it is more efficient for child-care duties to be assigned almost entirely to the mother. As a result, the mother's role as primary caregiver leads to a strong attachment between mother and infant, such that she becomes the main agent of socialisation in the child's early years. Social changes, particularly in industrial cultures, have meant that many women now work away from home in occupations that are incompatible with simultaneous child care. The impact of these changes on the development of children is the subject of much contentious debate (which we will look at on pages 70–5).

Individualist and collectivist cultures

We might explain cultural differences in attachment behaviours in terms of the childrearing methods used to socialise the child into a particular culture. We would, therefore, expect children born in an **individualist** culture (such as the US) to be brought up differently from children born in a **collectivist** culture (such as Japan). The emotional reaction of most US children to separation is anxiety, whereas for Japanese children it is sadness. This is consistent with the Japanese ideal of the importance of the group, and the Western emphasis on the importance of the individual. The Japanese child experiences sadness because of a sense of loss (he is no longer a member of the group), whereas the US child experiences anxiety because the absence of the mother threatens his newly developing autonomous self.

KEY TERM

Cross-cultural variations: The ways that different groups of people (e.g. members of a society or subcultures within a society) vary in terms of their social practices and the effects these practices have on development and behaviour.

---

star**STUDY**
Cross-cultural variations in attachment
(VAN IJZENDOORN & KROONENBERG, 1988)

Aims

Prior to this study, a number of other studies had found significant differences in attachment patterns in different cultures. Van IJzendoorn and Kroonenberg questioned whether there really are such differences or whether the apparent differences are due to research error. For example, different researchers in different cultures may classify infant behaviours in the Strange Situation slightly differently or may conduct the Strange Situation with minor variations. Therefore, the question is whether cross-cultural differences really exist. Van IJzendoorn and Kroonenberg were also interested in finding out whether there were *intra*cultural differences – differences in the findings from studies conducted within the same culture. In order to investigate these inter- and intracultural differences, Van IJzendoorn and Kroonenberg aimed to collect a larger sample of data than previously examined.

Procedures

This study is not an experiment or an observational study. It is called a **meta-analysis**, which means that findings from a variety of different studies are looked at with a view to drawing some general conclusions.

Van IJzendoorn and Kroonenberg looked through various databases to find studies on attachment. They decided only to select those studies of mother–infant interaction that used the Strange Situation procedure. Studies were excluded if they looked at special groups such as Down's syndrome or twins, or those that involved fewer than 35 infants. Altogether they examined over 2,000 Strange Situation classifications from 32 studies conducted in 8 different countries.

Research methods
Cross-cultural studies

Psychologists quite often compare behaviours in different cultures. This is a way of seeing whether cultural practices affect behaviour. It is a kind of **natural experiment** where the IV is childrearing technique and the DV is some behaviour, such as attachment.

There are many limitations with such studies. For example, researchers may use tests or procedures that have been developed in the US and are not valid in the other culture. This may make the individuals in the other culture appear 'abnormal' or inferior. The term that is used to describe this is an **imposed etic** – using a technique in one culture when it has been designed for use in another culture.

A second limitation is that the group of participants may not be representative of that culture, and yet we make generalisations about the whole culture – or even the whole country.

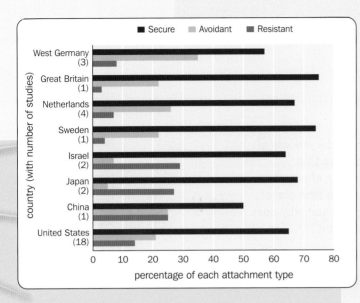

Key: ■ Secure ■ Avoidant ■ Resistant

country (with number of studies):
West Germany (3), Great Britain (1), Netherlands (4), Sweden (1), Israel (2), Japan (2), China (1), United States (18)

percentage of each attachment type (0–80)

Other research on cross-cultural variations in attachment

Cross-cultural differences

Grossmann and Grossmann (1991) found that German infants tended to be classified as insecurely rather than securely attached. This may be due to different childrearing practices. German culture requires keeping some interpersonal distance between parents and children, so infants do not engage in proximity-seeking behaviours in the Strange Situation and thus *appear* to be insecurely attached.

Cross-cultural similarities

Tronick *et al.* (1992) studied an African group, the Efe, from Zaire. The infants are looked after and even breastfed by different women, but usually sleep with their own mother at night. The infants still show one primary attachment.

Fox (1977) studied infants raised on Israeli kibbutzim who spend most of their time being cared for in a communal children's home by a *metapelet*. They were nevertheless most closely attached to their mothers.

Findings

The findings are shown in the table. With reference to variation *between* cultures/countries, Van IJzendoorn and Kroonenberg found that the differences were small. Secure attachment was the most common classification in every country. Insecure/avoidant attachment was the next most common in every country except Israel and Japan.

With reference to variation *within* cultures, they found that this was *1.5 times* greater than the variation between cultures.

Conclusions

The global pattern across cultures appears to be similar to that found in the US. Secure attachment is the 'norm' – it is the most common form of attachment. This supports the idea that secure attachment is 'best' for healthy social and emotional development. Van IJzendoorn and Kroonenberg suggest that the cross-cultural similarities might be explained by the effects of mass media (e.g. TV and books), which spread ideas about parenting so that children all over the world are exposed to similar influences.

Criticisms

The validity of the Strange Situation in different cultural settings

The Strange Situation may not be a valid measure of attachment in all cultures. The Strange Situation is based on the notion that autonomy, individuation and exploration (i.e. independence) are the outcomes of secure attachment. Western cultures (like the US) are **individualist** cultures which value independence. In contrast, other cultures are described as **collectivist** (e.g. Japan).

Takahashi (1990) reports that Japanese infants rarely experience separation from their mothers and this would explain why they were more distressed in the Strange Situation than their American counterparts – making them *appear* to be insecurely attached.

Different countries are not the same as different cultures

One explanation for the large within-culture variation is that some studies involved middle-class infants, whereas other studies involved working-class infants. Some US studies looked at urban populations, whereas others were more rural. Rural societies in the US may be more similar to rural societies in Israel than they are to urban societies in the US. What this means is that data were collected on different *subcultures* within each country.

Explaining attachment

W e have considered, in this module, many aspects of the process of attachment – the stages in its development, the ways that individuals differ and how child-rearing methods may affect an individual's development. But what leads to attachment in the first place? How and why does an infant become attached to a caregiver, and why does an infant become attached to one caregiver rather than another?

Behaviourists are psychologists who assume that all behaviour is learned. You are born like a blank slate (so they say) and are conditioned to learn new responses which gradually become more complex.

Classical conditioning

Pavlov, a Russian physiologist, first described classical conditioning. He was conducting research on salivation in dogs, recording how much they salivated each time they were fed – or at least, he was trying to do this when he observed that they started salivating *before* they were fed. The dogs salivated as soon as they heard the door open signalling the arrival of food. The dogs had come to *associate* the sound of the door with food. They had *learned* a new stimulus response (S-R). They learned to salivate (response) when the door opened (stimulus).

Operant conditioning

The second explanation used by the behaviourists is called **operant conditioning**. Learning also occurs when we are rewarded for doing something – rewards can be anything such as money or praise. Each time you do something and it results in a *pleasant state of affairs*, the behaviour is 'stamped in' or *reinforced*. It becomes more probable that you will repeat that behaviour in the future. If you do something and it results in an *unpleasant state of affairs*, it become less likely that you will repeat that behaviour. These two possibilities are called **reinforcement** and **punishment**, respectively.

Explanation 1: The behaviourist approach: Learning theory

Behaviourists suggest that attachment is learned either through classical or operant conditioning (see descriptions on the left).

Classical conditioning involves learning through association. Food (an unconditioned stimulus) produces a sense of pleasure (an unconditioned response). The person who feeds (a conditioned stimulus) the infant becomes *associated* with the food. The 'feeder' eventually produces the conditioned response – pleasure. This association between an individual and a sense of pleasure is the attachment bond.

Dollard and Miller (1950) offered a more complex explanation, based on operant conditioning. They suggested that a hungry infant feels uncomfortable and this creates a drive to reduce the discomfort. When the infant is fed, the drive is reduced and this produces a sense of pleasure (a reward). Food is therefore a **primary reinforcer** because it 'stamps in' (reinforces) the behaviour in order to avoid discomfort. The person who supplies the food is associated with avoiding discomfort and becomes a **secondary reinforcer**, and a source of reward in his/her own right. This 'rewardingness' is attachment.

This approach has been called the *cupboard love* theory of attachment because it suggests that the infant becomes attached because he/she is fed, and that the infant becomes attached to the person who feeds him/her.

Classical conditioning: Learning a new response

1 Before conditioning

Unconditioned stimulus (UCS) produces an unconditioned response (UCR)

Food (UCS) makes the dog salivate (UCR)

2 During conditioning

Food and door opening occur together a number of times

3 After conditioning

Conditioned stimulus (CS) produces a conditioned response (CR)

Door opening (CS) makes the dog salivate (now a CR)

Criticisms

Support

We *do* learn through association and reinforcement. However, food may not be the main reinforcer. Attention and responsiveness from a caregiver are also rewarding.

Counter-evidence

Schaffer and Emerson (see page 47) found that infants were *not* most attached to the person who fed them, nor to the person who spent most time with them. They were most attached to the person who was most responsive and interacted with them. A person's constant presence is no guarantee that interaction will occur.

A classic study by Harlow (1959) further demonstrated that food isn't everything. This study concerned rhesus monkeys who were raised on their own by two 'wire mothers'. One wire mother had a feeding bottle attached and the other was wrapped in soft cloth but offered no food. According to learning theory, the young monkeys should have become attached to the 'mother' associated with food and offering drive reduction. In fact, the monkeys spent most time with the cloth-covered mother and would cling to it especially when they were frightened (a proximity-seeking behaviour which is characteristic of attachment).

These studies suggest that 'cupboard love' is not likely to be an explanation for attachment, though we must remember that this research concerned monkeys and it may not be wholly appropriate to generalise the findings to human behaviour.

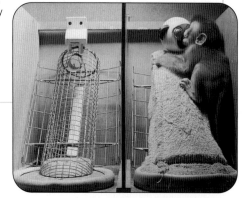

Orphan monkeys spent most time with the cloth-covered 'mother', visiting the 'mother' with the feeding bottle only for food. This suggests that attachment is related to comfort and not food.

Explanation 2: The psychoanalytic approach: Freud's theory

Sigmund Freud developed a theory of personality – an explanation of how each individual's personality develops. This theory can be used to explain many aspects of behaviour, including attachment.

Freud proposed that attachment grows out of the feeding relationship. In essence Freud claimed that infants are born with an innate drive to seek pleasure. He called this the **pleasure principle**, and suggested that one 'structure of the personality' (the **id**) was motivated by this principle. The id is the primitive, instinctive part of our personality that demands immediate satisfaction. In infancy the id demands oral satisfaction. The person providing this satisfaction becomes the love object, and an attachment is formed.

Freud's approach is described in more detail on pages 134 and 137.

Criticisms

This is another 'cupboard love' theory and can be dismissed with the same evidence as for behaviourist theory; see previous page.

The psychoanalytic approach *analyses* the psyche (your mind), i.e. it breaks it down into constituent parts such as the id, ego and superego.

The evolutionary approach was described on page 47 (under the heading 'What is adaptive value?').

Explanation 3: The evolutionary approach: Bowlby's theory

Infants are born with a drive to become attached

Bowlby (1969) proposed that infants become attached to a caregiver because attachment is **adaptive**. In other words, it is good for their reproductive success. Infants who do not become attached are less likely to survive and reproduce. Thus the attachment 'gene' is perpetuated and infants are born with an innate drive to become attached.

There are two reasons why attachment is good for survival and reproduction:

1 It means the infant is more likely to be well cared for when young and defenceless.
2 Attachments form the basis for later social relationships. They provide a template for how to have relationships with other people, and this promotes survival and reproduction.

Infants elicit caregiving

What specific behaviours promote attachment in infants? Infants are born with **social releasers**. The obvious example of a social releaser is when a baby smiles or when it cries. Such behaviours *elicit caregiving* from others nearby. If a baby didn't have these innate social releasers, potential caregivers would happily go about their business, ignoring the baby.

Adults respond to social releasers

But social releasers alone don't explain why the infant becomes attached to certain people rather than others. As we have seen, such attachments don't simply form because individuals spend a lot of time together. Attachments form because infants and caregivers *interact*.

Infants form one special relationship (monotropy)

Infants become most strongly attached to the person who interacts best – the person who responds *most sensitively* to the infant's social releasers. This person becomes the infant's **primary caregiver** and plays a special role in the infant's emotional development. This concept is called **monotropy** – focused on one person.

The infant's relationship with his/her primary caregiver has a particular significance. It is important for emotional and social development because it has emotional intensity. Bowlby suggested that the infant develops an **internal working model** of relationships based on this special emotional relationship with his/her primary caregiver. The internal working model is like a **schema**. It is a cluster of concepts about relationships – expectations about whether relationships involve consistent or inconsistent love, whether others make you feel good or anxious, and so on. The primary caregiver's behaviour is a model for what the infant will expect from others. The infant *internalises* this model.

Criticisms

Support: The continuity hypothesis

It follows, from Bowlby's theory, that we would expect securely attached infants to develop different social and emotional relationships in comparison to those who were insecurely attached (who have less trusting internal working models). This is called the **continuity hypothesis** – the idea that emotionally secure infants go on to be emotionally secure, trusting and socially confident adults. A number of studies support this and are described on the next page.

Alternative explanation: The temperament hypothesis

However, this continuity in development can be explained without using Bowlby's theory. An alternative explanation is that some infants are born trusting and friendly. This would explain why they become securely attached and also why they later form similar kinds of relationship. This is called the **temperament hypothesis** (described earlier on page 51).

The cute face of a baby acts as a social releaser – it elicits caregiving. It is no accident that all young animals have 'cute' faces: big eyes, small nose and chin, high forehead.

Research related to Bowlby's theory of attachment

Bowlby's theory of attachment is an example of an evolutionary approach to explaining behaviour. It is the most thorough explanation of attachment and the one that is best supported by research studies. We looked briefly at the support for Bowlby's theory on the previous page, and now will examine further studies.

Review: Three explanations of attachment

The behaviourist approach: An infant learns that certain individuals are associated with feelings of pleasure and reduce feelings of discomfort. The infant becomes attached to these individuals.

The psychoanalytic approach: A caregiver provides oral pleasure through feeding, thus satisfying innate drives and creating a love bond.

The evolutionary approach: Attachment is adaptive and innate. Infants elicit caregiving and become attached to those individuals who respond most sensitively to their signals. The relationship with a primary caregiver acts as a template for all later relationships.

Research related to Bowlby's theory of attachment

Imprinting in non-human animals

Bowlby drew on the concept of **imprinting** when he was developing his theory of attachment. We described this, and Lorenz's research, in the introduction to this section (page 45). Newborn animals, such as ducks, imprint on their parents. They appear to form an indelible picture of their parent(s) within hours of birth, and this helps them stick closely to this important source of protection and food. A young animal who wanders away from its parent would have to find its own food and is likely to be eaten rather quickly.

Since imprinting is innate there is likely to be a limited window of development – a **critical period**. (Aspects of development that are biological can only develop during a restricted period; for example when a baby is growing in the womb there is a particular time when the arms develop. If the mother is ill during this period the arms may not grow normally and the window for arm development passes forever.) If the infant has not been exposed to a suitable object during this critical period, no imprinting will take place. Later research has shown that the concept of a **sensitive period** is probably more appropriate. Development of all biological systems takes place most rapidly and easily during a critical period but can still take place at other times.

Sensitive periods

Bowlby applied the concept of a sensitive period to attachment. He claimed that infants who did not form attachments by a certain age would find it more difficult to become attached later. In the next section we will look at research on the effects of privation – when infants lack any attachments early in life (pages 64–7). This can tell us whether a lack of attachments does have long-term effects.

Is Lorenz's study an experiment, and if so, what kind is it? Can you identify the IV and DV? What variables might not have been controlled?

The continuity hypothesis

There is evidence to support the view that individuals who are securely attached in infancy *continue* to be socially and emotionally competent, whereas insecurely attached children have more difficulties, i.e. there are continuities from early to later experiences.

The study by Hazan and Shaver (1987) was mentioned earlier (page 50). They printed a 'Love Quiz' in a newspaper, seeking to find out about adults' early attachment experiences and about their later attitudes and experiences in love. **Secure attachment** types had happy, lasting and trusting love relationships. **Insecure/resistant** types worried that their partners didn't really love them. **Insecure/avoidant** lovers typically feared intimacy. This appears to support Bowlby's theory, though the data are correlational. This means we can't be certain that early attachment experiences caused later attachment types. This evidence merely shows that individual differences are related to early attachment experiences. It could be that the reason for continuity is because an individual was born friendly and this led to secure attachment and also determined the kind of relationships they had later in life (the **temperament hypothesis**, described on page 51).

The Minnesota longitudinal study (Sroufe *et al.*, 1999) used the Strange Situation to classify the attachment types of participants when they were infants. The participants have been reassessed as they have gone through childhood. The study has found that the securely attached infants were highest rated for social competence, were less isolated and more popular, and more empathetic. This again demonstrates continuity.

According to Bowlby, an infant becomes most strongly attached to an adult who responds sensitively to the infant's social signals (social releasers). 'Maternal' sensitivity is not exclusive to women. Men can 'mother' their children and some children are more strongly attached to their fathers.

Monotropy

Schaffer and Emerson (1964) found that most infants were specially attached to one primary caregiver, but many children had two or more equivalent attachments. Tronick *et al.*'s study of the Efe from Zaire (see page 53) found that infants aged 6 months had one primary attachment despite having many caregivers.

On the other hand, Lamb (1981) believes that different attachments simply serve different purposes rather than being in a hierarchy.

The importance of responsiveness and sensitivity

Harlow's monkeys (see page 54) preferred the cloth mother but had no responsive care. The monkeys all became quite maladjusted adults – they had difficulties in reproductive relationships and were poor parents. This underlines the importance of *interaction* in attachment. It is not enough to have something to cuddle – you need to be cuddled back.

The importance of sensitivity was expressed by Ainsworth in the **caregiver sensitivity hypothesis** (the importance of maternal sensitivity was discussed on page 51). Ainsworth *et al.* (1978) found that securely attached infants had mothers who responded more sensitively, whereas insecurely attached infants had mothers who responded less sensitively.

COMMENTARY

CORNER

Consider the extent to which psychological theories have been successful in explaining attachments.

A characteristic of all psychological theories is that they are constructed as an attempt to explain known facts and empirical (i.e. research) findings. How *successful* a theory is largely depends on three factors:

1 Does it fit the facts?
2 Is it consistent with existing research findings?
3 Does subsequent research support its claims?

One way to evaluate any chosen theory (i.e. the **AO2** content) is to assess its 'success' in explaining attachments. Such evaluations are covered in the *Criticisms* sections on pages 54–5.

Consider the major theories of attachment we have covered:

• **The behaviourist approach:** An infant learns that certain individuals are associated with feelings of pleasure and reduce feelings of discomfort. The infant becomes attached to these individuals.

• **The psychoanalytic approach:** A caregiver provides oral pleasure through feeding, thus satisfying innate drives and creating a love bond.

• **The evolutionary approach:** Attachment is adaptive and innate. Infants elicit caregiving and become attached to those individuals who respond most sensitively to their signals. The relationship with a primary caregiver acts as a template for all later relationships.

In a 300-word answer to this question, you may be tempted to apply the three paragraphs rule by covering each theory in one paragraph. Simple mathematics allows for about 100 words per paragraph, and within that paragraph a split of about 30/70 for **AO1/AO2**. Nothing is ever as exact as that, but these are rough guidelines to aim for. This would mean being able to **précis** each theory in 30 words or so. You may feel that this is too limited and therefore choose just two theories to form the basis of your answer. This immediately frees up a lot more words, and is a perfectly legitimate alternative.

These are not the only ways in which the requirements of this question can be met. You may choose to focus on two or more theories, but then in your final paragraph look further afield for your concluding evaluation – perhaps in the section on cross-cultural variations in attachment. If the test of a good theory is its ability to 'fit the facts', then does it fit these? A *really* successful theory of attachment would be able to explain the cultural differences and similarities that we met on pages 52–3.

A **précis** is a more compact version of a piece of text. There are many occasions when it is necessary to reduce the number of words used to express an argument – and your mini-essay is one of them because you have a limited amount of time to say as much as possible. It is important to restrict yourself to writing about only those things that will be creditworthy.

Deprivation and privation

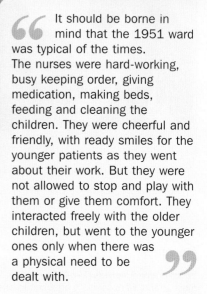

> It should be borne in mind that the 1951 ward was typical of the times. The nurses were hard-working, busy keeping order, giving medication, making beds, feeding and cleaning the children. They were cheerful and friendly, with ready smiles for the younger patients as they went about their work. But they were not allowed to stop and play with them or give them comfort. They interacted freely with the older children, but went to the younger ones only when there was a physical need to be dealt with.
>
> Robertson and Robertson, 1989

specification breakdown

Specification content	Comment
Bowlby's maternal deprivation hypothesis, including evidence on which it was based.	Bowlby's **maternal deprivation hypothesis** is specifically identified which means you must be able to describe and evaluate it. You must also be able to describe and evaluate the **evidence** on which the hypothesis is based, such as Bowlby's own studies and those of the Robertsons.
Research into the effects of privation (e.g. studies of extreme privation and institutionalisation), including the extent to which the effects of privation can be reversed.	Deprivation refers to the *loss* of attachments through separation; **privation** refers to the *lack* of attachments (i.e. no attachments were ever formed between an infant and his/her mother figure). Studies of extreme privation and studies of children in institutional care permit us to consider whether the effects of such privation can be reversed.

Many Romanian orphans suffer extreme deprivation and a lack of attachment. Such experiences may have devastating long-term consequences for emotional development.

John spent just nine days in a residential nursery. He went from being happy and well-adjusted to being depressed and distressed. Even temporary disruption of attachment can have serious consequences.

The quotation on the left, taken from James and Joyce Robertson's book, *Separation and the Very Young*, describes the surgical ward of the Central Middlesex Hospital, where James Robertson, armed with a cine camera, began his groundbreaking studies of young children in brief separation. Over the next few years, Robertson was to film a number of children who, for one reason or another, were separated from their primary caregiver. Robertson's films took the medical world by storm. In the year that his studies began, few hospitals in Britain that admitted children allowed daily visiting (a survey by the *Nursing Times* in 1952 found that of 1,300 hospitals, only 300 allowed daily visiting, and 150 prohibited visiting altogether). Robertson's films confirmed what had been widespread knowledge in the community for a long time – that young children could be 'changed' by a spell in hospital (Robertson and Robertson, 1989).

Robertson's films were not restricted to studies of children in hospital. It was the Robertsons' study of John, a healthy 17-month-old child placed in a residential nursery for 9 days, that remains one of the most powerful demonstrations of the disruptive effects of separation from the attachment figure. Over the course of just 9 days, John went from a happy, well-adjusted child to a child so distressed by the experience that upon reunion with his mother, his rejection of her was all too clear:

'A few minutes later his father entered the room and John struggled away from his mother into his father's arms. His crying stopped, and for the first time he looked directly at his mother. It was a long hard look, one she had never seen before.' Robertson and Robertson, 1989

More recently, we have become aware of the extreme deprivation suffered by children in orphanages in the former 'Iron Curtain' countries such as Romania. If temporary disruption of the attachment bond had such devastating effects on children such as John, what would be the consequences of prolonged deprivation? Psychologists have looked carefully at the long-term effects of bond disruption (deprivation) as well as cases where the absence of appropriate caregiving meant that the bond never formed at all (privation). Although children have proved remarkably resilient in such situations, inevitably there are costs.

One thing to note about this section is that most of the research is very old. This is mainly because the research on deprivation and privation relied on access to individuals who experienced deprivation and privation – largely children in institutions. Institutional care changed dramatically after the 1950s, as a result of the early psychological research, and this meant it was no longer possible to conduct such studies (there was no one to study). Recently, however, events in Eastern Europe have sadly led to an increase in cases to study, and this is the only modern research that we will look at in this section.

Breaking attachment bonds

I n the previous section, we looked at the use of the Strange Situation technique to explore different attachment styles (pages 48–9). Ainsworth and her colleagues used the Strange Situation to study how a mother's presence or absence affected her infant's behaviour. It is clear that for most young children, *physical* **separation** from their primary caregiver is distressing. However, in many cases, some degree of physical separation is unavoidable, as children must spend time in hospital, in day care, or even be left with a babysitter. Because the attachment bond is so important to the healthy emotional development of the child, psychologists have been particularly concerned with how the child copes when the bond is disrupted in this way.

For most children, physical separation from the primary caregiver has no lasting ill effects, *provided* that suitable substitute emotional care is available during that separation. In the absence of this (or where the separation is particularly prolonged), **deprivation** may ensue. To be *deprived* means to lose something, so in this case the child has lost the emotional care usually provided by his/her caregiver, and this loss is not compensated for by suitable levels of care from another person. As with separation, the child's attachment bond is disrupted, but the absence of suitable emotional care during the separation period may have more serious consequences.

Bowlby's maternal deprivation hypothesis

Evidence on which the maternal deprivation hypothesis is based

In the 1930s and 1940s a number of psychologists studied children who had experienced prolonged separations from their families. They observed that such children were often profoundly disturbed and lagged behind in intellectual development. For example, Spitz and Wolf (1946) observed that 100 'normal' children who were placed in an **institution** became severely depressed within a few months. Skeels and Dye (1939) also studied children placed in institutions. They found that these children scored poorly on intelligence tests.

These effects were quite a surprise because, before the findings of these studies became known, no one really thought about the effects of separation on infants and children. It was assumed that a good standard of physical care was all that would be required when infants and children were separated from caregivers. However, these studies showed that separation may affect emotional and cognitive development. John Bowlby also conducted research into the effects of deprivation (see research on opposite page).

Bowlby's hypothesis

Bowlby's research, and the other studies conducted in the 1930s and 1940s, led Bowlby to formulate the **maternal deprivation hypothesis**. This was a statement of Bowlby's belief about the psychological effects of separation. He believed that emotional care was as important for development as physical care. He famously said that 'mother-love in infancy and childhood is as important for mental health as are vitamins and proteins for physical health' (Bowlby, 1953, p. 240).

Bowlby believed that it wasn't enough to make sure that a child was well fed and kept safe and warm. He thought that infants and children needed a mother's emotional care to ensure continuing normal *mental* health. 'An infant and young child should experience a warm, intimate and continuous relationship with his mother' (Bowlby, 1953, p. 13). Bowlby believed that a child who is denied such care because of frequent and/or prolonged separations will become emotionally disturbed *if* this happens before the age of *about* 2½ years, and *if* there is no substitute mother-person available (Bowlby, 1953, p. 33). Bowlby also felt there was a continuing risk up until the age of 5.

Bowlby used the words 'mother/maternal' and 'deprivation'. 'Maternal' referred to a child's natural mother or his/her 'permanent mother-substitute – one person who steadily "mothers" him' (Bowlby, 1953, p. 13). 'Deprivation' referred to the *effects* of *prolonged* separation. Separation alone may not be harmful, but Bowlby claimed that a child who is *deprived* of emotional care will suffer permanent consequences in terms of mental health. This will only happen if a child is separated from his/her mother-figure *and* is offered no substitute emotional care. In other words, separation need not necessarily result in deprivation.

Criticisms

Positive influences

This hypothesis had an enormous impact on postwar thinking about childrearing and also on how children were looked after in hospitals. Before the research by Bowlby children were separated from parents when they spent time in hospital or if their mother spent time in hospital. Visiting was discouraged or even forbidden. Bowlby's maternal deprivation hypothesis changed all that.

The critical period

Bowlby claimed that the years up until about 2½ were critical in the child's development. This is called a **critical period hypothesis**. Bowlby claimed that if a child was denied emotional care during this time, permanent harm was fairly inevitable. Some research has challenged this. For example, some studies of isolated children (described on page 74) demonstrate good recovery despite many years of deprivation.

On the other hand, support for the critical period hypothesis comes from the study by Hodges and Tizard (see page 64), which found some permanent effects from early privation. So Bowlby may be right after all, though his concept of a 'critical period' may be rather strong. It might be preferable to talk about a **sensitive period** during which emotional care is especially important.

The effects of maternal deprivation: 44 juvenile thieves

(Bowlby, 1944)

In the 1930s John Bowlby worked as a psychiatrist in a Child Guidance Clinic in London, where he treated many emotionally disturbed children. Part of this treatment would involve interviews with parents about the child's early experiences. This work led Bowlby to formulate his belief about the link between early separations and later maladjustment.

Aims

The aim of this study was to test the maternal deprivation hypothesis. Bowlby was specifically interested in one group of adolescents attending the clinic – the 'thieves'. All the children referred to the clinic were emotionally maladjusted but, Bowlby argued, some of them were unable to understand how other people felt. These children lacked normal signs of affection, shame or a sense of responsibility. Such characteristics enabled them to be 'thieves' – they could steal from others because it didn't matter to them. So Bowlby decided to compare 44 juvenile *thieves* (children referred to the clinic because they had been involved in thefts) with another group of emotionally disturbed teenagers who were not thieves. Were 'thieves' more likely to have experienced early separations during which they received little substitute care? This would suggest that early separations could lead to emotional maladjustment, supporting the maternal deprivation hypothesis.

Procedures

The children interviewed ranged in age from 5 to 16. They all attended the Child Guidance Clinic. The **experimental group** consisted of 44 children who had been referred to the clinic because they were caught stealing. A further 44 children acted as a **control group**. This group were not thieves but had experienced emotional problems, for which they had been referred to the clinic. In addition Bowlby diagnosed 14 of the thieves as **affectionless psychopaths** – individuals who particularly lacked emotional sensitivity.

The children and their parents were interviewed by Bowlby and his associates. Information was collected about their early life experiences, with particular attention paid to early separations.

What was the IV in this experiment? What was the DV?

You should note that Bowlby's maternal deprivation hypothesis was developed almost *twenty years* before his attachment theory, which was described on page 55. It was the forerunner of the attachment theory.

Findings

It was found that the affectionless thieves had experienced frequent early separations from their mothers. The figures in the table show that 86% of the affectionless thieves (12 out of 14) experienced frequent separations compared with 17% (5 out of 30) of the other thieves.

Furthermore, almost none of the control participants experienced early separations, whereas 39% of all the thieves had experienced early separations. These early separations often consisted of continual or repeated stays in foster homes or hospitals, when the children were often not visited by their families.

	Separations from mother before the age of 2		Total
	Frequent	None	
Affectionless thieves	12 (86%)	2 (14%)	14
Other thieves	5 (17%)	25 (83%)	30
All thieves	17 (39%)	27 (61%)	44
Control participants	2 (4%)	42 (96%)	44

Graph showing separations from mother before the age of 2

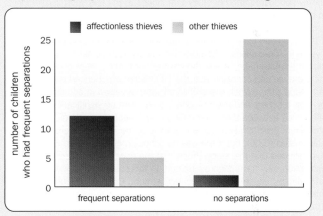

Conclusions

These data suggest a link between early separation and becoming a thief (i.e. someone lacking a social conscience). They also suggest that early separations are linked to affectionless psychopathy. In other words, lack of continuous care may well cause emotional maladjustment, especially in the extreme form of affectionless psychopathy.

Criticisms

Unreliable data

The information about early separation was collected *retrospectively*. Parents were asked to recall events from up to 14 years previously about when they had been separated from their children. It is likely that such recall was not completely accurate (as we know from our study of memory!). The data collected may also have been unreliable because people don't always answer interviewer's answers truthfully – parents might be expected to present themselves in a better light (**social desirability bias**) and report *fewer separations*.

Causal relationship not demonstrated

This study is a natural experiment. (The IV (separations) varied naturally.) This means that a causal relationship is not demonstrated. Rutter (1981) suggested that there may be a linking factor which causes both separations and maladjustment and that is why they are linked. A possible factor would be stress in the home due to marital discord or a lack resources to care for the children.

Further evidence related to the maternal deprivation hypothesis

A photograph of Laura from the book by Robertson and Robertson, *Separation and the Very Young*, 1989

Bowlby's maternal deprivation hypothesis predicted that children who experienced prolonged early separations would experience long-term emotional problems. His own study of juvenile delinquents (described on the previous page) supported this hypothesis. However, this study involved a correlational analysis; therefore we cannot conclude that early separations caused later maladjustment. The box below examines issues surrounding the use of correlational analysis.

Subsequent research, by Bowlby and others, has further examined the maternal deprivation hypothesis. We will look at this research now.

Separation or deprivation?

Bowlby conducted another study that looked at the effects of separation on development (Bowlby *et al.*, 1956). In this study the participants were a group of 60 children under the age of 4 who had TB. Treatment of this condition used to involve a prolonged stay in hospital (as long as 2 years in some cases). The nurses in the TB hospital did not provide substitute maternal care and the children were only visited once a week. Therefore we can conclude that the TB children experienced prolonged early *deprivation*. When these children were assessed in adolescence (by their teachers and psychologists), there were no significant differences between them and their 'normal' peers in terms of intellectual development. Some members of the TB group were more maladjusted (63%), but there was no serious maladjustment. Bowlby *et al.* concluded that this study shows that the dangers of maternal deprivation may have been overstated. In this case early deprivation did not invariably cause emotional maladjustment. One explanation for the individual differences may be that some children were more securely attached and therefore able to cope better.

Reversibility of deprivation

It may be that, even when children suffer deprivation, they are able to recover. In other words, the effects are reversible. The study described earlier by Skeels and Dye (1939) produced data supporting this. Some of the institutionalised children who showed IQ deficits were transferred to a home for mentally retarded adults. When the children's IQs were tested again, they had increased! Why? Could it be that the retarded adults enjoyed having children to look after and provided the missing emotional care? To test this belief, Skodak and Skeels (1949) arranged for some more infants to be placed in a home for the mentally retarded while a control group remained in the orphanage. When the children's IQs were tested after 1.5 years they found that the IQs of the control group had, on average, fallen from 87 to 61 points, whereas the transferred group's IQ rose from 64 to 92 points.

There are many other studies that support the view that deprivation effects can be reversed. For example, Bohman and Sigvardsson (1979) studied over 600 adopted children in Sweden. At the age of 11, 26% of them were classified as 'problem children', probably the result of early experiences of deprivation prior to adoption. In a follow-up study 10 years later, they concluded that none of the children were any worse off than the rest of the population. This would suggest that early, negative effects were reversed.

What is the difference between deprivation and separation?

Separation refers to a situation where a child is separated from his/her primary caregiver(s). If suitable replacement care is available, and this meets the emotional needs of the child, then separation need not have any adverse consequences. If suitable replacement care is not available, and particularly if the separation is prolonged, the disruption of the attachment bond may be classified as *deprivation*.

Deprivation refers to being deprived of emotional care. When a child is separated this may result in deprivation if no substitute emotional care is offered. Deprivation, therefore, is not the same as separation, but *may* accompany physical separation in certain circumstances.

| Physical separation | ▶ Alternative emotional care offered | ▶ Bond disruption avoided |
| Emotional deprivation | ▶ Loss of emotional care | ▶ Bond disruption |

A two-year-old goes to hospital

Our understanding of the effects of separation and of how to improve the experience of separation is due to the pioneering work of James and Joyce Robertson. Some of their research, especially with a young boy called John, was described in the introduction to this section. Robertson and Bowlby (1952) were alarmed by the despair they observed in hospitalised children, but found that the medical profession was reluctant to acknowledge this. Perhaps a film would 'pierce the defenses' in a way that the spoken word failed to do. A two-year-old child, Laura, was selected at random. She was admitted to the hospital for an eight-day stay to have a minor operation. Robertson was concerned that he might be accused of only filming at the times when Laura was distressed so he used an unbiased **time-sampling** technique, filming two 40-minute sessions at the same time each day.

The film shows Laura alternating between periods of calm and distress. Her parents visit occasionally and she begs to go home. Laura's obvious struggle to control her feelings is hard to watch. One doctor was very angered by the film and felt that his profession had been slandered. However, the next time he walked down his children's ward, he saw things differently: 'I really heard the children crying for the first time.' (Robertson and Robertson, 1989, p. 54). The doctor immediately introduced unrestricted visiting and encouraged parents of under-5s to stay. Gradually attitudes all over the world changed. It was this film, and the PDD model, which were responsible for these major social changes.

Children in residential care: Young children in brief separation

James Robertson and his wife Joyce (1968–73) produced further films, recording how five children coped with brief separation while their mothers were hospitalised. Some children were in foster care (with Joyce Robertson) and had substitute emotional care; one child was in a residential nursery where substitute emotional care was not provided. These films aimed to compare situations with or without substitute emotional care.

Jane, Lucy, Thomas and Kate – These children were all under 3 years of age, spending time in foster care for up to 27 days. To help the children the Robertsons kept routines similar to those at home, father's visits were arranged to maintain emotional links with home, and children were taken where possible to visit their mothers in hospital. All the children seemed to adjust well and did not reject their mothers when reunited.

John – John spent 9 days in a residential nursery and had quite different experiences to the fostered children, as we saw at the start of this section. The film of John is so distressing that many viewers say they can't bear to watch it again. During the first 2 days in the nursery John behaved much as normal, confident that nurses would respond to his needs as his parents had done. When this does not happen he becomes increasingly bewildered. He makes more determined efforts to get attention from the nurses, but he cannot compete with the other, more assertive children in the nursery. The nurses are always friendly but also always busy. When John fails to find anyone who will respond to him, he seeks comfort from an over-sized teddy bear. Over the next few days he gradually breaks down and refuses food, stops playing, cries a great deal, and gives up trying to get the nurses' attention.

John's father visited often and at first John greets him enthusiastically but soon he also rejects these visits. On the 9th day, when his mother comes to take him home, John struggled to get away from her. For many months afterwards he continued to have outbursts of anger towards his mother.

Conclusions – The observational record demonstrates a clear difference between those children placed in a foster care situation and a child placed in an institutional setting. The key explanation is **bond disruption** (disruption of emotional support). As long as children are given continuing emotional support they appear to cope with separation; otherwise they become despairing and detached.

Criticisms

Using case studies

The conclusions of this study are based on observations of only a few children. It is probable that each of these children is unique in different ways and we should not make **generalisations** about all human behaviour. For example, John's rejection of his mother may have been due to the new baby she had during his stay in the residential nursery.

High validity

We could say that this study has high **external validity** because it was in a realistic setting which makes us more confident about generalising the findings to real life. The study also has high **internal validity** because the observations were filmed in a rigorous way unbiased by observer expectations (lack of **observer bias**) and the record is available for others to inspect and draw their own conclusions (**replication** of analysis)

The concepts of **external** and **internal validity** are explored in detail later in this book (pages 182–7) Validity concerns the legitimacy of a study and its conclusions.

Research methods *Generalisability*

'Generalisability' refers to the idea that the findings of any particular study should apply to all human behaviour. It is rarely true that we can generalise from particular research studies to all human behaviour but it is a goal of research studies. For this reason researchers aim to use a **representative sample** of the target **population**. More of this when we look at **sampling** (on page 108).

Research methods *Naturalistic observation*

Naturalistic observation is both a **research technique** and a **research method**. In this particular study the method could be described as a **natural experiment** because there is a naturally varying IV: whether the children did or did not receive substitute emotional care. The technique involved was naturalistic observation (simply recording everything that happened at set time intervals).

COMMENTARY CORNER

To what extent do research studies support the view that disruption of the attachment bond has lasting effects for the individual?

Caution – be careful when choosing what material to include. The question asks for *research studies*, not theories or other explanations.

Studies that have demonstrated that disruption of the attachment bond *does* have lasting effects on the individual include those carried out by Skeels and Dye (1939), Bowlby (1944), and Spitz and Wolf (1946). Each of these has demonstrated different effects, but all have provided evidence for disruption having a significant adverse effect on subsequent development.

Caution – are the studies being used as **AO1** or **AO2**?

In order to balance the debate, you should also refer to those studies which suggest that the disruption of an attachment bond may *not* have lasting effects for the individual. These include Skodak and Skeels (1949), Bowlby *et al.* (1956), and Bohman and Sigvardsson (1980). However, *describing* alternative studies does not qualify as *evaluation*. Description would be credited as AO1. For **AO2** credit you must weave the material into a critical argument that pits the insights and conclusions of one study against those of another.

Caution – remember the **AO1/AO2** split (one-third/two-thirds) when compiling material.

You must make a special effort to include evaluation and commentary. There are important general points that might be made in response to this question. Rutter (1981) suggested that it is wrong to assume that early separations *caused* later maladjustment. Other factors (e.g. family discord) may be responsible for *both* the disruption of the bond (perhaps through temporary fostering) *and* any subsequent maladjustment.

Caution – deprivation and privation are different.

It is important to be clear about the distinction between the terms *deprivation* and *privation* (which we cover on page 64). Deprivation refers to the physical disruption of an attachment bond, whereas privation means an attachment bond has never developed in the first place. You must be clear about whether the question concerns deprivation only, or whether material on privation would be relevant or could be made relevant. The question given here refers to the 'disruption of attachment bonds' and is therefore specifically related to deprivation.

What is meant by privation?

In Bowlby's maternal deprivation hypothesis (Bowlby, 1953), he stated that a child who is *deprived* of emotional care will suffer permanent consequences in terms of mental health. Rutter (1981), in his book *Maternal Deprivation Reassessed*, criticised this view of deprivation because it did not make clear whether the child's attachment bond had formed but been broken, or in fact had never formed in the first place. Rutter's view of deprivation was that the latter (the *lack* of an attachment bond) would have potentially far more serious consequences for the child than the former (the *loss* of an attachment bond). He therefore used the term **privation** to refer to situations where the child fails to develop an attachment bond with one primary caregiver, and deprivation to refer to situations where a bond does develop, but through prolonged or traumatic separations is disrupted or lost. Privation may be evident if the primary caregiver is 'lost' prior to the development of an attachment bond (and no substitute caregiver is available). This may happen in conditions of abuse and neglect, or in other conditions of inconsistent or inadequate parental care.

Psychologists have typically studied children raised in institutions to see whether a lack of cognitive and emotional stimulation had the later consequences predicted by Rutter.

What is the difference between privation and deprivation?

Bowlby suggested that infants need a close continuous relationship. It wasn't clear in his original theory whether deprivation meant a disruption of this relationship (i.e. the loss of an attachment figure) or a lack of it altogether.

Michael Rutter said that the concept of 'deprivation' was misleading because there was an important difference between being separated from loved ones (deprivation) and never having formed a relationship with anyone in the first place (privation). Rutter felt that deprivation may not have irreversible consequences, whereas privation might.

KEY TERM

Privation: A term originally introduced by Michael Rutter to distinguish children who had never managed to develop an attachment bond (privation) from those who had developed a bond that had been broken (deprivation).

---

star STUDY

The effects of privation
(HODGES & TIZARD, 1989)

Aims

Bowlby's **maternal deprivation hypothesis** suggested that a discontinuous relationship between a mother-figure and infant would result in emotional maladjustment. But some of the research evidence indicates that children can and do recover from early deprivation – this might not be the case with privation. To test whether early privation did have long-term effects, Jill Hodges and Barbara Tizard undertook a long-term study (a **longitudinal study**), following a group of children from early life to adolescence.

Procedures

The study focused on a group of 65 children who had been placed in one institution when they were less than 4 months old. At this age children have not yet formed attachments. There was an explicit policy in the institution against the 'caretakers' forming attachments with the children and there was also a high turnover of staff. This meant that the children had little opportunity to form a close, continuous relationship with an adult. An early study of the children found that 70% were described as not able 'to care deeply about anyone'. Thus we can conclude that most if not all of these children had experienced early emotional privation (a lack of attachment rather than a loss of attachment).

By the age of 4, 24 of the institutionalised children had been adopted, 15 had returned to their natural homes and the rest remained in the institution. The children were assessed at this time and again when they were 8 years old, at which time the sample was reduced to 51 children. The children were assessed again at age 16 – by then the researchers were only able to locate 23 of the adopted children (some of whom had been adopted after the age of 4), 11 'restored' children and 5 children who had remained in institutional care.

At each assessment the children, their parents and teachers were interviewed and asked to fill in questionnaires. The data collected concerned attitudes and behaviour.

At all ages there was also a **control group** of children raised in a 'normal' home environment.

http://www.gsm.uci.edu/~mckenzie/rethink/mck97-ch8.htm
Research on the psychological effects of institutional care, with useful table of research studies.

In the follow-up study at age 16 there were two experimental groups and one control group. What were they?

All of the ex-institutional children had one thing in common – they all had difficulty in peer relationships. This suggests that their abilities to form relationships may have been damaged by early privation.

Findings

At age 4: The institutional caretakers reported that the children did not have any deep relationships. The children, in general, were more attention-seeking and more indiscriminately affectionate than non-institutional children.

At age 8: Most of the ex-institutional (restored or adopted) children had formed close attachments with their parents or adopted parents. The children's teachers reported that the ex-institutional children still tended to be more attention-seeking and also more 'over-friendly' than 'normal' peers. They also tended to be unpopular, but did not lag cognitively when compared to 'normal' peers.

At age 16 *two important findings emerged*:

1 **Relationships within the family**: In general the adopted children were about as closely attached to their parents as the control group, whereas the 'restored' group were much less likely to be closely attached.

2 **Peer relationships**: All the ex-institutional adolescents were less likely to have a special friend, to be part of a crowd, or to be liked by other children. They were also more quarrelsome and more likely to be bullies.

Conclusions

The findings at age 4 and 8 suggest that the children did show signs of permanent damage as a result of their early institutional life.

The findings at age 16 suggest that early privation had a negative effect on the ability to form relationships when the relationship involved someone who wasn't going to work hard at it. The adopted children were doing fine at home, but not in peer relationships. This suggests that they hadn't fully recovered from their early privation because they were less able to form relationships.

Criticisms

Attrition

The original sample was reduced in subsequent follow-ups. This is called **attrition** and is a problem in longitudinal studies because particular kinds of participants are likely to be the ones who 'drop out'. It is possible that more troubled children dropped out – though this should have affected both the adopted and restored children equally and therefore not have biased the findings.

Sample bias

It is also possible that the adopted and restored groups were different because the children first selected for adoption might have been the less troubled children. Parents select which child to adopt and they are likely to select those easier to get on with. This could explain why the adopted children got on better at home (because they were 'easier' children), but doesn't explain why they had more difficulties with peers. According to the **temperament hypothesis** 'easier' children should have easier relationships with everyone. This means that the Hodges and Tizard findings do support the view that privation has negative long-term effects.

Alternative explanations for the findings

Hodges and Tizard suggest that the findings, at age 16, might be explained in other ways. For example, it could be that the adopted children suffered from poor self-esteem stemming from being adopted, which would explain their problems outside the home. Another explanation could be that the ex-institutional children lag behind their peers in emotional development and this would explain their poor peer relationships – they are simply not yet ready to cope.

This study is a natural experiment. At the final follow-up, at 16 years, what was the naturally occurring IV?

Research methods *Longitudinal design*

When a study is conducted over a long period of time it is said to have a **longitudinal design**. Such studies make it possible to observe long-term effects and to make comparisons between the same individual at different ages. An alternative way to do this (which takes a lot less time) is to use a **cross-sectional design**. In this design one group of participants of a young age is compared with another, older group of participants. The problem with a cross-sectional study is that the two groups of participants may be quite different. The **participant variables** in a cross-sectional design are not controlled, in the same way that they are not controlled in an independent groups design (which we discussed on page 13). This means that, in a cross-sectional design, differences between groups may be due to differences between participants rather than the independent variable (age).

Can the effects of privation be reversed?

A variety of other studies have considered the long-term effects of privation. The conclusions tend to be negative, though this is by no means the universal finding. There are many individuals who spend their early years in extreme privation and yet go on to be quite content and able to form good interpersonal relationships.

Other research findings on the effects of privation

Case studies of isolated children

Through the course of history there have been cases recorded where individual children have been raised in conditions of extreme isolation – and privation, i.e. *apparently* lacking emotional care. Two of the best-known cases are those of Genie and of the Czech twins (PM and JM). What can the findings from the study of these children tell us?

Genie was locked in a room by her father until she was 13½ (because he thought she was retarded). When she was 'found' she could not stand erect, and could not speak. She never fully recovered, socially or in terms of being able to speak. She apparently showed a *disinterest* in other people. In other words, she lacked social responsiveness. Her lack of recovery may be due to her extreme early emotional privation, though her mother claimed to have formed a relationship with her. Or it may be due to the late age at which she was 'discovered' (well past Bowlby's sensitive period for effective attachment), which would mean that recovery was not possible. Or it may be that the *physical* deprivation she experienced could explain her poor development (Curtiss, 1977; Rymer, 1993).

The Czech twins (Koluchová, 1976) spent the first seven years of their lives locked up by a stepmother. When they were first 'discovered' they couldn't talk. After discovery they were cared for by two loving sisters and by age 14 had near normal intellectual and social functioning. By the age of 20, they were of above-average intelligence and had excellent relationships with the members of their foster family (Koluchová, 1991). It is possible they were 'discovered' at a young enough age and therefore could recover. It is also possible that they provided emotional care for each other, and thus did experience early attachment rather than privation.

Studies of institutionalised children

We have already considered some of the very early studies of institutionalised children, for example, the studies by Spitz and Wolf (1946) and Skodak and Skeels (1949) – see pages 62-63. It is difficult to say whether these are studies of deprivation or privation – a case could be argued either way. Goldfarb (1943), who also studied institutionalised children, concluded that 'strong anchors to specific adults were not established' during the early years of such children's lives. Goldfarb found that the children he studied were more emotionally withdrawn in early adolescence than 'normal' children. This suggests that privation does have permanent long-term effects.

Quinton et al. (1985) also studied the long-term effects of institutional care. They compared a group of about 50 women who had been reared in institutions (children's homes) with a control group of 50 women reared at home. When the women were in their 20s it was found that the ex-institutional women were experiencing extreme difficulties acting as parents. For example, more of the ex-institutional women had children who had spent time in care and more of the ex-institutional women were rated as lacking in warmth when interacting with their children.

However, not all studies have found that the effects of privation are permanent. Triseliotis (1984) studied 44 adults who had been adopted late in childhood. It was not expected that they would recover but the children showed good adjustment, which was attributed to the fact that they had been placed in good, caring environments.

Recent studies of institutionalised children

Rutter et al. (1998) have been studying a group of 111 Romanian orphans, who spent their early months and years in extreme physical and emotional privation in institutions. These children were adopted by British families before the age of 2. By the age of 4 the children had apparently recovered. This shows that recovery from extreme privation can be achieved given adequate care. However, it is important to note that the age of adoption is within the period that Bowlby regarded as critical (i.e. under 2½ years of age).

Criticisms

One of the main difficulties with all of this research is that we don't know whether or not the children were attached to someone during the sensitive years, and what the quality of that attachment was. In order to test the hypothesis that *lack* of attachment can have a profound effect, we need to be able to assess whether an infant/child did or did not form any attachments along the way, or at least did not form any continuous and secure attachments.

Research methods Case studies

Case studies are full of problems. They concern unique individuals who provide us with a rich record of human experience, but it is hard to generalise from such individual cases and hard to uncover what did actually happen in the past (when retrospective data are used). It would seem that some children can recover if they are discovered early enough and given good subsequent care.

Effects of privation

The 'cycle of privation'

It may be that children who experience early privation are in some way 'driven' to recreate the conditions of their own childhood when they themselves become parents. This idea of a 'cycle of privation' is an extremely controversial area. However, there is some research support for this proposition. In terms of theoretical support there is the argument that children who lack early attachments are less able to form relationships later in life. In terms of empirical support there is the study by Quinton *et al.* (reported on the previous page), which found ex-institutional women experienced extreme difficulties as parents, and a high proportion of their children spent time in care themselves.

Reactive attachment disorder

This condition was made popular by the movie *Good Will Hunting*. Children with reactive attachment disorder have learned that the world is unsafe, and have learned not to depend on adult caregivers. They develop a protective emotional 'shell', which isolates them from the pain of their attachment failure. These shells become very difficult to remove, as children depend on them as their sole means of coping with the world. Anyone who tries to remove this shell is seen as a threat and so they turn against the very people who want to help them the most, the caregivers. Individuals with this disorder (also known as attachment disorder), if left untreated, may grow up to become **sociopaths** who fail to develop a conscience and do not learn to trust others. They also show a complete lack of ability to be genuinely affectionate with others or to form loving and lasting intimate relationships.

In the film *Good Will Hunting*, psychiatrist Sean McGuire (Robin Williams) tries to get through to Will Hunting (Matt Damon), diagnosed with reactive attachment disorder.

http://www.radzebra.org/
Read about reactive attachment disorder.

CORNER

COMMENTARY

To what extent has research supported the claim that privation in infancy will have adverse effects on later development?

On this and the previous spreads, there are many studies that have demonstrated the long-term effects of privation. In attempting to answer the question, however, it pays to be selective. Each of the studies represents just one part of the overall picture regarding the effects of privation on subsequent development. In choosing and describing research to represent this area, a précis of the main findings and/or conclusions is all you would need.

The question above asks you to consider the extent to which research has *supported* the stated claim. Most research *does* support this claim, but other research studies reach rather different conclusions. Indeed, some research suggests that although there *are* adverse effects associated with early developmental privation, these effects are *reversible* if the child is given the right sort of stimulation later on. As a debate includes all aspects of this argument, so research that suggests a *lack* of long-term effects is as relevant as research that shows that they *do* exist.

All of the research included in this section can be criticised in one way or another, and this is an important way to attract AO2 credit. For example, you might consider the issue that much of the research depends on recalling events from many years ago. Such comments would balance the research claims made regarding the long-term effects of privation with some words of caution regarding the interpretation of that research.

As well as the criticisms that can be levelled against specific research studies (which *limit* their value in the debate concerning long-term effects), there are other more general evaluative points that can be made. One of these concerns the tendency to ignore fathers as attachment figures. Most developmental literature has considered fathers in terms of their absence (and the effects of this on subsequent development) rather than their inclusion in the parenting process. Apart from media representations of 'new men' holding babies as a sign of new-found intimacy, dominant representations of child care treat 'parent' as equivalent to 'mother' (Burman, 1997). We must also guard against interpreting the conditions of privation too literally. The development of children is susceptible to many influences, of which the presence or absence of the primary caregiver is only one, albeit an important one.

CRITICAL ISSUE:
Day care

Q We're thinking of putting our 2-year-old into day care, and I'm nervous. The school seems great, but I've heard that toddlers in day care get sick all the time and are not as close to their parents. Is that true?'

specification breakdown

Specification content	Comment
The effects of day care on children's cognitive and social development.	The research on attachment led some people to believe that when a child is placed in **day care**, the consequent separation from his/her primary caregiver would have detrimental effects on the child's development. The separation might affect **cognitive** and/or **social development**.

WHAT DO YOU THINK ABOUT DAY CARE?

Do you think mothers should stay home to look after babies under the age of 2?

☐ Yes ☐ No ☐ Matter of personal choice ☐ Don't know

Does it have to be the mother? Can children be looked after as well by their father or another relative?

☐ Mother ☐ Father ☐ Mother or father ☐ Grandparents are just as good

Do you think that children whose parents both work are harmed by the separation from their attachment figure?

☐ Yes ☐ No ☐ Don't know

What kind of child care did you experience?

☐ Childminding ☐ Day nursery ☐ Other care outside the home ☐ Cared for by family (parent or other) ☐ Other

Ellen Galinsky

A Answer from Ellen Galinsky,
President of Families and
Work Institute:

'In the last few decades, there has been a great deal of research into the effects of various types of child care on kids' well-being. What's emerged on all fronts is that quality of child care is what matters – not where it takes place. If the people who care for your child are warm and caring, then it doesn't matter whether they do that in your home or in a group setting. Despite the cost difference, nannies are no more likely to provide good nurturing than day-care center employees, and vice versa.

What you need to do is closely observe the teachers at the day-care center. Do they connect with the children? Or spend most of their time cleaning up and talking to each other? Do the kids seem busy and involved? If they cling to you when you walk in the door, that is a sign the teachers aren't giving them enough attention.

As to whether children become ill more in group care, the answer is yes. But usually that is only initially, until they build up their immunities. You also have to remember that if you keep your kids at home until they're ready for public school, they'll probably just get sick more then, when they're exposed to a host of viruses and bugs for the first time.

As for your concern that kids in group care are less attached to their parents, that depends on the parents, not the type of child care they use or even their relationship with their provider. I'm not advocating one kind of provider over another, but I strongly believe – and research supports – that parents have to choose what is right for their child. The bottom line: Look for someone who is nurturing and who will help your child thrive, no matter where she spends her day.'

Source: http://www.lifetimetv.com/family/QA_ellen08.html

What is meant by day care?

The concept of day care is not a precise one. In general it refers to a form of temporary care (i.e. not all day and night long), not provided by family members or someone well known to the child, and it usually takes place outside the home. This includes childminding and day nurseries. Many of you will have been left with childminders or in a day nursery if both your parents worked – therefore, you have had first-hand experience of day care!

Leaving their child with a childminder is seen as a preferable form of day care for many parents, because the care the child receives is more likely to be similar to the care he or she would receive at home. The other commonly used form of day care is the day nursery. Day nurseries can be found in a variety of locations, including schools, churches, women's shelters and so on. One of the most rapidly growing forms of day care is nurseries within the workplace. These are gaining popularity because employers recognise that providing on-site day care is not only a good benefit for employees, but it also makes good business sense. Other types of day care include home day care, where a child-care professional cares for the child in the child's own home.

Difference between day care and institutional care

As well as knowing what day care *is*, it is important to understand what it is *not*. Other forms of care that are part of a more formal institutional programme of childrearing (such as fostering and community homes) or that are health-related (such as hospitalisation) are not what is meant by day care in this context.

KEY TERM

Day care: A form of temporary care (i.e. not all day and night long), not given by family members or someone well known to the child, and usually outside the home.

What is high-quality care?

This is measured in terms of low child-to-adult ratios (about 1:3 for infants and 1:5 for toddlers); small overall numbers of children in the day-care setting; and a sensitive, stimulating and warm environment.

The day-care debate

Is day care good, bad or indifferent? Are children harmed by spending time away from their mothers (or mother-substitutes)? Do they actually benefit from this extra care? Does it matter how old they are when placed in day care? Does the quality of the care matter? Are the effects different for different children?

This is a very hot debate, with so many questions and hundreds of answers. Some individuals strongly oppose day care. For example, Kathy Gyngell of the Full-time Mothers Association claims: 'When a child's mother dies that is a terrible tragedy. But we impose that tragedy on every child when we go out to work.' On the other hand, Tony Munton of London University's Institute for Education reports with certainty that: 'We know that day care doesn't do children any harm, especially if it is of good quality.'

You may not think that this debate has anything to do with you – but what of recent research that suggests that children do worse in exams if they have spent time in day care? Would you like to know if this is true?

http://www.geocities.com/Wellesley/Garden/2010/
Arguments strongly against day care.

The arguments against day care

Argument 1: *Separation from one's primary caregiver is bad*

Bowlby's **maternal deprivation hypothesis** (page 60) and his theory of attachment (page 55) suggested that prolonged separation from a primary caregiver will have both short- and long-term effects. Some people argue that day care is a form of prolonged separation which affects the *continuous* relationship between a mother-figure and child. If this is true, day care is likely to result in deprivation and have negative effects on development.

Argument 2: *The quality of care offered in day care may not be as good as that given by parents*

Parents have a much greater investment in the well-being and development of their child, and may provide a different kind of attention for the child as well as more intense empathy (consideration of the child's feelings). Day-care providers and childminders may look for peace and quiet rather than stimulation and empathy, especially when they are caring for a number of young children at the same time.

This view has been supported in various research studies. For example, Bryant *et al.* (1980) found that some children in a childminding setting were actually disturbed, and suggested that this may be because childminders feel that they don't have to form emotional bonds with the children. Howes and Hamilton (1992) found that secure attachments only occurred with 50% of caregivers as opposed to 70% of mothers. The lower rate of attachment probably reflects the lower quality and closeness of the caregiver relationship, which is probably due to the fact that day-care assistants are less committed to the child, less attached, and engage in less intense interactions.

As we know from our earlier studies of separation and bond disruption, separation is likely to result in deprivation when no substitute emotional care is offered. This means that day-care provision that is lacking emotional support may well be detrimental. Of course it is not fair to say that *all* day-care providers offer unstimulating and disinterested care, but a large number do. A study conducted in the US by the National Institute of Child Health and Human Development (NICHD, 1999) found that 90% of day-care providers are providing less than 'excellent' day care.

Argument 3: *Studies show that day care is related to negative outcomes*

Many studies of day care have found that children in day care come out worse in all sorts of ways than children who spend their early years at home. These studies are considered in relation to cognitive and social development on pages 74 and 76.

The arguments supporting day care

Argument 1: *Day-care providers can provide lots of fun and stimulation*

Many children and parents look at a well-run nursery and think 'What an exciting place to be!' There are daily activities (such as painting, play house, sand pits, story time), friends to have fun with, and staff specially trained to look after the children. This may not be the case for all day-care situations, but many are very good and may even be better than care provided at home. Often mothers and infants at home are quite isolated; some mothers plonk the baby in front of the television for hours at a time – so day care may in fact provide a more stimulating environment.

Argument 2: *Mothers have to work and/or get bored at home*

For those mothers who feel isolated or bored at home, day care may provide a better alternative for their child. Brown and Harris (1978) conducted a classic study on depression in women. They found that many depressed women blamed their depression on being at home with children. A depressed mother will not provide good child care.

It is also true that for some mothers there is no choice about working, such as in the case of single parents or families where a joint income is needed. This means that society has a duty to provide high-quality care.

Argument 3: *Quality counts more than quantity*

Many of the negative effects of day care may 'simply' be due to poor-quality care. When children are placed in high-quality care, there are rarely negative effects and there can be positive effects. For example, Andersson's (1992) study of day care in Sweden found that those children who were placed in day care before the age of 1 did best of all at school (compared to those who entered day care later and those who didn't attend day care). Day care in Sweden is of a very high quality.

Therefore, the issue may not be about whether day care is good or bad, but how high-quality care can be provided. Quality care is important at home, too. Mothers who work can't provide a high quantity of care but may still be able to provide a high-quality care. The study by Schaffer and Emerson (see page 47) found that children were not always attached to the person who spent most time with them. This shows that good care is not related to quantity. Sensitive caregiving (Ainsworth's caregiver sensitivity hypothesis) is more crucial than the amount of time a person spends with a child.

Argument 4: *Research evidence shows that day care is related to positive outcomes*

Many studies of day care have found that children in day care do better on various measures. In fact, most people would be happy to know that there are simply no negative effects, let alone the possibility that day care may actually be *better*! Studies of the positive effects of day care are considered in relation to cognitive and social development on pages 75 and 77.

Lots of fun, but what sort of effects does day care have on young children?

Evaluating the arguments for and against day care

Individual differences

Some children may find day care harder to cope with than others. For example, children who are shy may find it quite frightening (Pennebaker *et al.*, 1981). Children who are insecurely attached at home may also find that separation is hard to cope with. An NICHD study (1997) found that children whose mothers lacked responsiveness (and thus might be insecurely attached) did less well in day care. On the other hand, a different study found that insecurely attached children did best in day care (Egeland and Hiester, 1995), whereas securely attached children became more aggressive. This might be due to the fact that insecurely attached children *needed* compensatory education, and therefore benefited from day care, whereas the securely attached children did not need this extra attention.

Number of hours

An important variable, when considering whether day care has good or bad effects, is how long a child spends each day or week in day care. It may be that there is a limit to how much a small child can take. A recent NICHD study (2001) found that babies in day care for more than 10 hours a week were more aggressive once they reached school. On the other hand, Clarke-Stewart *et al.* (1994) found no difference in attachment between children spending a lot of time in day care (30 hours or more a week from age 3 months) and children who spent less time (fewer than 10 hours a week). Scarr and Thompson (1994) also found that placing a child in day care before the age of 1 year and for more than 20 hours per week had no significant effect on his or her later school performance.

Methodology of the studies

Many of the studies involve a **correlation**. Therefore, day care may be related to certain outcomes but may not be the *cause* of them. There may be other variables. For example, working mothers may be more stressed, on average, than those who stay home, and this causes increased aggressiveness in their children. The problem with day-care studies is that there are so many variables which may affect the outcomes that it is hard to produce a clear-cut answer.

It is also worth considering the fact that some studies involve children who were in day care more than 10 years ago. Improved conditions may mean that the conclusions from these studies are no longer relevant.

Research methods *Investigations using a correlational analysis*

A **correlation** is a relationship between two things or variables. Do two things, such as amount of time in day care and later achievement at school vary together? It could be that the *more* time spent in day care, the *better* achievement at school. Or the *less* time spent in day care, the *better* achievement at school. In both cases the factors or co-variables are changing in a consistent and related way.

We might expect less time spent in day care to be related to better achievement at school. This is called a **negative correlation**.

A correlation is not a research method. It is a technique for analysing data. Therefore we don't talk about a correlational investigation but an investigation using a correlational analysis.

	Advantages	Weaknesses
Experiments (lab and field)	Cause can be determined because we observe the effect of an IV on a DV. The procedures can be repeated again relatively easily which means that the findings can be confirmed (the same is true of studies using a correlational analysis).	May lack **ecological validity** because behaviour is reduced to a set of variables that don't represent real-life behaviour – the same may be true of a study using a correlational analysis.
Investigations using correlational analysis	Can be used when it would be unethical or impractical to manipulate variables. Useful to help decide whether a more rigorous investigation into the apparent relationship is justified. If no correlation found then a causal relationship can be ruled out.	May lack ecological validity. People often misinterpret correlations and assume that a cause and effect have been found whereas this is not possible. There may be other, unknown variables that can explain why the co-variables being studied are linked.

Research methods *Positive, negative and zero correlation*

In the study above, the co-variables are educational attainment and number of hours mother worked. Co-variables may not be linked at all. This is called **zero correlation**. If co-variables vary together this can happen in two ways. Either they may both increase together, as is the case with height and age – as children get older their height increases; this is called **positive correlation**. Alternatively, two co-variables may vary *inversely* – as one co-variable increases, the other decreases, as is the case with alcohol and reaction time. An individual who has drunk more alcohol will have a slower reaction time. This is called **negative correlation**. Note that co-variables that are negatively correlated are linked just as much as co-variables that are positively correlated.

These are called **scattergraphs** because there is a scatter of dots. Each dot represents one participant.

The first scattergraph (a) shows a **negative correlation** between hours worked by mother and average GCSE score – the more hours worked, the lower the GCSE score – the co-variables vary together but inversely. The second scattergraph (b) shows a **positive correlation** – the two variables increase together. The third scattergraph (c) illustrates a **zero correlation** – there is no consistent relationship between the co-variables.

(a)   (b)   (c)

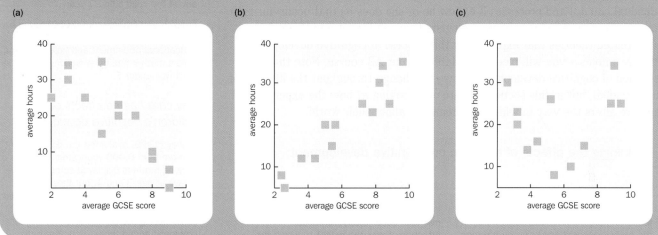

What other descriptive statistics would you use to illustrate your data?

Consider the effects of day care on children's development.

Some students think that a general question such as this is a gift because it means they have lots to write about. But the danger is that you have *too* much to say and, in an effort to cram it all in, you lose marks for lack of selectivity and insufficient detail. One of the greatest problems in an exam is reducing what you know to a compact set of statements – selecting what is important from material that is less important. This is the art of **précis**. We think it is vital to learn how to précis, and to improve this skill with regular practice.

Here is a paragraph of 150 words. Try to reduce it by 50%. It won't be easy but, in an exam, you must aim to present the bare bones, plus a few important details. At the end the key points should still be there, and it should be readable.

Day care can have good and bad effects on young children. One reason to think that it would be bad for children comes from Bowlby's maternal deprivation hypothesis. He suggested that children who are separated from their parents experience bond disruption and this causes them permanent harm, because they need emotional care for good emotional development as much as they need vitamins for good physical development. There is some evidence to support this view, such as Bowlby's study of 44 thieves, where he found that those children who experienced frequent early separations were more likely to become affectionless psychopaths than children who weren't separated from their parents. On the other hand, another study by Bowlby looked at children in a TB sanatorium and found that they didn't have problems later, despite having no substitute emotional care in hospital. It is possible that individual differences are important.

When you have done this, compare your version with our effort:

One argument against day care comes from Bowlby's maternal deprivation hypothesis. He suggested separation leads to bond disruption, and supported this with a study where he found that those children who experienced frequent early separations were more likely to become affectionless psychopaths. However, Bowlby also studied children in a TB sanatorium. These children didn't have problems later, despite having no substitute emotional care in hospital. It is possible that individual differences are important. [73 words]

You can try this exercise with any chunk of material in this book. If it makes you feel better, it is a task we have had to engage in constantly while writing this book – in order to squeeze our vast knowledge into a limited number of pages. We have lots of practice in the art of précis!

What is meant by cognitive development?

Cognitive development is one of those terms in psychology that covers a wide range of behaviours, such as the development of memory, intelligence, reasoning, problem solving and so on. It is, therefore, generally used to refer to any and all of the changes in a person's cognitive (mental) structures (i.e. how knowledge is organised), abilities (i.e. what the individual can do) and processes (i.e. how he or she does it) that occur during a person's lifespan. A number of psychologists (such as Piaget and Vygotsky) have created theories that explain how this process of cognitive development actually unfolds – you will meet these later in your A2 course. Note that the definition of cognitive development allows for change throughout the lifespan of the individual, but in this section, we are only looking at how the experience of day care alters the way in which children *think* about their world.

Explaining the effects of day care on cognitive development

Stimulation

Holding babies and interacting with them leads to more connections being made in the brain – connections between **neurons**. The more an infant is stimulated, the more neural connections are made. The nervous system relies on experience for development. Greenough *et al.* (1987) found that rats reared in an enriched environment had larger brains than those raised in an impoverished environment. The neurons in the brain had more connections, and these rats were smarter.

The question, in relation to day care, is whether day care provides more or less stimulation than a child's home environment. Or it may be equivalent, in which case cognitive development would not be harmed.

Secure base

In the Strange Situation, one of the methods used to assess secure attachment was the extent to which the infant was happy to explore freely when his or her mother was present. This willingness to explore the environment is important for cognitive development. The more you explore, the more you learn. Separation through day care may harm the continuous relationship between mother and child, and this may lead to insecure attachment. Children who are insecurely attached will be less willing to explore, and their cognitive development may suffer as a result.

KEY TERM

Cognitive development:
This refers to the changes in a person's mental structures, abilities and processes that occur over his or her lifespan.

Research on the effects of day care on children's cognitive development

Day care has negative effects on children's cognitive development

Ruhm (2000) surveyed 4,000 babies and found that 3- and 4-year-olds tend to have lower verbal ability if their mothers worked during the child's first year. Five- and 6-year-olds tend to have worse reading and maths skills if their mothers worked during any of the child's first 3 years.

Ermisch and Francesconi (2000) found a negative correlation between a child's educational attainment and how much the child's mother had been working when the child was under 5.

Day care has no effects on children's cognitive development

Harvey (1999) evaluated the development of more than 6,000 youngsters. Children of working mothers displayed some cognitive delays at age 3 and 4, but these had disappeared by the age of 12. Harvey said: 'The message should be that being at home during the early years, or being employed during those years, are both good choices. Both can result in healthy, well-developed children.'

HI DAD, WHAT A DAY I'VE HAD, SHE'S DONE NOTHING BUT CRY

ROBERT THOMPSON

Designing a day-care questionnaire

A recent study (Ermisch and Francesconi, 2000) found a negative correlation between a child's educational attainment and how much the child's mother had been working when the child was under 5. In other words, the more a mother worked, the less good the educational achievement – or, to put it a different way, a mother who didn't work at all was likely to have a child who did well at school.

Would you find the same results? To collect suitable data you need:

1 A means of **operationalising** 'educational achievement' so that you can measure it. One way to do this would be to give each participant a GCSE score (10 points for a grade A, 8 points for a grade B and so on), and then divide by the number of GCSEs taken. This gives an 'educational attainment score'.

2 A means of assessing how much time the participant's mother had worked before the age of 5. For this you need to design a **questionnaire survey**. In order to collect the data, it is best to use as few questions as possible and make the answers easy to record.

Day care has positive effects on children's cognitive development

High-quality care associated with positive outcomes

Andersson (1992) conducted a **longitudinal study** in Sweden. Over 100 children were assessed at age 8 and 13. School performance was highest in those children who entered day care before 1 year, and lowest for those who did not have any day care. The Swedish government invests in a good public day-care system which is high in quality.

Burchinal et al. (2000) studied 89 African American children from the age of 3 months to 3 years. Those placed in high-quality child care had improved cognitive development, language development, and communication skills. On the basis of this, Burchinal et al. recommended that policymakers should strive to improve the quality of child care to enhance early development of vulnerable children.

Day care may benefit low-income children

The Headstart project was begun in the US in the 1960s with the intention of enriching the cognitive and social development of disadvantaged children. This would enable such children to start school on a more equal footing. Zigler and Styfco (1993) reported that, in general, Headstart children show IQ gains of about 10 points in the first year, but this usually disappeared. However, long-term effects were observed such as participants being more likely to obtain a high school certificate.

The Abecedarian Project was another project with low-income children. It was started in 1972; 50 infants were assigned to high-quality child care, while the remaining 50 had a variety of child-care arrangements. Campbell et al. (2001) studied the children 20 years later and found that those who had received high-quality care were twice as likely to continue in school and scored significantly higher on reading and maths achievement tests. They were also more likely to have a job.

To what extent has research shown that day care has positive effects on the cognitive development of the child?

You may remember from an earlier Commentary Corner that one effective way to tackle a question such as this is to decide what your conclusion is first, then construct your arguments in such a way as to support that conclusion. Of course, there will be some fairly powerful evidence for the opposite view, so you will need ways of discounting or qualifying the conclusions that might be drawn from it. Here are the main ingredients of an argument in favour of day care's effects on cognitive development.

Research studies showing positive effects

- Andersson (1992) – school performance was higher in those children who had received high-quality day care before 1 year.
- Burchinal *et al.* (2000) – children in high-quality day care showed improved cognitive and language development.
- Zigler and Styfco (1993) – Headstart children showed significant IQ and educational gains over their non-Headstart peers.

What do these studies tell you about day care? Each of them stresses the beneficial effects of *high-quality* day care on cognitive development, particularly amongst children from low-income families where day care *enriches* their cognitive environment.

But what about research that doesn't show cognitive gains?

- Ruhm (2000) – children demonstrated worse reading and maths skills if their mother had worked during the first 3 years of their life.
- Ermisch and Francesconi (2000) – found a negative correlation between the mother's working hours in the first 3 years of a child's life and the child's educational achievement.

How can you explain these findings, which appear to contradict your previously stated research evidence? The answer may lie in the material from the previous spread (evaluating the arguments for and against day care). These arguments can be used to *qualify* the conclusions from your quoted research and to *explain* why there may be some apparent contradictions in their findings. You might consider weaving the following insights into your answer.

- Individual differences – some children cope better with (and are more likely to benefit from) day care than others. This may, in part, explain the different findings of research studies regarding the benefits of cognitive development.
- Number of hours – it is possible, as claimed by Ermisch and Francesconi (2000), that the more a mother worked, the worse the child's educational achievement, but other research (e.g. Clarke-Stewart *et al.*, 1994) does not support this conclusion.
- Methodology – all the studies quoted are correlational only, therefore tell us little about the cause of any improvement (or otherwise). Other possible variables make firm conclusions impossible.

> ❝ If God gave you the choice between putting a child in a well-functioning, well-resourced family but lots of crummy child care or into a poorly functioning, poorly resourced family and lots of good child care, there's no choice. ❞
>
> Jay Belsky, a psychologist with a special interest in the effects of day care (cited in Azar, 2000)

You might use **closed questions** such as those shown below. Using closed questions makes it easier to use the data because there are only a few possible answers. On the other hand, **open questions** allow for people to give a more exact answer to suit their circumstances. An example of an open question would be: 'If you worked when you had preschool children, how do you think that this may have affected your children?' (Open and closed questions are discussed again on page 99.)

Analysing the data

When you have collected the data you can calculate two scores for each participant: one for educational attainment and one for average number of hours mother worked. Now plot these on a scattergraph, like the ones above. Is there a negative correlation, as predicted?

How many hours a week did you work when your son/daughter was under 1 year old?

- ☐ 0 hours
- ☐ Less than 10 hours
- ☐ Between 10 and 20 hours
- ☐ Between 20 and 30 hours
- ☐ More than 30 hours

What is meant by social development?

When psychologists consider the *social* development of children, they are interested in two related aspects of the growing-up process. First is the development of **sociability** in children, i.e. the tendency to seek and enjoy the company of others and to make personal relationships with them. Sociability is thought to be an **innate** part of a child's temperament, which makes this process more or less difficult for the child. Sociability is an important characteristic because so much of our lives is helped by having good relationships with others (such as friends, colleagues and love partners). Second is the **socialisation** process, i.e. the process by which an individual acquires the knowledge, values, social skills and sensitivity to others that enables him or her to become a part of society. With both of these aspects of social development, there is an assumption that children acquire *appropriate* behaviours that are adaptive for their particular society. This is really the argument surrounding the value of day care in this respect – does it *help* or *hinder* this process?

KEY TERM

Social development: That aspect of a child's growth that is concerned with the development of sociability, where the child learns how to relate to others, and with the process of socialisation, in which the child acquires the knowledge and skills appropriate to that society.

Explaining the effects of day care on social development

Attachment theory

Bowlby's theory suggested that continuous emotional care with a primary caregiver was the basis of later relationships. He proposed that one special relationship acts as a template (**internal working model**) for later relationships. Separation as a result of day-care arrangements may disrupt the bond between mother and child, and this would harm development. However, appropriate substitute emotional care may prevent this.

Interactions with other people

Day care has the potential for providing children with plenty of opportunity to interact with other children and adults. This may enable them to learn interpersonal negotiation skills that will be helpful when starting school. There is less opportunity for such experiences at home, especially for only children.

Research methods *Operationalise*

The idea of **operationalisation** is that a concept such as 'educational attainment' or 'social development' needs to be specified more clearly if it is going to be investigated. In other words, it means recording component parts – the operations. So, for example, you used GCSE scores as a way of operationalising 'educational attainment'. For social development you can list various behaviours that can be measured: the tendency to seek the company of others, to show enjoyment when with others, to have a number of friends, to display social skills such as negotiating with friends, and so on. These are the 'operations' that equal social development.

> While they are babies or young toddlers, even the very best daycare seldom gives them anything they positively need, and being there all day and every day, often deprives them of what they need from mothers. The vital continuous one-to-one attention can rarely be achieved in group care, however excellent the facility may be.
>
> Penelope Leach, 1994, p. 70

Kristin Droege, a research associate at Milken Family Foundation, argues that children in high-quality child-care arrangements tend to be less timid and fearful than children who spend much of their time at home. Her conclusion: quality day care breeds well-adjusted children who tend to be more outgoing and cooperative with unfamiliar peers.

Research on the effects of day care on children's social development

Day care has negative effects on children's social development

Belsky and Rovine (1988) assessed attachment (using the Strange Situation) in infants who had been receiving 20 hours or more of day care per week before they were 1 year old. These children were found to be more likely to be insecurely attached compared with children at home.

Violata and Russell (1994) did a meta-analysis of the findings from 88 studies, concluding that regular day care for more than 20 hours per week had an unmistakably negative effect on socio-emotional development, behaviour and attachment of young children.

DiLalla (1998) found that children who experienced little or no day care were more likely to behave prosocially, suggesting that day care may inhibit socialisation.

A recent NICHD report (2001) concluded that children who are separated from their mothers for more than 10 hours a week early in life are more aggressive once they reach kindergarten, as rated by their mothers and by their teachers.

Day care has no effects on children's social development

Clarke-Stewart et al. (1994) found no difference in attachment security when comparing children spending a lot of time in day care (30 hours or more a week from age 3 months) with children who spent less time (fewer than 10 hours a week). This might lead us to expect no differences in social development.

Day care has positive effects on children's social development

Vandell et al. (1988) reported that children in better-quality care have more friendly and fewer unfriendly interactions than those in lower-quality care.

Day-care programs for disadvantaged children have shown positive effects on social as well as cognitive development. Schweinhart et al. (1993) did follow-up studies of 66 children involved in the High/Scope Perry Preschool Project. They found decreased rates of self-reported delinquency at age 14, decreased official chronic delinquency at age 19, and, in the most recent follow-up at age 27, lower adult criminality.

Clarke-Stewart et al. (1994) found that those children who attended day care could cope better in social situations and negotiate better with peers.

Creps and Vernon-Feagans (1999) found that infants who started day care before the age of 6 months were more sociable later than those who started later. This suggests that early day care may be better for social development.

Using your knowledge of psychological research, what are the implications for improving day care?

Psychologists are committed to understanding what makes for high-quality day care, and what, on the other hand, makes for low-quality day care. Armed with this information, child-care professionals can begin to provide the right kind of day care to maximise the positive consequences for the child, whilst minimising the negative consequences. The following are some insights from the psychological research used in this section and their possible applications for improving day-care provision.

In most technological societies, maternal employment is no longer exceptional – it is the norm. The burning issue is not whether children should or should not be in day care, but rather how we can make sure their day-care experience is as rewarding as possible. Schaffer (1998) suggests that, provided certain safeguards are met, care outside the home may be positively beneficial as a supplement to home experiences – especially for some children. But what are these safeguards? Schaffer lists the two main ones as consistency and quality.

Consistency of care

- This issue was highlighted in Fox's study (Fox, 1977) of *metapelet* on kibbutzim (see page 53). Fox suggested that the reason why the children may have been less securely attached to the *metapelet* was because of the high turnover, thus not giving children the opportunity to attach to any one individual. Of course, this is part of a two-way process, because the same lack of consistency affects the feelings of the caregiver for the child. If a relationship is only likely to last for a brief time, the caregiver makes less of a commitment – perhaps even because of his or her own fear of being hurt when the child goes away. On the other hand, if the caregiver knows that he or she is to have a continuing and lasting relationship with the child (as in a parent–child relationship), the investment in that child is much greater, leading to a more secure attachment.

- The NICHD study (1999 – see page 71) supported this conclusion, with the finding that low child-to-staff ratios were related to more sensitive and positive interactions between caregiver and child. The authors of this study reported that even a child-to-caregiver ratio as low as 3:1 was sometimes overwhelming to the caregiver, therefore resulting in him or her being unable to offer consistency of care to any one child.

- The implications of these findings for the improvement of day-care arrangements are clear, according to Schaffer. Day nurseries and other day-care centres need to find a way of ensuring minimal turnover of staff, thus increasing *consistency* of care for the child. They should also arrange that each child is assigned to one specific substitute caregiver who is more or less constantly available and feels responsible for that child.

Quality of care

Most of the research studies that report *positive* effects for day-care experiences have one important thing in common – they provide *high-quality* substitute care. When children are placed in high-quality care, there are rarely negative effects, and there can be significant positive effects. But what constitutes high-quality care? Schaffer suggests a number of factors that might be consistent with this aim:

- The amount of verbal interaction between caregiver and child is related to how cognitively enriching the day-care experience is. Tizard (1979) discovered that the conversations between nursery teacher and child were far less complex than those between mother and child, *regardless* of class. Nursery teachers had fewer verbal exchanges with their charges, and in turn elicited less from the children themselves.

- Having sufficient stimulation, such as suitable toys, books and other playthings. This is particularly important where the day-care provision is part of an 'enrichment' programme such as Headstart, which aimed to give disadvantaged children a better start at school through enriched learning experiences in nursery schools.

- Caregivers should offer sensitive emotional care. The NICHD study found that about 23% of infant-care providers give 'highly' sensitive infant care, 50% of them provide only 'moderately' sensitive care, and 20% are 'emotionally detached' from the infants under their care.

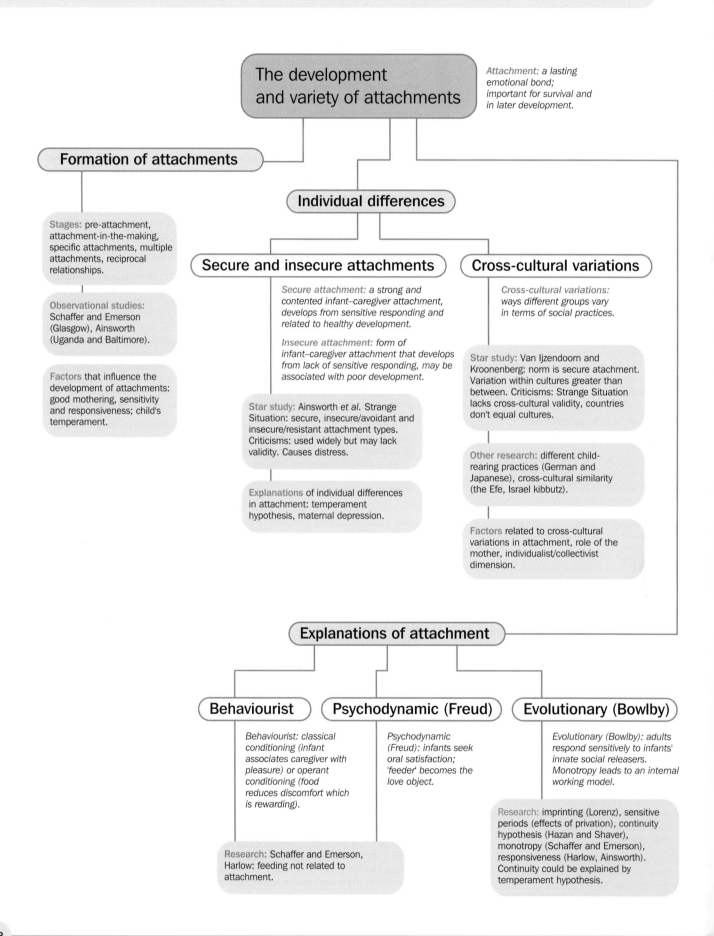

The development and variety of attachments

Attachment: a lasting emotional bond; important for survival and in later development.

Formation of attachments

Stages: pre-attachment, attachment-in-the-making, specific attachments, multiple attachments, reciprocal relationships.

Observational studies: Schaffer and Emerson (Glasgow), Ainsworth (Uganda and Baltimore).

Factors that influence the development of attachments: good mothering, sensitivity and responsiveness; child's temperament.

Individual differences

Secure and insecure attachments

Secure attachment: a strong and contented infant–caregiver attachment, develops from sensitive responding and related to healthy development.

Insecure attachment: form of infant–caregiver attachment that develops from lack of sensitive responding, may be associated with poor development.

Star study: Ainsworth *et al.* Strange Situation: secure, insecure/avoidant and insecure/resistant attachment types. Criticisms: used widely but may lack validity. Causes distress.

Explanations of individual differences in attachment: temperament hypothesis, maternal depression.

Cross-cultural variations

Cross-cultural variations: ways different groups vary in terms of social practices.

Star study: Van Ijzendoorn and Kroonenberg: norm is secure atachment. Variation within cultures greater than between. Criticisms: Strange Situation lacks cross-cultural validity, countries don't equal cultures.

Other research: different child-rearing practices (German and Japanese), cross-cultural similarity (the Efe, Israel kibbutz).

Factors related to cross-cultural variations in attachment, role of the mother, individualist/collectivist dimension.

Explanations of attachment

Behaviourist

Behaviourist: classical conditioning (infant associates caregiver with pleasure) or operant conditioning (food reduces discomfort which is rewarding).

Research: Schaffer and Emerson, Harlow: feeding not related to attachment.

Psychodynamic (Freud)

Psychodynamic (Freud): infants seek oral satisfaction; 'feeder' becomes the love object.

Evolutionary (Bowlby)

Evolutionary (Bowlby): adults respond sensitively to infants' innate social releasers. Monotropy leads to an internal working model.

Research: imprinting (Lorenz), sensitive periods (effects of privation), continuity hypothesis (Hazan and Shaver), monotropy (Schaffer and Emerson), responsiveness (Harlow, Ainsworth). Continuity could be explained by temperament hypothesis.

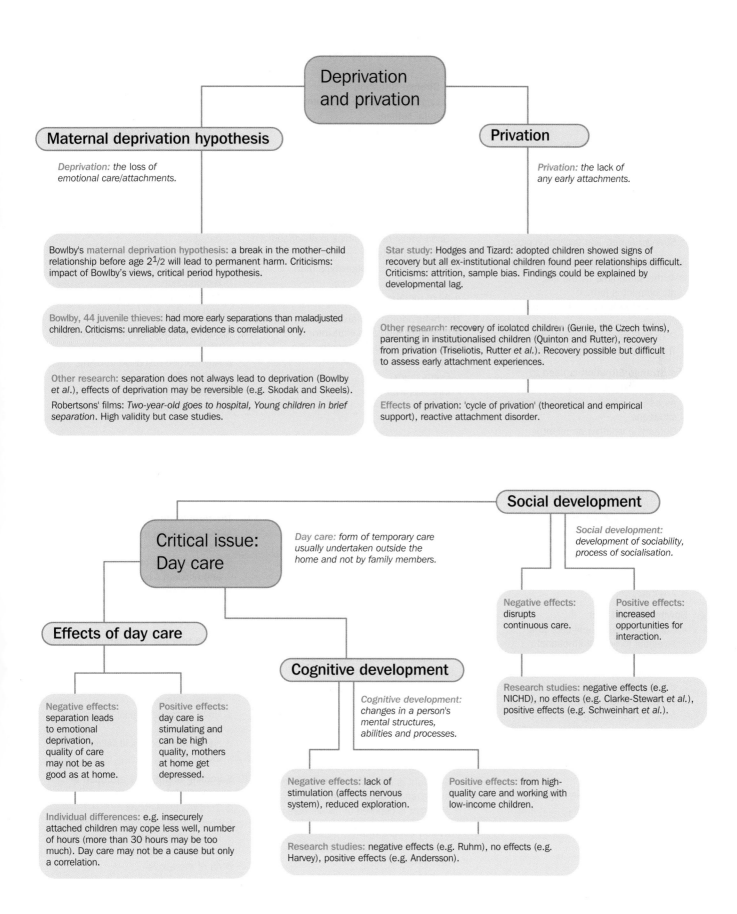

Deprivation and privation

Maternal deprivation hypothesis

Deprivation: the loss of emotional care/attachments.

Bowlby's maternal deprivation hypothesis: a break in the mother–child relationship before age $2^1/2$ will lead to permanent harm. Criticisms: impact of Bowlby's views, critical period hypothesis.

Bowlby, 44 juvenile thieves: had more early separations than maladjusted children. Criticisms: unreliable data, evidence is correlational only.

Other research: separation does not always lead to deprivation (Bowlby *et al.*), effects of deprivation may be reversible (e.g. Skodak and Skeels).
Robertsons' films: *Two-year-old goes to hospital, Young children in brief separation*. High validity but case studies.

Privation

Privation: the lack of any early attachments.

Star study: Hodges and Tizard: adopted children showed signs of recovery but all ex-institutional children found peer relationships difficult. Criticisms: attrition, sample bias. Findings could be explained by developmental lag.

Other research: recovery of isolated children (Genie, the Czech twins), parenting in institutionalised children (Quinton and Rutter), recovery from privation (Triseliotis, Rutter *et al.*). Recovery possible but difficult to assess early attachment experiences.

Effects of privation: 'cycle of privation' (theoretical and empirical support), reactive attachment disorder.

Critical issue: Day care

Day care: form of temporary care usually undertaken outside the home and not by family members.

Social development

Social development: development of sociability, process of socialisation.

Negative effects: disrupts continuous care.

Positive effects: increased opportunities for interaction.

Research studies: negative effects (e.g. NICHD), no effects (e.g. Clarke-Stewart *et al.*), positive effects (e.g. Schweinhart *et al.*).

Effects of day care

Negative effects: separation leads to emotional deprivation, quality of care may not be as good as at home.

Positive effects: day care is stimulating and can be high quality, mothers at home get depressed.

Individual differences: e.g. insecurely attached children may cope less well, number of hours (more than 30 hours may be too much). Day care may not be a cause but only a correlation.

Cognitive development

Cognitive development: changes in a person's mental structures, abilities and processes.

Negative effects: lack of stimulation (affects nervous system), reduced exploration.

Positive effects: from high-quality care and working with low-income children.

Research studies: negative effects (e.g. Ruhm), no effects (e.g. Harvey), positive effects (e.g. Andersson).

MULTIPLE-CHOICE QUESTIONS

Section 1 The development and variety of attachments

1 **In the pre-attachment phase of development, the infant**
   a Smiles more at familiar people
   b Smiles at anyone
   c Is uninterested in people
   d Is afraid of strangers

2 **Attachment-proper is indicated by**
   a No stranger anxiety
   b Stranger anxiety
   c Separation protest
   d Stranger anxiety and separation protest

3 **Infants develop multiple attachments**
   a At the same time as the first attachment is formed
   b Shortly after the first attachment is formed
   c Prior to forming one strong attachment
   d They never develop multiple attachments

4 **The Strange Situation is used to**
   a Assess stranger anxiety
   b Assess an infant's response to novel situations
   c Determine whether an infant is securely or insecurely attached
   d All of the above

5 **The Strange Situation**
   a Is appropriate to use in different cultural settings
   b Is not appropriate to use in different cultural settings
   c Has found there are large variations in different cultural settings
   d Has been altered for use in different cultural settings

6 **Secure attachment leads to**
   a Good social relationships in childhood
   b Higher self-esteem
   c Adult romantic relationships that are trusting
   d All of the above

7 **The behaviourist explanation of attachment suggests that infants become attached to a person who**
   a Spends time with them
   b Feeds them
   c Interacts with them
   d Loves them

8 **In the behaviourist explanation of attachment, food is**
   a A primary reinforcer
   b A secondary reinforcer
   c Both of the above
   d Neither of the above

9 **Bowlby's theory is an example of the evolutionary approach because he claimed that**
   a All infants become attached to a caregiver
   b Attachment is genetic
   c Attachment promotes survival and reproduction
   d Attachment leads to good social and emotional relationships

10 **An example of a social releaser is**
   a When a baby follows a caregiver
   b Any learned response to being looked after
   c Hugs and kisses
   d When a baby cries or smiles

Section 2 Deprivation and privation

1 **In Bowlby's maternal deprivation hypothesis, 'maternal' refers to**
   a An infant's biological mother only
   b Any woman who provides mothering
   c Any individual who provides mothering
   d Any caregiver

2 **Bowlby claimed that**
   a Continuous emotional care was essential to normal emotional development
   b Vitamins were important in development
   c Children without mothers would become emotionally maladjusted
   d Children needed mothers

3 **Affectionless psychopaths are individuals who**
   a Have no parents
   b Have experienced early separations
   c Lack a social conscience and empathy for the feelings of others
   d All of the above

4 **A 'critical period' is when**
   a An infant becomes aware of his/her surroundings
   b An important characteristic develops
   c A behaviour must develop or it will never be acquired
   d Infants are sensitive to certain stimuli

5 **Separation**
   a Always leads to deprivation
   b Sometimes leads to deprivation
   c Never leads to deprivation
   d Is the same as deprivation

6 **Bond disruption refers to situations where**
   a An infant has formed no bonds
   b An infant is separated from a caregiver and given substitute emotional care
   c An infant is separated from a caregiver and given no substitute emotional care
   d An infant is deprived of his/her caregiver

7 **Privation occurs when**
   a A child experiences the loss of attachments
   b A child has never experienced any attachments
   c A child has poor attachments
   d No attachments form before the age of 2½ years

8 **The term 'institutional care' refers to**
   a The care given in any kind of institution
   b Care for young children in hospitals and children's homes
   c Care involving fixed routines and a lack of individual attention
   d Care outside a child's home

9 **Studies that use correlational analysis**
   a Do not demonstrate cause-and-effect relationships
   b Can demonstrate cause-and-effect relationships
   c Have better ecological validity than experiments
   d Have lower ecological validity than experiments

10 **Sampling techniques are used in observational studies to**
   a Control observations
   b Ensure that observer bias is reduced
   c Reduce the number of observations that have to be made
   d All of the above

Section 3 Critical issue: Day care

1 The term day care refers to
- a Any care outside the home by non-relatives
- b Care during the day only
- c Care in day nurseries
- d State-funded care provision

2 Bowlby's view of the effects of maternal deprivation suggests that
- a Day care inevitably leads to deprivation
- b Poor-quality day care will lead to deprivation
- c Day care will harm emotional development
- d Mothers shouldn't work

3 Day care may have negative effects because
- a The quality of some day-care provision is poor
- b Separation may lead to disruption of emotional bonds
- c Children spend too long away from their mothers
- d All of the above

4 Day care may have a negative effect on cognitive development because
- a Children in nursery get less holding and stimulation
- b Day-care providers are less intelligent
- c Mothers provide better care than people working in day care
- d All of the above

5 Day care may have a positive effect on cognitive development because
- a Mothers may be bored at home and provide little stimulation for their children
- b Mothers may be depressed at home
- c Day-care centres can provide lots of stimulation
- d All of the above

6 Day care may have a negative effect on social development because
- a Day care provides no substitute emotional care
- b Children have to struggle with more boisterous peers
- c Day care disrupts the continuous relationship with the primary caregiver
- d All of the above

7 Day care may have a positive effect on social development because
- a Children have to learn to negotiate with other children
- b Children learn to fight with other children
- c Children get extra emotional care
- d All of the above

8 The day-care experience may affect children differently because
- a Some children are shyer than others
- b Some children are insecurely attached
- c Some children come from single-parent families
- d Both (a) and (b)

9 Longitudinal studies are used in order
- a To compare the same person at a different point in time
- b To compare different people at the same point in time
- c To conduct studies on long-term effects
- d Both (a) and (c)

10 One methodological problem with studies of day care is
- a There are no control groups
- b The samples are often quite small
- c Many of them were conducted in the US
- d The data are often correlational and therefore we can't say that day care was the cause

Section 3 answers
1a 2b 3d 4a 5d
6d 7a 8c 9d 10d

Section 2 answers
1c 2a 3c 4c 5b
6c 7b 8c 9a 10d

Section 1 answers
1a 2d 3b 4d 5b
6d 7b 8a 9c 10c

RESEARCH METHODS
terms covered

- Closed questions
- Controlled observation
- Correlation
- Co-variables
- Cross-cultural studies
- Cross-sectional design
- Ecological validity
- Ethical issues
- Event sampling
- External validity
- Generalisability
- Informed consent
- Longitudinal design
- Naturalistic observation
- Negative correlation
- Observation checklist
- Observer bias
- Observer reliability
- Open questions
- Operationalisation
- Participant variables
- Positive correlation
- Questionnaire survey design
- Replication
- Representative sample
- Sampling technique
- Scattergraph
- Social desirability bias
- Target population
- Time sampling
- Zero correlation

END OF MODULE REVIEW

Revision list

Key terms

You may be asked 'explain what is meant by ...' any of the following. Each explanation may be for 2 or 3 marks (and very rarely 6 marks). Make sure that what you write is related to the number of marks. Use examples to amplify your explanations where appropriate.

✓

☐	Attachment	p. 46
☐	Cognitive development	p. 74
☐	Cross-cultural variations	p. 52
☐	Day care	p. 70
☐	Deprivation	p. 60
☐	Insecure attachment	p. 48
☐	Privation	p. 64
☐	Secure attachment	p. 48
☐	Social development	p. 76

Factors that influence

You should be able to write about at least two factors of the following:

✓

☐ The formation of attachments	p. 47
☐ Cross-cultural variations in attachment	p. 52

Theories/explanations

You may be asked to describe or outline a theory/explanation for six marks. You are also likely to be asked an AO2 question about theories/explanations and discuss their strengths and limitations. When discussing a theory it is useful to refer to other research (theories and/or studies) as a means of evaluation.

✓

☐ The stages in the formation of attachments	p. 46
☐ Ways to explain individual differences in attachment	p. 51
☐ Learning theory explanation of attachment	p. 54
☐ Freud's explanation of attachment	p. 55
☐ Bowlby's theory of attachment	p. 55
☐ Maternal deprivation hypothesis	p. 60
☐ The reversibility of deprivation	p. 62

Star studies

This is the 'apfcc question'. You need three-minutes worth of writing on aims, procedures, findings and conclusions for each of these. You may also be asked for one or two criticisms of these studies. Criticisims can be positive or negative.

✓

☐	Individual differences in attachment (Ainsworth *et al.*, 1978)	pp. 48–9
☐	Cross-cultural variations (Van IJzendoorn and Kroonenberg, 1988)	pp. 52–3
☐	Effects of privation (Hodges and Tizard, 1989)	pp. 64–5

Research

You need to be able to outline the findings and conclusions of research (theories and/or studies). Such material is sometimes presented in a feature called 'Research on ...' but studies are also described in other places.

✓

☐	The formation of attachments	p. 47
☐	Cross-cultural variations	p. 53
☐	Related to Bowlby's attachment theory	pp. 56–7
☐	Evidence related to the maternal deprivation hypothesis	pp. 62–3
☐	Effects of privation	pp. 64–7
☐	Effects of day care on children's cognitive development	pp. 74–5
☐	Effects of day care on children's social development	pp. 76–7

Effects

You should be able to write about several effects of the following:

✓

☐	Secure/insecure attachment	p. 50
☐	Cross-cultural variations	p. 53
☐	Privation	p. 67
☐	Day care	p. 71
☐	Day care on children's cognitive development	p. 74
☐	Day care on children's social development	p. 77

Sample attachment question with students' answers and examiner's comments

1 (a) Explain what is meant by the terms secure and insecure attachment.

(3 marks + 3 marks)

Alison's answer: A child is said to be 'securely' attached if they are able to cope well with separation from the mother (e.g. in the Strange Situation test). This is because they know they will be reunited with the mother after separation.

A child is said to be insecurely attached if they show an adverse reaction to separation from the mother. Ainsworth found two types of insecure attachment in her Strange Situation test.

Nigel's answer: A child is said to be securely attached if they have formed a strong attachment with a caregiver. They are able to function independently of the caregiver because they have a strong emotional base from which to explore the world. In Ainsworth's Strange Situation test, the securely attached infant shows distress at separation from the caregiver, but greets them positively when reunited.

A child is said to be insecurely attached if they have formed a bond with the caregiver that is not optimally suited for future healthy development. Insecure attachment may be associated with poor cognitive and emotional development later on. In Ainsworth's Strange Situation test, the insecurely attached infant either avoided the caregiver on reunion (avoidant type) or was not easily soothed by them (resistant type).

Examiner's comments: The first of Alison's explanations is reasonably accurate and does contain a brief reference to why a securely attached child is better able to cope with separation. The answer needs development for the full 3 marks. The same is true of her second explanation – generally accurate with some slight elaboration, but lacking appropriate detail for full marks. What, for example, are these types of insecure attachment? This answer would get **2 + 2 marks**. Both terms have been accurately explained in Nigel's answer, and he has integrated the insights from Ainsworth's Strange Situation test effectively into the answer. This would be worth **3 + 3 marks**.

1 (b) Describe the procedures and findings of **one** study that has investigated cross-cultural variations in attachment.

(6 marks)

Alison's answer: Ainsworth studied mothers and children in Africa to see if they went through the same sort of attachment as in the US. She found that they did show more or less the same patterns of development of their attachments, and at about the same time as in US children (about 6 months). She concluded that there was little difference between the development of attachments in different parts of the world, and that all children appeared to go through the same stages of development in the same order at the same time. The conclusion that she reached is therefore that there is little or no difference between different cultures.

Nigel's answer: Van IJzendoorn and Kroonenberg analysed the findings of over 30 studies of attachment in many different cultures. The method they used is called a meta-analysis, where you look at the findings from a number of different studies to reach a general conclusion. They selected studies conducted in many different countries, which means that findings from a variety of different studies are looked at with a view to drawing some general conclusions. Each of the studies they looked at had used the Strange Situation to measure attachment style. This involves a number of episodes where the caregiver (usually the mother) leaves their infant alone or with a stranger.

Van IJzendoorn and Kroonenberg found that there were many similarities in attachment styles in the different cultures studied. They found that secure attachment was the attachment style most common across different cultures (at a rate of about 65%), and insecure (resistant) attachment was the least common (except in Israel and Japan, where avoidant attachment was least common). They also found that there were greater differences within cultures than between cultures.

Examiner's comments: We have to sift through Alison's answer looking for material relevant to *procedures* and *findings*. She does say that 'Ainsworth studied mothers and children in Africa', which is true, so counts as a *procedure*, although the rest of that sentence is an aim, so does not count. There is a brief statement of Ainsworth's *findings* in the middle of the answer, and then a (repetitious) statement of her *conclusions*, which likewise do not count here. This answer would be worth **2 marks**. Despite the fact that the study Nigel has chosen is a meta-analysis rather than a single study, it is perfectly appropriate as a response to this question. An accurate and detailed description has been provided, though, strictly speaking, the description of the Strange Situation is not creditworthy here. The procedures of this study relate to the meta-analysis, whereas the procedures of the Strange Situation would be relevant when describing one of the individual studies. Nevertheless, there is sufficient information on meta-analysis and on the findings to give the maximum **6 marks**. The findings are more detailed than the relevant procedures, but you are not required to present both elements in the same detail.

1 (c) Consider the claim that day care has positive effects on social development. (18 marks)

Alison's answer: Research into the effects of day care supports the claim that it has positive effects on social development. The most famous study in this area was Operation Headstart, which began in the USA in 1965. This took disadvantaged children and gave them a 'head start' by exposing them to preschool education. The children who went through the Headstart programme showed IQ gains over the children who did not, but this advantage soon disappeared. In a follow-up study however, the Headstart children did show a number of advantages, including less likelihood of them becoming delinquent in adulthood.

A study by Andersson (1992) of children in Sweden found that if children started day care before the age of 1, they would subsequently perform much better at school. However, a criticism of this study is that the children may have come from better-off families who could afford the day care, and so this might have affected the findings and therefore explain why these children did so well at school.

Another study by Alison Clarke-Stewart (1994) found that of those children who had just started school, those who had previous experience of day care were able to cope much better with social situations and get on better with their peers than those who had no experience of day care. Although there are other studies that suggest that day care may have a harmful effect on social development, the studies discussed above lend support to the claim that day care has mainly positive effects on both cognitive and social development.

Nigel's answer: Belsky (1986) claimed that children who experience more than 20 hours per week of day care are at increased risk of becoming aggressive and socially withdrawn in their early school years. In particular, Belsky claimed that full-time day care in the first year of life puts children at particular risk, and he suggested that the primary caretaking during this period should be done by a parent. Claims such as this are often based on research studies using the Strange Situation (e.g. Clarke-Stewart, 1988). These studies have shown that infants of full-time employed mothers are more likely to show insecure attachment relationships than infants of part-time or non-employed mothers.

One problem with research that links maternal attachment and maternal employment is that it tells us nothing about the kind of alternative care experienced by the infant. Howes *et al.* (1998) point out that the quality of the child's attachment to the mother does not necessarily predict the quality of the child's attachment to the alternative caregiver. A child with an insecure maternal attachment may have a secure attachment relationship with their alternative caregiver. This suggests that positive relationships with infant day-care caregivers may compensate for insecure maternal attachments.

Clarke-Stewart (1988) points to the fact that balancing a job and a family can create stressful circumstances. These stresses may make employed parents less available and less sensitive to their infants and this, in turn, may contribute to the problems that some may attribute to the day-care situation. Research that has attempted to compare the relative influences of family and day care on the social-emotional development of infants suggests that the combination of day care and family influences is the best predictor of the social development of the infant (Howes, 1998). Infants in high-quality care and cared for by families low in stress and high in social support tend to be more socially competent. Children with a history of high-quality care inside and outside the family show better adjustment to school than less fortunate children (Howes, 1998).

In conclusion, research evidence does not suggest that infant day care as such is detrimental to the child's future social and emotional development. It does, however, raise concerns for the child who experiences insensitive care both at home and in day care.

Examiner's comments: Although the Headstart programme is generally considered to be a study of *cognitive* gains in children, it also made a contribution to the debate on later *social* development. This is clearly in evidence in follow-up studies that demonstrated the decreased likelihood of adult delinquency among the day-care children. Alison seems to have a bit of a cavalier attitude to the exact requirements of this question, and has not really stressed the implications for *social* development as much as she might have done. The Andersson study makes a useful contribution to the discussion, and it is good that Alison shows an awareness of reading too much into its findings. The Clarke-Stewart study is described accurately, but not really used effectively as part of the developing argument. Overall, this is a 'reasonable' commentary on the topic, yet the analysis of material is limited and the material is used in only a 'reasonably effective' manner. This would receive **4 marks** for the AO1 content, and **5 marks** for the AO2 content, giving a total of **9 marks**.

Nigel's answer is a clearly written and thoughtful response to the question. He has started with Jay Belsky's claim for the detrimental effects of early day care, but has also supported this claim with appropriate research evidence *and* argument. He then moves on to consider the inherent problems of disentangling the influences of both home and day care and comes to a suitable conclusion. This is an excellent response because it makes the most of the material being used. All the material here is subjected to critical scrutiny so is used effectively. This would receive **6 marks** for the AO1 content, and **10 marks** for the AO2 content, giving a total of 16 marks. The choice of 10 rather than **12 marks** for AO2 is because the answer has a greater emphasis on description – it fails to use the material in a *highly* effective manner and does not provide a *thorough* analysis, both of which are criteria for the top marks (see mark schemes on page 216).

> **Total marks: Alison 15/30 (probably a Grade B) and Nigel 28/30 (clearly a Grade A).**

Developmental psychology question to try

2 (a) Outline **one** explanation of attachment. (6 marks)

(b) Outline findings of research into the effects of day care on children's cognitive development. (6 marks)

(c) To what extent does psychological research support the view that deprivation has irreversible effects? (18 marks)

Physiological psychology seeks to explain behaviour in terms of the systems that operate in our bodies – such as the action of blood, hormones, nerves and the brain. The way we think and feel has important influences on these physiological systems, as is illustrated by the study of stress.

Physiological psychology
Stress

Stress as a bodily response

Surveys and research reports over the past two decades have revealed that:

Recent research has increasingly confirmed the important role of stress in cardiovascular disease, cancer, gastrointestinal, skin and emotional disorders, and a host of disorders linked to immune system disturbances, ranging from the common cold and herpes to arthritis, cancer and AIDS.

Nearly half of all American workers suffer from symptoms of burnout, a disabling reaction to stress on the job.

43% of all adults suffer adverse health effects due to stress.

An estimated 1 million workers in the US are absent on an average workday because of stress-related complaints. Stress is said to be responsible for more than half of the 550,000,000 workdays lost annually because of absenteeism.

The market for stress management programs, products and services was $9.4 billion in 1995 in the US, and $11.31 billion in 1999.

A 3-year study conducted by a large corporation showed that 60% of employee absences were due to psychological problems such as stress.

Source: American Institute of Stress, www.stress.org

specification breakdown

Specification content	Comment
The body's response to stressors (e.g. pituitary – adrenal system); the General Adaptation Syndrome (Selye).	Here you are expected to know how the body responds to stressors, for example the role of the **autonomic system** and the **pituitary gland**. You are specifically required to know about Selye's **General Adaptation Syndrome** and should be able to summarise its three stages of stress response.
Research into the relationship between stress and cardiovascular disorders and the effects of stress on the immune system.	The use of the term 'research' should alert you to the possibility of questions relating to research studies that have explored the relationship between stress and **cardiovascular disorders** and the effects of stress on the **immune system**.

Stress, you might imagine, is a characteristic of modern living. We all experience stress in one form or another – in our personal relations, at school, in our job, or in just trying to make ends meet. In fact, it's hard to go through a day without hearing or reading something about stress and its destructive impact on people. Back in 1983, *Time* magazine referred to stress as 'The Epidemic of the 80s', as if it were some new kind of plague. Yet for our ancestors, what we call 'stress' enabled them to respond effectively to the everyday threats that they encountered in their world. Nowadays, however, the threat from sabre-toothed tigers and other ancestral inconveniences has all but vanished, and yet we are still left with the legacy of the stress response. So, although the *nature* of the situation causing us stress has changed, the response stays the same. To the motorist stuck in a traffic jam it can be the hassles of heavy traffic and an overheating car, whilst to the student it can be the pressure of an impending examination. To the textbook writer it can be the threat of deadlines and malfunctioning computers.

Most people see stress as a destructive, disabling force, but not all stress is negative. The word *eustress* has been coined to describe the kind of positive stress you might experience as a result of an exhilarating event. It is the type of stress you are likely to experience if you pass a driving test, complete your first parachute jump or win a fortune on the National Lottery. Negative stress, on the other hand,

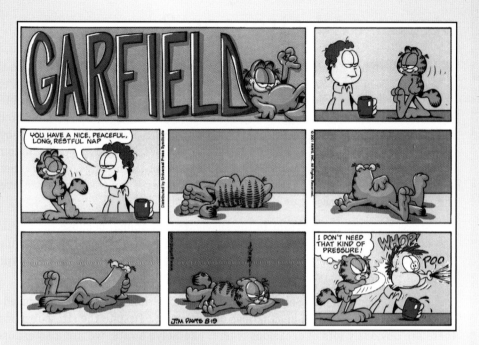

is *distress*. It is the stress of losing, failing, or simply not coping. We all experience distress from time to time. In fact, stress is an unavoidable consequence of life. Without stress, there would be no life. Just as distress can disable us, good stresses can offset this and promote well-being.

Speculations about the link between stress caused by psychosocial factors and illness are almost as old as medicine itself. In 1897, William Osler – often called the father of internal medicine – described the typical heart disease patient as 'a keen and ambitious man, the indicator of whose engine is always at "full speed ahead"'. Ongoing stress tends to lead to a range of physical or psychological illnesses. The major problem with long-term stress tends to be cardiovascular disease (such as raised blood pressure or heart disease).

Psychological disorders such as clinical depression and anxiety can occur too. With very severe stress, even death may occur. For example, during earthquakes, more people than usual die from heart attacks.

But how do we manage stress? For many, the key stress management strategy is simply to distract themselves by watching more television. In fact, watching television has been shown to be a good stress buster (Palmer and Strickland, 1995). Other often-used techniques include excessive drinking or even just having a bath. However, none of these techniques actually helps to deal with the stressful situation itself, only its symptoms. These types of stress management may not be that helpful in long-term management of stress, and because of the worrying statistics about stress and illness, professional stress management has become big business.

What is meant by stress and stressors?

Much of our understanding of the nature of stress can be traced back to the pioneering work of Hans Selye in the 1930s. Selye reported that the rats he was experimenting on showed distinctive physiological changes that were directly attributable to the daily injections they received during his experiments. What was injected appeared to be less important than the fact they were being injected (obviously an unpleasant event). After several months of these daily injections, the rats began to show a number of physiological symptoms, including the development of stomach ulcers. This led Selye to describe the physiological reaction whenever an organism is exposed to an unpleasant stimulus as **stress**, and the unpleasant event that led to this response as a **stressor**.

> Remember that 'physiological' means 'of the body'. Whenever you see the word 'physiology', just say 'of the body' quietly to yourself.

The stress response is important to the survival of an animal because the physiological changes associated with stress are essential in conditions of fight or flight (i.e. attacking or running away). It is somewhat surprising, then, to find that the stress response is **adaptive**, and an essential part of our survival.

The physiological changes Selye observed in his experimental rats were caused by *prolonged* exposure to a stressor, often in situations of low control. Despite the stress response being adaptive, there are obviously lots of occasions where, like Selye's rats, we are also exposed to prolonged stressful situations and feel powerless to escape. It is in these conditions that stress becomes more problematic, and may lead to similar physiological changes to those experienced by the rats.

The body's response to stressors

What's the difference between stress and a stressor?

When the terms 'stress' and 'stressor' are used together, the former term (stress) might be used to refer to the way the body reacts to a stressful situation (e.g. 'I feel really stressed' is a little like saying 'I feel really ill'). The latter term (stressor) would then be used to refer to whatever event led to this physiological reaction (e.g. a stressful job).

When someone says 'I feel stressed', we assume that it is a bad thing. However, we have already pointed out that stress is an *adaptive* response, or it least it sometimes is. Back in the **EEA** (environment of evolutionary adaptiveness), quick responses would have been a matter of life or death. Stress responses have evolved to provide animals with this ready responsiveness in times of danger, called 'fight or flight'. An animal that does not respond in this way is less likely to survive and reproduce.

What does this stress response feel like? Imagine you are sitting in a car about to take your driving test – you see the examiner walking towards you. Your hands feel clammy, your heart is racing, your rate of breathing speeds up, you feel slightly flushed. These are all signs of the stress response. They occur due to activity in the **autonomic nervous system** (ANS).

Some stress experiences are flash in the pan – a stressor appears and the body responds. This is an *acute* stress response. Other stressful experiences last for a long time, such as worrying about your AS level exams for months beforehand! These are *chronic* stressors. The body responds differently to these two types of stressor.

Stress response 1: Acute stress and the SAM system

Immediate (acute) stressors arouse the autonomic nervous system. It is called 'autonomic' because it governs itself (automatic). This system is necessary because some bodily functions, such as your heart beat, might not work very reliably if you had to think about them.

The ANS governs the release of **hormones**. These are chemical substances that circulate in your blood. One of these is called **adrenaline** (the Americans call it epinephrine). You may have heard the phrase 'adrenaline rush', meaning the physiological sensation that accompanies being scared or thrilled, i.e. being 'aroused' (in a physiological sense). At such times of **arousal** the **sympathetic branch** of the ANS is activated, and causes the hormone adrenaline to be released by the adrenal medulla in the adrenal glands (lying above the kidneys). Adrenaline creates all those sensations we described above, such as sweatiness and increased heart and breathing rate. It also stops you wanting to go to the lavatory and slows down digestion (to conserve resources for fight or flight).

> The word 'chronic' may suggest to you that it is 'bad' (e.g. 'That was a chronic film'), but here it means 'persisting for a long time'.

Stress response 1: SAM system (acute stress)
Involves the adrenal medulla

ANS (sympathetic branch) ▶ adrenal medulla ▶ adrenaline

Stress response 2: HPA axis (chronic stress)
Involves the adrenal cortex

Hypothalamus ▶ pituitary ▶ ACTH ▶ adrenal cortex ◀ cortisol

The General Adaptation Syndrome (GAS) model

Selye's (1936, 1950) research on rats and other animals led him to conclude that when animals are exposed to unpleasant stimuli (injections and other 'nocuous agents' such as extreme cold or severing limbs), they react in the *same way*. He described this universal response to **stressors** as the **General Adaptation Syndrome** (GAS): 'general' because it was the same response to all agents, 'adaptation' because it actually was an adaptive response – the healthiest way to cope with extreme stress – and 'syndrome' because there were several *symptoms* in the stress response.

Stage 1: Alarm reaction

The threat or stressor is recognised and a response made to the alarm. Adrenaline is produced, leading to 'fight or flight' activity. There is some activation of the HPA axis, producing cortisol.

Stage 2: Resistance

If the stress continues, it is necessary to find some means of coping and resisting collapse. The body is adapting to the demands of the environment, but at the same time resources are gradually being depleted. The body appears to be coping whereas, in reality (physiologically speaking), things are deteriorating.

Stage 3: Exhaustion

Eventually the body's systems can no longer maintain normal functioning. At this point the initial ANS symptoms may reappear (sweating, raised heart rate, etc.). The adrenal gland may be damaged from previous overactivity, and the immune system may not be able to cope because production of necessary proteins has been slowed in favour of other needs. The result may be seen in stress-related illnesses such as ulcers, depression, **cardiovascular** problems, and other mental and physical illnesses.

Summary of the GAS model

Stage 1 (alarm)	Stress response
Stage 2 (resistance)	Apparent coping
Stage 3 (exhaustion)	Breakdown, onset of stress-related illness

Stress response 2: Chronic stress and the HPA axis

If stress continues (becomes *chronic*), then the **hypothalamic-pituitary-adrenal axis** is increasingly activated. This 'axis' may sound complicated but isn't. An important part of the brain – the **hypothalamus** – stimulates another important part of the brain – the **pituitary** – to secrete a hormone called adrenocorticotropic hormone (**ACTH**) – which stimulates the adrenal glands to produce a hormone called **cortisol**.

The function of cortisol is to maintain a steady supply of blood sugar for continued energy. This enables the body to cope with the stressor, as distinct from the burst of energy needed for 'fight or flight' activity. This means that the body directs its energy towards maintaining sugar supplies.

HPA axis

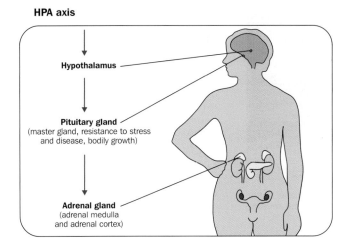

- **Hypothalamus**
- **Pituitary gland** (master gland, resistance to stress and disease, bodily growth)
- **Adrenal gland** (adrenal medulla and adrenal cortex)

A note for the terminologically challenged

If the phrase 'hypothalamic-pituitary-adrenal axis' stresses you, don't worry. You will not lose marks if you cannot use such terms or phrases – understanding and being able to describe the system are far more important. But if you can remember fancy words, it will lead to higher marks.

Criticisms

Support from research

The GAS model has had an important influence on our understanding of the relationship between stress and illness. It led to a vast amount of research, some of which we will look at on the next few pages. This research supports the view that stress does affect the body's systems and may lead to illness.

Is it an appropriate model for explaining human stress responses?

The fact that the GAS model is derived from research with non-human animals may explain why the model emphasises *physiological* factors. Humans are capable of thinking about their situation, which is certainly less true of non-human animals. This ability to think may mean that humans have the potential to control the extent to which an experience is stressful. For example, in the driving test situation, it is possible to practise relaxation techniques and thus reduce activity in the ANS. The GAS model does not incorporate cognitive influences.

On the other hand, individuals who have no adrenal glands need to be given additional amounts of certain hormones in order to respond to stressors, otherwise they may die. This shows that part of the human stress response *can* be explained in terms of physiological systems.

What are stress-related illnesses caused by?

The GAS model proposes that resources become depleted so that the body can no longer fight infections. However, more recent research has shown that many 'resources' do not become depleted even under extreme stress. The current view is that the exhaustion phase is associated with increased hormone activity, such as cortisol, and it is this rather than depletion of resources that leads to stress-related illness (Sheridan and Radmacher, 1992) (see page 92).

(see page 92).

KEY TERMS

Stress: Although this term may be used interchangeably with 'stressor' and 'stress response', it may also be seen as the subjective experience of a lack of fit between a person and his or her environment (i.e. where the perceived demands of a situation are greater than a person's perceived ability to cope).

Stressor: This refers to any event that causes a stress reaction in the body. Stressors include environmental stressors (such as the workplace) and life events (such as illness or divorce).

General Adaptation Syndrome: Selye's GAS model describes how, through physiological changes in the body, an organism copes with stress in an adaptive way. The model is characterised by three progressive stages that are part of this adaptive process: alarm, resistance and exhaustion.

What is meant by cardiovascular disorders?

In the previous spread, we described the stress response as a person's reaction to physical, chemical, emotional or environmental factors (i.e. *stressors*). More and more evidence suggests a relationship between prolonged exposure to such stressors and the risk of cardiovascular disorders. Acute and chronic stress may affect many different aspects of the cardiovascular system (i.e. the heart and circulatory system), such as the following:

- Hypertension (high blood pressure).
- Coronary heart disease (CHD) caused by **atherosclerosis** (the narrowing of the coronary arteries). Atherosclerosis is likely to produce angina (chest pain caused by reduced blood supply to the heart muscle), heart attack (myocardial infarction), or both.
- Stroke (brain damage caused by disruption of blood supply to the brain).

Although such cardiovascular disorders (also known as cardiovascular *disease*) are affected by lifestyle, diet, smoking etc., *stress* has become increasingly implicated in the development of all the disorders listed above.

The relationship between stress and physical illness

Stress may cause physical illness directly (as described by the GAS model) or indirectly, because stressed individuals are more likely to smoke and drink and these habits lead to illness. On the next few pages we will examine research on the relationship between stress and physical illness by looking at two examples of illness: cardiovascular disorders and the action of the immune system.

The effects of stress on cardiovascular disorders

A number of suggestions have been put forward to explain how stress might *directly* cause cardiovascular problems. For example:

- Stress increases heart rate, which may wear away the lining of the blood vessels.
- Stress increases blood pressure and this causes damage as high pressure would in any 'pipe'.
- Stress leads to increased glucose levels, leading to clumps blocking the blood vessels (*atherosclerosis*).

Stress may indirectly cause cardiovascular disorders, as suggested above.

Cardiovascular disease is a major cause of death in the UK. Therefore, understanding the causes of cardiovascular disease is very important.

star**STUDY**
The relationship between stress and cardiovascular disorders
(KRANTZ ET AL., 1991)

One cause of cardiovascular disorders is a condition called myocardial ischemia, which occurs when the heart muscle doesn't get the blood supply it needs ('ischemia' means reduced blood supply). This can happen during physical exertion, but research has found that it can also be brought on by psychological stress.

Aims

This study aimed to investigate the extent to which mental stress could be shown to increase myocardial ischemia (i.e. decrease the flow of blood to the heart). An additional aim was to see if patients with coronary artery disease (i.e. their blood vessels were thickened) reacted differently from individuals with no cardiovascular problems.

Procedures

Thirty-nine patients and 12 controls were studied while they performed three mental tasks: an arithmetic task, a Stroop task, and a task where they simulated public speaking. Each of these tasks was designed to create mild stress. The Stroop task involves asking someone to read a list of colour words (such as 'RED' or 'BLUE') in conflicting colours (e.g. **RED** and **BLUE**). In general the Stroop task slows reading down because of the cognitive conflict caused.

Measurements were taken of the participants' blood pressure and of the extent to which blood vessels around the heart contracted (high, medium or low ischemia).

Other research on the relationship between stress and cardiovascular disorders

Cardiovascular disorder and anger (an example of acute stress)

Williams *et al.* (2000) conducted a study to see whether anger was linked to heart disease. Thirteen thousand people completed a 10-question anger scale, including questions on whether they were hot-headed, or whether they felt like hitting someone when they got angry. None of the participants suffered from heart disease at the outset of the study. Six years later, the health of participants was checked; 256 had experienced heart attacks. Those who had scored highest on the anger scale were 2.69 times more likely to have a heart attack than those with the lowest anger ratings.

Cardiovascular disorder and work-related stress (an example of chronic stress)

Russek and Zohman (1958) looked at heart disease in medical professionals. One group of doctors was designated as high-stress (GPs and anaesthetists), while others were classed as low-stress (pathologists and dermatologists). Russek found heart disease was greatest among GPs (11.9% of the sample) and lowest in dermatologists (3.2% of the sample). This supports the view that stress is linked to heart disease, but it does not indicate whether the link is direct or indirect.

Cardiovascular disorders and individual differences

Recent research suggests that the sympathetic branch of the ANS in some individuals is more reactive than in others (Rozanski *et al.*, 1999). This would mean that some people (described as '*hyperresponsive*') respond to stress with greater increases in blood pressure and heart rate than others, and this would lead to more damage to the cardiovascular system in hyperresponsive individuals.

Later in this module (pages 102–5) we will look further at research into the relationship between individual differences and stress – at evidence that some *types* of people get more stressed and that they are more likely to have heart attacks and other cardiovascular disorders.

Findings

The cardiovascular patients who displayed greatest myocardial ischemia during the mental tasks also had the highest increases in blood pressure. The control participants showed the lowest levels of both myocardial ischemia and blood pressure when performing the mental tasks.

There was an intermediate group of patients who had either mild myocardial ischemia or none at all when performing the mental tasks. They also had only moderate increases in blood pressure.

Conclusion

These findings support the idea that there is a direct link between performing a mildly stressful cognitive task and physiological activity that could damage the cardiovascular system. However, not all cardiovascular patients responded in the same way, which leads us to conclude that there are important individual differences in responsiveness.

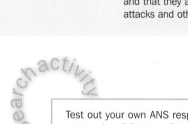

Test out your own ANS responses. Arrange for volunteers to engage in mildly stressful tasks, such as talking to the class or doing the Stroop task. Take physiological measurements before and after (repeated measures), such as measuring pulse, size of pupils (when the ANS is aroused they are dilated), dryness of mouth (again related to ANS arousal), sweat (check underarms!) and perhaps even blood pressure. You could also ask participants to produce a subjective report of their sensations.

Criticisms

Ethical issues

One could ask whether the mild stress given here is acceptable, especially to cardiovascular patients. The justification offered would be that the patients gave their informed consent and they were not subjected to stress greater than they would experience in everyday life.

Validity of the conclusion

A control group was used in order to see if the behaviour of cardiovascular patients was different from that of 'normal' individuals, but no controls were used to compare a patient's behaviour when stressed and not stressed. It is possible that the cardiovascular patients might show signs of muscle ischemia and raised blood pressure when relaxed as well as when mildly stressed, and this would mean that stress was not the cause of the ischemia or raised blood pressure. In this case, the conclusions of the study would not be justified.

COMMENTARY CORNER

To what extent does research support a link between stress and the development of cardiovascular disorders?

After reading this spread, you may have a sneaking feeling that stress *does* increase the risk of developing cardiovascular disorders. In constructing a response to this question, therefore, you could work up a series of arguments to support that feeling. If you look back at what you've just read, you will see a number of different possibilities for justifying that relationship. Some of these are *research*-based (Krantz *et al.*, Williams, Russek and Zohman, etc.), and some are *explanations* about why such a relationship might exist. Although the question specifies 'research', the explanations of *why* there might be a link between stress and cardiovascular disorders would be useful as **AO2** commentary. Whatever you use as part of your **AO2** response must be used *effectively* in order to gain high marks. Here is one possible way in which you could integrate research and explanation in an effective manner:

Russek and Zohman's study of medical professionals (Russek and Zohman, 1962) provided evidence for a link between workplace stressors and the development of cardiovascular disorders. They found that those in high-stress occupations (such as GPs) were more likely to develop heart disease than those in low-stress occupations (such as dermatologists). Although this study supports the view that high levels of stress are linked to heart disease, it does not indicate whether this link is direct or indirect. It is possible that Russek's high-stress individuals showed a greater incidence of heart disease because of elevated levels of stress hormones associated with their job. However, it is also possible that these individuals engaged in other compensatory behaviours (such as smoking and increased use of alcohol) or experienced lifestyle differences (e.g. sleep disruption), and these, not the stress itself, were responsible for the development of their cardiovascular disorder.

This extract provides **AO1** content (first two sentences) and **AO2** content (everything else) in the appropriate ratio (1/3 : 2/3) and *uses* the **AO2** in an obviously critical way. You might like to complete this answer using other material in a similar format.

What is meant by the immune system?

The **immune system** is designed to defend the body against millions of **antigens** (i.e. bacteria, viruses, toxins and parasites) that would otherwise invade it. It protects the body in three different ways:

1 It creates a barrier that prevents antigens from entering the body.
2 If an antigen does get into the body, the immune system tries to detect and eliminate it before it can make itself at home and reproduce.
3 If the virus or bacterium is able to reproduce and start causing problems, the immune system is responsible for eliminating it.

Probably the most crucial part of the immune system is the white blood cells, known as **leucocytes**. One of the most important types of white blood cell is the **lymphocyte.** Lymphocytes develop either as B-cells or as T-cells. One specific B-cell is tuned to a specific germ, and when the germ is present in the body the B-cell produces millions of antibodies designed to eliminate the germ. T-cells (Killer T-cells) detect cells in the body that are harbouring viruses, and when they detect such a cell, they bump up against it and kill it.

The effects of stress on the immune system

The GAS model proposed that stress leads to illness because the body's resources (e.g. glucose reserves) become depleted under extreme stress. This means that proteins for the immune system cannot be manufactured and the body is less able to fight invading viruses, bacteria and other toxins. However, many 'resources' do not in fact become depleted even under extreme stress; thus this is an unlikely explanation for the effects of stress on the immune system.

The second more likely explanation is that cortisol directly suppresses the immune system. This happens because **cortisol** decreases the production of lymphocytes (especially T-cells) and antibodies. There are positive effects of suppressing the immune system; for example cortisol is thought to help lower a temperature and it also reduces inflammation.

> **KEY TERM**
>
> Immune system: A system of cells within the body that is concerned with fighting intruders such as viruses and bacteria. White blood cells (leucocytes) identify and kill foreign bodies (antigens).

starSTUDY

The relationship between stress and the immune system

(KIECOLT-GLASER ET AL., 1995)

Aims

This study by Kiecolt-Glaser et al. sought to demonstrate the direct effects of stress on the immune system by looking at how quickly wounds heal. There are clearly ethical problems in creating stress in a group of participants in order to observe how this might affect their immune system. Therefore it is desirable to find a group of participants where high levels of chronic stress occur naturally. Kiecolt-Glaser et al. used a group of women who were caring for relatives suffering from senile dementia, a task which has been shown to be associated with chronic stress.

Procedures

In order to assess the effects of stress on the participants, a **matched participants design** was used. Participants were recruited by using advertisements in newspapers (thus it was a **volunteer sample**). Thirteen women aged 47–81 years were carers and placed in the **experimental group**, and a further 13 were matched with the carers on the basis of age and income but not marital status. This was the **control group**.

All participants were given a wound – a 'punch biopsy', which is a cut of 3.5mm just below the elbow. The wounds were dressed and treated by a nurse in the same way for each participant.

In addition, a second measure of immune response was taken. The researchers assessed levels of cytokines – biochemical substances involved in regulating the body's immune response.

Participants were also given a 10-item perceived stress scale to check how stressed they actually did feel.

Findings

First, complete wound healing took significantly longer in the carers than the controls. It took an average of 9 days (24%) longer in the carers.

Second, it was also found that cytokine levels were lower in the carers than the control group.

Third, on the perceived stress scale, the carers did actually indicate that they were feeling more stressed.

Conclusions

The findings support the view that chronic stress depresses the functioning of the immune system – because wound healing was slower in individuals who experienced chronic stress. The lower levels of cytokines in chronically stressed individuals support the view that stress lowers immune response directly.

Other research on the relationship between stress and the immune system

The effects of stress depress the immune system

Cohen et al. (1993) used the 'viral-challenge technique' to study the effects of stress on over 400 volunteers. Individuals were exposed to the common cold virus and also given a questionnaire to assess their levels of perceived stress. Cohen et al. found a positive correlation between levels of stress and the likelihood of catching a cold.

Riley (1981) experimented with mice, inducing stress by placing the mice on a rotating turntable. Within 5 hours this led to a lowered *lymphocyte* count. Some mice were implanted with cancer cells. After 3 days of 10 minutes of rotation per hour, mice were more likely to develop tumours than control mice given no stress. This shows that stress reduced immune activity (lymphocyte count) and was related to illness (more tumours).

Kiecolt-Glaser et al. (1984) looked at *T-cell activity* (another indicator of immune system activity) in the blood of students taking exams. Levels of T-cells were higher during the month before the students took exams, and dropped during the examination period itself.

The effects of stress may sometimes enhance the immune system

Evans et al. (1994) looked at the activity of one particular **antibody**, sIgA, which coats the mucous surfaces of the mouth, lungs and stomach and helps protect against infection. They arranged for students to give talks to other students (mild but acute stress). These students showed an increase in sIgA, whereas levels of sIgA decreased during examination periods that stretched over several weeks. Evans et al. (1997) propose that stress appears to have two effects on the immune system: up-regulation for very short-term acute stress, and down-regulation for chronic stress. This fits with the SAM/HPA distinction (see pages 88–9), and the essence of the GAS model.

One study found that people were more likely to catch a cold if they were stressed. This might be explained in terms of lowered immune responses as a consequence of being stressed.

How does a white blood cell know what to attack and what to leave alone? There is a system called the Major Histocompatibility Complex (MHC) that marks all the cells in your body as part of 'you'. Anything the immune system finds that does not have these markings is definitely 'not you', and is therefore fair game to be attacked.

Stress and separation

An interesting link can be made between maternal separation, the effects of stress and healthy development. Studies of rats have shown that taking a young rat away from its mother for 24 hours leads to an excess production of stress hormones. Stress hormones cause adrenaline to surge and the heart to beat faster, pumping more blood and nutrients to muscles needed for escape or defence, but may also reduce the ability of the brain to perform other important functions associated with physical and mental growth. As a result, such hormones can be damaging over time. In humans, babies who suffer stress because of neglect tend to be physically smaller (deprivation dwarfism) and mentally slower than their peers. Studies of Romanian children have shown that they had higher levels of a human stress hormone (cortisol) on weekdays when they were in a badly run day-care centre than at weekends when they were home with their parents (Carlson et al., 1995). Interestingly, high levels of stress hormones are reduced when infants are given substitute emotional care (Eliot, 1999).

Criticisms

Applications

These findings have important implications for treating people with infections, particularly in situations where people are recovering from surgery. Clearly it would be important to reduce stress as far as possible in such patients and thus speed their recovery.

Sample bias

The matching of participants was rather inexact, for example more of the carers were married and were non-smokers. However, both of these participant variables are related to *lower* stress. Social support is known to *reduce* stress, and non-smoking is related to *better* immune functioning. Therefore this **sample bias** would suggest that carers, if anything, should have better immune functioning. This strengthens the validity of the findings of this study.

Matched participants design was discussed on page 13. What are the advantages and weaknesses of this design? The study by Kiecolt-Glaser used a matched participants design. What was the research method? (Hint: Think about the IV.)

COMMENTARY CORNER

Consider whether research (theories and/or studies) supports a link between stress and the immune system.

When you are stuck for what to use as evaluation of a research study, you can always look a little closer at the research *methods* being used. This is one of the reasons why we've chosen to integrate the research methods content into these spreads rather than putting them in a separate area of the book. In this way, it gives you an added dimension of understanding *and* a critical appreciation of the strengths and limitations of a particular research approach.

In constructing your response to this question, you may well adopt the approach we used in the last Commentary Corner (on stress and cardiovascular disorders). However, for variety, you could offer some methodological criticism instead (or as well). For example, you would probably make reference to the study by Janice Kiecolt-Glaser and colleagues (Kiecolt-Glaser et al., 1995). We described their research design as a *matched participants* design and their sample as a *volunteer* sample. In what way does this design *strengthen* the value of the conclusions drawn? Similarly, how might the nature of the sample detract from the value of these conclusions? This is simply another way of evaluating material (considering the *value* of the study), and you might look for further opportunities in future spreads.

Sources of stress

Deciding exactly what constitutes a stressor is not that straightforward. Generally, people regard stressors as unpleasant events in their life, but it may surprise you to find out that they do not have to be negative events. Many of the things we look forward to (leaving home, going to university, getting married, having a baby) are significant sources of stress because they all require the individual to adapt in many different ways. Even something as relatively minor as going on holiday or Christmas can be significant stressors in a person's life. They are stressful because we are not always able to cope with the perceived demands of these situations. Over time, these stressors can add up and take a considerable toll on our health and well-being. Persistent on-the-job hassles, for example, can lead to

specification breakdown

Specification content	Comment
Research into sources of stress, including life changes (e.g. Holmes and Rahe), and workplace stressors (e.g. Johansson, Marmot).	You are expected to know about the **sources of stress**, and specifically required to know about research studies of the role of **life changes** and **workplace stressors** as sources of stress. Unlike specification entries that are preceded by the term 'including', you cannot be asked specifically about the work of Holmes and Rahe, or about workplace stressors (e.g. Johansson, Marmot). These are merely examples to help you decide what is an appropriate way to answer a question in this area.
Individual differences in modifying the effects of stressors, including the roles played by personality (e.g. Type A, hardy personality) and gender (e.g. physiological reactivity, social support).	Stress does not affect everybody in the same way. Here you are required to show your understanding of how the effects of stress might be modified by **personality** differences (e.g. the Type A and non-Type A difference demonstrated by Rosenman and Friedman), **cultural** differences and **gender** differences.

For some people, the thrills associated with 'living on the edge' are what they exist for. If you enjoy bungee jumping, whitewater rafting or off-piste skiing, or if you travel the world looking for the ultimate roller-coaster ride, you may fit the description of the Type T personality, where the T stands for thrills.

'You may not have heard of this personality, but I will wager that you know some people who show these characteristics. I believe Type T is at the basis of both the most positive and constructive forces in our nation (for example, creativity of all kinds)...and the most negative and destructive forces (such as vandalism, theft, joy-riding, taking hard drugs and excessive use of alcohol)' (Farley, 1990).

a condition of physical, mental and emotional exhaustion known as *burnout*. Teachers, nurses and police officers may simply become worn down by the never-ending stress of their job.

Rates of stress-related illnesses such as hypertension (high blood pressure) are also high for those who live in urban ghettos, where the everyday stresses that accompany poverty (unemployment, single parenting, overcrowding) are accompanied for many by racial intolerance and discrimination. The dramatic effects of high levels of stress became apparent in Russia in the early 1990s. Following the collapse of the former Soviet Union, Russia experienced mushrooming divorce, suicide, murder and stress-related disease rates. Life expectancy for Russian men also dropped a staggering 5 years.

Before we plunge into this next section, two things are particularly important.

- First, it may not be possible to define objectively the sort of events or situations that qualify as stressors. Psychologists have emphasised the significance of *cognitive appraisal* in the experience of stress. To qualify as a stressor has more to do with how a person thinks about a particular situation than any inherent stress-inducing characteristic of the situation itself. The most successful sportsmen and sportswomen get a positive high when thinking about a forthcoming competition, while others get incredibly nervous thinking about the same event, so creating a handicap before they even get started.

- The second important point to bear in mind when considering sources of stress is that the relationship between stressor and stress reaction is not a completely straightforward one. This relationship is moderated by individual differences such as personality, culture and gender. For example, it may well be the case that women have a mechanism that protects them from life-threatening diseases. The hormone oestrogen, for instance, appears to offer some resistance to cardiovascular disease. Evidence from post-menopausal women and women who have had their ovaries removed (both resulting in lower levels of oestrogen) has established that these women have higher rates of cardiovascular disease than pre-menopausal women.

Women too have an advantage over men when it comes to the moderating personality variables. Women are less likely to have Type A personalities (a cluster of personality characteristics that supposedly makes individuals more prone to coronary heart disease) and are less hostile than men (hostility increases the vulnerability of Type A individuals). So, if women win out in terms of biological and personality variables, why is the gap between male and female mortality rates decreasing? The answer may well lie in another source of stress – lifestyle. Davison and Neale (2001) suggest that lifestyle differences between men and women may account for the sex difference in mortality and that these differences are decreasing. Traditionally men have smoked and drunk more alcohol than women, but in recent years women have closed the gap in both of these activities. More women have entered the workforce, and as well as facing the same workplace stressors as men, for many women there is the dual responsibility of wage earner and mother.

What is meant by life changes?

So far we have concentrated on how stress affects us, and how prolonged exposure to stressful situations can sometimes make us ill. But what sort of things actually cause the chronic stress reaction we described earlier? In this section we look at two main types of stressors: life changes and workplace stressors. Life changes are those events (such as getting married, retiring or dealing with bereavement) that necessitate a major transition in some aspects of our life. Because they have such an impact on us, they are sometimes referred to as *critical* life events. There is, of course, considerable variation in the impact of these 'critical' life events. What might be profoundly stressful for one person (such as the death of a spouse) may be a blessed relief for another. Likewise, something as minor as the death of a much-loved pet or changing schools may be devastatingly stressful to some people.

Although the term 'life change' suggests something must happen in order to cause a person such stress, the same reaction can be found when something *does not* happen. For example, *not* being promoted or *not* getting to university are extremely stressful life 'not-changes' for many people.

KEY TERM

Life changes: Events (such as divorce or bereavement) that necessitate a significant adjustment in various aspects of a person's life. As such, they can be seen as significant sources of stress.

SOURCES OF STRESS

The Social Readjustment Rating Scale (SRRS)

Rank	Life event	LCU
1	Death of a spouse	100
2	Divorce	73
3	Marital separation	65
4	Jail term	63
5	Death of a close family member	63
6	Personal injury or illness	60
7	Marriage	53
8	Fired at work	47
9	Marital reconciliation	45
10	Retirement	45
11	Change in the health of family member	44
12	Pregnancy	40
13	Sex difficulties	39
14	Gain new family member	39
15	Business readjustment	39
16	Change in financial state	38
17	Death of a close friend	37
18	Change to a different line of work	36
19	Change in number of arguments with spouse	35
20	Mortgage over $10,000	31
21	Foreclosure on mortgage or loan	30
22	Change in responsibilities at work	29
23	Son or daughter leaving home	29
24	Trouble with in-laws	29
25	Outstanding personal achievement	28
26	Wife begins or stops work	26
27	Begin or end school	26
28	Change living conditions	25
29	Revision of personal habits	24
30	Trouble with boss	23
31	Change in work hours/conditions	20
32	Change in residence	20
33	Change in schools	20
34	Change in recreation	19
35	Change in church activities	19
36	Change in social activities	18
37	Mortgage or loan less than $10,000	17
38	Change in sleeping habits	16
39	Change in number of family get-togethers	15
40	Change in eating habits	15
41	Holiday	13
42	Christmas	12
43	Minor violations of the law	11

Why do life changes lead to stress?

Two medical doctors, Holmes and Rahe (1967), played a key role in developing the idea that life changes are linked to stress and illness. In the course of treating patients, they observed that it was often the case that a range of major life events seemed to precede physical illness. These events were both positive and negative experiences that had one thing in common – they involved change. Change requires 'psychic energy' to be expended, i.e. it is stressful. Holmes and Rahe suggested that this affected health.

Using life changes to measure stress

In order to test the idea that life changes are related to physical illness, it was necessary to have some means of measuring life changes. Holmes and Rahe (1967) developed the Social Readjustment Rating Scale (SRRS), based on 43 life events taken from their analysis of over 5,000 patient records.

To establish the stressfulness of each event, they enlisted the help of about 400 participants. The participants were asked to score each event in terms of how much readjustment would be required by the average person. The participants were asked to provide a numerical figure for this readjustment, taking marriage as an arbitrary baseline value of 500. If an event would take longer to readjust to than marriage, they should give the event a larger score. Scores for all participants were totalled and averaged to produce life change units (LCUs) for each life event.

star**STUDY**

Life changes as a source of stress

(RAHE *ET AL.*, 1970)

Aim

Rahe *et al.* used the SRRS to test Holmes and Rahe's hypothesis that the number of life events a person experienced would be positively correlated with illness. Rahe *et al.* aimed in particular to study a 'normal' population as distinct from the populations previously studied of individuals who were already ill in hospital.

Procedures

A military version of the SRRS was given to all the men aboard three US Navy Cruisers, a total of over 2,700 individuals. This is an **opportunity sample** (see page 108). The men completed the questionnaire just before a tour of duty, noting all the life events experienced over the previous 6 months.

An illness score was calculated on the basis of the number, type and severity of all illnesses recorded during the tour of duty (about 7 months). Rahe *et al.* did not include sick bay visits that appeared to be due to a desire to get out of work (because the individual wasn't actually ill).

Findings

An LCU score and an illness score were calculated for each man. Rahe *et al.* found a positive correlation between these scores of

Research methods
What does 'significant' mean?

Exactly what it says – anything that is 'significant' is important and meaningful. Some correlation coefficients are bigger than others; a significant result is a more important result. How do we know it is important? Statisticians work out what numbers count as 'meaningful' and record these in tables of significance. You will learn more about these when you do your coursework. All you need to know for now is that a 'significant result' means that there is a real correlation or difference in the findings, and that we can accept the research **hypothesis**. A result that is non-significant means there is not enough correlation/difference, and that we must accept the **null hypothesis** (a new concept).

+0.118. (This number is a correlation coefficient, which is explained on the right.) A positive correlation is one where both co-variables increase together. This relationship is illustrated in the scattergraph below. The number 0.118 expresses how closely the co-variables varied together. 0.118 is not a very strong correlation, but given the number of participants it is **significant**.

Correlation between total life change unit and mean illness score for that LCU

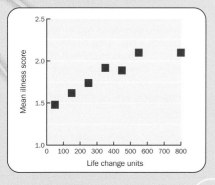

Research methods
Understanding correlation coefficients

'Coefficient' is a mathematical word meaning 'number'. On page 73 we looked at correlational analysis, including the idea that a correlation can be zero, positive or negative. These three kinds of correlation are illustrated in **scattergraphs** on page 73. Here we come to the final part of the story. When a correlational analysis is used, it is possible to calculate a number to represent the extent to which the co-variables are related. In the study by Rahe *et al.*, the co-variables are (1) illness score and (2) life unit score. In order to calculate the number or coefficient of their correlation, we use a formula found in a book (or computer program). This formula is not our concern here – all you need to know is that the numbers for each of the co-variables are put in, the formula is applied, and out comes the coefficient.

If the co-variables are closely correlated, the coefficient will be 1.0 or very close to it. If there is no correlation between the co-variables, the coefficient will be zero or close to it. In the study by Rahe *et al.*, 0.118 was found to be a significant correlation despite the fact that it is fairly close to zero. This is because there were thousands of participants. Usually, in psychological research, there are only 20 or 30 participants. If there are 20 participants, 0.45 would be a significant coefficient; if there are 30 participants, 0.36 would be significant. For 12 participants, 0.58 would be a close correlation and over 0.72 would be extremely close.

Notice that all correlation coefficients are less than 1. Some correlation coefficients are written as –0.52, whereas others are +0.52. The plus or minus sign shows whether it is a positive or negative correlation. The coefficient tells us how closely the co-variables are related. –0.52 is just as closely correlated as +0.52, only –0.52 means that as one variable increases the other decreases (**negative correlation**), and +0.52 means that both variables increase together (**positive correlation**).

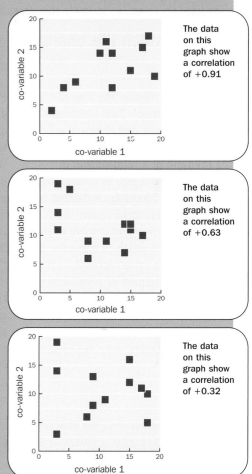

The data on this graph show a correlation of +0.91

The data on this graph show a correlation of +0.63

The data on this graph show a correlation of +0.32

Conclusions

The findings support the hypothesis of a link or positive correlation between life changes/events and physical illness. It is possible that the link is stress: life changes cause stress, and we know that stress causes illness. Therefore life changes are sources of stress. Both positive and negative events are included in the SRRS, so we see that it is change rather than negativity that is important. It is the overall amount of psychic energy required to deal with an event that creates stress.

Criticisms

Unreliable data

The LCUs were calculated by asking the men to recall life changes over the previous months. It is possible that they didn't remember these events accurately. For example, a man might repress the memory of an event that was a negative experience or might not recall exactly when it took place.

Is the SRRS a valid measure?

The SRRS was a landmark development in stress research. However, many psychologists have suggested that it is not a valid measure of stress. Other measures of life stressors are examined on the next page. The main complaints are that the SRRS focuses on acute life events rather than ongoing (chronic) stressors; it does not distinguish between desirable and undesirable events; and it does not take into account social resources, which may moderate the effects of stress. This means that the checklist is a rather crude measure of stress, which could explain why such a weak correlation was found in the study by Rahe *et al.*

More on life changes

SOURCES OF STRESS

The Social Readjustment Rating Scale paved the way for a whole new field of research, investigating the link between life changes and physical illness. Many psychologists have developed alternative scales for measuring life change, improving on the original SRRS. Other psychologists have used these scales to study the stress factors that are related to illness.

Ways in which life changes cause stress

Bereavement

Bereavement means 'the loss of something valued'. This loss usually involves a death, but it can also be applied to other situations, including the breakup of a relationship or divorce, loss of a job, or coming to terms with a disability. Research into comparative levels of stress connected with important life events shows that the death of a spouse is regarded as the most stressful event. The stressful impact of bereavement is more pronounced if the death is sudden or violent, or if the relationship was one in which one or both partners were very dependent.

Post-traumatic stress disorder

PTSD can be an extremely debilitating condition that can occur after exposure to a traumatic event in which grave physical harm occurred or was threatened. The sorts of traumatic events that can trigger PTSD include violent personal assaults, accidents, or military combat. People with PTSD may re-experience their ordeal in the form of flashbacks, nightmares or frightening thoughts, especially when they are exposed to events or objects that remind them of the trauma. They may also experience emotional numbness and sleep disturbances, depression, anxiety and outbursts of anger. Feelings of intense guilt (called survivor guilt) are also common, particularly if others did not survive the traumatic event.

Other ways of measuring life changes

Daily hassles – DeLongis et al. (1982) suggested that the ongoing (chronic) strains of daily living – hassles – would provide a better measure of stress than looking at acute events. Hassles include worries about money, current affairs, your job, your friends, sex, the weather, looking after your home, losing things, and so on. It is likely that people will differ in the amount of stress related to each hassle, and some people might experience the hassle as an uplift. For example, friends, money or sex could be a hassle or an uplift. DeLongis et al. developed a 'Hassles and Uplifts Scale' that included 53 items.

Perceived importance – Moos and Swindle (1990) produced the LISRES (Life Stressors and Social Resources Inventory). They identified eight areas of ongoing life stressors: health, home, finance, work, partner, child, extended family, friends. The LISRES also includes an assessment of social resources available to the individual as these moderate the effect of stressors.

Research methods
Pilot studies

It makes sense to conduct a small-scale trial run of any research design before doing the real thing in order to find out if certain things don't work. For example, participants may not understand the instructions or they may guess what the experiment is about. They may get very bored because there are too many tasks or too many questions. This trial run is called a **pilot study**.

Note that daily hassles are not an example of 'life changes'. Therefore the daily hassles scale would not be credited in a question about life changes, except as an evaluation.

---

research activity

You could construct your own life change scale, drawing on the ideas represented here: life events, chronic hassles, personal relevance, social support and so on. Schafer (1992) suggested that items such as some of the following might be suitable for a scale used by students: parking problems around campus, careless bike riders, library too noisy, too little time, too little money, boring teacher, not enough close friends, room temperatures, conflicts with family, too little sleep, writing essays, fixing hair in the morning, etc. In order to conduct a study you need some way to assess illness (or health). The issue of questionnaire design is considered on the next page.

Other research on life changes as a source of stress

Life changes are related to physical health

Jacobs and Charles (1980) investigated a possible link between life events and cancer in children. They asked parents to complete the SRE (an adaptation of the SRRS) in order to assess family stress. Children who developed cancer had families with a higher life change rating than a control group of children being treated for non-cancerous illnesses.

Life changes are not related to physical health

DeLongis et al. (1988) studied stress in 75 married couples. They gave the participants a life events questionnaire and the Hassles and Uplifts Scale, finding no relationship between life events and health, nor any relationship between uplifts and health. They did find a significant positive correlation of +0.59 between hassles and next-day health problems such as flu, sore throats, headaches and backaches. However, as all participants were over 45, it may not be reasonable to generalise from these findings.

Research methods *Designing a questionnaire*

Writing good questions on questionnaires

There are three guiding principles:

1 Clarity – Questions need to be written so that the reader (respondent) understands what is being asked. There should be no ambiguity. *(This question lacks clarity: '**Do you like working?**' It does not make it clear what kind of work – it might be paid work or school work.)*

2 Bias – Any bias in a question might lead the respondent to be more likely to give a particular answer. The greatest problem is **social desirability bias**. Respondents prefer to select answers that portray them in a positive light rather than reflect the truth.

3 Analysis – Questions need to be written so that the answers provided are easy to analyse. If you ask 'What kind of job do you do?' or 'What makes you feel stressed at work?' you may get 50 different answers from 50 people. These are called **open questions**. Alternatively one can ask **closed questions** where a limited range of answers are provided, such as a list of 10 job categories or 10 sources of stress. These are easier to analyse.

Designing good questionnaires

Filler questions: it may help to include some irrelevant questions to mislead the respondent from the main purpose of the survey. This acts as a **single blind** (see page 5).

Sequence for the questions. It is best to start with easy ones, saving difficult questions or questions that might make someone feel anxious or defensive until the respondent has relaxed.

You need to decide on **sampling technique**, i.e. how to select respondents. Sampling techniques are discussed on page 108.

In order to produce good questionnaires it may be necessary to do a **pilot study** where the questions can be tested on a small group of people . This means you can refine the questions in response to any difficulties encountered.

Closed questions, for example:

Which of the following factors at work makes you feel stressed? (Tick as many as you like)

☐ Noise at work ☐ Lack of control ☐ Workmates
☐ No job satisfaction ☐ Too much to do ☐ Other

Using a Likert scale where respondents can indicate the extent to which they agree or disagree with a statement, for example:

Work is stressful

☐ Strongly disagree ☐ Agree ☐ Not sure ☐ Disagree ☐ Strongly disagree

---

Advantages of **open questions**	Advantages of **closed questions**
• Allow respondents to express themselves • Unexpected information is collected	• Easy to analyse data • Easier for respondents to fill in

---

	Advantages	Disadvantages
Quantitative data	Easy to analyse, can produce descriptive statistics such as bar charts and means. Produces neat conclusions.	Oversimplifies reality. Experimenter bias and demand characteristics can be problems
Qualitative data	Represents the complexity of human behaviour. Provides rich detail.	More difficult to detect patterns and reach conclusions.

Research methods
Qualitative and quantitative data

Open questions may produce **qualitative data**. This is data that represents what people think or feel. Such data cannot be counted or *quantified* whereas this is what we do with **quantitative data** (e.g. drawing bar charts or producing tables of numbers).

CORNER

COMMENTARY

**'Life changes, no matter if they are positive or negative, are always a source of stress.'
To what extent have life changes been shown to be a source of stress?**

Some students tend to panic when they see a quotation, feeling that it presents an extra problem that needs to be addressed. Quotations are subtle hints about some of the issues that you *might* want to consider in your answer.

In this question, the quotation suggests that both positive and negative changes (e.g. marriage and divorce) are sources of stress. This is certainly something that Holmes and Rahe found in their research using the SRRS scale, but this also constitutes one of the *criticisms* of this scale – that it doesn't differentiate between desirable and undesirable life changes.

Of course, there are important differences in terms of what people regard as 'desirable' and 'undesirable'. From the discussion of bereavement, you'll remember that the impact

of this life change is more pronounced if the death is sudden or violent, or if the relationship was one in which one or both partners were very dependent. But what if the death was not sudden, or the partners were not even close? In some cases, the death of a spouse (if they have been seriously ill for many years, or have made their partner's life a misery) might be received as a positive event. In these cases, the initial stressful impact of the event would be lessened, and this would mark the transition to a new and more fulfilling part of the person's life.

In short, don't be put off by quotations, and feel free to explore the issues they suggest, but the question itself is what you have to respond to. The quotation is just a suggestion for a route through it.

What is meant by workplace stressors?

Stress at work is a priority issue for all of us who work, and for all who employ us. The European Foundation's 1996 report on working conditions in the European Union reported that over half of the workers questioned believed that their work affected their health. A particular stressor may or may not cause a stress reaction in an individual, depending on how that person perceives its demands and his or her ability to cope. So, to label 'responsibility' or 'workload' as automatic stressors without considering their impact on any given individual ignores the important fact that each of us interacts with our working environment differently, and so perceives it differently.

That said, there are still a number of characteristics of the working environment that are commonly reported as being 'stressful' and therefore would constitute a **workplace stressor**. These might be divided into *physical stressors* (such as noise, length of working day and inherent danger) and *psychosocial stressors* (such as relationships with co-workers, organisation of work and role responsibility). Each of these two broad types of workplace stressor has the *potential* to cause a stress reaction, and thus affect physical and psychological health. Whether they do or do not have this effect depends on many other factors, including an individual's ability to cope and available social support.

> ### KEY TERM
>
> **Workplace stressors**: Some aspect of our working environment (such as work overload or impending deadlines) that we experience as stressful, and which causes a stress reaction in our body.

star STUDY

A study of workplace stressors
(MARMOT *ET AL.*, 1997)

Most people would agree that work is a source of considerable stress, and some would agree that this stress may lead to illness. The question for researchers is to find out what aspects of the workplace are the most important sources of stress.

Aims

Marmot *et al.* sought to test the *job-strain model*. This model proposes that the workplace creates stress and illness in two ways: (1) high demand and (2) low control. Marmot *et al.* suggested that this could be tested in the context of civil service employees where the higher grades would experience high job demand, and low-grade civil servants would experience low job control.

Procedures

Civil service employees (men and women) working in London were invited to take part in this study. A total of 7,372 people agreed to answer a questionnaire and be checked for signs of cardiovascular disease. About 5 years later each participant was reassessed. For each participant the following information was recorded: signs of cardiovascular disease (e.g. ischemia or chest pains), presence of coronary risk factors (e.g. smoking), employment grade (a measure of the amount of job demand an individual experienced), sense of job control (measured by a questionnaire) and amount of social support (also measured by a questionnaire).

Findings

At the end of the study it was found that participants in the higher grades of the civil service had developed the fewest cardiovascular problems. Participants in the lower grades expressed a weaker sense of job control and also had poorest social support. It was also found that cardiovascular disease could in part be explained in terms of risk factors such as smoking (i.e. people who developed cardiovascular disease were more likely to be smokers and be overweight).

Conclusions

The main conclusion is that low control appears to be linked to higher stress and also linked to cardiovascular disorder, whereas high job demand is not linked to stress and illness. This does not fully support the job-strain model because it does not show that high demand is linked to illness, but lack of control does appear to be linked to stress and illness.

Criticisms

Can the findings be explained in terms of socio-economic status?

We can classify individuals in terms of **socio-economic status** (SES) – a measure of the kind of job they do (e.g. skilled or unskilled), how much money they have, the kind of house they live in and so on. People who are of low SES are more likely to smoke, live in more stressful environments and have poorer diets – all factors linked to cardiovascular problems. This means that low-grade civil servants may have more cardiovascular problems than high-grade civil servants because of factors related to low SES rather than because they lack job control.

However, Marmot *et al.* argue that other studies have demonstrated that lack of control does increase stress (see page 101). If low control is generally a source of stress, it may well be an important factor of stress in the workplace in *addition* to other SES factors.

Biased sample

The conclusions of this study are based on the sample studied – civil servants. The responses of such individuals may be not be typical of all adults as they are urban dwellers who are probably quite job-oriented and ambitious, in contrast with rural inhabitants whose jobs may play a less significant role in their lives. One study found that ambitious individuals were more affected by workplace stressors (Caplan *et al.*, 1975). Therefore, we might conclude that not everyone will be affected by low control in the way that these individuals were.

Factors in the workplace that act as stressors

Work overload

The study by Marmot et al. found that job demand was not a factor in stress. However, other studies have examined different aspects of 'demand' or 'workload'. For example, Johansson et al. (1978) looked at the effects of performing repetitive jobs that require continuous attention and some responsibility. The sawyers in a Swedish sawmill (high-risk group) have stressful jobs – a repetitive task, with an unrelenting pace and a sense of responsibility for the whole company because, if they fall behind on their work, everyone else's production is slowed down. The high-risk group was found to have higher illness rates and also higher levels of adrenaline in their urine than a low-risk group (e.g. maintenance workers who had less monotonous jobs and more flexibility). The high-risk group also had higher hormone levels on workdays than on rest days. This is evidence of a direct link between job demand, stress hormones and illness.

Lack of control

Stress occurs as a result of an interaction between the perceived demands from the environment and a person's perception of their ability to cope. When perceived demands exceed perceived ability to cope, we feel out of control. Lack of control is stressful because we feel at the mercy of outside forces. However, there may be individual differences. Schaubroeck et al. (2001) found that some workers respond differently to lack of control – they are *less* stressed by having no control or responsibility. In this study Schaubroeck et al. measured saliva, from which they could assess immune system functioning directly. They found that some people had higher immune responses in low-control situations. Some people view negative work outcomes as being their fault. For these employees control can actually exacerbate the unhealthful effects of stress.

Role conflict and role ambiguity

Conflict is stressful, and for many workers there are conflicts between different demands at work, and also between demands at work and at home. Shirom (1989) found a positive correlation between perceived role conflict and coronary heart disease (CHD).

'Role ambiguity' refers to the lack of definition given to a worker's job. This leads to a feeling of frustration and makes it hard to achieve a sense of satisfaction. Kahn et al. (1964) surveyed workers and found that 35% felt unclear about their job responsibilities and what they actually had to do.

Environmental factors

There are many environmental factors in the workplace that increase aggression and stress. These include noise, heat, poor lighting and overcrowding. The effects of unpredictable noise were demonstrated in a study by Glass et al. (1969). Sixty undergraduates completed various cognitive tasks in one of five conditions: loud or soft noise that was either random (unpredictable) or played at fixed intervals (predictable); there was also a no-noise condition. Stress (ANS arousal) was measured using the **galvanic skin response** (GSR). After the task, participants were asked to complete four puzzles, two of which couldn't be solved – in order to create frustration. Participants showed greatest stress in the random noise condition (highest GSR and lowest task persistence indicating frustration). Participants in the predictable noise condition showed more stress than those in the no noise condition. Overall this shows that noise creates stress, especially when it is unpredictable. Glass et al. suggested that random noise is particularly difficult because we can 'tune out' constant stimuli, but unpredictable stimuli require continued attention, and this reduces our ability to cope with stress.

The galvanic skin response (GSR)

When the ANS is active one of the effects is increased sweating. This increase in moisture can be detected if electrodes are placed on the skin, because water conducts electricity and the electrodes detect greater electrical conductivity in the skin. Thus GSR is used to measure increased stress (ANS activity → sweating → increased electrical conductivity).

A note about aims

In each Star Study the aims of the study have been described. This is in order to help you in the examination should you be asked to 'Describe the aims of one study of something'. If you are struggling to write enough about aims, you might ask yourself the following: What was the study trying to find out? What was the study going to illustrate? Was a possible connection between two things being investigated? Was the study seeking to confirm a previous finding? The answers to these questions will help you write enough about the aims of the study.

http://workhealth.org/index.html
The job stress network.

What is meant by individual differences?

There are important differences in the way that people react to stress, as there are differences in the way they react to many other influences in their life. Some people appear to be able to face horrendously stressful living conditions and still remain relatively healthy, whereas others buckle at the slightest bit of pressure. There are many different ways in which the differences between individuals might moderate the effects of stress, including personality, gender and cultural background. **Individual differences** are not always acknowledged in psychology. In many areas of the discipline, differences between individuals in terms of these important variables are ignored in order to present a more *general* view of human behaviour. This has often led to accusations of gender and cultural bias in psychological theories and research.

SOURCES OF STRESS

When Mike attended his first psychology lecture at university, the lecturer related what was essentially a fact sheet about human behaviour. This was the way that memory worked, this was the way that children reacted to bad parenting, and so on. 'Of course,' continued the lecturer, 'all this is subject to individual differences.' Individual differences? Having been socialised into the relative certainty of A-level biology just 6 months earlier, the idea that people didn't necessarily react in the same way was a bit of a puzzle. Surely earthworms didn't react differently if you cut them in two, or rats didn't learn mazes differently (actually they do), so why was it such a problem for the study of humans? We all know that this is indisputably true from our own experiences of life, but somehow it seems alien in the academic study of psychology.

What is meant by personality?

'Personality' is an elusive term that defies precise definition. In its broadest sense, personality can be thought of as a set of characteristic behaviours, attitudes and general temperament that remain relatively stable and distinguish one individual from another. Perhaps an easier way to define it is in more lay terms – it is that fundamental 'thing' that makes us who we are, and different from everybody else. Of course, we are different because of the peculiar mix of temperament, attitudes and so on that define *us*, but there are inevitably some personality **traits** that we share with others. It is this fact that interests psychologists who study the mediating influence of personality on the impact of stressors. Research has established that *some* personality characteristics make us more vulnerable to the negative effects of stress, while others make us more resistant.

Research on the role of personality in modifying the effects of stressors

Type A

Various studies have identified clusters of different behaviours (personalities) that appear to be present in individuals susceptible to heart disease and/or cancer. The first personality type identified was **Type A**. Friedman and Rosenman (1959) described a Type A individual as aggressive and ambitious with a competitive drive and a chronic sense of time urgency. These characteristics would lead to both raised blood pressure and raised levels of hormones, both linked to ill health. In contrast, *Type B* was proposed as a personality relatively lacking these characteristics.

In order to assess the hypothesis that coronary heart disease (CHD) was associated with Type A personality, Friedman and Rosenman set up the Western Collaborative Group Study (WCGS) in 1960. Approximately 3,000 men aged 39 to 59, living in California, were examined for signs of CHD (in order to exclude any individuals who were already ill) and their personalities were assessed using a **structured interview**. The interview included 25 questions concerned with how the individual responded to everyday pressures. For example, respondents were asked how they would cope with having to wait in a long queue. The interview was conducted in a provocative manner to try to elicit Type A behaviour. For example, the interviewer might speak slowly and hesitantly, so that a Type A person would want to interrupt.

The findings were frightening. After 8.5 years twice as many Type A participants had died of cardiovascular problems. Type As also had higher blood pressure, higher cholesterol, higher lipoproteins (a measure of immune system activity) and more cases of manifest CHD (i.e. CHD was diagnosed but the individuals were not dead – yet). Type As were also more likely to smoke and have a family history of CHD, both of which would indirectly increase their risk.

Research methods *Questionnaire surveys*

One method of collecting data in research is the use of the interview (see page 105). Questionnaire surveys (questionnaires) are similar to structured interviews except that they are written down, so there is no chance that an interviewer might bias the answers in the way he or she asks the questions. All the same, the way the questions are phrased may lead to biased answers – think about **leading questions**.

Advantages	Disadvantages
A lot of data can be collected from large numbers of people relatively cheaply and quickly.	As with interviews, there may be problems with **leading questions** and **social desirability bias**.
Questionnaires do not require specialist administrators.	The sample is biased because only certain kinds of people do fill in questionnaires – literate individuals who are inclined to spend time filling them in.

Type C for cancer

Type Cs suppress emotions, particularly negative ones, and are unassertive, likeable people who rarely get into arguments and are generally helpful to others. Temoshok (1987) suggests that such individuals cope with stress in a way that ignores their own needs, even physical ones, in order to please others, and this has negative physiological consequences. All stresses are suppressed, but eventually such stresses take their toll.

Why is Type C associated with cancer rather than cardiovascular disorder? Temoshok suggests that this is because some stressors activate the ANS and endocrine system (acute stress), and this is related to CHD. More chronic stressors affect the immune system and increase the risk for cancer.

Type D for depressed or distressed

People who are gloomy, socially inept and worriers may also be at risk of heart attacks – a mixture of Eeyore and Marvin the paranoid android from *The Hitch Hiker's Guide to the Galaxy* (Burne, 1999). Denollet *et al.* (1996) first identified Type D in a study that looked at approximately 300 men and women who suffered heart attacks. The participants filled in a personality questionnaire at the time of their first attack. Ten years later, those who had had a tendency to suppress emotional distress and to experience negative emotions were four times more likely to have had a further heart attack. This was termed a 'distressed personality' or Type D personality. This personality was associated with depression and social alienation.

The hardy personality type

Kobasa (1979a) suggested that some people are more psychologically 'hardy' than others. Hardiness enables people to cope better with stress. Kobasa proposed that hardiness can be taught and used as a stress management technique.

- *Control* – Hardy people see themselves as being in control of their lives. They attribute control to themselves rather than to external factors that are beyond their control.

- *Commitment* – Hardy people are involved with the world around them, and have a strong sense of purpose. They do not stand aside and watch.

- *Challenge* – Hardy people see life changes as challenges to be overcome rather than as threats or stressors. They enjoy change as an opportunity for development.

Marvin the paranoid android, from *The Hitch Hiker's Guide to the Galaxy*, had a personality similar to Type D, which might (had he been human) have made him more prone to having a heart attack.

Are the effects of personality a cause or an effect?

It may be that anxiety or depression is the *result* of stress rather than the cause. However, one study showed that the cancer-prone behaviour patterns can be reversed to reduce illness. Type C individuals are characterised as being unassertive and unwilling to fight against adversity. Greer *et al.* (1979) found women with a 'fighting spirit' were more likely to recover from cancer. This suggests that such behaviour patterns are a cause of health or illness, rather than an effect.

Are the effects of personality direct or indirect? A cause or a correlation?

There appears to be evidence that some aspects of personality are linked to CHD and other illnesses. But is this because some aspect of personality actually *causes* the immune system to underperform and/or *causes* blood pressure to increase (i.e. it is a direct effect)? Or is it that personality has an indirect effect, for example making it more likely that an individual would smoke and this would increase the likelihood of CHD?

Nemeroff and Musselman (2000) found evidence of a direct link between personality and illness. This study found that depressed people had 41% more sticky platelets in their blood than normal participants. Sticky platelets block arteries and increase risk of heart attack. Musselman found that giving these patients Prozac, an anti-depressant, almost got rid of these platelets. You might think that it was the Prozac that reduced the platelets, but if some patients were given a **placebo** (told they were taking Prozac but actually given a substance with no pharmacological effects), the number of blood platelets dropped! This suggests that mood itself is influencing the body's systems.

CORNER

Consider the role of personality in moderating the impact of stressors.

There is a tendency among students to 'compartmentalise' their knowledge. In other words, what is offered in response to a question is limited to the material that surrounded it at the time it was learned. This is not necessarily a bad thing, and we have certainly tried to give you all that you need to answer even the trickiest examination questions in these spreads. However, occasionally it pays to think a little wider. Personality is a case in point. If you have read the material on these two pages, you will be aware of the nature of the Type A personality and its role in the development of CHD in response to stress. However, if you wander through some of the other pages in this physiological psychology section, you will find lots more useful material that could be marshalled together to form an effective response. For example, research on hardiness as a personality variable (page 114) shows how some people possess personality characteristics that make them relatively vulnerable to the negative effects of stress. Hardy personalities are also more likely to show high levels of personal control – a vital factor in the moderation of stressors. Finally, in the introduction to 'Sources of stress' (page 94), you may remember that women are less likely to possess Type A personality characteristics, and therefore less likely to be vulnerable to their consequences. Making these links does not *have* to form the basis of your response to this question, but it stops you developing a blinkered view of psychology that may one day have you floundering in the dark.

COMMENTARY

Our understanding of personality may point the way to more effective treatments for stress-related illnesses. For example, cognitive therapy may help Type D individuals learn to think less negatively, and this may alter their susceptibility. Cognitive therapy is discussed on pages 112 and 139.

What is meant by gender?

'Gender' technically refers to the psychological characteristics displayed by an individual rather than his or her physical characteristics, denoted by the term 'sex', although the two terms – gender and sex – are often used interchangeably. Psychologists have increasingly argued for the existence of gender differences in stress reactivity. Some of these differences may be physiological, with females showing less arousal of the sympathetic nervous system in stressful situations, and some behavioural, with females tending to engage in different *types* of coping behaviour. Of course, nothing is quite that simple, and as with the other forms of individual difference covered in this section, the influence of gender on stress is itself subject to important age, personality, cultural and other mediating factors. We can, however, explore some of the significant differences between males and females in their response to stressful situations.

Research on the role of gender in modifying the effects of stressors

Biological explanations

Taylor *et al.* (2000) suggest that women may be biologically programmed to be less affected by stress, because of the action of the hormone **oxytocin**. Oxytocin has been studied largely for its role in childbirth, but it is also secreted in men and women as a response to stress. Individuals with high levels of oxytocin are calmer, more relaxed, more social and less anxious. In several animal species, oxytocin has been shown to lead to maternal behaviour and to affiliation. This might explain why, under stressful situations, women seek the support of others, which further serves to reduce their stress levels. Men also secrete oxytocin, but its effects appear to be reduced by male hormones, so oxytocin may have reduced effects on men's physiology and behaviour under stress. Oxytocin, along with other stress hormones, may play a key factor in reducing females' response to stress.

This finding has been supported by Hastrup *et al.* (1980), who found that women showed lowered stress responses when their cardiovascular reactions were tested during the time of their menstrual cycle. At this time their levels of **oestrogen** (which is released at times of stress in women and lowers blood pressure) were highest, and therefore it would seem that oestrogen might also be reducing the stress – a biological explanation for why women are less stressed.

Social explanations

Males have less social support, more unhealthy habits and more stressful occupations. All of these factors can explain why men are more prone to cardiovascular disorders than women.

In terms of social support, research shows that women are more likely to have confidantes and friends than men, and women report making use of social support networks more than men (Carroll, 1992).

In general, women engage in fewer unhealthy behaviours than men, or at least they used to. Men smoked more and drank more alcohol, which might have explained their higher rates of CHD. However, such habits are changing – women are smoking and drinking more and their CHD rates have risen, whereas men are smoking and drinking less. This would lead us to expect a narrowing of the gender gap in CHD mortality rates. Carroll (1992) reports that this has been happening.

In terms of occupational stress, Frankenhauser (1983) found that females in non-traditional roles (e.g. lawyers, bus drivers, engineers) had higher **neuroendocrine** levels than women in traditional roles. This suggests that male stress may be a consequence of the activities they engage in. As women enter the workforce they become more stressed

▼ As men and women begin to take on the same occupational roles, so their stress experiences may become more similar.

and display more typically male patterns such as raised adrenaline levels. This again could explain why the gender gap is narrowing.

All of this evidence suggests that the gender gap in cardiovascular disorders is likely to narrow even more.

Cognitive explanations

Males react to stressful tasks with higher blood pressure than females. It could be that such a difference is due to the effects of sex hormones (e.g. testosterone and oestrogen). However, studies of pre-pubescent boys and girls have still found gender differences, which suggests that reactivity cannot be explained in terms of sex hormones (because these are not present in sufficient quantities prior to puberty). An alternative explanation is that males and females differ in the way they learn to handle (or *think about*) social conflict situations. Vögele *et al.* (1997) suggest that females learn to suppress anger and so show low reactivity in stress situations, whereas when males have to suppress anger, this results in raised blood pressure.

Do females in fact react more than males?

Stone *et al.* (1990) tested the hypothesis that males show greater cardiovascular reactivity to stressors than females. They looked at the effects of two stressors: a video game and cigarette smoking, and 6 measures of stress (e.g. heart rate, blood pressure). On 5 out of 6 measures females actually had a higher reactivity to both stressors.

SOURCES OF STRESS

Many studies of stress use male participants. If males do respond differently to females, this challenges the validity of much stress research.

Gender differences in definitions

THINGY (thing-ee) n.
female: Any part under a car's bonnet.
male: The strap fastener on a woman's bra.

VULNERABLE (vul-ne-ra-bel) adj.
female: Fully opening up one's self emotionally to another.
male: Playing cricket without a box.

FLATULENCE (flach-u-lens) n.
female: An embarrassing by-product of digestion.
male: An endless source of entertainment, self-expression and male bonding.

From:
http://www.lollie.com/happy/giggle7.html

Research methods
Interviews

Psychologists aim to find out about behaviour. One way to do this is to conduct experiments to test a hypothesis. Another way is to ask people questions about their experiences and/or beliefs. This method is called an **interview**.

	Advantages	Disadvantages
Interviews	• Can collect information about people's attitudes, which cannot be found out in an experiment. • Interviews can be conducted by telephone.	• The interviewer's expectations may influence the answers the interviewee gives (this is called **interviewer bias**). This may especially be true because people don't always know what they think. They may also want to present themselves in a 'good light' and therefore give 'socially desirable' answers (this is called the **social desirability bias**). • People may be less willing to answer personal questions in an interview than a questionnaire.
In a **structured interview** all the questions are predetermined and the interviewer tries hard to stick strictly to his/her script.	• Such interviews can be more easily repeated.	• The answers are limited by the range of questions asked. • This technique requires skilled interviewers.
In an **unstructured interview** the interviewer starts with a few predetermined questions but then creates new questions in response to the answers given by the participant. This is sometimes called a *clinical interview* because it is the kind of technique used by a doctor when talking to a patient.	• The information collected can be very revealing because the questions have been shaped to the interviewee. This produces 'rich' data.	• The creative element of an unstructured interview means that there is greater potential for the interviewer to influence the interviewee's answers. • The answers from unstructured interviews are less easy to analyse because they are unpredictable.

COMMENTARY CORNER

To what extent has research provided evidence for gender differences in the impact of stress?

Engaging in effective commentary involves more than simply *criticising* a particular point of view, but may also involve a more subtle examination of the whole area under consideration. For example, in response to the AO2 requirements of the above question, the following material could be effectively woven into your response.

Why have studies tended <u>not</u> to show gender differences in the past?

Early research on the impact of stress emphasised the 'fight or flight response' as being a universal reaction to stressful situations. With situations that the individual perceives as being out of his or her control, the so-called 'defeat response' has also been proposed as a universal phenomenon. Several studies have described the physiological and behavioural responses associated with stressful situations, but is this a fair representation of gender-related reactions? Until recently, most laboratory studies of physiological reactions in response to stress have been carried out on males. Even when these studies have been carried out on animals, there has been a preponderance of male rats! Likewise, field trials of anti-anxiety drugs have often found that women report more side effects than men when taking these drugs, yet this has usually been dismissed as a greater tendency among women to report physical symptoms. Newer, less gender-biased research has suggested important gender differences in the *way* that males and females react to stress.

What is the evolutionary significance of gender differences in stress reactions?

Research by Taylor *et al.* (2000) provided support for the contention that gender differences in the reaction to stress may be rooted in our evolutionary history. The value of the fight or flight response to male survival has led, through the processes of *natural selection,* to the development of higher levels of cardiovascular performance (e.g. elevated blood pressure) and the activation of the sympathetic nervous system and the HPA axis in stressful situations. However, different considerations would apply to females who have made a greater biological investment in pregnancy and nursing their offspring. This maternal investment in offspring should result in the selection of female stress responses that do not jeopardise the health of the female or her offspring, and maximise the likelihood that they survive. According to this view, and contrary to early research findings, biological mechanisms should evolve that inhibit the fight or flight response in females and shift their attention to *tending* (attachment behaviour) and *befriending* (forming defensive networks of females) behaviour. Taylor *et al.*'s research found evidence that male and female sex hormones activate behaviours that conform to these predicted gender-related differences in stress reaction.

Are there alternative explanations for biological explanations of gender differences in this area?

Eagley and Wood (1999) disagrees with the claim that these gender differences have an evolutionary basis. She suggests that different behaviours can be 'learned on the job', so we don't know how many of these gender differences are due to hormonal differences and how many are learned. It is possible that differences in the way that males and females deal with stress have nothing to do with biological factors but are simply a part of the gender-role socialisation that males and females experience as they grow up.

Recent research by Heinrichs *et al.* (2001) found lowered levels of stress response among men exposed to a stressful situation if they had been given oxytocin in the form of a nasal spray. However, the participants showed much greater relaxation of their stress response if a friend was also present (as well as having the oxytocin administered), and the lowest levels of relaxation when only the oxytocin was available. This suggests that although oxytocin may have important stress-relieving properties for both males and females, the importance of social factors in stress reduction cannot be overlooked.

CRITICAL ISSUE:
Stress
management

The Bristol Stress and Health at Work Study published in June 2000 revealed that 1 in 5 workers (around 5.5m nationally) reported feeling extremely stressed at work.

A poll of NHS nurses found widespread disillusionment, with the majority of nurses reporting that workload and stress levels had increased.

UNISON report, 1999

specification breakdown

Specification content	Comment
Methods of managing the negative effects of stress, including physiological (e.g. drugs, biofeedback) and psychological approaches (e.g. stress inoculation and increasing hardiness).	The use of the word 'methods' tells you that you should be prepared for questions that might ask for more than one **physiological** method and/or more than one **psychological** method of stress management. The examples given are just that – examples – and there are other examples of each approach that would be relevant. Make sure you are clear about the *difference* between a physiological and a psychological approach to stress management.
The strengths and weaknesses of methods of stress management	You are also required to know about the **strengths** and **weaknesses** of each of your chosen methods of stress management as well as be able to summarise these in an overview of the strengths and weaknesses of physiological and psychological methods in general.

It is estimated that fatigue caused by excessive stress accounts for around 1,000 deaths on the road each year in the UK.

ROSPA

Sickness absence in Britain's police forces accounted for 1.5 million days in the year 1996–7. The Metropolitan Police alone lost 400,000 days to sickness absence at a cost to the taxpayer of £88 million.

National Audit Office

Estimates of the cost of stress and stress-related illness range from £5 billion (TUC) to £12 billion (CBI) each year (that's around £500 each year for every working adult). Sickness among staff cost the NHS more than £300 million in 1997 in England alone.

Daily Telegraph, 25 March 1998

Figures like those on the left remind us how serious a problem stress is in all of our lives. They paint a gloomy picture, yet there are positive steps that we can take to minimise the negative impact of stress. Over the next few pages we look at two very different approaches to stress management: those based on physiological intervention, such as the use of prescribed drugs, and those based on psychological intervention, such as improved coping skills. The jargon involved in these techniques, however, can sometimes blind us to the fact that there are very practical things we can all do to lower our stress levels. If you are taking an exam in the near future, you will find stress management is a vital consideration for you too (see below).

An important factor in all forms of stress management is control. We frequently feel more stressed because we have little control over events around us. Nervous flyers tend to feel nervous because they have very little control over what is happening at any given time. With exam revision, however, taking control is more straightforward. Learning what is on the specification, how the examination is constructed, deciding when and what you are going to revise, and putting it all in perspective can help to minimise the stress you will otherwise experience.

There are other techniques as well – relaxation, meditation, even watching television helps, provided these are used as part of your overall plan. For many, however, the measures used to reduce stress (excessive drinking, denial, constantly putting things off) are clearly not as constructive. We also need to be realistic.

With major life changes such as family breakdown, bereavement or chronic illness, the same sequence is involved – identifying the stressor, planning some way of managing the stress involved, and looking to take control – yet we still feel stressed. The stress management techniques on the next few pages are all strategies that are based on sound psychological principles, but even when we use them, life can still be stressful. Stress management is certainly a vital skill for us all, but living with the illusion that life is – or should be – stress free is, paradoxically, one of the biggest stressors of them all.

Applying stress management techniques to exam performance

Tips for the revision period

✓ Leave plenty of time to revise so that you don't have to do last-minute cramming.

✓ Develop a timetable so that you can track and monitor your progress. Allow time for fun and relaxation so that you avoid burning out.

✓ As soon as you notice you are losing concentration, take a short break. You will then come back to your revision refreshed.

✓ Regular moderate exercise will boost your energy, clear your mind and reduce any feelings of stress.

✓ Try out some relaxation techniques. They will help to keep you feeling calm and balanced, improve your concentration levels and help you to sleep better.

Tips for the exam itself

✓ Avoid panic. It's natural to feel some exam nerves prior to starting the exam, but getting excessively nervous is counterproductive as you will not be able to think as clearly.

✓ The quickest and most effective way of eliminating feelings of stress and panic is to close your eyes and take several long, slow, deep breaths. Breathing in this way calms your whole nervous system. Simultaneously, you could give yourself a mental pep-talk by silently repeating 'I am calm and relaxed' or 'I know I will do fine'.

✓ If your mind goes blank, don't panic! Panicking will just make it harder to recall information. Instead, focus on slow, deep breathing for about 1 minute. If you still can't remember the information, move on to another question and return to this question later.

✓ After the exam don't spend endless time criticising yourself for where you think you went wrong. Often our own self-assessment is far too harsh. Congratulate yourself for the things you did right, learn from the bits where you know you could have done better, and then move on.

Source: http://www.isma.org.uk/exams.htm

What is meant by stress management?

W e saw from earlier definitions that stress might be experienced whenever we are challenged beyond our perceived ability to adapt. These challenges may be psychological, social or physical. The emotions and physiological arousal created by stressful situations are highly uncomfortable, and this discomfort motivates the individual to take action. The process by which a person attempts to manage stressful demands is called coping or **stress management**.

Some approaches to stress management may reduce the stress in one area of a person's life, but at the same time increase stress in another area, or in those close to the person. Such 'misadaptive' approaches to stress management include excessive drinking or sleeping, reducing personal stress by 'taking it out' on others, or becoming a 'fanatic' about a particular approach to stress management (e.g. working out) to the point that it becomes a source of stress in itself. Other forms of stress management are more adaptive in that they are focused on reducing the negative effects of the stressful situation without developing equally stressful situations elsewhere in the person's life.

What is meant by physiological and psychological approaches to stress management?

A person can focus on alleviating the emotions associated with the stressful situation, even if the situation itself cannot be changed. This may be achieved in a number of ways, including the use of drugs that reduce the anxiety associated with stress, or through learning how to control some aspects of the body's stress reaction. Such approaches are referred to as the *physiological* approach to stress management. The second approach involves the use of techniques that help the person to cope with the situation itself, rather than just dealing with the symptoms of stress. A person can focus on the specific problem or situation that has arisen, trying to find some way of changing it or avoiding it in the future, or may learn techniques that minimise the negative effects of stressful situations. This second approach is known as the *psychological* approach to stress management.

KEY TERMS

Stress management: The different ways in which people try to cope with the negative effects of stress. We may attempt to change the way our body responds to stress (the physiological approach), or change our relationship with the stressful situation (the psychological approach).

Physiological approaches to stress management: The use of techniques (such as drugs and biofeedback) designed to change the activity of the body's stress response system.

Psychological approaches to stress management: The use of techniques (such as relaxation, hypnosis, or specific cognitive techniques such as stress inoculation) that are designed to help people cope better with stressful situations, or to alter their perception of the demands of a stressful situation.

Research methods *Sampling techniques*

Studies of the effects of drugs rely on looking at their effects on a small group of people. How does a researcher *select* (i.e. sample) that group of people (participants)? The intention is to make this selection with as little bias as possible so that the participants represent the entire **target population**. If you select only women, the **sample** would be unrepresentative – unless you only wanted to make statements about female behaviour.

How does this selection take place? There are several methods, but we need only to consider the three main ones:

- **Random sample**. If you require 20 participants, you would put the names of all possible participants (for example, everyone in the school) in a 'hat' and select 20 names. This means that every member of the **target population** (the school) has an equal chance of being selected. This is an unbiased sample – though the population from which the names are drawn is biased. Note that if you take every 10th name in the school register this is *not* a random sample. This is called a *systematic sample* or *quasi-random sample* (i.e. not quite random).

- **Opportunity sample**. This is the most common method used to select a sample. You simply approach anyone who happens to be available, for example asking people in the street or friends in your school. This method is sometimes mistakenly regarded as random, whereas it is invariably biased. It is the easiest method to use.

- **Volunteer sample**. In many studies advertisements are used to attract participants. Ads are placed in a newspaper or on a noticeboard. The participants then volunteer themselves. This results in a **volunteer bias** because such participants are usually more highly motivated than randomly selected participants.

	Advantages	Disadvantages
Random sample	Potentially unbiased.	Needs to be drawn from a large population to be unbiased.
Opportunity sample	Easy.	Very biased.
Volunteer sample	Access to a variety of participants.	**Volunteer bias**.

What do you feel like when you are stressed? Uptight, anxious, irritable? These are all symptoms of the body's response to stress and can be treated by directly treating the body – with drugs. Drugs that combat anxiety are called anti-anxiety or anxiolytic drugs.

Benzodiazepines: Reduce nervous system activity

The group of drugs most commonly used to treat anxiety is **benzodiazepines** (BZs). These are sold under various trade names such as Librium, Valium, Halcion and Xanax.

BZs slow down the activity of the central nervous system. They do this by enhancing the activity of a natural biochemical substance called *GABA* (gamma-amino-butyric acid). GABA is the body's natural form of anxiety relief. This enhancement is achieved in several ways.

- One way is that GABA slows down nerve cell activity. GABA allows chloride ions into **neurons**, slowing the activity of the neuron. This causes relaxation.

- A second way is that GABA also reduces **serotonin** activity. Serotonin is a **neurotransmitter** (see diagram) that has an arousing effect, i.e. it stimulates some neurons. People who are depressed have low levels of serotonin and one form of treatment is to take drugs to increase the levels of this neurotransmitter to reduce depression. People with anxiety need to reduce levels of serotonin. GABA reduces serotonin, which then decreases arousal of neurons, causing reduced anxiety.

BZs imitate the activity of GABA and thus reduce arousal of the nervous system and reduce anxiety.

Beta-blockers: Reduce autonomic (ANS) activity

Beta-blockers act on the **sympathetic nervous system** rather than the brain. As we saw earlier (page 88), stress leads to arousal of the sympathetic nervous system and this creates increased blood pressure, heart rate, elevated levels of **cortisol**, and so on. These symptoms in themselves lead to cardiovascular disorders and also reduce the effectiveness of the immune system. Beta-blockers reduce the activity of the sympathetic nervous system and reduce the associated undesirable symptoms. Beta-blockers are often used by sportsmen and women to reduce arousal because ANS arousal may have a negative effect on performance.

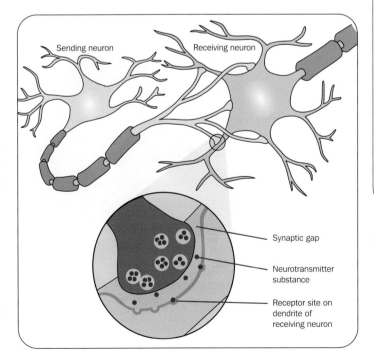

Sending neuron | Receiving neuron

Synaptic gap

Neurotransmitter substance

Receptor site on dendrite of receiving neuron

◀ Neurotransmitters are released by one neuron into the synaptic gap between two neurons. The neurotransmitter stimulates the receiving neuron, thus transmitting the nerve impulse (electrical signal)

Strengths

Effectiveness

Anxiolytic drugs work. One way to assess effectiveness is to compare outcomes when some anxious patients are given a drug and others are given a **placebo** – a substance that has no *pharmacological* effects (i.e. it has no effect on the body). Patients are given medication but do not know whether it is the real thing or the placebo. This enables us to determine whether the effectiveness of the drug is due to its pharmacological properties or to something psychological, such as simply believing that taking the drug will make you better. Kahn *et al.* (1986) followed nearly 250 patients over 8 weeks and found that BZs were significantly superior to placebo.

Easy to use

One of the great appeals of using drug treatment for stress (or any other problem) is that the therapy requires little effort from the user. You just have to remember to take the pills. This is much easier than the time and effort needed to use stress management techniques such as biofeedback and the psychological methods described later in this section.

Weaknesses

Addiction

BZs were first introduced over 40 years ago and replaced barbiturates, which tended to be addictive, i.e. patients exhibited withdrawal symptoms when they stopped taking the drug, indicating a physiological dependence. It is only recently that the problems of addiction and BZs have been recognised, especially the problems of low-dose dependence on BZs. Patients taking even low doses of BZs show marked withdrawal symptoms, though individuals with passive-dependent personalities appear to be more likely to experience withdrawal symptoms than other patients. Because of such addiction problems there is a recommendation that BZs should be limited to a maximum of 4 weeks' use (Ashton, 1997).

Side effects

Side effects include drowsiness, dizziness, tiredness, weakness, dry mouth, diarrhoea, upset stomach, changes in appetite, blurred vision, changes in sex drive or ability, or, more seriously, seizures, severe skin rash and irregular heartbeat, all of which require immediate medical attention.

Treating the symptoms, not the problem

Drugs may be very effective at treating symptoms, but this lasts only as long as the drugs are taken. As soon as you stop taking the drugs, the effectiveness ceases. It may be that the problem has passed, but, in cases of chronic stress, it may not be appropriate simply to put a temporary 'bandage' on the problem, especially if the treatment produces further problems of its own (such as addiction). This means that it may be preferable to seek a treatment that addresses the problem itself rather than one that deals only with the symptoms.

Ethical issues: Comparing therapies

One way of assessing the effectiveness of any method of stress management is to give the treatment to some participants and withhold the treatment from a control group. There are ethical objections to doing this because the researcher is determining who gets help and who does not.

Physiological methods of stress management (continued)

W e now look at a second physiological method of stress management – **biofeedback** – and consider how it is similar to, and different from, the use of drug therapy.

Physiological approach 2: Biofeedback

Biofeedback, like drugs, also deals with the physiological symptoms of stress. These physiological symptoms, such as raised blood pressure and increased muscle tension, are *involuntary*. We are unable to control them consciously because they are governed (for a good reason) by our **autonomic nervous system** (ANS). If these systems were controlled consciously, we would spend our time thinking about nothing else! Biofeedback is a method by which an individual learns to exert voluntary control over involuntary (autonomic) behaviours by being made aware of what is happening in the ANS.

Biofeedback involves four processes:

- *Feedback*. The patient is attached to various machines which provide information (feedback) about various ANS activities. For example, the patient can hear his/her heartbeat or is given a signal (light or tone) to show higher or lower blood pressure.

- *Relaxation*. The patient is taught techniques of relaxation. These have the effect of reducing activity of the **sympathetic nervous system** and activating the **parasympathetic nervous system**. The result should be reduced heart rate, blood pressure and all symptoms associated with stress.

- *Operant conditioning*. Relaxation leads to a target behaviour, for example heart rate is decreased or muscle tension is relaxed. This is rewarding, which increases the likelihood of the same behaviour being repeated. Such learning (conditioning) takes place without any conscious thought. The reward leads to an unconscious 'stamping in' of the behaviour.

- *Transfer*. The patient then needs to transfer the skills learned to the real world.

Operant conditioning occurs when a behaviour is 'stamped in' as a result of reinforcement. Reinforcement increases the probability that a behaviour is repeated (see page 54).

A good way to illustrate this is to consider a classic study on feedback by Miller and DiCara (1967). They used curare to paralyse 24 rats, keeping the rats alive using artificial respiration. Half of the rats were rewarded whenever their heart rates slowed down, and the other half were rewarded when their heart rates speeded up. The reward was 'a sense of pleasure' – this was achieved by electrically stimulating a part of the brain known as the pleasure centre. The result was that the heart rates of the rats in the 'fast' group speeded up, and the heart rates of the rats in the slow group slowed down. Two things are important. First, the learning that took place was entirely involuntary as the rats were paralysed. It was the automatic ANS responses (heart rate) that were conditioned. Second, the learning was the result of operant conditioning – behaviour stamped in because it was rewarded.

Other explanations

Miller and DiCara's study has never been directly replicated, so it is not clear whether biofeedback is in fact due to operant conditioning. It is possible that biofeedback may work for reasons other than operant conditioning. The success of biofeedback may be due simply to learning to relax, and relaxation reduces sympathetic activity and increases parasympathetic activity. Or it may be that the method offers patients a sense of increased control and this produces beneficial effects (lack of control is discussed on page 101).

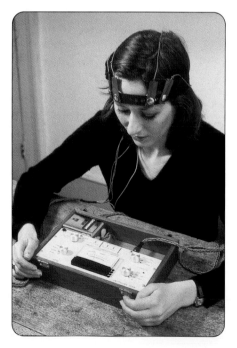

Biofeedback (biological feedback)

▶ Patient connected to a machine that provides information about autonomic (ANS) activity.

▶ Uses relaxation to learn how to control ANS behaviours.

▶ Successful behaviours are repeated because they are rewarding.

▶ Patient learns to transfer to everyday situations.

---

http://webideas.com/biofeedback/index/
Clinical applications and technique on biofeedback around the world, related sciences and stress disorders.

▶ A biofeedback machine provides feedback about ANS activities so a person can learn to control them.

Research on biofeedback

Biofeedback in non-human animals

Gruber and Taub (1998) successfully trained four monkeys to raise and lower body temperature and reduce muscle tension using biofeedback. This demonstrates that biofeedback learning does not depend on conscious thought because non-human animals cannot be using the power of thought.

Biofeedback with children

Attanasio et al. (1985) trained children and adolescents to use biofeedback with stress-related disorders, mainly muscle-contraction headache. They identified various advantages of training children: increased enthusiasm, less scepticism about the procedure, fewer previous failures with treatment and generally more positive attitudes. This may explain why biofeedback can be more successful with children.

Strengths

Effectiveness

Biofeedback has been found to be successful in treating a wide assortment of behaviours (e.g. heart rate, blood pressure, skin temperature and brain waves) and disorders (curvature of the spine, migraine headaches, asthma and Raynaud's disease, where there is restricted blood flow to fingers and toes). Bradley (1995) compared the effectiveness of using biofeedback versus relaxation to control muscle-tension headaches. The biofeedback group was given seven 50-minute sessions with feedback about muscle activity (using EMG – electromyogram – which provides information about electrical activity of the muscles). After treatment the biofeedback group had significantly fewer headaches than the relaxation group.

No side effects

Biofeedback is not an invasive technique. In other words, it does not alter the body in any permanent way as drugs do. The only effects (or side effects) are increased relaxation, which can only be desirable.

Weaknesses

Expensive

The technique requires specialist equipment, which means that it is expensive and can only be undertaken with specialist supervision. If the success of biofeedback is mainly due to relaxation rather than feedback and conditioning, there is no need for these expensive and time-consuming procedures.

Treating the symptoms, not the problem

The aim with biofeedback is to reduce symptoms associated with stress, such as reducing heart rate or muscle tension. Biofeedback does not treat the source of stress, such as workplace tension. However, it does provide the patient with a potentially long-lasting means of dealing with stress symptoms – by applying relaxation techniques.

Similarities and differences between drug therapy and biofeedback

- Both treat the symptoms rather than the cause.
- Biofeedback may provide a more lasting solution to stress management through relaxation.
- Drug therapies have potential problems with withdrawal and side effects, whereas biofeedback is not invasive.
- Drug therapies require no effort on the part of the patient, whereas biofeedback requires specialist training and an investment of time and effort.

research activity

A good way to try to conduct your own naturalistic observation would be to use material from TV or videos to record behaviour. As we are currently studying stress, you might make observations of how people respond to stressful situations, i.e. record stress responses. Previously we suggested how you might conduct a controlled observation (see page 49). In a naturalistic observation all variables are free to vary. Some of the techniques you might use are on page 49.

COMMENTARY CORNER

Consider the effectiveness of physiological approaches to stress management.

One effective way of handling the requirements of the **AO1 + AO2** question is to decide at the outset what your conclusion will be and work towards it. After all, that's what J. K. Rowling did with the final volume in her *Harry Potter* series, so it should be good enough for us here!

You may decide that physiological approaches are not particularly effective forms of stress management and proceed to justify that claim in your choice of material. For example, most psychologists appear to conclude that the claims for biofeedback are greatly exaggerated, despite the wide popularity of the technique. Davison and Neale (2001) concluded that there is little evidence that biofeedback involves anything more than relaxation and increased control. Likewise, drugs may be very effective at treating the symptoms of stress, but this lasts only as long as the drugs are taken. As soon as you stop taking the drugs, the effectiveness ceases.

On the other hand, you may decide that physiological approaches *are* effective in the management of stress, and so choose to emphasise slightly different aspects of the same material. For example, biofeedback has been shown to be particularly effective with children, as demonstrated in the research by Attanasio *et al.* (1985). Likewise, anxiolytic drugs do appear to work, particularly in the way they reduce the general anxiety associated with stressful situations. This claim is supported by the research of Kahn *et al.* (1986), who followed nearly 250 patients over 8 weeks and found that BZs were significantly superior to placebo in the treatment of stress-related anxiety.

It is a useful exercise for you to construct *two* answers to this question, one the case for the prosecution (i.e. that physiological approaches are *not* effective in the management of stress), and one the case for the defence (i.e. that they *are* effective).

Having thought about the arguments from both sides, you are then in a much better position to construct the sort of debate we talked about on page 13. It is unlikely that physiological approaches are *completely* ineffective, but then again it is equally unlikely that they are *completely* effective on their own without some form of concurrent psychological technique being used. We are going to look at psychological techniques next.

What is meant by psychological methods of stress management?

The *psychological* approach to stress management involves the use of techniques that help the person to cope with the situation itself rather than just dealing with the symptoms. A person can focus on the specific problem that has arisen, trying to find some way of changing it or avoiding it in the future, or may learn techniques that minimise the negative effects of stressful situations. Although some of the most often used psychological approaches to stress management are relaxation and meditation, the really effective psychological techniques involve specific psychological interventions that train individuals either to appraise stressful situations differently, or to increase resistance to the negative effects of stress.

'There is nothing either good or bad, but thinking makes it so.'
William Shakespeare, *Hamlet*

Note that here we talk of a 'client', whereas in the context of physiological therapies it is the 'patient' who is receiving treatment. This reflects the view of each kind of therapy. Cognitive (psychological) therapies regard the client as an active participant in the therapy process rather than a passive patient.

What's the difference between physiological and psychological methods of stress management?

The main difference between a *physiological* and a *psychological* approach to stress management is that in the former a person focuses on alleviating the emotions associated with the stressful situation rather than dealing with the situation itself. This is a form of stress management known as *emotion-focused coping*. The psychological approach involves the use of techniques that help the person to cope with the situation itself rather than just dealing with the symptoms of stress. Because psychological approaches frequently involve learning constructive ways to deal with stressful situations (thus minimising their stressful impact), this approach to stress management is also known as *problem-focused coping*.

Psychological approach 1: Stress inoculation training (SIT)

Meichenbaum (1985) proposed a form of **cognitive therapy** to deal with stress. The essence of a cognitive therapy is that the problems that an individual encounters are often beyond his or her control. For example, stress in the workplace or the strains of urban life cannot be changed. What a person can change is the way that he or she *thinks* about these stressors. Positive thinking leads to changes in attitudes and feelings, which reduces the stress response and leads to being able to cope better.

There are different kinds of cognitive therapy. Meichenbaum's cognitive therapy, called stress inoculation training (SIT), was developed specifically to deal with stress. It is different to other stress treatments because Meichenbaum suggested that an individual should develop a form of coping *before* the problem arises; that is, you should *inoculate* yourself against the disease of stress in the same way that you receive inoculations against infectious diseases.

Meichenbaum proposed three main phases to this process.

Phase 1: Conceptualisation

The therapist (trainer) and client establish a relationship, and the client is educated about the nature and impact of stress. For example, the client is taught to view perceived threats as problems-to-be-solved and to break down global stressors into specific components that can be coped with. This enables the client to reconceptualise the problem.

Phase 2: Skills acquisition (and rehearsal)

Coping skills are taught and practised primarily in the clinic and then gradually rehearsed in real life. A variety of skills are taught and are tailored to the individual's own problems. These include positive thinking, relaxation, social skills, methods of attention diversion, using social support systems, and time management. Clients may be taught to use self-statements, such as those shown on the left. The skills taught are both cognitive and behavioural: cognitive because they encourage the client to think in a different way, and behavioural because they involve learning new behaviours through rewards (conditioning).

Phase 3: Application (and follow-through)

Clients are given opportunities to apply the newly learned coping skills in different situations, which become increasingly stressful. Various techniques may be used such as imagery (imagining how to deal with stressful situations), modelling (watching someone else cope with stressors and then imitating this behaviour) and role playing (acting out scenes involving stressors). Clients may even be asked to help train others. Booster sessions (follow-through) are offered later on.

Examples of coping self-statements

Preparing for a stressful situation
- You can develop a plan to deal with it.
- Don't worry; worry won't help anything.

Confronting and handling a stressful situation
- One step at a time, you can handle it.
- Relax, you're in control. Take a slow breath.

Coping with the feeling of being overwhelmed
- Keep the focus on the present.
- Label your fear 0 to 10 and watch it change.

Reinforcing self-statements
- It worked: you did it.
- It wasn't as bad as you expected.

Panel 1: THE REASON I DON'T GET STRESSED OUT IS THAT I PRIORITIZE THE THINGS I'M ASKED TO DO.

Panel 2: HOW?

Panel 3: WHEN A REQUEST COMES IN, I THROW IT AWAY.

Panel 4: IF IT COMES BACK, I DO IT.

Research on SIT

Meichenbaum (1977) compared SIT with another form of psychological treatment called desensitisation. This involves presenting clients with a hierarchy of fearful stimuli, starting with the least fearful. When a client can relax and cope with the least fearful stimulus, the therapist introduces the next most fearful situation. Patients used SIT or desensitisation to deal with their snake phobia. Meichenbaum found that both forms of therapy reduced the phobia but that SIT was better because it helped clients deal with a second, non-treated phobia. This shows that SIT can inoculate against future stressful situations as well as offering help in coping with current problems.

Fontana et al. (1999) examined the effectiveness of a peer-led stress inoculation programme in college students. After a 6-session treatment programme the participants had lower heart rate and state-anxiety levels than did controls. This difference was maintained at a 6 month follow up.

Jay and Elliot (1990) demonstrated the effectiveness of a stress inoculation programme for parents whose children are undergoing medical procedures. Parents were assigned to a stress inoculation programme (to cope with their own stress) or observed their child's participation in a cognitive therapy programme. Parents in the stress inoculation group reported less anxiety.

Strengths

Effectiveness

Meichenbaum (1996) claims that stress inoculation has been shown to be successful with acute and chronic stressors. Examples of acute stressors that have been treated with SIT include preparing for an athletic race or public speaking. Examples of chronic stressors that have been treated with SIT include medical illness (asthma, chronic pain), occupational stress (police work, combat) and stressful events (coping with divorce or rape).

Deals with causes, not symptoms: now and in the future

This method of stress management offers a two-pronged attack: skills to cope with current problems, and also skills and confidence to cope with future problems. The focus on skills acquisition provides long-lasting effectiveness. Skills are taught, practised and followed through. They are also dealt with on a cognitive and behavioural level, and tailored to the needs of the individual.

Weaknesses

Time-consuming and requires high motivation

The training programme requires a lot of time and effort, motivation and money. Its strengths are also its weaknesses – it is effective because it involves learning and practising many new skills, but this complexity makes it a lengthy therapy which would suit only a limited range of determined individuals.

Unnecessarily complex

It may be that the effectiveness of SIT is due to certain elements of the training, not all of it. This means that the range of activities (and time) could be reduced without losing much of the effectiveness. For example, it might be equally effective just to learn to talk more positively and relax more.

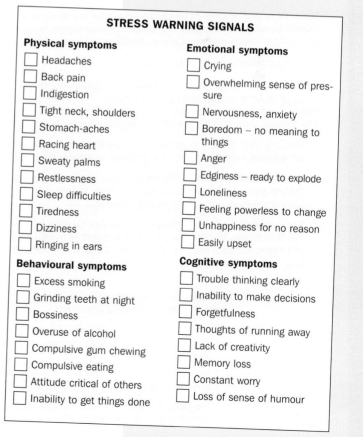

STRESS WARNING SIGNALS

Physical symptoms
- [ ] Headaches
- [ ] Back pain
- [ ] Indigestion
- [ ] Tight neck, shoulders
- [ ] Stomach-aches
- [ ] Racing heart
- [ ] Sweaty palms
- [ ] Restlessness
- [ ] Sleep difficulties
- [ ] Tiredness
- [ ] Dizziness
- [ ] Ringing in ears

Behavioural symptoms
- [ ] Excess smoking
- [ ] Grinding teeth at night
- [ ] Bossiness
- [ ] Overuse of alcohol
- [ ] Compulsive gum chewing
- [ ] Compulsive eating
- [ ] Attitude critical of others
- [ ] Inability to get things done

Emotional symptoms
- [ ] Crying
- [ ] Overwhelming sense of pressure
- [ ] Nervousness, anxiety
- [ ] Boredom – no meaning to things
- [ ] Anger
- [ ] Edginess – ready to explode
- [ ] Loneliness
- [ ] Feeling powerless to change
- [ ] Unhappiness for no reason
- [ ] Easily upset

Cognitive symptoms
- [ ] Trouble thinking clearly
- [ ] Inability to make decisions
- [ ] Forgetfulness
- [ ] Thoughts of running away
- [ ] Lack of creativity
- [ ] Memory loss
- [ ] Constant worry
- [ ] Loss of sense of humour

Source: http://www.suu.edu/ss/wellness/trauma.html

Psychological methods of stress management (continued)

W e now look at a second psychological method of stress management and consider how it is similar to, and different from, the use of stress inoculation training.

Most stress management courses actually draw on a variety of different techniques, from different programmes.

Psychological approach 2: Hardiness training

In Section 2 on sources of stress we considered the role of personality in modifying the effects of stress (pages 102–3). Suzanne Kobasa identified a personality type that was especially resistant to stress – the hardy personality. Kobasa argued that this concept could be turned into a stress management technique. If some people were naturally resistant to stress (because they were hardy), perhaps it would be possible to teach others how to become 'hardier', and thus manage stress better.

What is a hardy personality?

Hardy individuals demonstrate three characteristics – the three Cs:

- **Control** – Hardy people see themselves as being in control of their lives. They attribute control to themselves rather than to external factors that are beyond their control.

- **Commitment** – Hardy people are involved with the world around them, and have a strong sense of purpose. They do not stand aside and watch.

- **Challenge** – Hardy people see life changes as challenges to be overcome rather than as threats or stressors. They enjoy change as an opportunity for development.

The point is that all three of these characteristics will result in a reduced physiological arousal to potential stressors. The reduced arousal means lower blood pressure and so on, and this means that there is less likelihood of stress-related illnesses.

How can hardiness be taught?

Salvator Maddi, who worked with Kobasa, founded the Hardiness Institute in California (http://www.hardinessinstitute.com/default.htm). The aim of the training programme is to increase self-confidence and sense of control so that individuals can deal more successfully with change. Both Maddi and Kobasa suggested the followed ways to train hardiness:

- *Focusing*. The client is taught how to recognise signs of stress, such as muscle tension and increased heart rate, and also to identify the sources of this stress.

- *Reliving stress encounters*. The client relives stress encounters and is helped to analyse his or her stress situations. This helps the client to an understanding of *current* stressors and *current* coping strategies.

- *Self-improvement*. The insights gained can now be used to move forwards and learn new techniques. In particular the client is taught to focus on seeing stressors as challenges and thus learn to take control. Control, commitment and challenge are the basis of hardiness training.

Similarities and differences between SIT and the hardiness approach

- Both treat the problem rather than the symptoms.
- Both are concerned with skills acquisition, to provide lasting and varied strategies to cope with stress.
- Both teach clients to view stress as a problem-to-be-solved.
- Both require lengthy training and highly motivated clients.
- The success of stress inoculation may be mainly due to positive thinking, whereas the success of hardiness training may be due to increased control.

Strengths

Effectiveness

Maddi et al. (1998) assessed the progress of 54 managers in a hardiness training programme, comparing this with a relaxation/meditation condition and a placebo/social support control. The hardiness training condition was more effective than the other two conditions in increasing self-reported hardiness, job satisfaction and social support while decreasing self-reported strain and illness severity.

Deals with the problem rather than the symptoms

Hardiness training, like stress inoculation training, teaches individuals to manage all stressors in their lives, not just a particular set of symptoms related to a particular problem. This makes it a much more adaptable and effective therapy than using drugs. Skills acquisition leads to longer-term effectiveness.

Weaknesses

Limited to business executives

The research conducted by Kobasa and Maddi largely concerns white middle-class business men and women. It may not be reasonable to generalise these findings to other sections of the population. Control and challenge may be successful coping strategies for this target group, but not for all adults. We have seen elsewhere (page 101) that for some individuals high control is stress-inducing.

Does hardiness exist?

It is possible that hardiness is no more than being in control, and commitment and challenge matter less. Funk (1992) argues that low hardiness is the same as being negative, and it is negativity rather than lack of hardiness that leads to the ill effects of stress.

HOW HARDY ARE YOU?

Below are 12 items similar to those that appear in the hardiness questionnaire devised by Kobasa. Write down how much you agree or disagree with the following statements, using the following scale, and write in the number of your answer (0, 1, 2 or 3) beside the letter of each question on the score sheet.

0 = strongly disagree   1 = mildly disagree
2 = mildly agree   3 = strongly agree

☐ **A** Trying my best at work makes a difference.

☐ **B** Trusting to fate is sometimes all I can do in a relationship.

☐ **C** I often wake up eager to start on the day's projects.

☐ **D** Thinking of myself as a free person leads to great frustration and difficulty.

☐ **E** I would be willing to sacrifice financial security in my work if something really challenging came along.

☐ **F** It bothers me when I have to deviate from the routine or schedule I've set for myself.

☐ **G** An average citizen can have an impact on politics.

☐ **H** Without the right breaks, it is hard to be successful in my field.

☐ **I** I know why I am doing what I'm doing at work (school or office).

☐ **J** Getting close to people means I'm then obligated to them.

☐ **K** Encountering new situations is an important priority in my life.

☐ **L** I really don't mind when I have nothing to do.

TO SCORE YOURSELF: For half the questions, a high score (like 3) indicates hardiness; for the other half, a low score (like 0) does.

To get your score on 'control', add your answers to questions A and G; add your answers to B and H; and then subtract the second number from the first. $[(A+G) - (B+H)]$

To get your score on 'commitment', add your answers to questions C and I; add your answers to D and J; and then subtract the second number from the first. $[(C+I) - (D+J)]$

To get your score on 'challenge', add your answers to questions E and K; add your answers to F and L; and then subtract the second number from the first. $[(E+K) - (F+L)]$

Add your scores on commitment, control and challenge together to get a score for total hardiness. The highest possible score is 18.

What did you score?

Cara (who thought she was in control and quite hardy) scored 0, 3 and 1 for a total of 4.

Mike (who thought he was well hardy) scored 3, 2 and 0 for a total of 5.

Source: Adapted from http://www.suu.edu/ss/wellness/trauma.html

Research on the hardy personality

Kobasa (1979b) studied a group of about 800 American business executives (males and females), assessing stress using Holmes and Rahe's Social Readjustment Rating Scale (SRRS). Approximately 150 were classed as high-stress. Of these participants, some had a low illness record whereas others had a high illness record. This suggests that something else may modify the effects of stress because individuals experiencing the same stress levels had *different* illness records. Kobasa proposed that some individuals had a hardy personality type and this enabled them to be more resilient. She assessed various characteristics of the high-stress group, looking at control, commitment and challenge. The individuals in the high-stress/low-illness group scored high on all three personality variables (characteristic of the hardy personality), whereas the high-stress/high-illness group scored lower on these variables.

Wiebe (1991) assessed male and female undergraduates for hardiness and then gave them a task to do under stressful conditions. The hardy individuals displayed greater tolerance, reported that they found the task less threatening, and the men showed less increase in heart rate during the task.

Maddi (1999) found that hardy individuals had lower blood pressure (direct measure) and reported less stress (indirect measure) than individuals who measured low in hardiness.

COMMENTARY CORNER

So far we have represented physiological and psychological techniques as being two sides of the same coin – aspects of stress management that operate in quite different ways. In this Commentary Corner we summarise some of the main ways in which these techniques differ. It is important to be able to articulate these differences because, in an examination, you may well be asked to contrast physiological and psychological approaches to stress management. The points below are just to get you started. You might also like to consider how these approaches differ in terms of their strengths and weaknesses, and indeed how they are sometimes similar in their approach or their effect on the stressed individual.

- Physiological approaches tend to be based more on emotion-focused coping (i.e. focused more on the anxiety that accompanies stressful situations than the situation itself). Psychological approaches tend to be based more on problem-focused coping, helping the person find ways of minimising the impact of stressful situations, or increasing resistance to their negative effects. However, biofeedback does provide the patient with a means of dealing with stress (the problem) by applying relaxation techniques, making this a potentially long-lasting means of dealing with stress.

- Psychological techniques such as stress inoculation and hardiness training require lengthy teaching and highly motivated clients, whereas the most commonly used physiological treatment, drug therapy, requires little or no effort or training on the part of the client.

- The use of drug therapies as a means of stress management has important ethical considerations, particularly as anxiety-reducing drugs (anxiolytics) are prescribed by health professionals rather than by the individual themselves. Psychological therapies such as stress inoculation and hardiness training increase an individual's level of control over his or her own life, rather than leaving the initiative for stress management to others.

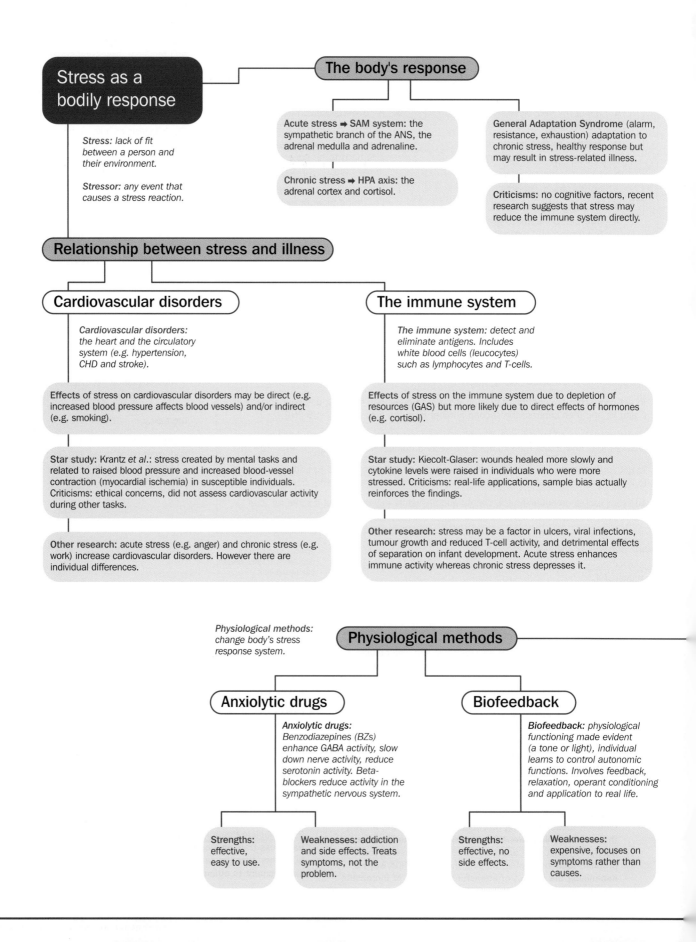

Stress as a bodily response

Stress: lack of fit between a person and their environment.

Stressor: any event that causes a stress reaction.

The body's response

Acute stress ➡ SAM system: the sympathetic branch of the ANS, the adrenal medulla and adrenaline.

Chronic stress ➡ HPA axis: the adrenal cortex and cortisol.

General Adaptation Syndrome (alarm, resistance, exhaustion) adaptation to chronic stress, healthy response but may result in stress-related illness.

Criticisms: no cognitive factors, recent research suggests that stress may reduce the immune system directly.

Relationship between stress and illness

Cardiovascular disorders

Cardiovascular disorders: the heart and the circulatory system (e.g. hypertension, CHD and stroke).

Effects of stress on cardiovascular disorders may be direct (e.g. increased blood pressure affects blood vessels) and/or indirect (e.g. smoking).

Star study: Krantz *et al.*: stress created by mental tasks and related to raised blood pressure and increased blood-vessel contraction (myocardial ischemia) in susceptible individuals. Criticisms: ethical concerns, did not assess cardiovascular activity during other tasks.

Other research: acute stress (e.g. anger) and chronic stress (e.g. work) increase cardiovascular disorders. However there are individual differences.

The immune system

The immune system: detect and eliminate antigens. Includes white blood cells (leucocytes) such as lymphocytes and T-cells.

Effects of stress on the immune system due to depletion of resources (GAS) but more likely due to direct effects of hormones (e.g. cortisol).

Star study: Kiecolt-Glaser: wounds healed more slowly and cytokine levels were raised in individuals who were more stressed. Criticisms: real-life applications, sample bias actually reinforces the findings.

Other research: stress may be a factor in ulcers, viral infections, tumour growth and reduced T-cell activity, and detrimental effects of separation on infant development. Acute stress enhances immune activity whereas chronic stress depresses it.

Physiological methods: change body's stress response system.

Physiological methods

Anxiolytic drugs

Anxiolytic drugs: Benzodiazepines (BZs) enhance GABA activity, slow down nerve activity, reduce serotonin activity. Beta-blockers reduce activity in the sympathetic nervous system.

Strengths: effective, easy to use.

Weaknesses: addiction and side effects. Treats symptoms, not the problem.

Biofeedback

Biofeedback: physiological functioning made evident (a tone or light), individual learns to control autonomic functions. Involves feedback, relaxation, operant conditioning and application to real life.

Strengths: effective, no side effects.

Weaknesses: expensive, focuses on symptoms rather than causes.

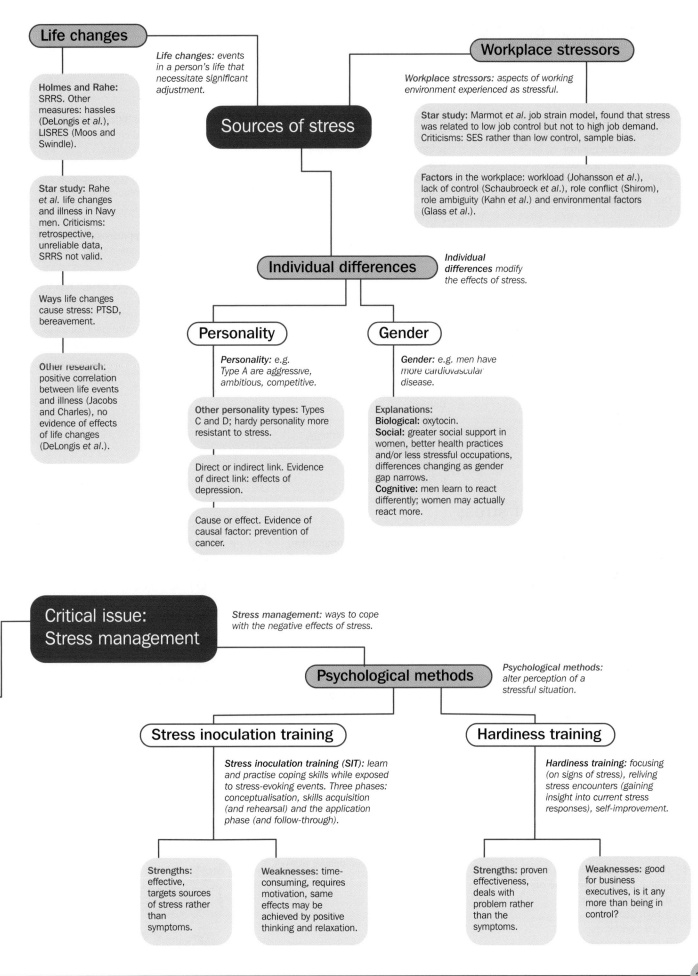

Life changes

Holmes and Rahe: SRRS. Other measures: hassles (DeLongis et al.), LISRES (Moos and Swindle).

Star study: Rahe et al. life changes and illness in Navy men. Criticisms: retrospective, unreliable data, SRRS not valid.

Ways life changes cause stress: PTSD, bereavement.

Other research: positive correlation between life events and illness (Jacobs and Charles), no evidence of effects of life changes (DeLongis et al.).

Life changes: events in a person's life that necessitate significant adjustment.

Sources of stress

Workplace stressors

Workplace stressors: aspects of working environment experienced as stressful.

Star study: Marmot et al. job strain model, found that stress was related to low job control but not to high job demand. Criticisms: SES rather than low control, sample bias.

Factors in the workplace: workload (Johansson et al.), lack of control (Schaubroeck et al.), role conflict (Shirom), role ambiguity (Kahn et al.) and environmental factors (Glass et al.).

Individual differences

Individual differences modify the effects of stress.

Personality

Personality: e.g. Type A are aggressive, ambitious, competitive.

Other personality types: Types C and D; hardy personality more resistant to stress.

Direct or indirect link. Evidence of direct link: effects of depression.

Cause or effect. Evidence of causal factor: prevention of cancer.

Gender

Gender: e.g. men have more cardiovascular disease.

Explanations:
Biological: oxytocin.
Social: greater social support in women, better health practices and/or less stressful occupations, differences changing as gender gap narrows.
Cognitive: men learn to react differently; women may actually react more.

Critical issue: Stress management

Stress management: ways to cope with the negative effects of stress.

Psychological methods

Psychological methods: alter perception of a stressful situation.

Stress inoculation training

Stress inoculation training (SIT): learn and practise coping skills while exposed to stress-evoking events. Three phases: conceptualisation, skills acquisition (and rehearsal) and the application phase (and follow-through).

Strengths: effective, targets sources of stress rather than symptoms.

Weaknesses: time-consuming, requires motivation, same effects may be achieved by positive thinking and relaxation.

Hardiness training

Hardiness training: focusing (on signs of stress), reliving stress encounters (gaining insight into current stress responses), self-improvement.

Strengths: proven effectiveness, deals with problem rather than the symptoms.

Weaknesses: good for business executives, is it any more than being in control?

MULTIPLE-CHOICE QUESTIONS

Section 1 Stress as a bodily response

1 Chronic stress is associated with the
   a SAM system and adrenaline
   b HPA axis and cortisol
   c SAM system and cortisol
   d HPA axis and adrenaline

2 The effect of the hormone adrenaline is to
   a Make you sleepy
   b Wake you up
   c Arouse the body
   d Make you hungry

3 The three stages of the GAS model are
   a Alarm, resistance, exhaustion
   b Alarm, resistance, recovery
   c Alarm, adaptation, exhaustion
   d Alarm, adaptation, recovery

4 'Cardiovascular' refers to the
   a Heart
   b The blood vessels
   c The heart and circulatory system
   d The heart and the brain

5 Stress may cause cardiovascular disorders because
   a Stress increases heart rate
   b Stress increases blood pressure
   c Stress raises levels of glucose
   d All of the above

6 Myocardial ischemia is
   a A Japanese name for heart disease
   b A condition that affects the muscles around the heart
   c Reduced blood supply
   d All of the above

7 Which of the following is *not* a part of the immune system:
   a Killer T-cell
   b Antibody
   c Lymphocyte
   d Red blood cell

8 Cortisol
   a Maintains a steady supply of blood sugar for continued energy
   b Reduces the body's immune response
   c Both (a) and (b)
   d Neither (a) nor (b)

9 Stress may have different effects:
   a Both acute and chronic stress depress the immune response
   b Both acute and chronic stress enhance the immune response
   c Acute stress enhances the immune response whereas chronic stress depresses it
   d Acute stress depresses the immune response whereas chronic stress enhances it

10 Matched participants design has the advantage of
   a Controlling for order effects
   b Controlling for participant variables
   c Reducing the number of participants needed compared to repeated measures design
   d All of the above

Section 2 Sources of stress

1 Positive life changes are stressful because
   a They are more significant
   b Some people prefer to be miserable
   c All change involves psychic energy
   d None of the above

2 Which of the following is *not* an example of a life event from the SRRS:
   a Christmas
   b Addition of new member to the family
   c Bad weather
   d Sex difficulties

3 The social readjustment rating scale by Holmes and Rahe has been criticised because:
   a The life changes were all negative
   b The scale did not take into account the personal significance of the changes
   c It was difficult to understand the scale
   d There were too many life changes

4 The workplace has been found to be a source of stress because of
   a Environmental factors
   b High demand
   c Low control
   d All of the above

5 Individuals who are competitive, aggressive, ambitious and in a hurry have been classified as
   a Type A
   b Type B
   c Type C
   d Type P

6 Personality may modify the effects of stress because
   a Personality directly affects physiological responses
   b Personality indirectly affects physiological responses
   c Both of the above
   d Neither of the above

7 The action of oxytocin may cause women to
   a Drink more and so become less stressed
   b Become more aggressive
   c Seek the support of others
   d Become more competitive at work

8 It is proposed that men may have higher rates of cardiovascular disease than women because
   a Of male hormones
   b They learn to react differently to stress
   c They have unhealthy habits that lead to illness, such as smoking and drinking
   d All of the above

9 A correlation coefficient is
   a A number
   b A research method
   c A graph
   d None of the above

10 Closed questions have the advantage of being
   a Harder to analyse
   b Harder to answer
   c Both of the above
   d Neither of the above

Section 3 Critical issue: Stress management

1 Why are benzodiazepines effective in reducing stress?
a They mimic the body's natural stress reliever
b They act as a placebo
c They causes people to think more clearly
d None of the above

2 What effect do beta-blockers have?
a They reduce activity in the autonomic nervous system
b They reduce activity in the sympathetic nervous system
c They reduce activity in the parasympathetic nervous system
d None of the above

3 Which of the following is a major weakness in using drugs to treat stress?
a They treat the causes and not the symptoms
b They treat the symptoms and not the causes
c It is difficult to remember to take them
d They are expensive

4 Biofeedback involves giving patients feedback about
a How they are coping
b Their anxiety levels
c Activity in their autonomic nervous system
d Levels of stress hormones

5 The success of biofeedback may be due to
a Operant conditioning
b Relaxation
c Reduced activity in the sympathetic nervous system
d All of the above

6 SIT stands for
a Stress injection treatment
b Stress inoculation therapy
c Stress inoculation training
d Sunday idleness therapy

7 The essence of SIT is that people
a Learn how to cope after a problem arises
b Learn how to cope before a problem arises
c Learn how to ignore stress
d Learn how to shift stress onto others

8 Hardiness training involves three Cs. These are:
a Challenge, commitment, concern
b Commitment, concern, control
c Control, commitment, challenge
d Control, consciousness, challenge

9 Hardiness training involves
a Focusing on stress symptoms and gaining insights into one's own methods of dealing with stress
b Focusing on ways of dealing with stress and gaining insights into new ways to deal with stress
c Focusing on techniques to deal with stress and gaining insights into what works
d Focusing on a training programme and gaining insights

10 Which of the following method of sampling produces the least biased sample?
a Random sample
b Opportunity sample
c Both random and opportunity sample
d Volunteer sample

Section 1 answers
1b 2c 3a 4c 5d
6b 7d 8c 9c 10d

Section 2 answers
1c 2c 3b 4d 5a
6c 7c 8d 9a 10d

Section 3 answers
1a 2b 3b 4c 5d
6c 7b 8a 9a 10a

RESEARCH METHODS
terms covered

- Alternative hypothesis
- Closed questions
- Correlation coefficient
- Directional hypothesis
- Experimental hypothesis

- Forced-choice questions
- Interview
- Interviewer bias
- Leading questions
- Likert scale
- Matched participants design

- Negative correlation
- Non-directional hypothesis
- Open questions
- Opportunity sample
- Pilot study
- Population

- Positive correlation
- Qualitative data
- Quantitative data
- Quasi-random sample
- Questionnaires

- Random sample
- Sample
- Sample bias
- Sampling
- Significant
- Social desirability bias

- Structured interview
- Systematic sample
- Unstructured interview
- Volunteer bias
- Volunteer sample

Revision list

Key terms

You may be asked to 'Explain what is meant by' any of the following. Each explanation may be for 2 or 3 marks (and very rarely 6 marks). Make sure that what you write is related to the number of marks. Use examples to amplify your explanations where appropriate.

✓

- [ ] Cardiovascular disorder   p. 90
- [ ] General Adaptation Syndrome   p. 89
- [ ] Immune system   p. 92
- [ ] Life changes   p. 96
- [ ] Physiological approaches to stress management   p. 108
- [ ] Psychological approaches to stress management   p. 108
- [ ] Stress   p. 88
- [ ] Stress management   p. 108
- [ ] Stressor   p. 89
- [ ] Workplace stressors   p. 100

Star studies

This is the 'apfcc' question. You need three minutes' worth of writing on aims, procedures, findings and conclusions for each of these. You may also be asked for one or two criticisms of these studies. Criticisms can be positive or negative.

✓

- [ ] The relationship between stress and cardiovascular disorders (Krantz et al., 1991)   pp. 90–1
- [ ] The relationship between stress and the immune system (Kiecolt-Glaser et al., 1995)   pp. 92–3
- [ ] Life changes as a source of stress (Rahe et al., 1970)   pp. 96–7
- [ ] Workplace stressors (Marmot et al., 1997)   p. 100

Research

You need to be able to outline the *findings* and *conclusions* of research (theories and/or studies) into the following:

✓

- [ ] The relationship between stress and cardiovascular disorders   p. 91
- [ ] The relationship between stress and the immune system   p. 93
- [ ] Life changes as a source of stress   p. 98
- [ ] Workplace stressors   p. 101
- [ ] The role of personality in modifying the effects of stressors   pp. 102–3
- [ ] The role of gender in modifying the effects of stressors   p. 104
- [ ] Biofeedback   pp. 110–11
- [ ] SIT   pp. 112–13
- [ ] The hardy personality   pp. 114–15

Effects

You should be able to write about several effects of the following:

✓

- [ ] Stress on cardiovascular disorders   p. 90
- [ ] Stress on the immune system   p. 92

Factors that influence

You should be able to write about at least two factors of the following:

✓

- [ ] Factors in the workplace that act as stressors   p. 101

Ways that...

You should be able to write about several ways that ...

✓

- [ ] Life changes cause stress   p. 98
- [ ] Personality may modify the effects of stressors   pp. 102–3
- [ ] Gender may modify the effects of stressors   p. 104

Theories/explanations

You may be asked to describe or outline a theory/explanation for 6 marks. You are also likely to be asked an AO2 question about theories/explanations and to discuss their strengths and limitations. When discussing a theory, it is useful to refer to other research (theories and/or studies) as a means of evaluation.

✓

- [ ] The body's response to stressors   p. 88–9
- [ ] The General Adaptation Syndrome (GAS)   p. 89
- [ ] How gender modifies the effects of stressors   p. 104–5
- [ ] Two physiological methods of stress management   pp. 108–9
- [ ] Two psychological methods of stress management   pp. 112–13

Sample stress question with students' answers and examiner's comments

1 (a) Outline **two** ways in which gender may modify the effects of stress. (3 marks + 3 marks)

Alison's answer: Different genders appear to react differently to stressful situations. Women have been found to show a much smaller increase in blood pressure during stressful situations. This might be due to physiological differences between the sexes, or it may indicate that men and women differ in their attitude to stressful situations. Men have been shown to be more competitive and are therefore more aroused (and stressed) by competitive situations.

It is also possible that gender differences in reactions to stress are the product of evolutionary differences between the sexes. Females show the 'tend and befriend' response in times of stress. This might be caused by the action of a hormone oxytocin, which is released at times of stress and makes us calmer and more social. It has been shown that women have higher levels of oxytocin.

Nigel's answer: Men have more of a stress response. Some psychologists think this is because their autonomic nervous system operates differently to women's. Women's autonomic nervous system doesn't produce such a big response and it doesn't last as long.

Women tend to turn to others when they are stressed. Men drink.

Examiner's comments: Alison has provided two clear and well-detailed accounts of possible gender differences. Note that both of these are speculative to a degree. This is okay, because the question does say 'ways in which gender *may* modify'. The first of these ways is a *physiological* difference, and the second a difference that has developed through evolution. These are fairly broad explanations, but can be counted as two for the purposes of this question. Both answers are accurate, making full use of the time available for this type of question, and would be worth **3 + 3 marks**.

Nigel's first outline of a gender difference is recognisable as a description of the increased reactivity of the ANS in males. Whether this is true or not is not the point, it is a possibility that Nigel has identified here. The description is somewhat clumsy and vague, but the essence is here. The second way is less clear, but there is a sense of familiarity about it in that Nigel is *identifying* a gender difference, but no more. As the first way is limited and not particularly detailed (although generally accurate), it would be worth **2 marks**. The second way is not as clear although has *some* relevant psychology, so is worth **1 mark**.

1 (b) Describe **one** strength and **one** weakness of one approach to stress management. (6 marks)

Alison's answer: A strength of drugs as a form of stress management is that they are cheap and they work quickly.

A weakness of drugs is that they don't do anything about the underlying cause of the stress, because that is still going to stress the person if they stop taking the drugs.

Nigel's answer: Relaxation is a valuable form of stress management because it is so easy to practise it, even in unusual circumstances such as a traffic jam. This means that the person is able to use it wherever and whenever they feel the need, without having to worry about the presence of other people or equipment.

Relaxation techniques may reduce the levels of the stress response but their action is non-specific. For effective long-term stress reduction, a more focused intervention on the source of the stress is needed.

Examiner's comment: If we discount Alison's claim that drugs are cheap (compared to what? – certainly not compared to relaxation), we can accept the claim that they work quickly. This *is* a strength of using drugs (such as BZs), but the description is very basic and lacking in detail. The weakness is better, although more elaboration would be needed for the full 3 marks. Alison would receive **1 mark** for the strength and **2 marks** for the weakness.

In Nigel's answer to this question, both the strength and the weakness of relaxation as a method of stress management are described in sufficient detail and with sufficient clarity and accuracy. It is difficult sometimes to know how to elaborate quite simple principles, but Nigel has achieved that admirably with this answer. Description of both the strength and weakness asked for is concise, yet also accurate and detailed, and so Nigel would receive **3 + 3 marks**.

1 (c) To what extent have factors in the workplace be shown to be a significant source of stress? (18 marks)

Alison's answer: Two factors known to be linked to stress in the workplace are work overload and role-related responsibility. Work overload is common in Western industrialised societies, and is a frequent cause of stress-related illnesses such as coronary heart disease and depression. Johansson *et al.*'s study of employees in a Swedish timber mill found that for those workers involved in 'finishing' the timber, stress levels were high. This is because they were responsible for the wages of the whole factory, their work was boring and repetitive, and also it was machine-paced. The effects of work overload may be influenced by other factors such as the Type A personality type. These are characterised by being under constant time pressure and always struggling to meet deadlines. However, Kobasa claims that the reason why some people do not experience stress-related illness when under excessive workload is because they are high in hardiness, and see all work-related issues as simply challenges to be overcome.

A second work-related factor is role-related responsibility. This is illustrated by Cobb and Rose's study of male air traffic controllers. These men were found to be four times more likely to be suffering from high blood pressure than other workers without such high levels of responsibility in their job. One of the problems with this study is that it only uses men. There is a lot of evidence to show that men and women act differently in stressful situations. Men show larger increases in blood pressure in stressful situations. So, sex differences may have something to do with the findings of the Cobb and Rose study. The impact of work factors on stress levels has been shown to be affected by other factors at work and in the home, particularly in terms of relationships. Research has shown that supportive relationships in the workplace have a significant beneficial effect on workers' stress levels.

continued...

Nigel's answer: Stress in the workplace is one of the main sources of illness and absenteeism. The sort of things that have been shown to cause stress in the workplace include poor supervision, too much work to do, falling out with workmates and not having enough pay for the job. Another important factor is the amount of responsibility you have. A study of workers in a timber yard found that the men who had to finish off all the jobs were much more stressed than the others. The researchers found that they stayed off work more and were ill more. Another study looked at air traffic controllers who also had a lot of responsibility at work. They had higher levels of blood pressure, which is a cardiovascular disorder.

One of the things that contributes to our feelings of stress at work is the amount of control we have. Brady's work on executive monkeys demonstrated this. It was not the monkey with the responsibility that got the ulcers, but the one that had no control. The most stressful situations for workers are also those where they have no control over what happens to them. Seligman called this learned helplessness where someone is so frustrated that they have no control over things that happen to them that they just give up the ghost.

Examiner's comments: Alison has provided a decent response to this question. Two relevant 'factors' form the central 'core' of the answer, but she does more than simply describe research on their impact. She takes issue with each and shows how each may be mediated by other factors. Excessive workloads can be stressful, but the hardy personality type copes better than most. This is a good point to make and shows evidence of Alison's ability to *engage* with the material in an effective way. The second factor is also similarly treated. First the research supporting the assertion, and then a critical look at the mediating factors, in this case gender and supervisory relationships. These are not just conjured up for a few extra words, but are cleverly tied into the argument. The point about blood pressure and gender differences is a nice touch. This is *informed* commentary with perhaps *slightly* limited analysis of the content chosen. The material has been used *effectively* but perhaps a little more could have been made of it at times. The answer would receive **6 marks** for the AO1 component, and **10 marks** for the AO2 component, a total of **16 marks**.

Nigel has produced a pretty general response that is mostly descriptive content only. The only point of evaluation is the statement that 'Brady's work on executive monkeys demonstrated this' in the second paragraph. He seems at a loss to know what to do with this material to develop an AO2 response. The material here could form the basis of a decent answer, but Nigel has given insufficient thought to how he might use it to construct an evaluative argument that answers the question set. The second paragraph contains a lot of studies and concepts, but these are treated far too superficially, and the examiner would be left to work out any possible relevance for him/herself. This would receive **4 marks** for the AO1 component (this is generally accurate but not as detailed as it might have been), and just **2 marks** for the AO2 component (this is just discernible in his answer), a total of **6 marks**.

Total marks: Alison 25/30 (undoubtedly a Grade A) and
Nigel 15/30 (approximately equivalent to a Grade B).

Research methods question with students' answers and examiner's comments

A group of students decide to conduct a study to see if stress is positively correlated with illness. In order to do this, they decide to construct a questionnaire that includes questions about stress experiences and also about recent episodes of ill health. After writing a first draft of the questionnaire, the students conduct a pilot study.

The final version of the questionnaire is given to 20 participants (respondents). The data from the questionnaire produce two scores for each participant: a stress score and a health score (based on the number of days they had been free of illness in the previous 3 months). The data from all 20 participants are shown in the scattergraph. The correlation coefficient is −0.56.

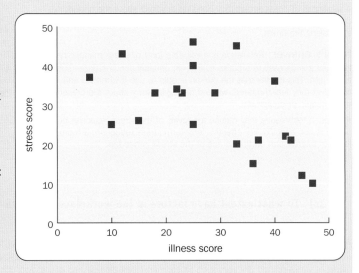

(a) Outline the research aims for this study. (2 marks)

Alison's answer: To see if stress affects illness.

Nigel's answer: The aim of this study is to see if there is a relationship between stress and illness.

Examiner's comments: Alison has fallen into the trap of expecting a *causal* relationship between the two, whereas the study is simply trying to see if they are correlated. This would receive **0 marks**.

Nigel's answer is accurate and detailed, and correctly representing the focus of the study. This would receive **2 marks**.

(b) Identify one of the variables in this study. (1 mark)

Alison's answer: The level of stress.

Nigel's answer: One of the variables in this study is the stress score.

Examiner's comments: Alison's answer is vague – the study was specifically using stress scores derived from previous stressful experiences rather than the current level of stress, so would receive **0 marks**.

Nigel's answer is accurate and sufficiently clear for **1 mark**.

(c) Explain the purpose of conducting a pilot study in the context of this research. (3 marks)

Alison's answer: A pilot study is useful because it gives the researcher the chance to try everything out before the proper study. If there are any problems, then they can be addressed and changes made before the proper study is carried out.

Nigel's answer: Because the questionnaire contains questions about stress and illness, the researchers would need to make sure that the questions were understood by the participants, and that they were sufficiently sensitive to get the right sort of information about how much stress the person was generally under, and how much poor health they had experienced.

Examiner's comments: Alison has given an appropriate reason why a pilot study would be used, but it is not placed in the context of this study, so would receive only **2 marks** rather than the full 3 marks.

Nigel's reason is similar to that described in Alison's answer, but he has placed it solidly in the context of this study, so would receive the full **3 marks**.

(d) Describe one advantage and one disadvantage of using a questionnaire to collect data. (2 marks + 2 marks)

Alison's answer: One advantage of using a questionnaire is that the person asking the questions can follow up a respondent's answers with more searching questions that will give more specific information.

A disadvantage is that you never know if the person is telling the truth, they may just be saying what the researcher wants to hear.

Nigel's answer: Questionnaires have the advantage of much greater anonymity, and so respondents are more likely to give truthful answers because of this.

Questionnaires may contain questions that are leading or ambiguous, meaning that the responses that people give may not be how they really feel about the subject of the questionnaire.

Examiner's comments: Alison appears to be confusing a questionnaire with an *interview*, since the advantage she gives is really applicable to an interview. This would not be an advantage of a questionnaire, so gets **0 marks**. The disadvantage is probably also aimed at an interview, but this social desirability bias is also a problem with questionnaires, so even though she has not made this explicit, the answer would be worth **1 mark**.

What is particularly effective about Nigel's answers is that he *identifies* the advantage and disadvantage, and then goes on to explain *why* this would be advantageous (or disadvantageous) when questionnaires are used as part of a study. His answers receives the full **2 + 2 marks**.

(e) Describe two issues that the students might have considered when writing good questions for this questionnaire. (2 marks + 2 marks)

Alison's answer: Two things that people should bear in mind when writing questions for a questionnaire are that they should make sure that the questions are not ambiguous (i.e. have more than one meaning). Second, they should make sure that the questions are not leading in any way (i.e. they might lead the respondent to answer in a certain way).

Nigel's answer: It is important for all questions to be clear and unambiguous. For example, it would not be appropriate in the health questionnaire to ask someone if they had felt 'down' in the previous 3 months, as this could be interpreted in different ways. It would also be important to include a number of more neutral filler questions, so that respondents would not become aware of the purpose of the questionnaire and begin to respond in a way that confirms the relationship between stress and ill health.

Examiner's comments: Alison's answer points to undoubtedly important issues in the construction of *all* questionnaires, but she has failed to make these explicitly relevant to *this* study. She has gained marks for describing the issues, but lost marks through failing to embed her answer in the specified study. She would receive **1 + 1 marks** for this answer.

Unlike Alison, Nigel has clearly embedded his answers in the context of this study. These issues are relevant and accurately described *and* they have been constructed in the context of the questionnaires used in this study. This answer would receive **2 + 2 marks**.

(f) Identify a suitable method for selecting participants and explain how you could put this into practice. (3 marks)

Alison's answer: The researchers could use a volunteer sample. In order to get their 20 participants, they could distribute a letter to all members of the college staff at their sixth form college, and ask for volunteers to participate. From those that respond to this initial letter, they could take the first 20, and ask them to complete the two questionnaires anonymously.

Nigel's answer: A random sample could be used here. The researchers could take a list of all the members of the sixth form (200 in total) and select every 10th person to get their 20 participants. To make it even more accurate, they could divide the list into boys and girls (e.g. 120 girls and 80 boys), and take every 10th girl and every 10th boy to give a total of 12 girls and 8 boys in the sample.

Examiner's comments: Alison has correctly identified an appropriate sampling method (volunteer sample), and given sufficient details about how this would be put into practice to guarantee the full **3 marks**. Note that she has avoided the use of vague terms like 20 people, and has identified the population (i.e. college staff) from which the sample will be taken. It doesn't matter here that better sampling methods might have been used: this is still appropriate.

Nigel's answer, despite its loving attention to detail, contains one major flaw. Although he has *identified* random sampling as the appropriate method of obtaining participants, the description of how this would be put into practice is clearly *not* random sampling, but a mix of stratified and systematic sampling. He would receive **1 mark** for his identification of an appropriate method, but as the expansion of this method is wrong, he would get no more marks.

(g) Give **one** disadvantage of the method you have suggested in (f) for selecting participants. (2 marks)

Alison's answer: There is a possibility that volunteers are not representative of the population.

Nigel's answer: A disadvantage of random sampling is that with small sample sizes it is difficult to be confident that the sample is unbiased. As the size of the sample grows, so it is more likely to reflect the population from which is was taken.

Examiner's comments: What Alison says is true, but she needs to add a little more detail to demonstrate in what way they may be unrepresentative, or how this might impact on the interpretation of findings. This is worth **1 mark**.

Nigel has given an accurate and detailed account of a major problem with random sampling, worth **2 marks**. Note that because Nigel identified *random* sampling in part (f), his disadvantage had to be specific to that.

(h) Using the information from the scattergraph above, describe the relationship between stress and illness. (2 marks)

Alison's answer: There is a weak negative correlation between stress and illness.

Nigel's answer: This is a moderate negative correlation showing that as stress scores increase, so health scores decrease.

Examiner's comments: There *is* a negative correlation between the two variables, but this is more moderate than weak, so Alison gets only **1 mark**.

Nigel has accurately interpreted this as a *moderate negative* correlation, and has expanded that interpretation in terms of the two variables being investigated. This is worth **2 marks**.

(i) Explain whether or not these findings support the original aims of the study. (2 marks)

Alison's answer: The findings do not support the aim of the study. That was to see if stress and illness were positively correlated, but this study has shown a negative correlation between the two.

Nigel's answer: Although the scattergraph shows a negative correlation, this does support the original aim of the study, as it shows that illness (measured in terms of low health scores) is positively related to stress.

Examiner's comments: Alison has been misled by the scattergraph and the researchers' operationalisation of 'illness' in terms of low overall health scores. This answer would receive **0 marks**.

Although Nigel's answer is still a little unclear, what *is* certain is that he has understood that illness is represented by low health scores, and that the study has confirmed the original belief.
This would receive **2 marks**.

(j) The students decide to conduct some further research on stress. Suggest a set of aims and some suitable procedures for a further possible study. (6 marks)

Alison's answer: A study could be carried out to see if people become stressed when they are watching a scary movie. The aim of this study would be to investigate whether frightening movie scenes cause a physiological stress reaction (i.e. an increase in heart rate) in the person watching.

A random sample of students could be shown a scary movie (such as *Nightmare on Elm Street*) and their heart rate could be taken at regular intervals during the film so see if it goes up during the scary parts.

Nigel's answer: The aim of this study is to see if there are gender differences in students' responses to stressful situations.

Ten male students could be matched with ten female students of similar age, educational level and resting heart rate. Each participant could then be asked to prepare a 5-minute presentation to the rest of the class. For the purposes of monitoring heart rate and blood pressure, each participant could be wired up to a blood pressure monitor. This could be set to record heart rate and blood pressure each minute in the 5 minutes leading up to the presentation, during the presentation, and in the 5 minutes after the presentation. These readings could then be used to compare the stress reactions of the male and female participants.

Examiner's comments: Alison has designed an appropriate study and has made a brave attempt to elaborate her aims beyond the initial statement. Her procedures, however, are sadly lacking in appropriate detail. We are not given any information about, for example, the number or age of students, how the heart rate was to be taken (hands on the throat?), or even how the researchers would decide what was 'scary' in the film. This answer would be worth **3 marks**.

Although there is no need for the aims and procedures to be evenly balanced, Nigel might have written a little more for the aims. For example, the study would presumably be looking at *physiological* reactions to stress rather than psychological reactions, but this is not stated here. There are other things that might have been included in the procedures (e.g. sampling procedures, control of other variables), but what *is* here is accurate and detailed, so overall the answer would receive **5 marks**.

> **Total marks: Alison 13/30 (approximately equivalent to a Grade C) and Nigel 26/30 (a resounding Grade A).**

Stress question to try

1 **(a)** Outline **two** ways in which the body responds to stressors. (3 marks + 3 marks)

(b) Outline the findings of research on the role of gender in modifying the effects of stressors. (6 marks)

(c) Outline and evaluate the physiological approach to stress management. (18 marks)

Individual differences are those aspects of each of us that distinguish us from others, such as personality and intelligence. Each of us also differs in the extent to which we are 'normal'. For the most part, deviation from normal is not a problem, but in some circumstances it is – but how do we know when abnormality is unacceptable?

Individual differences

Abnormality

Section 1

Defining psychological abnormality

Section 2

Biological and psychological models of abnormality

Section 3

Critical issue: Eating disorders

End of module review

Defining psychological abnormality

> ❝ If sanity and insanity exist, how shall we know them? ❞

This question, posed by Stanford University psychologist David Rosenhan, signalled the beginning of one of the most audacious pieces of psychological research ever carried out (described on the far right). Rosenhan believed that although we may be convinced that we can tell the normal from the abnormal, the evidence for this ability is not quite as compelling. There are several conflicting views about what constitutes 'normal' and 'abnormal' behaviour. The situation is made even more confusing by the fact that what is considered normal in one culture may be seen as quite aberrant in another (Rosenhan, 1973).

Defining behaviour as 'abnormal' (and therefore requiring treatment) presupposes that we have a clear idea of what we mean when we refer to abnormal behaviour. After all, diagnosing a physical illness, such as chickenpox or measles, is fairly straightforward, so why can't we diagnose a mental 'illness' with equal certainty? The problem appears to be that the very

specification breakdown

Specification content	Comment
Definitions of abnormality: statistical infrequency, deviation from social norms, failure to function adequately, and deviation from ideal mental health.	You are required to study definitions of abnormality. Four definitions are named.
Limitations associated with these definitions psychological abnormality (including cultural relativism).	This subsection requires you to be able to define and criticise (i.e. offer **strengths** and **limitations** for) the four definitions listed here. Note that the problem of **cultural relativism** (the view that the cultural context of a behaviour must be taken into account before judging its abnormality) is given as an example of a limitation, although it is not the only limitation relevant here.

As touch, taste, sight, smell and hearing boarded the chartered flight to Havana, Professor Fitzherbert knew in his heart that he had lost more than good friends. In fact, he had finally lost his senses.

definitions of abnormality itself are considerably less real than we generally believe them to be. Many lay definitions of abnormality would focus on the fact that abnormal behaviours are somehow deviant or odd. Yet murder is deviant but not generally regarded as a mental disorder, and musical genius is odd but likewise would not be seen as requiring treatment.

Rosenhan had a plan for testing whether diagnosis of abnormal behaviour could be made as easily as was generally believed. He would send sane people to psychiatric hospitals to see if they would be unmasked as normal by health professionals unaware of their actual mental health status. If they were discovered to be sane, Rosenhan reasoned, this would mean that normality (and presumably abnormality) could be accurately diagnosed, regardless of the context in which the diagnosis is made. This would confirm that normality (and therefore also abnormality) was something that resided in the person and was independent of the context in which it was being assessed. If, however, they were not discovered, this would suggest that psychiatric diagnosis of 'abnormality' has less to do with the individual, and more to do with the (insane) environment in which he or she is found.

Schizophrenia

A group of psychotic disorders characterised by major disturbances in thought, emotion and behaviour; disordered thinking in which ideas are not logically related; faulty perception and attention; bizarre disturbances in motor activity; flat or inappropriate emotions; and reduced tolerance for stress in interpersonal relations. The patient withdraws from people and reality, often into a fantasy life of delusions and hallucinations. (Davison and Neale, 2001).

ON BEING SANE IN INSANE PLACES

Eight 'pseudopatients' (i.e. normal people pretending to be real psychiatric patients) gained secret admission to 12 different hospitals. They were a varied group consisting of a psychology graduate in his 20s, three psychologists, one psychiatrist, a paediatrician, a painter and a housewife. The thing they all had in common was that they were completely psychologically healthy.

These pseudopatients sought admission into a variety of different hospitals presenting one single symptom. They arrived at the admissions department complaining that they were hearing voices, which appeared to be saying 'empty', 'hollow' and 'thud'. Apart from these voices, no other symptoms or evidence of pathological behaviour was presented. Indeed, everything else about the pseudopatient (background, life history and general behaviour) suggested complete normality. Upon admission, each of the pseudopatients behaved on the ward as they would do normally. When asked by staff how they were feeling, they said they felt fine and no longer experienced any symptoms. When they were admitted, the pseudopatients had no idea when they might be released. They were told by staff that this would be 'when they had convinced staff they were sane'. As a result of this, they were motivated to behave sanely and to cooperate fully towards the goal of release.

Despite this public show of sanity, none of the pseudopatients were ever detected for what they really were (impostors). With one exception, they were admitted with a diagnosis of schizophrenia, a serious mental disorder. Upon discharge, they were diagnosed as having schizophrenia in remission (the symptoms were no longer evident but it seemed likely that the disease still lurked nearby). This research shows the profound impact of an 'abnormal' diagnosis. Once labelled as abnormal (in this case as a schizophrenic), individuals are stuck with the label and there is nothing they can do to remove the tag. This in turn profoundly colours others' perceptions of them and their behaviour. In a real-life situation, a patient may eventually accept the diagnosis and behave accordingly.

What is meant by abnormality?

One of the most difficult tasks for those working within the field of abnormal psychology is to *define* abnormality. Definitions of what constitutes abnormal behaviour have changed dramatically through history. Before the application of scientific thinking in this area, any behaviour that seemed outside of an individual's control was thought to be the product of supernatural forces. The way in which our ancestors dealt with abnormal behaviour (e.g. exorcism, the burning of witches, trepanning) reflected their very different beliefs about its nature and cause.

Although we have moved on in our understanding of what constitutes normal and abnormal behaviour (and therefore who requires treatment), the *definition* of abnormality itself inevitably remains a judgement. In this section, we consider some attempts to define this most elusive concept. As will become evident, no single definition is adequate on its own, although each captures some aspect of what we might expect from a true definition of the term. Consequently, abnormality is usually determined by the presence of several of the following characteristics at the same time, rather than being viewed solely in terms of just one alone.

Explanation 1: Statistical infrequency

If you love statistics like this, go to www.statistics.gov.uk.

Probably the most obvious way to define abnormality is in terms of statistical infrequency. How do we know what is 'normal'? Researchers and government agencies collect statistics to inform us. Such statistics inform us about things such as what age is most typical for women (and men) to have their first baby, the average shoe size for 10-year-old children, how many people read daily newspapers and which papers they read, and so on.

These statistics can be used to define the 'norm' for any group of people. A 'norm' is something that is usual or regular or typical. If we can define what is most common or normal, then we also have an idea of what is not common, i.e. abnormal. For example, it is not the norm to have your first baby when you are over 40 or under 20, as you can see from the graph below.

What is interesting is that if you draw a graph of most aspects of human behaviour, you get a **normal distribution** – this is illustrated by a symmetrical bell-shaped curve similar to the one shown in red on the graph. In a normal distribution, most people (the 'normals') are in the central group, clustered around the mean, and fewer people (the 'abnormals') are at either extreme.

Limitations

Is all abnormal behaviour undesirable?

The main objection to this approach is that there are many abnormal behaviours that are quite desirable. For example, very few people have an IQ over 150, yet we would not want to suggest that this is undesirable. Equally, there are some *normal* behaviours that are undesirable. For example, depression is relatively common, yet it is undesirable.

Therefore, using statistical infrequency to define abnormality means that we are unable to distinguish between desirable and undesirable behaviours. In order to identify behaviours that need treatment, there needs to be a means of identifying infrequent *and* undesirable behaviours.

Cultural relativism

If we attempt to define abnormality using the statistical infrequency approach, how do we cope with the fact that behaviours differ from one culture to the next? Behaviours that are statistically infrequent in one culture may be statistically more frequent in another. For example, one of the symptoms of schizophrenia is claiming to hear voices. However, this is an experience regarded as normal and even desirable in some cultures. Revered religious leaders often claim to have heard the voice of God.

This means that the statistical infrequency model is culturally relative, i.e. it only relates to a particular culture.

Strengths

In some situations it is appropriate to use a statistical criterion to define abnormality. For example, mental retardation is defined in terms of the normal distribution using the concept of **standard deviation** to establish a cut-off point for abnormality (explained on the next page). The statistical infrequency model works better for some human behaviours than others.

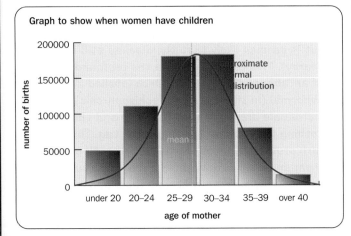

Graph to show when women have children

number of births / age of mother

(approximate normal distribution / mean)

◀ This graph shows the number of births per annum in England and Wales by age of mother. This is not a true normal distribution, as there are more births to the left of the mean. This distribution is positively skewed.

A **normal distribution** is what you get if you plot the frequency of any randomly determined events. For example, if you plot shoe sizes of all the women you know or if you plot the life of the light bulbs in your house, you should get a normal distribution.

Research methods *Range and standard deviation*

When considering a set of values (such as 3, 5, 6, 6, 8, 10, 11, 15, 18, 25), there are several ways to *describe* the data. For example, we can say there are 10 values and the **mean** of these values is 10.7, the **median** 9 and the **mode** is 6. These descriptions (about the numbers above) are all **measures of central tendency**, which we discussed earlier (see page 31).

Another way to describe the data is to use **measures of dispersion** (i.e. how dispersed or spread out the values are). The easiest way to do this is to use the **range**. Consider the values below:

3, 5, 8, 8, 9, 10, 12, 12, 13, 15	mean = 9.5	range = 12 (3 to 15)
1, 5, 8, 8, 9, 10, 12, 12, 13, 17	mean = 9.5	range = 16 (1 to 17)

The two sets of values have the same mean but a different range, so the range is helpful as a further method of *describing* the data. If we just used the mean, the data would appear to be the same.

A more precise method of expressing dispersion is called the **standard deviation**. To calculate the standard deviation, every value is subtracted from the mean of that set of data and the differences are added together and divided by the number of values. This tells us the average (mean) distribution of all values.

The standard deviation for the two sets of values above is 3.69 and 4.45, respectively.

	Advantages	Disadvantages
Range	Easy to calculate.	Affected by extreme values.
Standard deviation	More precise measure of dispersion because all values taken into account.	Harder to calculate.

DSM – the *Diagnostic and Statistic Manual* – is a list of mental disorders that is used for diagnosis. For each disorder a list of **clinical characteristics** is given, i.e. the symptoms that should be looked for. In order to diagnose a condition a **clinician** will look for symptoms. DSM-IVR is the current version in use in the US. In Britain clinicians use ICD (*Internal Classification of Diseases and Health-related Problems*).

A **clinician** or **clinical psychologist** is a person who is trained to diagnose and treat mental disorders. A **psychiatrist** is a person who is trained as a doctor and then studies psychology.

Explanation 2: Deviation from social norms

This model uses the concept of deviation in the sense of deviant behaviour – behaviour which is anti-social or undesirable. In any society there are standards of acceptable behaviour that are set by the social group. These social norms include morals as well as expectations about how people should think. These standards are often in place for good reasons. An example of a social norm is politeness. Politeness oils the wheels of interpersonal relations. People who are rude or surly are behaving in a socially deviant way.

Social standards are concerned with rules of etiquette as well as more serious moral issues, such as what is acceptable in sexual behaviour. Our culture permits sex between consenting adults of any gender but regards some other behaviours as sexually deviant. In the past homosexuality was classified as deviant behaviour. Currently the **DSM** classification scheme contains a category called 'sexual and gender identity disorders', which includes paedophilia and voyeurism. Such behaviours are socially deviant.

KEY TERMS

Abnormality: A psychological condition or behaviour that departs from the norm or is harmful and distressing to the individual or those around him or her. Abnormal behaviours are usually those that violate society's ideas of what is an appropriate level of functioning.

Cultural relativism: The view that behaviour cannot be judged properly unless it is viewed in the context of the culture in which it originates.

Limitations

Susceptible to abuse

The main difficulty with the concept of deviation from social norms is that it varies as times change. What is socially acceptable now was not socially acceptable 50 years ago. For example, today homosexuality is acceptable but in the past it was included under sexual and gender identity disorders. In Russia 50 years ago, anyone who disagreed with the state was regarded as insane and placed in a mental institution.

If we define abnormality in terms of deviation from social norms, we open the door to definitions that rely on prevailing social morals and attitudes. This then permits the incarceration of individuals who transgress social rules. Szasz (1974) claimed that mental illness was simply a way to exclude non-conformists from society.

Cultural relativism

Attempting to define abnormality in terms of social norms is obviously bound by culture because social norms are defined by the culture. Classification systems, such as **DSM** (see above), are almost entirely based on the social norms of the dominant culture in the West (white and middle class), and yet the same criteria are applied to people from different subcultures living in the West. Using one set of criteria for different cultural (subcultural) groups in differential diagnosis rates (e.g. African–Caribbean immigrants are seven times more likely to be diagnosed as schizophrenic than whites (Cochrane, 1977)).

The social deviance model is so affected by cultural norms that it is not a sound basis for defining psychological abnormality.

Strengths

This model does distinguish between desirable and undesirable behaviour, a feature that was absent from the statistical infrequency model. The social deviancy model also takes into account the effect that behaviour has on others. Deviance is defined in terms of transgression of social rules and (ideally) social rules are established in order to help people live together.

Behaviour that is deviant is socially unacceptable for the rest of us. This way of defining abnormality takes account of the greater good of society. According to this definition, abnormal behaviour is behaviour that damages others.

Definitions of abnormality (continued)

The first two attempts to define abnormality both focused on norms: statistical norms and social norms. Now we look at two further attempts to define abnormality, both of which are more concerned with the individual's subjective sense of abnormality.

Why do we need to define abnormality?

Whenever we talk about 'abnormality' or 'abnormal behaviour', we inevitably invoke one of the definitions given on these pages. You probably all have some idea about what constitutes abnormality, regardless of whether or not you could put this clearly into words. Such *implicit* definitions would not be acceptable among health professionals. If definitions remain implicit, they cannot be challenged, alternatives are ignored and our scientific understanding of abnormal behaviour cannot develop.

DEFINING PSYCHOLOGICAL ABNORMALITY

Explanation 3: Failure to function adequately

The first two definitions of abnormality focus on comparing behaviour to some kind of standard to determine normality. An alternative approach is to consider normality from the individual's point of view. Most people aim to be able to cope with day-to-day living. Abnormality can then be judged in terms of not being able to cope. For example, if you are feeling depressed this is acceptable as long as you can continue to go to work, eat meals, wash your clothes, and generally go about day-to-day living. So 'failure to function adequately' refers to the individual's ability (or inability) to cope with day-to-day living. This definition includes bizarre behaviour and/or behaviours that distress a patient or others.

Limitations

Who judges?

In order to determine 'failure to function *adequately*' someone needs to decide if what is 'adequate'. Some individuals may be quite content with the situation and/or simply unaware that they are not coping. It is others who are uncomfortable and judge the behaviour is abnormal. For example, many schizophrenics do not feel there is a problem; however their erratic behaviour is distressing to others and may even be dangerous as in the case of someone like Peter Sutcliffe, the Yorkshire Ripper.

Cultural relativism

Definitions of adequate functioning are related to cultural ideas of how one's life should be lived. The failure to function criteria are likely to result in differential diagnoses when applied to people from different cultures because the standard of one culture is being used to measure another. This may explain why lower-class and non-white patients are more often diagnosed with mental disorders – because their lifestyles are non-traditional and this may lead to a judgement of failing to function adequately.

Strengths

This model of abnormality does recognise the subjective experience of the patient, allowing us to view mental disorder from the point of view of the person experiencing it. In addition 'failure to function' is also relatively easy to judge objectively because one can list behaviours (can dress self, can prepare meals) and thus judge abnormality objectively i.e. when treatment is required.

Explanation 4: Deviation from ideal mental health

Marie Jahoda (1958) pointed out that we define physical illness in part by looking at the *absence* of signs of physical health. Physical health is indicated by having correct body temperature, normal skin colour, normal blood pressure and so on. Why not do the same for mental illness? Jahoda conducted a review of what others had written about mental health and identified 6 categories that were commonly referred to:

- Self-attitudes: having high self-esteem and a strong sense of identity.
- Personal growth and self-actualisation: the extent to which an individual develops his or her full capabilities.
- Integration, such as being able to cope with stressful situations.
- Autonomy: being independent and self-regulating.
- Having an accurate perception of reality.
- Mastery of the environment: including the ability to love, function at work and in interpersonal relations, adjust to new situations and solve problems.

This model proposes that the absence of these criteria indicates abnormality and potential mental disorder.

Limitations

Who can achieve these criteria?

According to these criteria most of us are abnormal and possibly mental disordered. Jahoda presented them as ideal criteria and they certainly are. We also have to ask how many need to be lacking before a person would be judged as abnormal.

Cultural relativism

Many if not most of the criteria of the ideal mental health model are culture-bound. If we apply these criteria to people from non-Western or even non-middle-class social groups, a higher incidence of abnormality will be found. For example, the criteria of self-actualisation is relevant to members of **individualist** cultures but not to **collectivist** ones where individuals strive for the greater good of the community rather than self-centred goals.

Strengths

The deviation from mental health is a positive approach to the definition of abnormality, and focuses on what is desirable rather than what is undesirable.

caseSTUDY

Robert's school phobia

Robert was an underweight 8-year-old who had always been very reluctant to go to school. Every school night he ate little, and even that was brought up later. He became increasingly anxious as the evening wore on. When he couldn't get to sleep he would cry, and his mother would come and sit with him and tell him stories.

In the morning Robert got up early and paced up and down or sat in a corner, occasionally rushing to the toilet to be sick. When it was time to go to school he had to be pushed out of the house, though often his tears and complaints of feeling unwell led his mother to relent and allow him to stay home.

If Robert did go to school, there was some comfort in the fact that his mother would visit at play time, bringing milk and biscuits. She came because that was part of the 'deal' about going to school, but also because she would otherwise worry about Robert.

Robert surprisingly got on quite well with the other children and was well liked, despite crying on the way to school and often acting like a baby. He was good at athletics and quite bright. He did not like being away from home for anything – he did not go to play at friends' houses. But it wasn't just being away from home that caused the problem – Robert was simply terrified of school.

Is Robert's behaviour abnormal? How does it fit our definitions?

- *Statistical infrequency*: Such school phobia is statistically rare. Most children go to school happily, some go to school unhappily but do not experience any of Robert's physical symptoms, nor his sense of terror. This suggests that his behaviour is abnormal when compared to the norms for his age group.

- *Deviation from social norms*: Robert is able to cope with social relations, so he is not deviant in that respect. His unwillingness to travel beyond his immediate environment is a deviation from social norms and undesirable for normal development.

- *Failure to function adequately*: Robert's phobia clearly prevents him attending school, which is a part of day-to-day life. However, his behaviour may *appear* to be dysfunctional in one sense but may serve another function – to prevent separation between him and his mother.

Source: Adapted from Oltmanns *et al*. (1999), *Case Studies in Abnormal Psychology*. John Wiley and Sons.

- *Deviation from ideal mental health*: Robert's behaviour demonstrates a lack of most of the criteria for ideal mental health, such as poor self-esteem, being unable to cope with stressful situations, lack of autonomy and lack of environmental mastery. It is likely that his behaviour, if it continued, would prevent personal growth.

- *DSM-IV*: School phobia is not listed as a category in the **DSM** but is discussed as an aspect of separation anxiety disorder (an excessive anxiety about being away from home lasting for more than a month).

Oltmanns *et al*. identified the key issue as being Robert's anxious nature. Robert received lots of love from his mother but worried that this would cease if he stopped being good. When he started school he was immediately thrown into a new fear of not succeeding. The anxiety of school coupled with the anxiety of being separated from his mother led to Robert's intense phobia. In the next section, on models of abnormality, we will look at further explanations of Robert's behaviour.

COMMENTARY CORNER

Outline and evaluate definitions of abnormality.

This type of question gives you the chance to utilise all of the techniques so far discussed. Let's review some of these here:

- The **AO1** content should be one-third and the **AO2** content two-thirds of your answer. The use of the word 'outline' in the question alerts you to the fact that only a summary description is needed (the **AO1** content) rather than a detailed account of each. The use of the word 'definitions' in the plural tells you that you should write about more than one (but there is no requirement to write about *all* the definitions covered here). In fact, trying to cover too broad a canvas in your outline of such definitions may result in either a very superficial coverage, or an unbalanced answer. Evaluation (the **AO2** content) may be specific (about particular definitions) or general (about the whole idea of trying to define abnormality).

- You are required by the specification to cover *limitations* of each of these definitions of abnormality, but there is no explicit mention of *strengths*. Evaluation, however, can include both limitations *and* strengths, so the strengths of each of these definitions are as relevant as the limitations for your **AO2** content. For example, the 'failure to function adequately' definition of abnormality recognises the subjective experience of the individual, and allows us to view mental disorder from the point of view of the person experiencing it.

- Whatever the evaluative material, it is a good idea to use appropriate link phrases to introduce your **AO2** content. These are fairly simple ('However, an alternative explanation is...', 'In support of this assumption...') but are also extremely effective in focusing the examiner *and* you on the fact that you are doing something different from just describing material.

- Remember that you do not have to restrict yourself only to the material on the preceding pages. There will be lots more accessible content that you can use (for example, the discussion of cultural relativism on the following pages). The most important thing to bear in mind is that there is no one set route to take when answering this question, and no one 'right' answer that an examiner will be looking for.

KEY TERMS

Statistical infrequency: Abnormality is defined as those behaviours that are extremely rare, i.e. any behaviour that is statistically infrequent is regarded as abnormal.

Deviation from social norms: Abnormal behaviour is seen as a deviation from implicit rules about how one 'ought' to behave. Anything that violates these rules is considered abnormal.

Failure to function adequately: By using practical criteria of adequate functioning, mentally healthy people are judged as being able to operate within certain acceptable limits. If abnormal behaviour interferes with daily functioning, it may, according to these criteria, be considered abnormal.

Deviation from ideal mental health: Abnormality is seen as deviating from an ideal of positive mental health. Ideal mental health would include a positive attitude towards the self, resistance to stress and an accurate perception of reality.

Biological and psychological models of abnormality

Although our knowledge of how our ancestors viewed abnormality is extremely limited, it is probable that most prehistoric societies viewed abnormal behaviour as being evidence of possession by evil spirits. Trepanning to release these evil spirits is probably the oldest form of psychosurgery. A less extreme form of treatment was *exorcism*, carried out by a shaman, or priest, who would attempt to remove the evil spirits through a mixture of prayers, insults, pleas or magic potions.

Evidence of the link between abnormality and demonology can be traced back to prehistoric times.

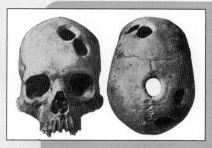

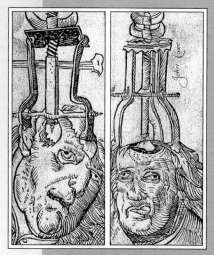

Historical methods of treating abnormality: skulls that have been trepanned to release evil spirits, and a cunning Egyptian device for doing this.

specification breakdown

Specification content	Comment
Assumptions made by biological (medical) and psychological (including psychodynamic, behavioural and cognitive) models of abnormality in terms of their views on the causes of abnormality.	Assumptions are beliefs that are held without proof. You will need to know two or three assumptions for each model of abnormality. There are *four* models specified here (**biological**, **psychodynamic**, **behavioural** and **cognitive**). Note that you are only required to know about assumptions on the **causes** of abnormality.

However, views about demonic possession were still much in evidence throughout the Middle Ages. These were times of great anxiety, as people were exposed to famine, war and plague. The incidence of abnormal behaviour, according to historians, increased dramatically during this period and, as usual, the devil was to blame. Treatments were still fairly barbaric, with starvation, whipping, scalding or stretching being commonly used to drive the devil out of the afflicted person's body (Comer, 1995). There was also a great fear of witchcraft during this period. Witches, mostly women, were thought to have made a pact with the devil in exchange for the power to bring harm upon their enemies. Although almost any form of extreme behaviour (including having a sharp tongue or a bad temper) was sufficient for a person to be branded a witch, for at least some of these unfortunates the cause of their strange behaviour appears to have been a mental disorder.

It would perhaps be an overstatement to say that we live in a period of widespread enlightenment about the origins of abnormal behaviour. Indeed, one fairly recent study (Murray, 1993) found that 43% of people believe that individuals bring on mental disorders themselves, and 35% believe they are caused by sinful behaviour. However, the latter half of the twentieth century saw some significant changes in the understanding of abnormal behaviour. Each of the models of abnormality covered in this section has very different views about the nature and causes of abnormality. Whereas demonic possession was the almost universally accepted explanation of abnormal behaviour in the Middle Ages, in the early twenty-first century we have a variety of more reasoned explanations for the same behaviours.

TREPANNING

Just imagine: a hole of 2.5 to 5cm in diameter, drilled by hand into the skull of a living person, without any anaesthesia, during 30 to 60 long minutes. This ancient form of brain surgery is called *trepanning* or *trephining*. Trepanning was performed either by bone abrasion (using a sharp-edged stone or knife) or by cutting (using semi-circular *trephines*, which cut by means of a swinging motion). The Egyptians invented the circular trephine, which cut much more easily by means of rotation. It was used extensively in Greece and Rome and gave rise to the 'crown' trephine, performed in Europe from the 1st to the 19th centuries.

Skulls with signs of trepanning have been found in practically all parts of the world where humans have lived. Evidence for trepanning has been found in 40,000-year-old Cro-Magnon sites, making it probably the oldest surgical operation known. We will never know how and when primitive humans came to discover trepanning, and can only speculate on the reasons for which it was carried out. One reason may have been the conviction that opening the skull would liberate 'bad spirits' or demons that inhabited the patient's body. From the Middle Ages well into the 18th century in Europe, trepanning was common as a medical procedure very much like bloodletting, i.e. it had no medical

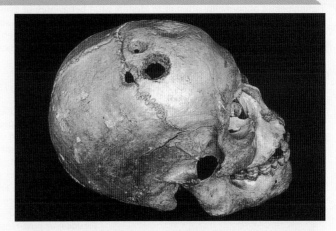

usefulness in itself. Repeated trepanning was common, for instance Prince Philip of Orange was trepanned 17 times by his physician!

It is hard to imagine how patients survived such a drastic operation without antibiotics or anaesthetics. Judging from the number of skulls which show healing and bone regeneration at the borders, the proportion of 'patients' who survived the ordeal was quite high, about 70%. In modern times (14th to 18th centuries) the proportion was much lower, sometimes approaching zero. One professional 'trepanator' named Mery lost all his patients in 60 years of activity!

Source: Sabbatini (1997), *The History of Psychosurgery.* http://www.epub.org.br/cm/n02/historia/psicocirg_i.htm

What is meant by a model of abnormality?

Many different models are used to explain and treat abnormal behaviour. Each is based on different assumptions about the nature of human behaviour, and therefore has different views on abnormal functioning. At one extreme, the **biological model** (also referred to as the *medical* model) stresses the importance of organic (i.e. bodily) processes in behaviour, and therefore sees abnormal behaviour as being caused by either anatomical or biochemical problems in the brain. **Psychological models** focus more on the psychological dimensions of human behaviour (e.g. the way a person thinks, feels or acts), and base their interpretation of abnormal behaviour on problems in these areas. Because these models are based on often very divergent assumptions and ideas about human behaviour, they also conflict in their interpretation of abnormal functioning. As with the definitions covered earlier (in Section 1), none of the models offers a *complete* explanation of abnormality, and none can explain the entire spectrum of abnormality.

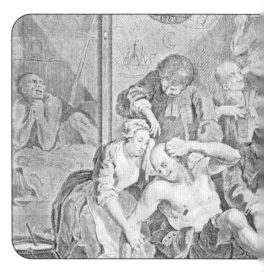

Overview of the four models of abnormality

Definitions of abnormality attempt to identify what behaviours or symptoms are abnormal. Here we look at explanations for how these abnormal behaviours might have come about. There are four main approaches in psychology to explaining abnormality: biological, psychodynamic, behavioural and cognitive. Each of these is called an 'approach' (sometimes called a 'perspective'), meaning that it represents a way to explain behaviour.

The biological approach

Module 3 explored the physiological approach to explaining stress. This involved considering how bodily systems can be used to explain the causes and effects of stress. The biological approach encompasses more than physiology. It includes genetic explanations of behaviour as well.

A biological psychologist explains behaviour in terms of physiological (body) and/or genetic causes, and explains mental disorder as the consequence of malfunctioning of these systems.

The biological model of abnormality is also called the **medical model** because it treats abnormality as a physical condition. The medical model of abnormality is the most widely accepted model of mental illness. In fact, that is why psychiatrists have used the term mental 'illness' rather than 'disorder' – because the dominant view in psychiatry is that mental problems are *illnesses* to be treated, much like physical illnesses (which also contain a psychological component).

The psychodynamic approach

Modules 1 and 2 briefly looked at the psychodynamic approach – when considering Freud's explanation of forgetting (repression) and his explanation of attachment. The essence of this approach is to explain behaviour in terms of its *dynamics* – what drives it. The best-known example of this approach is Freud's psychoanalytic theory of personality. There are many other psychoanalytic theories based on Freud's ideas (often called neo-Freudian or post-Freudian theories).

Sigmund Freud was first to challenge the medical model, claiming mental disorder was caused by psychological rather than physical factors.

The essence of the psychoanalytic approach is that much of our behaviour is motivated (driven) by unconscious desires. The result is that behaviour can often be explained in terms of deeper, hidden meanings. For example, *Freudian slips* are mistaken things that people say which unintentionally express their real feelings. Freud (1920) gave an example of this. A British Member of Parliament referred to his colleague as 'the honourable member from Hell' instead of from Hull. A psychoanalytic psychologist explains behaviour in terms of early experience and hidden meanings, and explains abnormality as the consequence of unresolved conflicts of childhood which are unconscious.

▼ 'Always look on the bright side of life', the song sung at the end of Monty Python's film *The Life of Brian*, is an example of the cognitive approach: dealing with a problem by thinking about it differently.

Assumptions about causes of abnormal behaviour

In the next four spreads we look at how each of the four approaches outlined here is translated into a model of abnormality.

What is meant by 'assumptions about causes of abnormality'?

Models of abnormality are based on different perspectives of the nature of *normality* and therefore the nature of *abnormality*. In order to make this distinction, the models must first make it clear how such 'normal' behaviour comes about in the first place. A biological perspective, for example, sees all behaviour as being a product of physiological processes in the brain and body. Abnormal behaviour, therefore, is what happens when these processes go wrong in some way. In the behavioural model, all behaviour is learned, either through direct reinforcement or as a result of the observation of others. What we classify as 'abnormal' behaviour is acquired in the same way, but is considered maladaptive even though it may serve some important purpose for the person concerned, i.e. it is rewarding for that person. For example, having panic attacks about meeting people or going out to work is clearly maladaptive. Yet this same behaviour may bring the person hidden rewards such as increased attention from a loved one or the avoidance of an unpleasant workplace. Thus something that appears maladaptive may actually be adaptive for that individual.

▼ This was the scene in Bedlam, the common name for the mental hospital outside London called Bethlem, as depicted by Hogarth (1735)

The cognitive approach

The first module of this book was an example of the cognitive approach in psychology – applied to the study of human memory. Cognitive psychology focuses on internal mental processes. It likens the mind to a computer: information is input, processed, stored and retrieved. The different components of the brain function as part of a network, just like a computer.

The emphasis of the cognitive approach is on how thinking shapes our behaviour – quite the antithesis of the behavioural approach, where the concept of the mind was banished from any explanations. The cognitive approach is more recent than the others outlined above, emerging in the 1950s along with the information-processing revolution. Today it is a dominant approach in the treatment of mental illness.

A cognitive psychologist explains all behaviour in terms of thoughts, beliefs and attitudes, and studies how these direct behaviour. Cognitive psychologists explain abnormality in terms of irrational and negative thinking. The problem is the way an individual is thinking – if you change the thinking, the problem will disappear. This is the essence of the therapies derived from the cognitive model.

The behavioural approach

Learning theory (classical and operant conditioning) is the bedrock of the behavioural approach, which is based on the claim that all behaviour is learned. We are born as a blank slate which is written on by experience. Behaviourists also believe that behaviour is all that should concern psychology – there is no need to search for the mind or analyse thoughts and feelings. They believe that, in order to develop a truly scientific and objective science of psychology, behaviour alone should be studied (which is why they are called 'behaviourists').

Behaviourism was first formulated around the start of the 20th century, at about the same time as Freud's early work. A later development of behaviourism was introduced by Albert Bandura in the 1960s. He pointed out that much of what we learn is not the consequence of direct rewards or punishments but of *vicarious* or second-hand reinforcement. We learn by watching what happens to others and, under certain conditions, *imitating* these behaviours. This is called **social learning theory** (SLT) – 'social' because the learning involves other people. SLT is also called 'neo-behaviourism' (a new behaviourism).

A behavioural psychologist explains all behaviour in terms of learning and observable phenomena, and explains abnormality in the same terms. Neo-behaviourists use the concept of social learning theory.

COMMENTARY CORNER

Can we equate mental disorders with physical diseases?

The main assumption of the biological model of abnormality is that diseases of the mind are actually diseases of the brain. The equation of the mind with the brain and of mental disease with brain disease is then used to justify the drug treatment of mental illness. Contrary to these views, Thomas Szasz (2000) asserts that mental functions are not reducible to brain functions, and that mental diseases are not brain diseases – indeed, that mental diseases are not diseases at all.

Szasz makes the distinction between diseases of the brain (such as epilepsy) and diseases of the mind (such as an irrational belief that one's body is already dead), and states that the two are not equally 'illnesses'. To Szasz, such irrational beliefs cannot be explained by means of physical defects or diseases and therefore cannot be called illnesses in the same way as we would call epilepsy a physical illness.

Of course, disorders such as anxiety and depression *do* exist, but they are not diseases in the pathological sense. Diseases are physical phenomena or processes, for example the abnormal metabolism of glucose (diabetes). Mental diseases, on the other hand, are patterns of personal conduct, unwanted by the individual or others. In short, medical diseases have a physical reality. They are discovered and named, as in the case of acquired immune deficiency syndrome (AIDS). Mental diseases do not have the same physical basis. they are not discovered. They are invented and then named, as in the case of post-traumatic stress disorder.

What is meant by the 'biological' model of abnormality?

The biological model represents the views of mainstream *psychiatry*. All behaviour is seen as rooted in underlying physiological processes in the body. Any abnormality must, therefore, have specific causes that lie in some bodily malfunction or in genetic factors. Cure is only possible by removing the root cause and returning the body to its 'normal' level of functioning. This model is called 'medical' because it suggests that mental illness should be diagnosed in the same way as physical disease is diagnosed. Mental disorders represented as mental *illnesses*. Because of its emphasis on *scientific* investigation and understanding, the biological model is the most widely respected model of abnormality. However, its representation of mental disorders as 'disease' states equivalent to physical illnesses also makes it one of the most controversial.

Assumptions of the biological (medical) model about the causes of abnormality

Abnormality is caused by physical factors

The biological (medical) model assumes that all mental disorders are related to some change in the body. Mental disorders are like physical disorders, i.e. they are illnesses. Such changes or illnesses may be caused by one of four possible factors: genes, biochemical substances, neuroanatomy and/or micro-organisms (such as general paresis, described opposite).

Abnormality is inherited

The genetic view is that mental illness is programmed in an individual's genetic material, passing from parent to child. One way of investigating this possibility is through the use of twin studies. For example, pairs of identical twins are compared to see if one twin has a disorder that the other twin shares. This provides us with a **concordance rate**. There are low concordance rates for some mental disorders (e.g. phobias) but quite high concordance rates for others (e.g. schizophrenia).

Certain genes lead to abnormal biochemistry and/or abnormal neuroanatomy

Genes tell the body how to function. They determine, for example, the levels of **hormones** and **neurotransmitters** (biochemistry). In the module on stress we mentioned the neurotransmitter serotonin. High levels of serotonin are associated with anxiety, whereas low levels have been found in depressed individuals. Genes also determine the structure of the brain (neuroanatomy). Some research has indicated that schizophrenics have large holes (ventricles) in their brains. The biological model assumes that such abnormalities are inherited and cause mental illness.

casestudy

Using the biological model to explain Robert's school phobia

Robert's separation anxiety may in part be caused by a predisposition to be anxious. He may be anxious by nature and even have inherited a tendency to develop phobias. There is evidence that certain personality traits are inherited. It may be that these innate tendencies, coupled with certain life experiences (e.g. maternal overprotection), could explain his separation anxiety disorder and his school phobia.

Criticisms

Humane or inhumane?

Historically, the emergence of the medical model in the 18th century led to more humane treatment for mental patients. Until then mental illness was blamed on demons or on evil in the individual. The medical model offered a different source of blame – the illness, which was potentially treatable.

More recent critics have claimed that the medical model is inhumane. Thomas Szasz (1972) wrote a book called *The Myth of Mental Illness* in which he argued that mental illnesses did not have a physical basis. He suggested that the concept of mental illness was 'invented' as a form of social control.

Cause or effect?

It is not clear whether abnormal biochemistry or abnormal neuroanatomy is a cause of abnormal behaviour or an effect. If it is an effect of the disorder, such changes may perpetuate the disorder. It may still be appropriate to treat the symptoms and alleviate some suffering.

Inconclusive evidence

There is no evidence that mental disorders are purely caused by biology. Concordance rates are never 100%. It is likely that, in the case of certain disorders, individuals inherit a susceptibility for the disorder but the disorder develops only if the individual is exposed to stressful life conditions. This is called the **diathesis-stress model** ('diathesis' means a constitutional disposition).

Murderous rampage

In 1966 Charles Whitman strangled his mother, murdered his wife while she was asleep, then installed himself in a tower on the Texas university campus (above) and shot down 14 people before eventually being shot down himself. In a letter written beforehand, he expressed a wish that his body be autopsied after his death to see if there was a physical cause for his mental anguish. A small tumour was discovered in his brain, though it is not clear whether this can explain his murderous rampage.

What is meant by the 'psychodynamic' model of abnormality?

When used in the context of abnormal behaviour, the term **psychodynamic** refers to any approach that emphasises the *dynamics* of behaviour, i.e. what drives us to behave in particular ways. As the individual is constantly changing and developing, so do the underlying drives of his or her behaviour. Those theorists who subscribe to a psychodynamic model believe that an individual's abnormal behaviour is determined by underlying psychological conflicts of which he or she is largely unaware (i.e. *unconscious* forces). Psychodynamic theorists focus mostly on past experiences, notably early parent–child relationships, because they believe the majority of psychological conflicts are rooted in these relationships. The best known of the psychodynamic theories of abnormality is Sigmund Freud's theory of **psychoanalysis**. Freud believed that unconscious forces determined all normal *and* abnormal behaviour.

Assumptions of the psychodynamic model about the causes of abnormality

Mental disorder results from psychological rather than physical causes

Freud believed that the origins of mental disorder lie in the *unconscious unresolved conflicts* of *childhood*. Medical illnesses are not the outcome of physical disorder.

Unresolved conflicts cause mental disorder

Conflicts between the id, ego and superego create anxiety. The ego protects itself with various defence mechanisms (ego-defences). These defences can be the cause of disturbed behaviour if they are overused. For example, repression is the blocking of unpleasant thoughts and placing them in the unconscious.

Early experiences cause mental disorder

In childhood the ego is not developed enough to deal with traumas and therefore they are repressed. For example, a child may experience the death of a parent early in life and repress associated feelings. Later in life, other losses may cause the individual to re-experience the earlier loss and this can lead to depression. Previously unexpressed anger about the loss is directed inwards towards the self, causing depression.

Unconscious motivations cause mental disorder

Ego-defences, such as repression, exert pressure through unconsciously motivated behaviour. Freud proposed that the unconscious consists of information that is either very hard to bring into conscious awareness. However, it exerts a powerful effect on behaviour which cannot be controlled until brought into conscious awareness.

Criticisms

Very influential

Freud's theory was the first attempt to explain mental illness in psychological terms. It has had an enormous influence on our understanding of normal and abnormal behaviour as well as on literature and the world in general. Much of this understanding has been absorbed into our culture so we are not aware of it.

Too much emphasis on sex

Freud was overconcerned with sexual (physical) factors and made little reference to the influence of society (social factors) on development. This may be a reflection of the times during which he lived – when there was much repression of sexual feelings.

Poor research evidence

Freud based his theory on his observations of behaviour – but these were largely of middle-class Viennese women suffering from mental disorders. So it is a major leap to make generalisations from this sample to that of the normal development of children.

Anna O

Anna O. (Freud, 1910) suffered severe paralysis on her right side as well as nausea and difficulty drinking. Freud demonstrated that these physical symptoms actually had a psychological cause. During discussions with her it became apparent that she developed a fear of drinking when a dog she hated drank from her glass. Her other symptoms originated when caring for her sick father. She could not express her anxiety for his illness but did express it later, during psychoanalysis. As soon as she had the opportunity to make these unconscious thoughts conscious her paralysis disappeared.

casestudy

Using the psychodynamic model to explain Robert's school phobia

Robert may have had a fear of failing and this created anxiety. In order to cope with this anxiety his feelings about school were repressed, and in order to deal with this he had to avoid the object creating the fear. The phobia is the ego's way of not confronting the repressed problem.

In addition to this phobia Robert also suffered from separation anxiety, which may have developed out of an insecure attachment with his mother. Such insecurity leads a child to feel anxious when separated. Such anxiety would have been repressed and the method of coping would be to avoid separation.

The implications of this are important. To simply try to get Robert to school (dealing with symptoms) would not overcome the real causes and his anxieties would remain.

COMMENTARY CORNER

Outline and evaluate the psychodynamic model of abnormality.

There are two skills to practise in this Commentary Corner.

First, **précis** Freud's psychoanalytic theory in about 100 words. (Hint: don't try to include *everything* and focus your outline explicitly on the explanation of abnormality.)

Second, what would you use to *evaluate* this theory in about 200 words? (Hint: think and read widely for an effective response to this part of the question. You might use other models as evaluation.)

What is meant by the 'behavioural' model of abnormality?

Behaviourists believe that our actions are determined largely by our life experiences rather than by underlying pathology or unconscious forces. Abnormality is seen as the development of behaviour patterns, established through classical and operant conditioning or through social learning, that are considered maladaptive for the individual. Most learned behaviours are **adaptive**, helping people to lead happy and productive lives, but maladaptive (and therefore undesirable) behaviours can be acquired in the same way.

Assumptions of the behavioural model about the causes of abnormality

Abnormal behaviours are learned through conditioning

All behaviour is learned through experience. Abnormal behaviour is no different from normal behaviour. We can use the principles of classical and operant conditioning to explain all behaviour. This includes the concepts of *association* and *reinforcement*.

Only behaviour is important

Behaviourists assume that the mind is an unnecessary concept; it is sufficient to explain behaviour in terms of what can be observed. There are no such things as mental illnesses because, to a behaviourist, the mind is an unnecessary concept.

The same laws apply to human and non-human animal behaviour

According to the principles of evolution, all animals are formed from the same basic units. 'Higher' animals just have more of them and this leads to more complex combinations – but the same basic laws apply. This means that it is reasonable to conduct research on non-human animals, like rats and pigeons, and make generalisations to human behaviour.

Conditioning theory

Classical conditioning – Learning occurs through association. A neutral stimulus is paired with an unconditioned stimulus, resulting in a new stimulus-response (S-R) link. The neutral stimulus is now a conditioned stimulus producing a conditioned response.

Psychological disorder is caused when an experience (neutral stimulus) produces an extremely unpleasant response such as fear (conditioned response) so that the situation will be avoided at all costs in the future.

Operant conditioning – Learning occurs through reinforcement. An animal responds to the environment and some responses are reinforced, increasing the probability that they will be repeated. If a response is punished this decreases the probability that it will be repeated.

A psychological disorder is produced when a maladaptive behaviour is reinforced. This means that such behaviours may be functional for the individual, at least at the time they are learned. For example, if a person finds that he or she gets increasingly more attention when behaving in a wild and erratic fashion, this behaviour will be repeated.

Little Albert

John B. Watson and Rosalie Rayner (1920) demonstrated how emotions could be learned through classical conditioning. They worked with an 11-month-old boy called 'Little Albert' (not to be confused with Little Hans). They first tested his reponses to white fluffy objects: a white rat, a rabbit and white cotton wool. He showed no fear response.

Next they set about creating a conditioned response to these previously neutral objects. To do this they used a steel bar that was four feet long. When he reached out for the rat they struck the bar with a hammer behind Albert's head to startle him. They repeated this three times, and did the same a week later. After this, when they showed the rat to Albert, he began to cry. They had conditioned a fear response in Little Albert.

Criticisms

Scientific and testable

The simplicity of the model makes it easy to conduct research to test how association and rewards affect behaviour. Experimental studies (such as Little Albert) have shown how abnormal behaviours can be learned, giving support to the model.

Can't account for all human behaviour

There is no doubt that learning theory can account for some aspects of normal and abnormal behaviour. For example, some individuals develop a phobia of dogs after being bitten (classical conditioning). However, much of human behaviour is more complex than this, as we saw in our study of stress. The way we *think* about things affects our experiences. Behaviourism disregards thoughts and emotions, and is not a complete explanation of human behaviour.

The symptoms not the cause

Part of the success of this model comes from the effectiveness of behavioural therapies for treating abnormal behaviour. However, these do not work with all disorders, suggesting that the symptoms are just the tip of the iceberg. The actual **causes** of the disorder may lie elsewhere.

caseSTUDY

Using the behavioural model to explain Robert's school phobia

The behavioural account for Robert's phobia simply suggests that it developed as a result of classical conditioning, as outlined in the account of Little Albert. School became associated with anxiety, and therefore Robert found that avoidance of the feared object (school) reduced his anxiety. Continued absence served to reduce the fear and was thus reinforcing.

Robert also received a kind of reward for staying away from school – he continued to enjoy his mother's company. In addition, when he did go to school she visited him. This meant his phobic behaviour was rewarded.

What is meant by the 'cognitive' model of abnormality?

Much of contemporary psychology is concerned with human *cognition*, e.g. how people perceive, reason and judge the world around them. The cognitive model of abnormality emphasises that cognitive distortions (dysfunctional thought processes) and cognitive deficiencies (the absence of sufficient thinking and planning) may be at the root of many psychological disorders. Cognitive distortions can be summarised thus:

- *Cognitive structures* refer to the internal organisation of information. Most of us think of dogs (or cats) as pets that are a source of companionship, sometimes able to do tricks, totally scatty, and so on. People who are afraid of dogs, however, view them on just one dimension – as objects of fear.
- *Cognitive content* is the actual material that the person is processing. We may focus on the negative aspects of a situation ('How can I possibly do this?' or 'I just know I'm going to fail') or the positive ('This is great' or 'I will survive').
- *Cognitive processes* are the ways in which we operate on this information. Anxious people process information differently to those who are less anxious. We may overhear a chance remark: 'She really gets on my nerves'. This is a statement that could apply to anyone, but the self-focused anxious person will be convinced that they are talking about her.
- *Cognitive products* are the conclusions that people reach when they have processed this material. In the example above, the person may conclude that she isn't liked or accepted, a conclusion based on faulty processing, i.e. an example of irrational thinking.

Cognitive psychologists therefore explain abnormality in terms of *irrational and negative thinking*. Such distortions in the way we process information have been implicated in depression, schizophrenia and several other mental disorders.

▲ The cognitive model emphasises that cognitive processing is an important influence in psychological adjustment. The sleeping dog, whose real nature is unknown, is seen differently by the two cats.

caseSTUDY

Using the cognitive model to explain Robert's school phobia

The cognitive view would be that Robert's phobia was a result of the fact that he placed undue emphasis on negative events in his environment and held irrational assumptions about his abilities to cope. An example of his irrational assumptions was his view that his mother's and teacher's approval was paramount. These 'faulty thoughts' prevented him changing his behaviour.

Assumptions of the cognitive model about the causes of abnormality

Abnormality is caused by faulty thinking

The cognitive model assumes that thinking, expectations and attitudes (i.e. cognitions) direct behaviour. Mental illness is the result of disordered thinking. The issue is not the problem itself but the way you *think* about it. Faulty and irrational thinking prevents the individual behaving adaptively. Examples of faulty thinking include maladaptive assumptions about oneself (thinking that there are perfect solutions to everything) and upsetting thoughts (fleeting images that go through one's mind without conscious control). Such thoughts lead to failure and depression.

The individual is in control

In each of the three previous models the view was that an individual's behaviour is determined by forces outside his or her control – physiological, genetic, unconscious or environmental factors. The concept of *determinism* will be discussed on the next spread. The cognitive model portrays the individual as being in control because the individual controls his or her own thoughts. Abnormality is faulty control.

Criticisms

Faulty thinking may be the effect rather than the cause of a mental disorder

It is not clear which comes first. Do thoughts and beliefs really cause disturbance, or does mental disorder lead to faulty thinking? It may be that, for example, a depressed individual develops a negative way of thinking *because* of the depression rather than the other way around.

Blames the patient, not situational factors

The cognitive model suggests that it is the patient who is responsible. This may lead situational factors to be overlooked, for example not considering how life events or family problems may have contributed to the mental disorder. According to the cognitive model, the disorder is simply in the patient's mind and recovery lies in changing that, rather than the individual's environment.

Therapeutic success

The success of cognitive therapies such as stress inoculation training (see page 112) lends support to the claim that many forms of abnormal behaviour are the result of disordererd thinking. Challenging these faulty cognitions is often more effective than concentrating on immediate behaviours (behavioural model) or deeper meaning (psychodynamic model).

Issues and debates in psychology

In your study of psychology you may have already noticed that certain topics keep coming up, such as the influence of cognitive factors and comments about ethical issues. These are sometimes referred to as issues and debates, or as **synoptic topics**. 'Synoptic' means 'having a general view of the whole'. In your second year of studying psychology (should you get that far), these synoptic topics will be very important. As a start we will introduce eight synoptic topics that you may study next year, and relate each of these to the models of abnormality. These synoptic topics offer a further way of evaluating each model. For example, many of the models are criticised for being both reductionist and determinist.

Gender bias

In the section on stress, we saw that most laboratory studies of physiological reactions to stress have been carried out on males. This has led to the claim that the 'fight or flight' reaction is a universal response to threatening stressors *despite* the under-representation of females in such research. However, more recent, less gender-biased research has suggested important gender differences in the *way* that males and females react to stress. Psychological theories are often based on studies of men only, yet generalisations are made about all human behaviour. This means that many psychological theories may be better described as a view of male, not human, behaviour (known as the **androcentric bias**). Psychologists have also become sensitive to the fact that many gender differences may be due to the different treatment of men and women (a bias).

Culture bias

We also considered cultural variations in the section on stress, as well as elsewhere in this book. It may be that some of the variations are due to bias in the way we perceive individuals from cultures other than our own. Psychology remains dominated by white middle-class Europeans and North Americans, and the interpretations produced by psychology cause us to view human behaviour in an inevitably biased way – not least because psychologists use 'tools' in other cultures such as intelligence tests and the Strange Situation procedure that were developed in a European cultural setting. Such tools (or imposed etics) may be inappropriate and produce biased findings.

Ethical issues

Ethical issues have recurred throughout this book, as with all synoptic topics. They are threads that run through the specification. In the next module on social psychology we will look in detail at ethical issues and ethical guidelines. It is paramount that psychologists are aware of their ethical responsibilities and judge the value of their methods with such issues in mind.

The use of non-human animals

This is a synoptic topic that has not been raised, though we have discussed studies involving the use of non-human animals such as Harlow's studies of monkeys (see page 54). Psychologists must consider whether it is *appropriate* to use non-human animals – can we make generalisations from non-human animal behaviour to human behaviour? If the answer is no, then we shouldn't conduct such research. Psychologists must also consider whether it is *right* to use non-human animals – is it ethically acceptable to cause any harm? Some psychologists argue that non-human animals should have the same rights as humans, while others argue that it is reasonable to inflict a high level of suffering on animals to avoid a smaller level of suffering in humans, up to a point. All agree that such research should be carefully monitored and that there should be restrictions on the number of animals used and number of studies conducted. It is worth remembering that even research that does not involve suffering, such as using animals for genetic engineering research, raises ethical concerns.

Determinism

Determinism is the view that behaviour is determined by forces other than the individual's will to do something. Many of the approaches examined in this section on models of abnormality represent a determinist view, because they suggest that our behaviour is determined by, for example, biology, early experience or rewards. 'Free will' is used to refer to the alternative end of the spectrum where an individual is seen as being capable of self-determination. As with all debates, the answer lies somewhere in between – our behaviour is probably a mixture of the two extremes. 'Soft determinism' is the compromise position – each of us exercises free will within a limited repertoire of options (i.e. determined but free).

Reductionism

Reductionism is any attempt to reduce a complex set of phenomena to more simple components. This is useful when trying to understand how things work. For example, if you want to understand how a windmill works you would look at a diagram of the parts. However, a knowledge of the individual parts may not give you an understanding of the way the whole thing operates or of its function. The sum of the parts does not always equal the whole.

Psychology as a science

Psychology is often defined as the 'science of behaviour and experience'. Most psychologists believe that science is an integral part of the study of behaviour and experience. Experiments are one way of being scientific, but other research methods are also scientific – such as observational studies and questionnaire surveys. The aim is to study behaviour and experience as *objectively* as possible to discover the causes of behaviour. Experiments do this best, but experiments are also beset with problems, such as **experimenter bias** (which is discussed on page 173). So we may be fooling ourselves that we really are discovering anything.

Nature and nurture

At the beginning of the module on attachment we commented on the fact that development can be explained from two positions: nature and nurture. You are either the product of your genes and biology (nature), or what you are is due to experience and environment (nurture). The answer to the question of 'nature or nurture' lies in looking at the way nature and nurture interact, as suggested by the **diathesis-stress** model and Freud's theory of development.

What is meant by an 'issue'?

The decision to preface the word 'Issue' with the modifier 'Big' for the magazine that is sold by and for homeless people was made because it suggested that homelessness was important, vital, not to be ignored. The same is true in psychology – some 'issues' are so important that we really cannot ignore them. These may potentially undermine the value of psychological theories and research (e.g. if we can demonstrate gender or cultural bias), or they may focus on important aspects of the subject's integrity (e.g. the use of animals in research). All of these issues are 'big' because we ignore them at our peril.

What is meant by a 'debate'?

Debates come in all shapes and sizes and, if on television, are also frequently accompanied by some pretty heated arguments and a fair amount of mudslinging. Academic debates involve a discussion of some topic, usually presenting both sides of an argument. Many of these are actually phrased as if they were somehow a contest (e.g. *nature versus nurture*), although invariably (rather like the debates we witness on television), the truth lies somewhere in between. Although the term 'debate' is used to describe an actual physical event (e.g. a debate about whether marijuana should be legalised), in psychology the term is used to describe an ongoing academic discussion about some fundamental aspect of human behaviour. The presentation of arguments might extend over many years, and with no real resolution to the topic being discussed.

▲ Biological and behaviourist psychologists conduct much of their research with non-human animals and make generalisations about human behaviour.

	The biological model	The psychodynamic model	The behavioural model	The cognitive model
Causes	Internal, physical.	Internal, biological/psychological.	External, psychological.	Internal, cognitive.
Patient	Passive.	Passive.	Passive.	Active.
Gender bias	Promotes the view that gender differences are real and related to the different effects of sex hormones. This may mask the effects of gender bias.	Freud's research involved mainly women, yet his views were male-biased. He suggested that men are morally superior because the resolution of the phallic stage is more successful.	Ignores the effects of gender, which is in itself a bias.	Bias is a cognitive process. The fact that we think there will be gender (or cultural) differences leads us to treat individuals differently and they may live up to this expectation. A self-fulfilling prophecy.
Culture bias	Ignores the effects of culture, which is in itself a bias.	May apply only to Victorian, middle-class, European women.	Cultural relativism can be explained in terms of different learning experiences.	
Ethical issues	Intended to be a more humane approach, but places patient in passive role. Therapies can be dangerous.	Places blame on parents, sometimes without real justification.	Removes blame from patient, but therapies manipulate behaviour in line with therapist's goals.	Blames the patient for his/her faulty thinking.
Use of non-human animals	Used in research, objections from anti-vivisectionists.	Use of non-human animals irrelevant.	Used in experiments but non-invasive methods.	Use of non-human animals irrelevant.
Determinism	We are determined by internal factors and/or inherited factors, both of which are outside our control.	Psychic determinism: causes of behaviour are unconscious and hidden from us.	Environmental determinism: we are controlled by external factors.	Thoughts determine behaviour; therefore the individual has control (free will). However, the therapy may be quite manipulative.
Reductionism	Reduces behaviour to basic biological components.	Reduces behaviour to a set of hypothetical mental structures and processes.	Reduces behaviour to stimulus-response units.	Reduces behaviour to thoughts, beliefs and attitudes.
Psychology as a science	Lends itself to experimental study. Often uses non-human animals because of ethical objections.	Relied on case studies and subjective interpretation. May better reflect the complexity of human behaviour.	Highly objective and experiment-based approach.	Highly experimental approach. Propositions can be easily tested.
Nature and nurture	Biological systems are innate (nature), but experience may modify them (e.g. changed hormone levels when stressed).	Behaviour is driven by innate systems but outcome is the result of an interaction with experience (nurture).	All behaviour is learned (nurture).	Faulty thoughts may be innate or due to experience. They may be a cause or effect of mental disorder.

CRITICAL ISSUE:

Eating disorders

Most of you are probably aware of the problem of eating disorders such as anorexia and bulimia. Many of you may know the symptoms and problems associated with such disorders. But probably few of you can imagine what it is like to have an eating disorder. The accounts below provide some insights.

A DAY IN THE LIFE OF A PERSON WITH BULIMIA

Do you lay in bed at night reviewing your day through the lens of everything you ate and how you looked? Mary did. Here's her typical day.

7:00 am	The alarm goes off. Mary wakes up and instantly checks her stomach to see if it's big or flat. She decides that it's BIG, bigger than it was yesterday. She knows immediately that she's going to have a bad day. As she showers, she touches her stomach and thighs. They all feel flabby. As she squeezes into her size 6 outfit, she looks in the mirror. 'I'm so fat and ugly,' she thinks, 'I hate myself.'
9:00 am	At work, Mary can't concentrate on anything but the tightness of her clothing. She drinks Diet Coke, coffee and water. After a morning of caffeine jitters, the bloating goes away but her self-consciousness does not. She wonders if everyone notices how fat she's looking. Though no one has said a word about her appearance, she's convinced that they're all making comments about her – which makes her feel even worse. Mary's day-to-day well-being depends on what she thinks others think of her, and today she's sure it's all in the minus column.
12:00 noon	The only thing that relieves Mary's misery is the growling of her stomach. If she's hungry, she's happy. She can picture how flat her stomach will look tonight and how good she'll feel. All she has to do is keep fasting. Skipping lunch, she focuses instead on what she'll eat for dinner: 3 ounces of tuna and a salad – nothing more.
5:00 pm	Mary leaves the office. She drives home, unlocks her door, and runs straight for the kitchen. Her stomach has never felt emptier; she needs something to eat quickly, just to tide her over until she can make her salad. She opens the bread bin, thinking that one piece of bread won't hurt her. But suddenly she's in a frenzy; she tears open the wrapper – and snaps. As if in a dream, she devours the entire loaf, slathering each piece with globs of peanut butter and jam.
5:45 am	When Mary comes to her senses, she panics. 'Oh my God,' she thinks, 'I've got to get rid of this right away or I'll get fat.' She rushes to the bathroom and vomits until she is depleted. Then she drops on her bed and says to herself, 'Oh God, I'm so unhappy. I swear, I'll never binge and purge again. I promise. Tomorrow, I'll be perfect.'

Source: www.healthyplace.com

Specification breakdown

Specification content	Comment
The clinical characteristics of anorexia nervosa and bulimia nervosa.	The requirement here is to cover the **clinical characteristics** of **anorexia nervosa** and **bulimia nervosa**, explanations (biological and psychological) and research studies relating to these explanations.
Explanations of these eating disorders in terms of biological and psychological models of abnormality, including research studies on which these explanations are based.	It is wise to cover more than one **biological explanation** (e.g. the influence of genes and biochemical explanations) and more than one **psychological explanation** (e.g. psychodynamic and behavioural).

> ## Anorexia, for me, is about the fear of growing up

I was around 13 when I 'discovered' the fine art of starving and 'getting sick'. It quickly became my biggest secret, my hidden world, and I protected it at all costs for over half my life. I was truly shocked to learn, back in 1970–71, that there were others who knew about this. I was enraged, terrified and insulted when a newspaper article appeared in the mail via my grandmother to my mother, a very hush-hush correspondence, but I saw it long enough to see a skeletal girl with the words 'anorexia nervosa' above her in bold black letters. My blood turned to ice as I realised for the first time that others knew. It made me mad because it made me less special. I'd finally found something to call my very own, and others had to take it for their own. I felt threatened and betrayed. I was confused by my affinity to and hate for this girl. It was as though I'd 'lost my innocence'. You know how once you see or know something, you cannot from then on not see it or not know it? I can still feel the chill that went through me as it sunk in that if others knew what I was doing they would know that something was wrong. This enforced the secrecy and the need to 'hide away' in isolation. It also enforced the guilt that began to overflow, however, to this day I cannot identify the sadness that accompanied the guilt. Like the guilt of knowing that you are doing something so against the law or so evil that to be found out would be the worst thing in the world, but you're so obsessed and controlled by it that the thought of being without it is unimaginable, like a piece of my very existence being ripped away.

There have been so many movies and books about anorexia and bulimia that the subject should be exhausted. I don't think it is, though, and I still have much, much more to add to this. There are so many levels of complicated thought processes and one-track behaviour rolled into an unreachable ball. I think when something like this takes over your life, and wraps itself so tightly around you, it overtakes reality-based perception and replaces it with some exaggerated image. There's not much that can be done by way of a quick cure to a healthy self-image, because it is everything we are. It takes just one disappointing look in the mirror, at a low and vulnerable point, to forever change a self-image. From then on the reflection is distorted, or more distorted than it was. It will never be perfect. It will never be good enough. No matter what the reflection is after that or what the scale says or what the size is, it will be regarded as a lie. A size 8 really only means something if you're not there yet. Once there, it isn't good enough. Once there, the novelty is gone, and it's time to move down to size 6. I guess everyone knows that anorexia is not about size, really. More the fear of growing up, being a woman and the responsibility that goes along with it, fear of men and sex, fear of having to operate as an adult world on an adult level. I found out years later that during the time spent absorbed with control of weight/life all other processes stop, meaning that the maturity I had as a teenager when I began this was the same maturity I had after 13 years of this. Do you know what I mean? No emotional development happens. It's like treading deep waters all the time, but never getting anywhere.

Having to face responsibilities and work with the 'big guys' in business was like being threatened with the guillotine every day. I mean, I'd wake up in the grip of fear and dread in the middle of the night, just begging to have the world or me end. I wanted to just not wake up anymore. I was so afraid. With life so out of control, and the overwhelming feelings of powerlessness and helplessness, I was dynamite just waiting for a match.

What is meant by eating disorders?

Many Western cultures appear to be preoccupied with food, and it seems that we can't switch on our television sets without coming across shows such as *Ready Steady Cook* or *The Naked Chef*. It is hardly surprising, therefore, to find that many people in Western cultures are overweight, even obese. As a natural consequence of this, we have also developed an obsession with *losing* weight through dieting. This obsession with food coupled with an obsession for losing weight has led to the emergence of disorders associated with food and eating. We might suppose that eating disorders would be rare in cultures less obsessed with eating and dieting, and this is generally the case.

In 1694 Richard Morton published the first medical case history of anorexia nervosa, and in the 1870s Sir William Gull gave it its name – which means 'nervous loss of appetite' (in fact, patients usually do not lose their appetite until the late stages of anorexia). Eating disorders did not appear in the **DSM** (an American classification system for mental disorders) until 1980, and with the publication of DSM-IV in 1994 eating disorders became a distinct category in their own right. The main types of eating disorders are **anorexia nervosa** and **bulimia nervosa** (from the Greek word meaning 'ox hunger'), although there are others.

◀ Jamie Oliver and many other TV cooks feed our Western preoccupation with food.

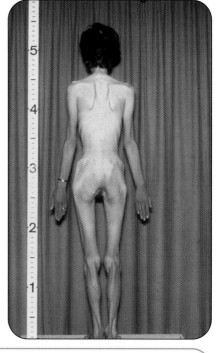

▼ The emaciated body of a girl with anorexia.

KEY TERMS

Eating disorder: A term that refers to a serious disruption of a person's eating habits or appetite and which may reflect abnormal psychological functioning. The most common eating disorders are anorexia nervosa and bulimia nervosa.

Anorexia nervosa: A type of eating disorder in which the person, despite being seriously underweight, fears that she or he might become obese and therefore engages in self-starvation to prevent this happening.

Bulimia nervosa: A type of eating disorder in which a person habitually engages in episodes of uncontrollable eating (known as bingeing) followed by self-induced vomiting or other compensatory behaviours (purging). People with bulimia have an abnormal concern with body size and a morbid fear of being or becoming fat.

Both anorexia and bulimia are most common in adolescent girls, but they do occur in older individuals and are also becoming increasingly frequent in men. They are also more common in European countries, but again incidence is increasing elsewhere.

A **clinical characteristic** is a symptom of a disorder that is used by clinicians to diagnose a syndrome. DSM-IV (*Diagnostic and Statistic Manual*) provides lists of such characteristics.

Note that weight loss, which is one characteristic of anorexia, is an example of defining abnormality in terms of a statistically infrequent behaviour.

Clinical characteristics of anorexia nervosa

DSM-IV lists four criteria for anorexia.

1 Anxiety

A key characteristic of anorexia is the anxiety associated with the disorder and excessive fear of being fat. People with anorexia are not simply obsessed with weight but fearful of weight gain.

2 Weight

Weight loss is considered abnormal when it drops below 85% of the individual's normal weight, based on age and height. People with anorexia develop unusual eating habits, such as avoiding food and meals, picking out a few foods and eating these in small quantities, or carefully weighing and portioning food. Individuals with anorexia may repeatedly check their body weight, and many engage in other techniques to control their weight, such as intense and compulsive exercise.

3 Body-image distortion

People with anorexia do not see their own thinness. They often continue to see themselves as fat despite the fact that their bones can be clearly seen. People with anorexia also deny the seriousness of their low body weight. They regard thinness as a vital component of their high self-esteem.

4 Amenorrhoea

'Amenorrhoea' means cessation of menstrual periods. The absence of periods for more than 3 months is a clinical characteristic of anorexia in girls who have begun menstruation. The lack of a menstrual cycle is caused by reduced weight. There are other associated physical symptoms such as paleness and hair falling out.

Clinical characteristics of bulimia nervosa

DSM-IV lists five criteria for bulimia.

1 Binge

People with bulimia engage in recurrent episodes of secret binge eating. Bingeing involves eating an excessive amount of food within a short period of time and feeling a lack of control over eating during the episode. One individual with bulimia described a typical binge as: a half-box of cereal, two pints of milk, a large sliced loaf of bread that is buttered, a packet of bacon, three eggs and sausages, accompanied by cooking oil to wash the food down (from the *Daily Telegraph*, 7 March 1998).

2 Purge

After bingeing the individual with bulimia is likely to purge her/himself to compensate for the overindulgence and in order to prevent weight gain. This is achieved by self-induced vomiting or misuse of laxatives or other medications. Alternatively, the individual with bulimia may stop eating for a long period as a means of purging.

3 Frequency

In order to be diagnosed as suffering from bulimia an individual should have been displaying binge eating and inappropriate compensatory behaviours, on average, at least twice a week for 3 months.

4 Body image

As with people with anorexia, the self-image and self-esteem of the individual with bulimia are unduly influenced by body shape and weight. Someone suffering from bulimia has an inappropriate perception of his/her own body.

5 Different from anorexia

Because purging or other compensatory behaviour follows the binge-eating episodes, people with bulimia are usually within the normal range of weight for their age and height. However, like individuals with anorexia, they may fear gaining weight, have a strong desire to lose weight, and feel intensely dissatisfied with their bodies. People with bulimia often perform the behaviours in secret, feeling disgusted and ashamed when they binge, yet relieved once they purge.

▲ Princess Diana captured the public's sympathy when she admitted to her bulimia in a television interview

It has been suggested that anorexia and bulimia are not easily distinguishable and it may be more appropriate to consider the eating disorder as a condition 'bulimarexia' (Boskind-Lodahl, 1976), which ranges from restricting individuals with anorexia at one end of the spectrum through to obese bulimia at the other. There are those with anorexia who are classified as 'bulimic anorexics' and many people with anorexia go on to develop bulimia. The table below shows some of the differences between anorexia and bulimia.

On the next four spreads we examine the biological and psychological explanations for anorexia and bulimia. The specification only requires that students are able to describe and evaluate biological and psychological explanations of *eating disorders*, which means that questions will not be set specifically on explanations of anorexia or bulimia. We have presented them separately because they are quite different as disorders. You may decide to study the first two spreads (biological and psychological explanations of anorexia) or the latter two spreads (biological and psychological explanations of bulimia). This would satisfy the requirements of the specification. You can also study all four spreads.

Differences between anorexia nervosa and bulimia nervosa

Difference	Anorexia nervosa	Bulimia nervosa
Weight	Severely underweight – below 85% of what is normal for age and height.	Only slightly underweight or near normal.
Hunger	Doesn't experience feelings of hunger which leads to reduced food intake.	Feels hungry which leads to eating and guilt, and then the need to purge to reduce weight and guilt.
Personality	Tends to be obsessional and to have greater self-control (overcontrolling). Also more compliant.	Tends to be impulsive and emotionally unstable leading to conflicts with family.

We have chosen to talk about 'individuals with anorexia/bulimia' rather than use the words 'anorexics' or 'bulimics'. This is in line with our attitudes towards physical illness. A person with measles is not a measlic. Having anorexia or bulimia does not change the whole person.

What causes anorexia nervosa?

On pages 144–5 we looked at the clinical characteristics of eating disorders. We now look at attempts to understand their causes. Are they biological or psychological? We start with anorexia.

One issue that arises is the distinction between a cause and an effect. People with anorexia have certain typical symptoms, such as abnormal levels of particular hormones. Such abnormalities may have precipitated the illness (i.e. they caused it). Or it may be that the illness was caused by some other factors, such as an early trauma, and then, once starvation set in, hormone levels became abnormal. We are interested in *causes* but we are also interested in the other factors that perpetuate the illness because these *continue to cause* the illness. It is important to distinguish between causes and effects, but it is also important to realise that effects cause further effects that become causes!

A second important issue is that there is no single explanation. As you will see, the explanations presented here fit together to make a long and complex account.

Genetic factors

Twin and family studies, such as the study by Holland *et al.*, indicate that anorexia is caused by inherited (genetic factors).

The main question is, if anorexia is caused by genetic factors, what is the mechanism by which the gene(s) actually lead(s) to disordered behaviour?

Gorwood *et al.* (1998) suggest that genes may dictate abnormal levels of neurotransmitters or abnormal development of the hypothalamus (both discussed below).

Klump *et al.* (2000) suggest that people with anorexia and their parents have an obsessive-compulsive personality disorder that produces perfectionist behaviour. This can be seen in an obsessive interest in food. What drives obsession? One possibility is that it is serotonin, and abnormal levels of serotonin could be genetically caused (discussed below).

star**STUDY**

The biological causes of anorexia nervosa

(HOLLAND *ET AL.*, 1988)

Aims

A variety of data suggest that anorexia may have a genetic basis. There is increasing evidence of inherited susceptibilities for other mental disorders such as manic depression, and evidence that weight is related to nature as well as nurture (environment). Both sets of evidence suggest that anorexia may have a genetic basis as well. This study aims to explore this possibility by comparing incidence of anorexia in identical (MZ) and non-identical (DZ) twins. Since twins are raised in the same environment, similarity may be due to nature or nurture. However, if MZ twins are more similar, this implies that genes play a greater role.

Procedures

Forty-five pairs of female twins were interviewed where at least one twin had had anorexia. The interviews established the clinical characteristics observed as well as the occurrence of eating disorders in any close relatives. Records were also made of body mass and length of amenorrhoea, and questions asked about drive to be thin and body dissatisfaction.

In order to determine whether twins were identical or not, a blood test was used. There were 25 MZ twins and 20 DZ twins in the study.

Findings

There was significantly higher concordance in the MZ twins; 25 (56%) of the MZ twins were concordant for anorexia whereas only 1 (5%) of the DZ twins was.

There was significantly more anorexia in relatives studied than found in the normal population. The rate of anorexia in the population in general is 0.1%. The study found 6 cases of anorexia among first-degree relatives (4.9%) and in second-degree relatives there were 2 cases (1.2%).

The measures of body mass, amenorrhoea, drive to be thin and body dissatisfaction indicated that these were heritable as there was greater similarity between MZ than DZ twins.

Conclusions

The findings from all three different methods of analysis suggest that anorexia has a large genetic component. The figure of heritability may be as large as 80%; in other words, 80% of the variation in anorexia is due to genetic factors and 20% to environmental factors. This high figure may be partly explained in terms of how genetic factors interact with the environment. What is inherited is a genetic sensitivity to environmental factors.

Criticisms

Unreliable diagnosis

One difficulty with studies of anorexia is that the actual diagnosis in any individual is not that certain. Some individuals suffer both anorexia and bulimia, though not always at the same time. This means that the genetic susceptibility may be a 'susceptibility to develop eating disorders' rather than anorexia in particular. Gorwood *et al.* (1998) suggest that if we want to identify the genetic causes of anorexia, we need to distinguish distinct subtypes more clearly.

MZ twins are treated more similarly

It may be that MZ twins are treated more similarly and this makes their environment more similar than DZ twins' environment, which would explain higher concordance rates. However, Holland *et al.* argue that MZ twins who actually look very different still have the same high concordance rates as MZ twins who look identical. Therefore this explanation is unlikely.

It is also possible that twins imitate each other and this is more likely in MZ twins. However, some twins who developed the disorder had been living in separate countries and they concealed the disorder from their other twin.

Biochemical factors

Serotonin – There is considerable evidence that increased serotonin activity in the brain is associated with a suppressed appetite and also with increased anxiety, obsessive behaviour, phobias and even vomiting – all characteristics of people with anorexia. It may be that restricted food intake alleviates related problems because, if no food is eaten, in particular a substance called tryptophan, then body serotonin levels drop. Therefore people with anorexia feel better by starving themselves.

Biochemical factors as a cause or effect of anorexia nervosa – The *starvation hypothesis* suggests that neurotransmitter and hormone disorders are a consequence rather than a cause of emotional distress. Fichter and Pirke (1995) starved normal individuals, which caused changes in neurotransmitter and hormone levels, supporting the view that starvation causes the changes rather than vice versa. It may be that, once starvation is under way, this leads to changes that then become symptoms of the disorder.

Neuroanatomy

The hypothalamus – Control of serotonin and of stress responses occurs in the hypothalamus (see pages 88–9). Perhaps people with anorexia have an innately malfunctioning hypothalamus. The hypothalamus controls the autonomic nervous system (mediates emotion) and endocrine system (governs hormones such as those for menstruation). It is also involved in the control of hunger – part of the hypothalamus produces feelings of hunger (the lateral hypothalamus, LH), whilst another part suppresses hunger (the ventromedial hypothalamus, VMH). The LH and VMH jointly regulate hunger. If the LH is damaged the

result is undereating because no feelings of hunger are produced and the VMH continues to send signals to suppress hunger.

The hippocampus – Stress hormones affect a tiny area in the middle of the brain called the hippocampus, which regulates the release of certain hormones such as **cortisol**. Prolonged stress leads to shrinkage of the hippocampus. The smaller the hippocampus, the more stress hormones are released. This could explain why people with anorexia get stuck in a vicious cycle and can't start eating again despite a desire to do so.

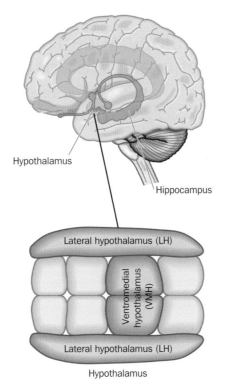

Hypothalamus

Hippocampus

Lateral hypothalamus (LH)

Ventromedial hypothalamus (VMH)

Lateral hypothalamus (LH)

Hypothalamus

Criticisms

Positive

Increasing research in this area is beginning to indicate that biological differences exist between people with anorexia and normal individuals, which may explain why the disorder develops and also why it is so resistant to treatment. If neurotransmitters and hormones can be shown to be critical, then successful drug therapies may be developed. For example, anti-depressants which reduce the effect of serotonin have been shown in some cases to be effective in treating anorexia.

On the negative side

Much of the research mentioned has relied on very small samples (often fewer than 10 participants). Even in these small groups, there are individual differences (for example, not all people with anorexia have shrunken hippocampi). This means that no one biological mechanism has been pinpointed as the source of the disorder.

In addition, biological explanations cannot account for the fact that anorexia has increased dramatically in the past 30 years. Nor can they explain why there is not 100% concordance for anorexia in twins.

The best model to use is the **diathesis-stress model**. Some individuals are born with a biological predisposition to develop anorexia, others may acquire this predisposition through, for example, birth injuries or illness. However, it is likely that the disorder is triggered by life stressors (psycho-social factors). Once the disorder begins, then biological mechanisms may perpetuate the illness. It is unlikely that biological factors alone can explain anorexia.

COMMENTARY CORNER

To what extent is it possible to explain anorexia nervosa from a biological perspective?

Each of the perspectives discussed on this spread offers a slightly different account of anorexia. However, one thing they all have in common is that they are *biological* explanations. Before we accept (or reject) biological explanations of anorexia, two further points should be considered.

- The **diathesis-stress** model proposes that rather than anorexia itself being directly inherited, people may inherit a *vulnerability* or risk factor (the diathesis), which puts them more at risk of developing anorexia during adolescence. This risk factor may interact with psycho-social stressors, which leads the individual to diet during adolescence, and this results in the emergence of a clinical eating disorder. A key vulnerability factor in the development of anorexia is *obsessionality*. Aspects of obsessive-compulsive disorder are common among individuals with anorexia *and* their

family members. Personality traits, such as perfectionism and inflexibility, are particularly common. Therefore, obsessional personality traits may be a specific familial risk factor (a diathesis) for anorexia. Research has established a strong genetic influence in the development of obsessive-compulsive disorder, which in turn suggests a common familial vulnerability for anorexia nervosa.

- The biological explanations proposed in this section focus principally on brain mechanisms that are relevant to hunger and satiety. This may explain why people with anorexia display abnormal eating patterns, but does not explain many of the more psychological aspects of the disorder, such as the intense fear of becoming fat or the distorted body image. It is clear that biological explanations *alone* are insufficient and we must also examine the role of psychological, social and cultural factors in the development of this disorder.

Causes of anorexia nervosa (continued)

We now consider psychological explanations for anorexia nervosa. Psychological explanations differ from biological ones in that they focus more on the psychological dimensions of human behaviour rather than the role of bodily processes. They also make different *assumptions* about the nature of behaviour, and therefore the nature of this particular form of abnormal behaviour.

starSTUDY · The psychological causes of anorexia nervosa (BECKER, 1999)

Imagine a country where the phrase 'You've gained weight' is considered a compliment. Until recently, this was the case on the island of Fiji.

Aims

Various explanations are offered as to how anorexia may be caused by psychological factors. One such explanation is that cultural factors create a desire for thinness and introduce ideas about dieting to young girls. However, no studies have demonstrated a relationship between cultural change and disordered eating habits. This study took advantage of a naturally occurring situation where television was first introduced to the island of Fiji to see what effects prolonged, novel exposure to Western television would have on attitudes towards eating and incidence of anorexia among adolescent girls.

Procedures

In 1995, at the time when TV was first introduced to the island, 63 native Fijian girls were asked to complete a questionnaire on attitudes towards eating and were questioned about their TV viewing habits.

Three years later, a further sample of 65 girls, aged 17 years on average, were re-questioned to assess the impact of TV on their eating habits. Girls were also interviewed about their views on eating and television.

Findings

Some findings are shown in the table. Both measures were significantly higher in the group with prolonged television exposure.

Behaviour	1993	1995
Girls who reported that they vomited to control weight	3%	15%
Girls with a high score on the eating questionnaire, indicating risk of disordered eating	13%	29%

Conclusions

The findings indicate a strong link between exposure to Western ideals of thinness and changed attitudes towards eating. The girls' desire to be slim is one sign that young Fijians are striving to conform to Western cultural standards. Such changed attitudes are likely to lead to the development of eating disorders such as anorexia.

Criticisms

The findings do not necessarily demonstrate a cause

It would be a mistake to assume that this study indicates that watching Western TV programmes *causes* eating disorders or even leads to changed attitudes. It is an experimental study but a natural one and therefore the IV was not manipulated. This means we are not justified in making causal assumptions. It may be, for example, that such changes are due to the strains on a traditional culture trying to keep up with a technologically more advanced global culture.

Changed attitudes may not lead to eating disorders

The assumption that changed attitudes may lead to eating orders may be mistaken. If eating disorders are caused by, or at least related to, biological factors, then the cultural explanation alone will be insufficient.

Psychological explanations of anorexia nervosa

The psychodynamic approach

Freud suggested that eating was a substitute for sexual activity. Therefore, not eating was a way to repress sexual thoughts and the onset of sexual maturity. Starvation in adolescence is also a means of avoiding the development of an adult's body. Restricted food intake prevents menstruation and development of secondary sexual characteristics, such as breasts and enlarged hips. By preventing adult development, an adolescent can avoid anxieties associated with adulthood and mature sexuality.

Bruch (1980) has proposed a more recent psychodynamic explanation of the development of anorexia in terms of poor parenting and a struggle for autonomy. The origins of anorexia are in early childhood, when the mother does not cope adequately with her child's needs. For example, she may offer the child food when the child was expressing anxiety. This leads the child to feel ineffectual because his or her signals are not appropriately responded to. Such children fail to develop self-reliance and are especially sensitive to criticism from others.

In adolescence, the conflict between maternal dependence and the child's wish for independence results in anorexia as a means of exerting self-control. At the same time, the mother's continuing relationship problems mean a desire on the mother's part to retain dependence and encourage immaturity in her child, both in body and mind.

Criticisms

The main issue with psychodynamic explanations is that they are difficult to falsify (prove wrong). Bruch developed her explanation on the basis of examining many case studies of anorexia and producing an interpretation of the causal factors.

CORNER

COMMENTARY

Consider whether anorexia nervosa is best explained from a biological or a psychological perspective.

Nigel: Okay, what's the biological take on this?

Alison: Well, in brief, the biological perspective emphasises the importance of bodily processes in the development of anorexia. There is evidence (such as Holland et al., 1988) to suggest that anorexia has a large genetic component, with as much as 80% of the variation in anorexia due to genetic factors. These genetic factors may lead either to

The behavioural approach

The principles of classical and operant conditioning – Step 1 is learning an association between thinness and admiration. An individual starts dieting and his/her new slimness receives admiration. The individual learns to associate slimness (previously a neutral stimulus) with admiration and feeling good about him/herself (a response).

Step 2 is operant conditioning. Continuing admiration is reinforcing. In addition, refusing to eat and excessive weight loss may attract increased attention, which is rewarding/reinforcing. The individual may gain personal satisfaction (reward) because weight loss acts as a punishment to parents.

Avoidance of feared stimulus (eating) perpetuates dieting through **negative reinforcement** – escaping from an undesirable situation, which results in a pleasurable state of affairs.

The influence of the media – It is the media (e.g. magazines, films, toys) that creates the social norm that 'thin is good'. We see that thin models and film stars receive admiration and attention (**vicarious reinforcement**), and therefore we imitate the behaviour. This media explanation centres around indirect (vicarious) learning through operant conditioning (social learning theory). It is supported by the study by Becker (see previous page)

Anorexia as a culture-bound-syndrome (CBS) – The media explanation is also a cultural explanation. The media transmits social norms and cultural values. It is our culture that values thinness. This means that one way to test this hypothesis is to look at the incidence of anorexia in other cultures. The incidence of anorexia in other cultures is rare. For example, Sui-Wah (1989) reported that anorexia is rare in black populations in Western and non-Western cultures, and in China. The Chinese have a cultural norm of respect for food, which means that thinness is not valued.

Criticisms

The behavioural view is appealing because it can explain many observed facts. It can explain gender differences (female stereotypes more associated with dieting and thinness), increased rates of anorexia in males (male thinness stereotypes are increasing), increased rates of anorexia in general (due to increasing emphasis on thinness) and cultural differences (different attitudes to eating and different social norms).

However, the behavioural model cannot explain individual differences. All of us in the West are exposed to thin models but very few develop anorexia. Equally, many people diet but very few develop anorexia. This means that behavioural explanations on their own are insufficient. It may require the addition of one of the other biological and/or psychological explanations to account for the development of the disorder in particular individuals.

The concept of anorexia as a CBS is not without objectors. Hoek *et al.* (1998) set out to test the view that anorexia is rare in other cultures. The researchers examined the records of 44,192 people admitted to hospital between 1987 and 1989 in Curacao, a non-Westernised Caribbean island where it is acceptable to be overweight. They found 6 cases, a rate that they claim is within the range of rates reported in Western countries.

The cognitive approach

Is anorexia related to disordered thinking? An individual with anorexia, according to the cognitive model, is an individual who is preoccupied with the way he or she looks – or thinks he or she looks. People with anorexia often perceive themselves as unattractive and/or overweight. The cognitive model can explain why only some dieters develop anorexia. We are all exposed to the thinness model but only those with faulty belief systems are affected because they don't 'see' their excessive weight loss.

Bemis-Vitousek and Orimoto (1993) pointed out the kind of faulty cognitions that are typical in people with anorexia. For example, a common cognition is that dieting is a means of exerting self-control, but at the same time most people with anorexia are aware that they are out of control because they can't stop dieting, even though they know it is threatening their life. These are faulty cognitions and maladaptive ways of thinking.

Criticisms

Distorted cognitions may be an effect rather than a cause of the illness. However, as with the other explanations, once an individual develops faulty cognitions it can be seen how these would help perpetuate the disorder.

One strength of the cognitive approach is that it has the potential to lead to useful therapies, enabling clients to tackle self-defeating statements and therefore start eating again. Garner and Bemis (1982) point out that whatever the cause, the end result appears to be the desire to become thin. It is this cognition that should be the focus of therapy.

---

abnormal levels of neurotransmitters such as serotonin, or to abnormal development of the hypothalamus. Both of these are important in the regulation of appetite, so abnormal development can lead to an eating disorder.

Nigel: Isn't it true that some individuals are both anorexic *and* bulimic, so how can they be said to inherit anorexia directly?

Alison: Ah, did I say that? What appears to be inherited is not the disorder itself, but a vulnerability to anorexia or bulimia. For example, a risk factor for anorexia is obsessionality, and this appears to run in families, so an individual may inherit an

obsessional personality, and this makes them more vulnerable to developing anorexia.

Nigel: What you seem to have missed out here is that in order to 'become' anorexic, there must be something else, a psychological stressor that triggers the disorder?

Alison: The diathesis-stress model. True, what they inherit is the risk factor, or diathesis, and this interacts with the psycho-social stressors of adolescence and so may produce anorexia.

Nigel: So what you're saying is that biological factors alone can't explain anorexia?

Alison: More or less. Don't forget, though, that research is beginning to show very real biological differences between individuals with anorexia and those with bulimia. For example, if levels of neurotransmitters *are* shown to be critical in anorexia, then drug therapies can be developed.

The debate continues...

Of course you wouldn't write *your* answer like this. However, exercises such as this help you to appreciate the arguments and counter-arguments for each perspective, so that when you *do* write a response to this question, these will spring more readily to mind.

What causes bulimia nervosa?

We now look at explanations of bulimia – both biological and psychological. It may be useful to recall some of the major distinctions between anorexia and bulimia. People with bulimia tend to have near normal weight, whereas people with anorexia are more than abnormally thin. Both anorexia and bulimia are associated with a *desire* to be thin, but people with bulimia cannot resist eating whereas people with anorexia have no appetite (though they may think a lot about food). Individuals with bulimia may even derive comfort from eating, whereas individuals with anorexia gain pleasure from starvation.

Despite these differences, many of the explanations offered for anorexia apply equally to bulimia, such as the effects of media images. However, some explanations apply more particularly to bulimia.

research activity

Conducting an interview

This might be a good opportunity to try to conduct an interview yourself. Your class might decide on a topic, such as dieting, and then develop a short set of questions to start the interview (the interview script). You (the interviewer) should then follow this with other questions and record the answers on tape, to be transcribed later. Data can be qualitatively and quantitatively analysed. (*Be sure to inform your interviewee about the purpose of the study.*)

starSTUDY

The biological causes of bulimia nervosa

(KENDLER *ET AL.*, 1991)

Aims

Kendler *et al.* aimed to establish whether the increased incidence of bulimia in families was due to genetic or environmental factors. This can be done by comparing incidence in MZ and DZ twins, as was done in the study by Holland *et al.* (page 146).

Procedures

The study contacted over 1,000 pairs of twins (2,000 individuals) by using data from the Virginia twin registry. All twins were interviewed by trained interviewers. The same interviewer never interviewed both members of a twin pair.

Findings

In MZ twins there was 26% concordance between twin pairs and 16% for DZ twins.

Of the sample interviewed, there were 123 cases of bulimia. Most of these participants also reported other mental disorders at some time in their lives, including anorexia (10%), depression (51%), phobia (42%) and anxiety disorder (11%).

Conclusions

The higher concordance for MZ twins indicates a strong genetic component in bulimia. However, this is lower than found for anorexia. Kendler *et al.* suggest a heritability estimate for bulimia of 55%, i.e. about half of the variation in bulimia is due to genetic factors and half to environmental factors. This is significantly less than the heritability estimate for anorexia (which was 80%).

The relationship between bulimia and other mental disorders suggests that what may be inherited is a general vulnerability for mental illness, not just for bulimia specifically.

Criticisms

Contradictory findings

A more recent study by Bulik *et al.* (2000) concluded that bulimia is 83% genetically influenced and anorexia nervosa is 58% genetic, which both supports and contradicts Kendler *et al.*'s findings. It is supportive because it is further evidence of a genetic cause. It is contradictory because it suggests a greater genetic component for bulimia. One of the difficulties may be the issue of reliability in diagnosis. All studies rely on identifying characteristics of a disorder, and inevitably different criteria may be employed, leading to different rates of diagnosis.

Twins may not be representative

There may be reasons why twins are more prone to mental illness than non-twins and therefore the findings may not generalise to the rest of the population. It is possible that twins experience more stress or that they are genetically more vulnerable.

Research methods
Conducting interviews

Earlier we looked at the advantages and disadvantages of different kinds of **interview** (page 105), and compared the interview method with using **questionnaires** (page 102). Both methods use questions, but the less structured interview method has one key advantage – the interviewer can adapt the questions to suit the interviewee. This makes the interview more natural and permits unexpected information to be collected. The open-endedness of adapting questions can of course be a disadvantage as well because the interviewer may ask impromptu questions which may be '**leading questions**' or biased in some other way. This is why interviewers should be specially trained.

One kind of interview method is called the **clinical method**, a semi-structured approach. It is called 'clinical' because it is the kind of method used by doctors and clinicians when interviewing patients. The doctor starts with a set of standard questions and then begins to adapt the questions depending on previous answers. For example, there would be little point asking a patient about dieting if that person has reported that his or her weight is normal.

The interview is 'semi-structured' because the questions start off as pre-determined (and easily codeable) and then become freer. 'Freer' questions usually require **qualitative** analysis (see page 99).

Genetic factors

The studies by Kendler *et al.* and Bulik *et al.* (on the previous page) both provided evidence that bulimia is inherited. Genetic factors may lead to biochemical or neuroanatomical abnormalities, or they may lead to dispositional differences. Lilenfeld *et al.* (2000) suggest that inherited factors may predispose some individuals to impulsivity and that such individuals develop bulimia, in the same way that others are predisposed to obsession and to develop anorexia.

Biochemical factors

Serotonin – It has been suggested that serotonin may be involved in bulimia but in a way that is different to its involvement in anorexia. Increased serotonin activity in the brain may be responsible for anorexia, whereas decreased serotonin activity may be responsible for bulimia (Galla, 1995). This makes sense because people with bulimia have an enhanced rather than absent appetite. People with bulimia overeat and then feel guilty because of the desire to be thin.

CCK – Another hormone, cholecystokinin (CCK), has been found to cause laboratory animals to feel full and stop eating. It has been found that people with bulimia have decreased levels of CCK after eating, which would explain why they are able to go on eating so much. In one study 25 people with bulimia and 18 controls were asked to binge. The people with bulimia consumed 3,500 calories during the meal compared to 1,500 for the controls (Kissileff *et al.*, 1996).

Neuroanatomy

As with anorexia, the hypothalamus plays a role in bulimia. Damage to the hypothalamus can result in either overeating or undereating. In animals, damage to the ventromedial hypothalamus (VMH) results in overeating. This happens because the lateral hypothalamus (LH) stimulates eating and the VMH usually stops eating. But if the VMH is damaged, there is no sense of satiety and overeating occurs, which may result in obesity. In an individual who wishes to be thin, overeating is controlled as far as possible but may then result in an excessive binge, which further results in compensation through purging.

Serotonin is linked to this process because it helps to regulate the feeding centres of the hypothalamus. Low levels of serotonin stimulate the LH.

VMH Stops eating	• Damage results in overeating because no sense of being full. May result in excessive binges. Explains bulimia. • High levels of serotonin stimulate VMH, suppress appetite, lead to anorexia
LH Stimulates eating	• Damage results in undereating because no feelings of hunger and VMH continues to send signals of fullness. Explains anorexia • Low levels of serotonin stimulate LH, increase appetite, lead to bulimia

Criticisms

The same issues that are related to biological explanations of anorexia apply to bulimia, namely the question of cause or effect as well as lack of consistency in findings. For example, some studies have found higher rather than lower levels of serotonin in people with bulimia and/or normal levels of CCK.

Bulimia, like anorexia, is probably the result of a 'collision' between vulnerabilities biological (e.g. abnormal serotonin levels) and developmental factors (such as abuse or exposure to the slimness ideal). However, there is good support for the importance of biological factors – these are discussed in the Commentary Corner below.

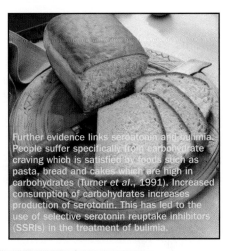

Further evidence links serotonin and bulimia. People suffer specifically from carbohydrate craving which is satisfied by foods such as pasta, bread and cakes which are high in carbohydrates (Turner *et al.*, 1991). Increased consumption of carbohydrates increases production of serotonin. This has led to the use of selective serotonin reuptake inhibitors (SSRIs) in the treatment of bulimia.

COMMENTARY CORNER

How convincing are biological explanations of bulimia?

The development of both anorexia and bulimia is presumed to be complex and influenced by many different developmental, social and biological processes. The exact way in which these different influences interact is not, however, fully understood. It seems clear that cultural attitudes towards physical attractiveness and the pursuit of thinness are relevant to the psychopathology of eating disorders, but unlikely that these *alone* could explain their development. There are three major reasons for this conclusion (Kaye *et al.*, 2000):

1 Dieting and the drive towards thinness are commonplace in industrialised countries throughout the world, yet anorexia affects only 0.3–0.7% and bulimia 1.7–2.5% of females in the general population. If such cultural pressures were the main reason behind eating disorders such as bulimia, then that figure would be considerably higher.

2 Numerous descriptions of eating disorders similar to anorexia and bulimia date from the middle of the nineteenth century. This suggests that something other than our present cultural norms plays a causal role in the development of bulimia.

3 Both anorexia and bulimia have a relatively stereotypic set of clinical characteristics, sex distribution and age of onset *regardless* of the culture concerned. This too suggests some common biological vulnerability for the development of bulimia.

Additional insights into the biological origins of bulimia have been obtained from the application of drug therapies in its treatment. Treatments using a variety of anti-depressant drugs (which alter the levels of neurotransmitter activity in the brain) have shown significant decreases in the episodes of binge eating associated with bulimia. Some studies (e.g. Walsh *et al.*, 1997) have compared the effectiveness of psychotherapy (a *psychological* treatment) and drug therapy (a *biological* treatment) for the management of bulimia. Although these studies typically show little short-term improvement from psychotherapy *plus* medication compared to medication alone, long-term follow-up studies have found that combined treatment is more effective than psychotherapy alone. The success of drug therapies for bulimia, compared to the limited success of similar drug treatments for anorexia, has made the case for a *biological* basis for bulimia that bit more convincing.

Causes of
bulimia nervosa (continued)

In this final spread, we look at alternative explanations for bulimia – those that are psychological in nature. As we have already seen, the main psychological explanations are psychodynamic, behavioural and cognitive. Psychodynamic explanations emphasise the influence of unresolved childhood conflicts, behavioural explanations are related to learning and social theory, and cognitive explanations refer to maladaptive thinking.

starSTUDY

The psychological causes of bulimia nervosa

(CUTTS & BARRIOS, 1986)

Aims

Many researchers have suggested that fear of weight gain underlies both anorexia and bulimia, yet few have tested this belief empirically. Fear of weight gain is an example of a distorted perception. This study aims to investigate whether such a fear is more prevalent in people with bulimia than in 'normal' controls.

Procedures

Thirty females aged 18–25 were assigned to an individual with bulimia or **control group** on the basis of questionnaires and interviews. Then all were tested in a laboratory. They listened to two descriptions: one of a neutral scene (sitting in a library) and one depicting weight gain (imagining they have gained 5 pounds). Both scenes were described by a man, and participants were asked to imagine themselves in this situation. Their accompanying physiological responses were recorded by measuring facial muscle activity, heart rate and skin resistance (indicates stress). They were also asked to report their own reactions using a self-report checklist, and their overt behaviour was rated by observers.

Findings

Both groups of participants showed similar responses to the neutral scene but different responses to the weight gain scene. People with bulimia had higher physiological activity when imagining the weight gain. They also reported greater subjective distress and their overt behaviour was rated as being higher.

Conclusions

The findings support the view that fear of weight gain may be a factor in bulimia. Such faulty perceptions could trigger biological responses and/or a behavioural cycle of reinforcement. If an individual fears weight gain, he or she diets and starvation leads to changes in neurotransmitters. If an individual starts dieting and loses weight, this leads to increased attention and attractiveness, encouraging further weight control.

Criticisms

Useful applications

The concept of faulty cognitions may also offer us a form of treatment for the disorder (by dealing with fear of weight gain) and may also offer ideas about how to detect potential individuals at risk of bulimia (by using checklists of faulty cognitions).

Extraneous variables

It may be that certain personality characteristics co-vary with faulty perceptions. For example, an individual who holds maladaptive assumptions may also have a more rigid cognitive style. It could be the rigid cognitive style rather than the faulty perceptions that is the cause of bulimia.

The psychodynamic approach

There are a variety of possible explanations.

McLelland et al. (1991) found that 30% of patients with eating disorders had reported abuse in childhood. Such experiences may be repressed and then expressed through the symptoms of bulimia. Bulimia is a means of punishing the body, and expressing self-disgust. The notion of bulimia as a coping mechanism could explain gender differences because females are taught to be self-critical, whereas males are taught to blame others. Thus an abused female turns the blame inwards and is more likely to develop bulimia. An abused male becomes hostile towards others and is less likely to develop bulimia.

Chassler (1998) suggests that bulimia represents conflicting wishes for merger and autonomy. Bingeing is an attempt to regain a momentary experience of the mother and merge with the engulfing maternal object. However, the terror of engulfment results in purging, rejecting this 'bad' object.

Criticisms

By no means all people with bulimia have experienced abuse, therefore this cannot explain all cases. And even in cases where an individual has suffered abuse, focus on this may distract attention away from other important factors.

Equally, issues of merger and autonomy are not apparent in all people with bulimia. This suggests that psychodynamic explanations may only be relevant to certain individuals.

Misconceptions about anorexia and bulimia

In discussions of eating disorders, an inevitable comment runs: '...and what I don't understand is that they just don't look good. If they're trying to look good, why can't they see that they're doing just the opposite?' The irony is that it is the observer who is failing to 'see' – failing to see that a desire to be attractive is not the problem.

This 'defective perception' is characteristic of people with eating disorders but it may be created by more than a desire to 'look good'. The American Psychiatric Association's

The behavioural approach

Direct and indirect conditioning – Bingeing is rewarding because it provides a sense of indulgence. However, it also causes anxiety that can be relieved by purging, which is therefore rewarding. Thus, both bingeing and purging are reinforced.

In some cases people with bulimia have mothers who also had the disorder and/or who continually diet themselves (Rodin, 1991). Such parents act as role models who are imitated (social learning theory).

The media also contributes to the development of bulimia by providing ideas about how to slim, such as the use of laxatives. Lee *et al.* (1992) suggest that one reason why eating disorders are relatively rare in Hong Kong is lack of specific information of how to do it.

Bulimia as a CBS – Lee *et al.* (1992) suggest that another reason that bulimia is relatively rare in Hong Kong is that the Chinese actually value fatness and dieting is rare. Their diet is low in fatty foods and eating is not associated with guilt. This suggests that it is socio-cultural factors that lead to bulimia rather than biological factors.

Nasser (1986) conducted an interesting comparative study to support the role of cultural factors in bulimia. He compared attitudes to eating (using EAT – the eating attitudes questionnaire) in two matched samples of undergraduate Arab females. One group was studying in London and the other group was in Cairo. Of those in London, 22% expressed abnormal eating attitudes (scored over 30) compared to 12% in Cairo. Six of the students in London could be classed as individuals with bulimia, whereas none had eating disorders in Cairo.

Criticisms

It is possible that there was an **extraneous variable** in Nasser's study. Arab students who decide to study abroad may possess certain personality characteristics that distinguish them from those who stay at home, and these may be related to stress vulnerability. Also they may experience greater stress being abroad.

Mumford *et al.* (1991) studied Asian girls living in the UK, finding that girls who scored highest on EAT were the ones most traditional in their dress and outlook. This is not what we would expect from the cultural model since these girls should be least affected by Western stereotypes. One explanation may be that conflict and stress were highest in this group because they went to school in the UK and experienced a greater culture clash. This supports the **diathesis-stress model** – vulnerable individuals develop bulimia when exposed to stressors.

The cognitive approach

The disinhibition hypothesis – Ruderman (1986) proposed that people differ in terms of the extent they are able to restrain their eating. There are unrestrained and restrained eaters. A 10-point 'restraint scale' was developed to assess this, with items such as 'How often are you dieting?' and 'Do you eat sensibly in front of others or do you splurge'?

Restrained eaters have a rigid cognitive style. Things are all or nothing, black or white. They also constantly monitor their weight. Various factors may lead to brief overeating – drinking too much or feeling depressed. If restrained eaters feel they have overeaten, they lose their sense of restraint ('I've blown it – I might as well continue to eat'). This leads to disinhibition of their normal restraint. They no longer feel inhibited about eating and this leads to a massive eating binge. This is a faulty cognition because they don't need to go over the top.

After eating too much, the individual feels guilt and self-disgust. This leads to purging to deal with the overeating, and more self-disgust. Once the cycle has commenced it may lead to physiological changes (biological model) that are self-perpetuating. Binge–purge may also be rewarding (behavioural model) because the bingeing allows self-indulgence while the purging offers a sense of relief. Furthermore, individuals may find that binge–purge offers a good way of dieting.

Other cognitive factors

Cooper and Taylor (1988) found that people with bulimia tend to have a distorted body image. This distorted thinking leads them to have a greater desire to lose weight. Vanderlinden *et al.* (1992) suggested that people with bulimia tend to perceive events as being more stressful than most people do and use binge–purge as a means of coping with stress or gaining a sense of control.

Criticisms

Herman and Mack's research (1975) supported the disinhibition hypothesis. They gave restrained and unrestrained eaters a 'pre-load' (a milkshake described as high in calories). They found that restrained eaters did eat more after the pre-load condition, presumably because they thought they had already overeaten, whereas unrestrained types actually ate less, presumably because they thought they were full.

As with cognitive explanations of anorexia, these explanations may be a cause or an effect of the eating disorder. However, they may still provide a useful form of treatment in order to break the binge–purge cycle.

---

textbook suggests: 'Abnormal eating behaviours are usually a smokescreen for certain unresolved psychological conflicts. These include grief, family conflict, lack of preparation for tasks of adolescence and adulthood, lack of sense of self and autonomy.'

The term 'unresolved psychological conflicts' delves into a boundless internal realm of wants and collisions. For example, anorexics often fear their own sexuality and seek to deny it by starving away all secondary sexual characteristics, by symbolically carving a new outer form. Bulimics often lack all the parental affection and involvement they need and soothe themselves with food as compensation.

Anorexia and bulimia are generally presented as strategies to gain mastery over a profound sense of chaos. The very last thing a person can do, when they generally feel that they've lost control, is discipline what they eat, perhaps in the hope that this will then lead to control over the rest of their lives.

So is thinness a 'smokescreen' for unresolved conflicts, or does dieting arise out of a need for control? In a culture of images, the anorexic/bulimic individual clearly emulates our culture's image of happiness and order: the slim figure. Wealth, popularity, beauty, love, sexual activity – the media links these desired items with icons of thinness. The idols of our culture, such as movie stars, are usually thin, and unusually so.

Couldn't these role models and their excessive slimness be the real culprits in anorexia and bulimia? If that were so, we would probably all be in therapy. These images work through association rather than by direct command. The statement, 'get thin or you won't be happy', is too subtle to alone push someone into a psychological disease. Eating disorders only fall within a sphere of social interests and concerns, they are not governed by it. Invisible conflicts are the real mechanisms. In other words, 'looking good' is only the tip of an iceberg whose true foundations are immense and submerged.

Source: Adapted from Jonathan Soverow (1997), *Thinking about Disease*.

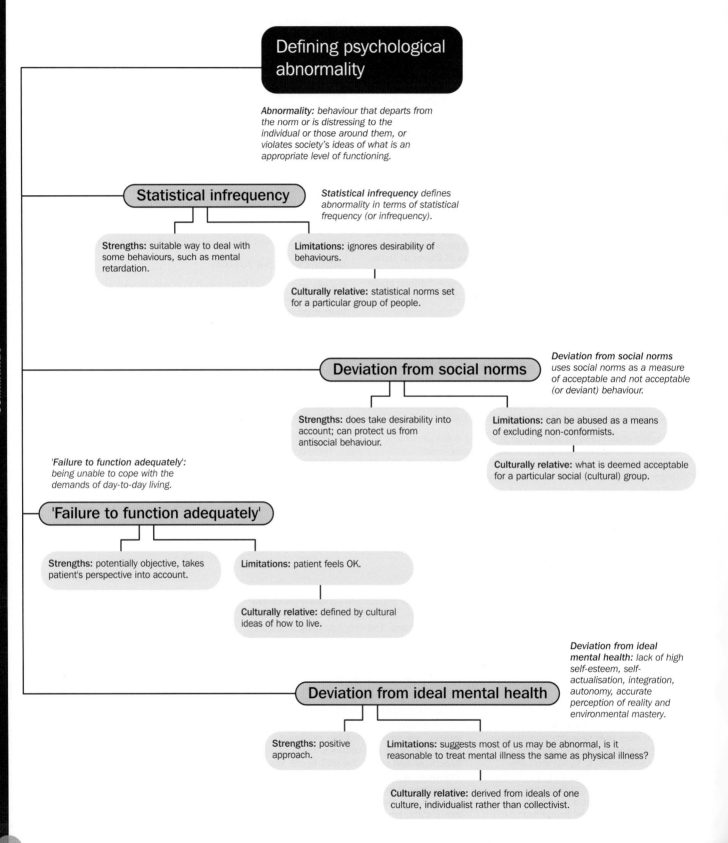

Defining psychological abnormality

Abnormality: behaviour that departs from the norm or is distressing to the individual or those around them, or violates society's ideas of what is an appropriate level of functioning.

Statistical infrequency

Statistical infrequency defines abnormality in terms of statistical frequency (or infrequency).

Strengths: suitable way to deal with some behaviours, such as mental retardation.

Limitations: ignores desirability of behaviours.

Culturally relative: statistical norms set for a particular group of people.

Deviation from social norms

Deviation from social norms uses social norms as a measure of acceptable and not acceptable (or deviant) behaviour.

Strengths: does take desirability into account; can protect us from antisocial behaviour.

Limitations: can be abused as a means of excluding non-conformists.

Culturally relative: what is deemed acceptable for a particular social (cultural) group.

'Failure to function adequately': being unable to cope with the demands of day-to-day living.

'Failure to function adequately'

Strengths: potentially objective, takes patient's perspective into account.

Limitations: patient feels OK.

Culturally relative: defined by cultural ideas of how to live.

Deviation from ideal mental health: lack of high self-esteem, self-actualisation, integration, autonomy, accurate perception of reality and environmental mastery.

Deviation from ideal mental health

Strengths: positive approach.

Limitations: suggests most of us may be abnormal, is it reasonable to treat mental illness the same as physical illness?

Culturally relative: derived from ideals of one culture, individualist rather than collectivist.

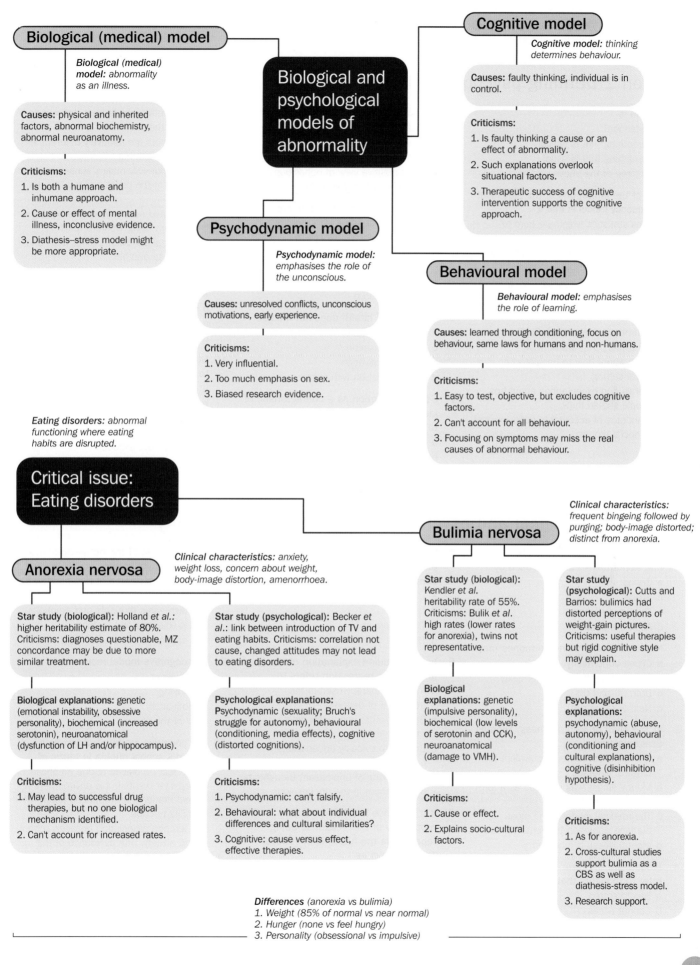

Biological and psychological models of abnormality

Biological (medical) model

Biological (medical) model: abnormality as an illness.

Causes: physical and inherited factors, abnormal biochemistry, abnormal neuroanatomy.

Criticisms:
1. Is both a humane and inhumane approach.
2. Cause or effect of mental illness, inconclusive evidence.
3. Diathesis–stress model might be more appropriate.

Cognitive model

Cognitive model: thinking determines behaviour.

Causes: faulty thinking, individual is in control.

Criticisms:
1. Is faulty thinking a cause or an effect of abnormality.
2. Such explanations overlook situational factors.
3. Therapeutic success of cognitive intervention supports the cognitive approach.

Psychodynamic model

Psychodynamic model: emphasises the role of the unconscious.

Causes: unresolved conflicts, unconscious motivations, early experience.

Criticisms:
1. Very influential.
2. Too much emphasis on sex.
3. Biased research evidence.

Behavioural model

Behavioural model: emphasises the role of learning.

Causes: learned through conditioning, focus on behaviour, same laws for humans and non-humans.

Criticisms:
1. Easy to test, objective, but excludes cognitive factors.
2. Can't account for all behaviour.
3. Focusing on symptoms may miss the real causes of abnormal behaviour.

Critical issue: Eating disorders

Eating disorders: abnormal functioning where eating habits are disrupted.

Anorexia nervosa

Clinical characteristics: anxiety, weight loss, concern about weight, body-image distortion, amenorrhoea.

Star study (biological): Holland *et al.*: higher heritability estimate of 80%. Criticisms: diagnoses questionable, MZ concordance may be due to more similar treatment.

Biological explanations: genetic (emotional instability, obsessive personality), biochemical (increased serotonin), neuroanatomical (dysfunction of LH and/or hippocampus).

Criticisms:
1. May lead to successful drug therapies, but no one biological mechanism identified.
2. Can't account for increased rates.

Star study (psychological): Becker *et al.*: link between introduction of TV and eating habits. Criticisms: correlation not cause, changed attitudes may not lead to eating disorders.

Psychological explanations: Psychodynamic (sexuality; Bruch's struggle for autonomy), behavioural (conditioning, media effects), cognitive (distorted cognitions).

Criticisms:
1. Psychodynamic: can't falsify.
2. Behavioural: what about individual differences and cultural similarities?
3. Cognitive: cause versus effect, effective therapies.

Bulimia nervosa

Clinical characteristics: frequent bingeing followed by purging; body-image distorted; distinct from anorexia.

Star study (biological): Kendler *et al.* heritability rate of 55%. Criticisms: Bulik *et al.* high rates (lower rates for anorexia), twins not representative.

Biological explanations: genetic (impulsive personality), biochemical (low levels of serotonin and CCK), neuroanatomical (damage to VMH).

Criticisms:
1. Cause or effect.
2. Explains socio-cultural factors.

Star study (psychological): Cutts and Barrios: bulimics had distorted perceptions of weight-gain pictures. Criticisms: useful therapies but rigid cognitive style may explain.

Psychological explanations: psychodynamic (abuse, autonomy), behavioural (conditioning and cultural explanations), cognitive (disinhibition hypothesis).

Criticisms:
1. As for anorexia.
2. Cross-cultural studies support bulimia as a CBS as well as diathesis-stress model.
3. Research support.

Differences (anorexia vs bulimia)
1. Weight (85% of normal vs near normal)
2. Hunger (none vs feel hungry)
3. Personality (obsessional vs impulsive)

Section 1 Defining psychological abnormality

1 A norm is
a A standard
b Something that is typical
c Something that is usual
d All three of the above

2 One of the limitations of the statistical infrequency model is that it
a Uses statistics which are hard to calculate
b Doesn't distinguish between desirable and undesirable behaviours
c Involves making a subjective judgement
d All of the above

3 Social norms are best defined as
a Behaviours that are normal
b Rules about how to behave when in a social setting
c Morals and expectations about how people should think
d Standards of acceptable behaviour set by social groups

4 One strength of the social deviancy model is that
a It takes subjective feelings into account
b It helps protect the rest of us
c It is a positive view of behaviour
d Deviance is easily identified

5 The 'failure to function adequately' approach to defining abnormality
a Can be assessed objectively
b Concerns the distress felt by the individual
c Concerns the distress felt by observers
d All of the above

6 Ideal mental health does *not* include
a High self-esteem
b Self-actualisation
c Lack of motivation
d Ability to get on with friends

7 Self-actualisation as a characteristic of ideal mental health is thought to apply to
a Individualist cultures only
b Collectivist cultures only
c Individualist and collectivist cultures
d Neither a or b

8 Cultural relativism is best defined as the view that
a Behaviours are relatively different in different cultures
b Behaviour only makes sense when viewed in the context of a particular culture
c We should not measure the behaviour of others using Western tests
d Abnormal behaviours differ from one culture to another

9 Methods of dispersion tell us about
a The average of a set of data
b The lowest numbers in a set of data
c The spread of a set of data
d The average spread of a set of data

10 Standard deviation is a better measure to use than the range because
a It is easier to calculate
b It can be done on a computer
c It is a statistical method
d It is more precise because all the numbers are included

Section 2 Biological and psychological models of abnormality

1 The biological model suggests that abnormality can be caused by
a Genes
b Stress
c The environment
d All of the above

2 Neurotransmitters and hormones may
a Cause abnormality
b May be the effect of abnormality
c Both (a) and (b)
d Neither (a) nor (b)

3 In *The Myth of Mental Illness*, Thomas Szasz claimed
a Mental illnesses were equivalent to physical illnesses
b Mental illness was invented as a form of social control
c The medical model is the most humane approach to mental illness
d Mental illness is inherited

4 Freud used the term 'unconscious' to refer to thoughts that an individual
a Has forgotten
b Cannot access
c Finds hard to bring into conscious awareness
d Pretends not to be aware of

5 Which of the following represents the primitive, pleasure-seeking part of the personality?
a The id
b The ego
c The superego
d The anal stage

6 In the Freudian explanation of abnormality, repression refers to
a A type of therapy used in the treatment of depression
b Blaming other people for life's misfortunes
c Bringing previously unconscious material into conscious awareness
d The blocking of unpleasant thoughts by placing them in the unconscious

7 If a response is reinforced, the probability of that response being repeated in the future is increased. This is known as
a Classical conditioning
b Operant conditioning
c Social learning
d Shaping

8 An advantage of the behavioural model of abnormality is that
a It is the only one that is supported by evidence
b It disregards thoughts and emotions
c It is scientific and testable
d It applies to all species equally

9 The cognitive model focuses on
a Behaviour
b Thinking
c Motivation
d All of the above

10 The cognitive model would explain Robert's school phobia in terms of
a The fact he placed undue emphasis on negative events in his environment and held irrational assumptions about his ability to cope
b A learned association between school and anxiety, with avoidance of the feared object reducing that anxiety
c Repressed feelings of anxiety associated with the fear of failing, with avoidance being the best way of dealing with that anxiety
d A predisposition to be anxious, which he may have inherited from his parents

Section 3 Critical issue: Eating disorders – anorexia nervosa and bulimia nervosa

1 What is 'amenorrhoea'?
a Intense religious belief
b Start of the menstrual cycle
c Cessation of the menstrual cycle
d Difficult menstrual cycle

2 Which of the following is *not* a clinical characteristic of bulimia?
a Excessive weight loss
b Binge and purge
c More frequent than once a week
d Distorted body image

3 One key difference between anorexia and bulimia is that only people with anorexia have
a A distorted body image
b A feeling of hunger
c No appetite
d A tendency to vomit or use laxatives

4 The diathesis–stress model proposes that
a Eating disorders such as anorexia nervosa are directly inherited
b Eating disorders are learned as a consequence of exposure to the media
c People inherit a vulnerability which puts them more at risk of developing an eating disorder
d Eating disorders are a direct result of high levels of life stress

5 The starvation hypothesis proposes that
a People with anorexia are starving
b Reduced levels of certain neurotransmitters lead to starvation
c Starvation leads to reduced levels of certain neurotransmitters
d Starvation causes shrinkage of the hippocampus

6 Bruch suggested that anorexia develops because poor parenting leads to
a An obsessive nature
b Phobias
c Overdependence on parent
d Desire for independence

7 People with anorexia may be reinforced for their behaviour by
a Increased attention
b A sense of greater attractiveness
c Avoidance of being fat
d All of the above

8 Bulimia is associated with
a High levels of serotonin
b Low levels of serotonin
c No differences in serotonin
d Other neurotransmitters

9 The disinhibition hypothesis proposes that people with bulimia are
a Inhibited about eating
b Uninhibited about eating
c Restrained eaters
d Unrestrained eaters

10 Cutts and Barrios (1986) discovered that
a Heritability in anorexia nervosa may be as high as 80%
b There is a strong link between Western ideals of thinness and changed attitudes towards eating
c There is a strong genetic component in bulimia
d Fear of weight gain may be a key factor in the development of bulimia

Section 1 answers
1d 2b 3d 4b 5d
6c 7a 8b 9c 10d

Section 2 answers
1a 2c 3b 4c 5a
6c 7b 8c 9b 10a

Section 3 answers
1c 2a 3c 4c 5c
6d 7d 8b 9c 10d

RESEARCH METHODS
terms covered

- Clinical method
- Content analysis
- Culture bias
- Determinism
- Ethical issues
- Gender bias
- Giving voice
- Grounded theory
- Mean
- Measures of central tendency
- Measures of dispersion
- Median
- Mode
- Nature–nurture
- Normal distribution
- Psychology as a science
- Qualitative analysis
- Quantitative analysis
- Range
- Reductionism
- Standard deviation
- Thematic analysis
- The use of non-human animals

Revision list

Key terms

You may be asked to 'Explain what is meant by' any of the following. Each explanation may be for 2, 3 or 6 marks. Make sure that what you write is related to the number of marks. Use examples to amplify your explanations where appropriate.

✓

☐ Abnormality	p. 128
☐ Anorexia nervosa	p. 144
☐ Bulimia nervosa	p. 144
☐ Deviation from ideal mental health	p. 131
☐ Deviation from social norms	p. 131
☐ Eating disorder	p. 144
☐ Failure to function adequately	p. 131
☐ Statistical infrequency	p. 131

Star studies

This is the 'apfcc' question. You need three minutes' worth of writing on aims, procedures, findings and conclusions for each of these. You may also be asked for one or two criticisms of these studies. Criticisms can be positive or negative.

You only need any one study of biological causes and any one study of psychological causes.

✓

☐ Biological causes of anorexia nervosa (Holland *et al.*, 1988)	p. 146
☐ Psychological causes of anorexia nervosa (Becker, 1999)	p. 148
☐ Biological causes of bulimia nervosa (Kendler *et al.*, 1991)	p. 150
☐ Psychological causes of bulimia nervosa (Cutts and Barrios, 1986)	p. 152

Research

You need to be able to outline the *findings* and *conclusions* of research (theories and/or studies) into the following:

✓

☐ Biological causes of eating disorders	p. 146–147, 150–151
☐ Psychological causes of eating disorders	pp. 148–9, 152–153

Assumptions about the causes of abnormality

You should be able to write about several assumptions of the following models about the causes of abnormality, and be aware of criticisms.

✓

☐ The biological (medical) model	p. 136
☐ The psychodynamic model	p. 137
☐ The behavioural model	p. 138
☐ The cognitive model	p. 139

Theories/explanations

You may be asked to describe or outline a theory/explanation for 6 marks. You are also likely to be asked an AO2 question about theories/explanations and to discuss their strengths and limitations. When discussing a theory, it is useful to refer to other research (theories and/or studies) as a means of evaluation.

✓

☐ Statistical infrequency	p. 128
☐ Deviation from social norms	p. 129
☐ Failure to function adequately	p. 130
☐ Deviation from ideal mental health	p. 130
☐ The biological (medical) model	p. 136
☐ The psychodynamic model	p. 137
☐ The behavioural model	p. 138
☐ The cognitive model	p. 139
☐ Biological explanations of eating disorders	p. 146–7, 150–151
☐ Psychological explanations of eating disorders	p. 148–9, 152–153

Sample abnormality question with students' answers and examiner's comments

1 (a) Give two limitations of the 'deviation from ideal mental health' definition of abnormality.   (3 marks + 3 marks)

Alison's answer: According to this view of 'ideal mental health' there are few people who would satisfy all its criteria at any given time. Therefore, many of us would be considered 'abnormal' despite the fact that we do not have any recognised form of abnormality.

It is difficult to measure ideal mental health with any degree of accuracy or even objectivity. This is more easily achieved with physical health, but is inevitably more subjective and culture specific with mental health.

Nigel's answer: This definition of abnormality is very restrictive because if it was applied strictly, it would be difficult for anyone to be considered in ideal mental health.

If we define abnormality in these terms, this might make people who do not appear to have ideal mental health very anxious about whether they are abnormal.

Examiner's comments: Alison provides two accurate and detailed criticisms of the 'deviation from ideal mental health' definition of abnormality. Each is elaborated carefully, and the extra detail adds that all-important clarity to the answer. This would be worth the full **3 + 3 marks**.

Nigel provides ideal examples of answers where there is just enough for 2 marks but not enough for 3. Each of these criticisms needs just that extra bit of elaboration. An example might help to achieve this in the first case. Perhaps Nigel might have explored the ethical problems of the second criticism in a little more detail. What, for example, is the problem with someone feeling 'anxious' about such a classification of abnormality? Nigel would receive **2 + 2 marks** for these criticisms.

---

1 (b) Describe the aims and conclusions of one study into the causes of anorexia nervosa.   (6 marks)

Alison's answer: Stoner (2000) interviewed 2,000 first-degree relatives of people who had been diagnosed with anorexia nervosa and compared them to relatives of people without anorexia. He looked at family histories of each of the interviewees, without knowing during the interview which group they were in. He found a much higher incidence of anorexia in the relatives of those already diagnosed with anorexia, and no evidence of anorexia in the relatives of those without the disorder.

Nigel's answer: Holland's study of anorexia aimed to see if anorexia was inherited. After the study, which showed a higher concordance rate for monozygotic twins compared to dizygotic twins, Holland concluded that this was because monozygotic twins have identical genetic make-ups and therefore this was why the concordance rate was higher for anorexia. This shows that anorexia may have a strong genetic component.

Examiner's comments: Ah... Alison has produced a very competent account of the procedures and findings of Stoner's study, but there is nothing at all about the aims and conclusions. It would have been easy enough to make a concluding statement here, but she has obviously not read the question closely enough and so fails to access any of the marks available. Unfortunately this has cost her dear, as she would receive **0 marks**.

Nigel's aims are very brief, although they do not have to be as detailed as the conclusions (or vice versa). However, he might have extended the aims to make them more explicit. The expression of conclusions is not all that clear, although we can follow what the main conclusions must have been. This is somewhere between 3 and 4 marks, but the lack of precision probably keeps it down to **3 marks**.

---

1 (c) Outline and evaluate one or more psychological models of abnormality   (18 marks)

Alison's answer: Freud's psychoanalytic model of abnormality explains abnormality in terms of unresolved childhood conflicts which have been repressed into the unconscious mind, where they continue to influence later behaviour. Freud also believed that different parts of the personality, the id, ego and superego, are in constant conflict, and this conflict creates anxiety. The ego must deal with the conflicting demands of id and superego and protects itself by using ego-defence mechanisms. If these are overused they can lead to disturbed behaviour. Finally, Freud believed that a young child's ego is not sufficiently mature to deal with childhood trauma (e.g. the loss of a parent), and therefore these may be repressed. However, these repressed feelings may contribute to the development of mental disorders such as depression in later life.

Freud can be criticised for his overemphasis on sex and his unwillingness to consider the possible influence of other factors in the development of abnormal behaviour (such as biological factors or learning). This can partly be explained in terms of the times in which Freud was writing: repression of sexual feelings was commonplace, and therefore Freud had good reason to believe that this was at the root of much of the abnormal behaviour he saw in his patients.

A problem for Freud's theory is that he based his work on a very narrow sample, mostly middle-class neurotic Viennese women. This meant that he relied on a small and abnormal sample, one that might not be representative of people in other cultures and at other times or even of normal people. It is not appropriate to generalise from this sample to an explanation of the development of abnormal behaviour in all other people. Compared with the behavioural model of abnormality, the Freudian approach is difficult to test scientifically. This is a strength of the behavioural model, in that it is relatively easy to conduct research to test the claims of the theory. The Freudian theory does not have this advantage, and is therefore less likely to be accepted as a scientific theory.

continued...

Nigel's answer: The psychodynamic model of abnormality explains abnormal behaviour in terms of unconscious forces that may be traced back to unresolved conflicts in childhood. Freud's view of abnormality can be criticised for being scientifically untestable, and relying too much on sex in his explanations of abnormal behaviour. He only studied a small sample of neurotic Viennese women, and relied too much on his own memory as he didn't take notes during sessions with patients.

The behavioural model explains abnormality in terms of the person learning maladaptive behaviour. This can be criticised because it only dwells on the learning aspect of abnormal behaviour and ignores other explanations like the psychodynamic and cognitive approaches.

The cognitive model explains abnormal behaviour in terms of faulty thought processes that give rise to unrealistic views on life. This is a good explanation because it focuses on the way that a person thinks which is not the case with the other two approaches. However, it focuses only on the cognitive aspect of abnormality and ignores other explanations like the psychodynamic and behavioural approaches.

An alternative model of abnormality is the biological model. This explains abnormality in terms of physical factors. These include genes, such as the genetic influence on schizophrenia and biochemical factors, such as the low levels of serotonin in people with depression. This approach can be criticised because concordance levels are never 100% so we can't be sure something really is inherited. Another criticism is that we can't be certain whether something like low levels of serotonin in depression are a cause or an effect of the disorder.

Examiner's comments: Alison has chosen to concentrate on just one model. The question allows for this, and as she can offer a detailed description of her chosen model, this is a wise decision. She would receive the full 6 marks for the AO1 component of this question.

Something that Alison does (which Nigel does not do in his answer) is to *elaborate* her criticisms. Thus we are told that Freud overemphasised the influence of sex in his explanations, but we are then given a commentary on why that might be expected. Her comparison with the behavioural model (i.e. its scientific basis) is both detailed and effective. Alison would receive 10 marks for the AO2 part of her answer (slightly limited, effective commentary) for a total of **16 marks**.

Nigel shows a decent understanding of the main assumptions of each of his chosen models. However, he has perhaps been a little ambitious trying to cover all three psychological models, with the result that his description is a little superficial. He would receive 4 marks for a limited AO1 description that is lacking in detail.

A characteristic of Nigel's AO2 material is that it lacks effectiveness. The criticisms of Freud's theory, for example, are appropriate but not linked explicitly to his explanation of abnormality, and certainly not sufficiently elaborated. Suggesting that one theory has ignored the other theories adds little to their evaluation. Nigel has included a description and evaluation of the *biological* model. This is not asked for in the question, and has not been used as part of an evaluative commentary on the *psychological* models. It would receive minimal credit if any. The AO2 mark would be just 5 (basic and reasonably effective at best) for a total of **9 marks**.

> **Total marks: Alison 22/30 (equivalent to a Grade A) and Nigel 16/30 (equivalent to a Grade B).**

Abnormality question to try

1 (a) What is meant by the terms abnormality, anorexia nervosa and bulimia nervosa?

(2 marks + 2 marks + 2 marks)

(b) Outline assumptions made by the cognitive model of abnormality in terms of the treatment of abnormality.

(6 marks)

(c) Outline and evaluate **two** or more explanations of anorexia nervosa based on the biological model of abnormality.

(18 marks)

Social psychology is the study of social behaviour, which occurs when two or more members of the same species interact. Social psychology may be concerned with how people influence each other's behaviour (social influence), or about how our thoughts influence our social behaviour (social cognition).

Social psychology
Social influence

Section 1

Majority and minority influence

Section 2

Obedience to authority

Section 3

Critical issue: Ethical issues in psychological research

End of module review

Majority and minority influence

The Cold War era, chilly for international relations between the superpowers, was also a fertile period for advances in social psychology. The work of Solomon Asch and Stanley Milgram, respectively, in the areas of conformity and obedience (both areas that involve the study of social influence) clearly demonstrated that human behaviour and mental processes cannot be adequately understood without reference to both personal and situational variables. Milgram's work in particular, published in 1963, demonstrated the existence of powerful situational forces that could induce normal and well-adjusted people to commit anti-social acts.

▲ Why did they tie the firework to the cat's tail? Because they are mean (a personal variable) or because the cat was naughty (a situational variable). Throughout this module you will find contrasting dispositional (personal) and situational explanations for behaviour.

specification breakdown

Specification content	Comment
Research studies into majority (conformity) and minority influence. Explanations of why people yield to majority and minority influence.	Here you are expected to know about **majority** and **minority influence** as forms of social influence. You are specifically required to know about *explanations* of why people yield to these two forms of social influence. Note that **majority influence** and **conformity** are the same thing, whereas **minority influence** is something completely different. You should be able to give aims, procedures, findings, conclusions and criticisms of one study each of majority and minority influence.

US Senator Joseph McCarthy speaking out against communist infiltrators.

McCarthyism – the age of conformity

Throughout the 1940s and 1950s America was overwhelmed with concerns about the threat of communism growing in Eastern Europe and China. Capitalising on those concerns, Senator Joseph McCarthy made a public accusation that more than 200 communists had infiltrated the US government. Though eventually his accusations were proved to be untrue, his campaigning brought about one of the most repressive times in 20th-century American politics. Known as McCarthyism, the paranoid hunt for communist infiltrators was notoriously difficult on writers and entertainers (including Arthur Miller, Orson Welles and Pete Seeger), many of whom were labelled as communist sympathisers and were unable to continue working. Some had their passports taken away, while others were jailed for refusing to give the names of other communists. The trials, which were well publicised, could often destroy a career with a single unsubstantiated accusation. In all, 320 artists were blacklisted, and for many of them this meant the end of exceptional and promising careers. By 1954, the fervour had died down and many actors and writers were able to return to work. The legacy of that time, however, stretched on for a number of years.

In the late 1950s a group of graduate students at the University of Chicago wanted to have a coffee vending machine installed outside the Physics Department for the convenience of people who worked there late at night. They started to circulate a petition to the Buildings and Grounds Department, but their colleagues refused to sign. They did not want to be associated with the allegedly radical students whose names were already on the document. This incident exemplifies the kind of timidity that came to be seen, even at the time, as the most damaging consequence of the anti-communist witch-hunt. To the despair of intellectuals, middle-class Americans became social conformists. A silent generation of students populated the nation's campuses, while their professors shrank from teaching anything that might be construed as controversial. Meaningful political dissent had all but withered away (Shrecker, 1994).

Jonestown

In 1963, the year Milgram's landmark work was published, a small-time Midwestern preacher from the US formed the People's Temple Full Gospel Church. By the time this movement self-destructed in 1978, 'Father' Jones had been directly responsible for the deaths of a US congressman and more than 900 of his own cult members. Reverend Jim Jones created the People's Temple church and congregation, first in Indiana, and later California. He convinced members of his congregation to give him all of their money and property, he came to see himself as a god, and demanded that everyone else see him as one also. If people refused, they were publicly humiliated and even beaten.

The US government began to have serious questions about the conduct of the church, so Jones moved it to South America, where he created Jonestown. Jones seemed to develop paranoia, and convinced his congregation that they too were unsafe. He had them practise trial suicide rituals.

In 1978, US congressman Ryan visited Jonestown to investigate whether US citizens were being held against their will. Ryan and the reporters travelling with him were killed before they could leave the airport to return to the US. Shortly after that Jones ordered his followers to perform another suicide ritual, but this was not a trial. Nine hundred people, including children, died by obeying Jones' orders to drink a combination of poison mixed with Kool-Aid. The tragic case of Jim Jones and the People's Temple demonstrates the powerful situational forces that influence our behaviour.

Mass suicide committed by the followers of the Reverend Jim Jones.

See http://www-rohan.sdsu.edu/~remoore/jonestown/

What is meant by social influence?

Although '**social influence**' has several meanings in psychology, it is most commonly used to summarise the field of social psychology that studies 'how the thoughts, feelings and behaviour of individuals are influenced by the actual, imagined or implied presence of others' (Allport, 1968). Our social life is characterised by many subtle (or not so subtle) social influences, some of which we are aware of, some of which we are not. Sometimes we give way to this social influence to 'fit in' with those around us, and sometimes we do it because we are not sure of the right way to think or act and so use others as a source of information.

If children learn by imitating what is the most common tradition amongst adults, and if adults follow what is the most common form of behaviour in their society, then **conformity** becomes common even in very large groups. Our social life is also characterised by **social norms**, which are generally accepted ways of thinking, feeling and behaving that are shared by the other members of our social group. We *should* act in a certain way in certain situations because otherwise we would be breaking an important social norm. When a social group has well-established norms that specify appropriate behaviour, pressures arise for individuals to maintain this norm (i.e. to *conform*). Deviants who go against social norms may experience considerable pressure to bring them back into line.

starSTUDY Majority influence
(ASCH, 1956)

Solomon Asch (1956) conducted a classic experiment on majority influence. Imagine you are sitting in a small group of strangers. You are all asked to look at three lines of different lengths (like the ones below). Then you are shown a fourth, 'standard' line and asked to say which one of the three lines is the same as the standard. The answer is obvious and definite yet, to your amazement, the other people in the group all select the same *wrong* answer. What do you do when it is your turn?

In *ambiguous* situations it makes sense for us to look to others to help us determine our behaviour and attitudes, for example deciding which knife to use in a restaurant. If you're not sure what to think or do, you look to see what everyone else is doing. But if there is a clearly right answer, are people still influenced by the behaviour of others?

Aim

The aim of this study was to find out how people would behave when given an *un*ambiguous task. Would they be influenced by the behaviour of others, or would they stick firmly to what they knew to be right? How much conformity to majority influence would there be?

Procedures

In total 123 American male undergraduates were tested. Asch showed a series of lines (the 'standard' line and the possible answers) to participants seated around a table. All but one of the participants were **confederates** of the researcher. The confederates were instructed to give the same *incorrect* answer on 12 *critical* trials. In total there were 18 trials with each participant. The true participant was always the last or last but one to answer.

What is meant by majority influence (conformity)?

An individual is said to *conform* if he or she chooses a course of action that is favoured by the majority of other group members or is considered socially acceptable. In contrast, an individual would be described as *deviating* if he or she chose to behave in a way that was not socially acceptable or which the majority of group members did not appear to favour. Because the individual is influenced by how the *majority* thinks or behaves, this form of social may be referred to as *majority influence*. The fact that an individual goes along with the majority in *public* does not indicate that the person has changed his or her *private* attitudes or beliefs. Therefore, most majority influence is characterised by **public compliance** rather than **private acceptance**.

Compliance is publicly acting in accordance with the wishes or actions of others. We can distinguish between public compliance (conformity) and private acceptance. Public compliance is behaving in a way consistent with a norm without accepting it internally.

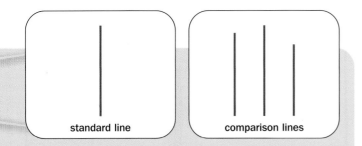

standard line

comparison lines

Findings

On the critical trials, 36.8% of the responses made by true participants were incorrect, i.e. conformed to the incorrect response given by the unanimous confederates. Twenty-five per cent of the participants never gave a wrong answer; thus 75% conformed at least once.

Just to confirm that the stimulus lines were unambiguous, Asch conducted a control trial with no confederates giving wrong answers. Asch found that people do make mistakes about 1% of the time.

Conclusions

This shows that there is a surprisingly strong tendency to conform to group pressures in a situation where the answer is clear. For Asch the important finding was that there was any conformity at all. However, Asch also saw the fact that on two-thirds of the trials his participants had remained independent as clear evidence of how people could *resist* the pressure to conform.

This study is represented in most social psychology textbooks as resounding evidence of people's tendency to conform when faced with a unanimous majority. It is also evidence of conditions under which people resist conformity.

Star study extra

Why did participants conform in Asch's study?

Asch (1956) interviewed some of his participants and found that they tended to give one of three reasons for why they conformed: (1) *distortion of perception* – they really did think their wrong answers were right; (2) *distortion of judgement* – they felt doubt about the accuracy of their judgement and therefore yielded to the majority view; (3) *distortion of action* – they didn't want to be ridiculed and therefore went along with the group.

Try the Asch experiment yourself online at:
http://library.thinkquest.org/C007405/exp/

Ethical issues raised in this study

Deception and lack of informed consent

The participants did not know they were being tricked – they did not know the real purpose of the experiment, nor did they know that the other 'participants' were actually confederates of the experimenter. They could not have been told the true purpose of the experiment, since then it would have been pointless. To some extent our objections can be overcome if the researchers properly informed the participants *after* the experiment (during **debriefing**) and offered them the right to withhold their data from the study. This right to withhold data is a means of compensating for the deception – the participants did not have the right to informed consent at the start of the study but, in a sense, are being offered this right afterwards.

Distress (psychological harm)

In Asch's experiment, the true participant may have found the experience quite distressing. Those who conformed must have experienced *pressure* to do so and may have felt distress at having behaved like 'sheep'. Those who resisted were also under pressure. Another study (by Bogdonoff *et al.*, 1961) tested the autonomic arousal of participants in an Asch-like task and found that they were aroused (high blood pressure, etc.), indicating the stress they were experiencing.

Research methods
Debriefing

This is a post-*research* interview in which the experimenter tries to restore participants to the same psychological state they were in when they entered the experiment. Debriefing is especially vital when participants have been deceived in any way during the experiment.

Debriefing is also useful for finding out if participants did believe in the original instructions or whether they were simply 'playing along', in which case their data might be rejected from the overall findings.

Criticisms

What does this study actually tell us about real life?

Asking people to judge the length of lines is a rather insignificant task and one where they would probably be willing to conform to save face. On a more important task we would expect conformity levels to drop. The fact that the participants had to answer out loud and in a group of strangers means that there were special pressures on them to conform, such as not wanting to sound stupid and wanting to be accepted by the group. The findings only tell us about conformity in special circumstances. For example, Williams and Sogon (1984) tested people who belonged to the same sports club and found that conformity may be even higher with people you know.

Is the study a 'child of its time'?

It is possible that these findings are particular to one culture – the participants were all men, all American and the research was conducted in America in the 1950s, the era of McCarthyism – a highly conformist society (described on page 163). This was the claim made by Perrin and Spencer (1980), who tried to repeat Asch's study in England in the late 1970s. They found only one student conformed on 396 trials. However, these were science students who may have felt more confident about their ability to estimate line length. Another study by Perrin and Spencer (1980) used youths on probation and found similar levels of conformity to Asch. Other studies (e.g. Larsen, 1974) have also found support for Asch in general, but Lalancette and Standing (1990) found no conformity and concluded that the Asch effect appears to be an unpredictable phenomenon rather than a stable tendency of human behaviour.

Majority influence (conformity) (continued)

Asch was not the first psychologist to investigate majority influence. Here we will consider research conducted prior to Asch's study, some of which focused more on *ambiguous situations*.

> Apparent non-conformity may actually be a case of not conforming to one set of norms but conforming to another set – for example, individuals who dress like Goths.

research activity

You could conduct a mini-investigation into conformity similar to Jenness' 'beans in the jar' experiment (below). Fill a jar with beans (ambiguous stimulus) and ask people to provide estimates on an answer sheet. Have two conditions: one sheet of paper with some high estimates, and the other a sheet of paper with low estimates. Participants in each condition should differ in their mean estimates, as a consequence of conforming to the estimates they see.

Take care to debrief your participants and inform them about the deception in the study so that they can provide truly informed consent.

THE FAR SIDE® BY GARY LARSON

Suddenly, Professor Liebowitz realizes he has come to the seminar without his duck.

Other research on majority influence

An ambiguous stimulus

Jenness (1932) asked students to guess the number of beans in a jar. After being given an opportunity to discuss their estimates they were asked to give their individual estimates again. Jenness found that individual estimates tended to converge to a group norm. It seems reasonable that, in an ambiguous situation, people look to others to get some ideas about a reasonable answer.

Sherif (1935) also investigated responses to an ambiguous stimulus, using the autokinetic effect. In the dark a point of light appears to move. This is the *autokinetic effect*. Sherif asked participants to estimate how far the light moved, then asked them to work with three others who had given quite different estimates of movement. After their discussion each was asked to provide individual answers again. These had become quite similar, demonstrating a tendency to establish and conform to group norms.

Fear of ridicule

Asch suggested that fear of ridicule is one reason that participants conformed in his study. This was supported in a study by Schachter (1951), where participants tried to influence a 'deviant' confederate (a confederate who disagreed with them). They were told the case history of a juvenile delinquent (Johnny Rocco) and asked to decide whether his behaviour would improve if he was given more loving attention or more punishment. The case was presented in such a way that they were likely to go for the loving attention approach. After this discussion the group was asked to select members to continue to participate in another task. If the confederate had disagreed and resisted attempts to change his view, the other group members rejected him for membership in a future group. However, if the confederate agreed, he was later included. This shows that lack of conformity does lead to group rejection.

Individual differences

Asch (1956) suggested that people low in self-esteem are more likely to conform, perhaps because they are more likely to fear rejection from the group. Burger and Cooper (1979) investigated another possible individual difference: the desire for personal control. Participants had to rate whether cartoons were funny or not in the presence of a confederate who was asked to do the same. Those participants who measured high on desire for personal control were less likely to rate cartoons in the same way as a confederate.

Gender differences

Some studies have found that women are more conformist than men (Eagly and Carli, 1981). This may be explained by the fact that women are more concerned with social relationships than men, which means that, in the experimental situation, they have different short-term goals. The result is that women *appear* to be more conformist than they are in the real world (Eagly, 1978).

People conform for all sorts of reasons, ranging from complete acceptance of the majority viewpoint at one extreme, to simply 'going along' with the crowd at the other.

Normative influence – following the crowd

If we simply go along with the majority without really accepting their point of view, we are conforming in behaviour alone. Psychologists have called this type of conformity **compliance**. A majority may be able to control other group members by making it difficult for them to deviate against the majority viewpoint, and thus exerting pressure on them to conform. Going against the majority isn't easy, as demonstrated in Asch's study, where participants clearly felt uncomfortable deviating from the majority position.

Informational influence – accepting the majority's viewpoint

In some cases individuals go along with the majority because they genuinely believe it to be right. As a result, we don't just comply in behaviour alone, we also *change* our own point of view in line with the majority viewpoint. Because we are conforming both publicly *and* privately, this form of conformity is known as **acceptance**. In conditions of uncertainty we may turn to the majority for *information* about how to behave. The majority, therefore, has *informational influence* over group members when they are uncertain how to behave.

> **Normative influence** is the result of wanting to be liked and part of a group (by following the social norms). **Informational influence** is the result of wanting to be right – looking to others for the right answer.

Factors that affect majority influence

Size of the majority

Asch (1956) found that the size of the opposing majority did affect conformity – up to a point. He found that as the size of the majority grew, so did the percentage of trials in which the naive participant conformed. There was a high percentage of conformity when a lone dissenter faced a unified majority of three people, but increasing the number of confederates beyond three did not raise conformity levels significantly.

Cultural factors

Compared to individualist cultures such as the UK and US, conformity appears to be higher in societies where group harmony is a priority. This is what Smith and Bond (1993) found in a review of 31 studies of conformity. Conformity may be seen as a *positive* feature in cultures where *interdependence* is more highly valued than *independence*.

In the West majorities often cause **public compliance** because of the need for apparent group harmony (normative social influence), whereas minorities (**minority influence**) often cause **private acceptance** because of informational social influence (the need to be right, a Western preoccupation).

COMMENTARY

> *To what extent has research supported the view that the majority exerts a significant degree of influence over the individual?*

Nigel: Well, Asch's research on majority influence certainly seems to have provided convincing evidence for the importance of conformity.

Alison: Maybe, but you seem to have forgotten that Asch also found that *despite* the pressure exerted by the majority, a large proportion of his participants remained independent in their judgements. Let's face it, asking people to judge the length of the lines is a pretty insignificant task. They would probably be willing to conform to save face.

Nigel: True, but his research still shows that group pressure can be so strong that people are willing to deny the evidence of their own eyes for the sake of conformity with the rest of the group.

Alison: Hmm... I remember reading Perrin and Spencer's claim that the Asch studies reflected a particular period of American history – the era of McCarthyism – when conformity was highly valued. In fact, when they tried to repeat Asch's study in England in the late 1970s they found that out of 396 trials, only once did they get a conforming response.

Nigel: Yes, but you have to remember that they used science and engineering students who may have felt more confident about their ability to estimate line length. In fact, another study by Perrin and Spencer where they used youths on probation as the participants and probation officers as the confederates produced very similar levels of conformity to those found by Asch in the 1950s.

Alison: I bet you were popular at school...

Nigel: I'll ignore that. Also, in a review of 31 studies of conformity all over the world, Smith and Bond found that conformity to a majority is more likely in collectivist cultures than in individualist cultures. They claim that conformity may be seen as a positive feature in cultures where *interdependence* is more highly valued than *independence*.

Alison: So how come the US was shown to be such a conformist society? You surely can't get a more individualist culture than that! Moscovici claimed that if everyone simply went along with the majority all the time, there would never be any social change or any innovations.

Nigel: Mosco... who?

Alison: Don't you ever read anything? Moscovici was critical of the emphasis on majority influence in the US. He emphasised the importance of the deviant minority for social change. Moscovici's research showed that the shift in opinion brought about by minority influence is more enduring than that brought about by majority influence. Although a majority can bring about compliance, individuals don't necessarily believe in it. A minority, on the other hand, can bring about internalisation of the minority position.

Nigel: Ah, but despite these claims, haven't studies failed to provide convincing evidence for strong minority influence in real-life situations where people have to go against the majority point of view? Remember, it takes great personal courage and uncommonly strong conviction for anyone to hold that firmly to an unpopular view, and that seems to be the main reason why people yield to majority influence.

Alison: Okay, enough, call it a draw?

Nigel: In your dreams.

What is meant by minority influence?

Many European social psychologists have been critical of the American preoccupation with conformity and the power of the *majority*. Serge Moscovici, one of the foremost critics of this perspective, claims that the idea of an all-powerful majority simply does not fit with historical reality. If the only form of social influence was majority influence, then we would all think and behave in the same way, and this would be unchanging from generation to generation. History has shown just how powerful minorities can be. For example, the suffragette movement of the 1920s gradually changed public and political opinion so that eventually women were given the vote.

Minorities tend not to have much power or status and may even be dismissed as troublemakers, extremists or simply 'weirdoes'. How, then, do they ever have any influence over the majority? Moscovici (1976) claims that the answer lies in their *behavioural style*, i.e. the *way* the minority gets its point across. The crucial factor in the success of the suffragette movement was that its proponents were *consistent* in their views, and this created a considerable degree of social influence. Minorities that are active and organised, who advocate and defend their position *consistently*, can create social conflict, doubt and uncertainty among members of the majority, and ultimately this may lead to social change. Such change has often occurred because a minority has converted others to its point of view. Without the influence of minorities, we would have no innovation, no social change. Many of what we now regard as 'major' social movements (e.g. Christianity, trade unionism or feminism) were originally due to the influence of an outspoken minority.

In a general sense, to 'conform' to something is to fit in with it or be moulded by it. This means that the term 'conformity' could be used in relation to majority or minority influence. However, technically, psychologists have restricted the use of 'conformity' to situations of majority influence only.

The difference between majority and minority influence

Innovation or status quo?

Majority influence is typically seen as maintaining the status quo, i.e. it is a form of social influence that is *resistant* to change. Majorities serve to promote uniformity among group members, and exert pressure on those who deviate from group norms. Minority influence, on the other hand, is associated with change and innovation, as the views of a deviant minority generate a social conflict with mainstream ideas, values and norms, the resolution of which may be represented as a movement towards the minority position (i.e. social change).

Conversion is a shift from one set of beliefs to another.

KEY TERM

Minority influence: A form of social influence where people reject the established norm of the majority of group members and move to the position of the minority.

Compliance or conversion?

In order for minority influence to take place, there must be a **conversion** within individuals who were formerly part of the majority. This conversion involves a careful thinking through of the arguments of the minority and the gradual acceptance of its point of view. As a result, the process of minority influence is relatively slow to take place. Majority influence, on the other hand, is a far more passive process, as individuals comply with the majority position without a great deal of thought. This is referred to as the **dual-process model** of social influence (Moscovici, 1980), with majority influence representing the need for social approval and minority influence representing the need for information about reality. Both lead to behavioural change, but each through different processes.

Imitation or originality?

Because minorities must work harder to get their position across, their arguments are thought to produce more cognitive effort in the majority than is the case with majority influence. Nemeth (1995) argues that by focusing the thoughts of the majority on the issue itself rather than the need to fit in with everyone else, the minority can set up processes that lead to far more creative thinking about the issue in question. She suggests that majority influence leads to restricted 'convergent' thinking based simply on imitation, whereas minority influence leads to more 'divergent' thinking as alternatives are considered. As a result, a minority position, even if it is later not accepted, can lead to cognitive reappraisal among the majority that eventually leads to a better quality outcome.

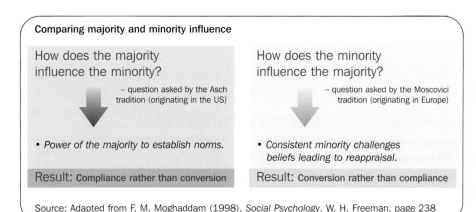

Comparing majority and minority influence

How does the majority influence the minority?	How does the minority influence the majority?
– question asked by the Asch tradition (originating in the US)	– question asked by the Moscovici tradition (originating in Europe)
• *Power of the majority to establish norms.*	• *Consistent minority challenges beliefs leading to reappraisal.*
Result: Compliance rather than conversion	Result: Conversion rather than compliance

Source: Adapted from F. M. Moghaddam (1998), *Social Psychology*. W. H. Freeman, page 238

Ethical issues raised in this study

Deception and lack of informed consent

It was necessary to deceive participants about the purpose of the experiment in order to investigate the hypothesis. Participants were told the true purpose at the end of the experiment, which serves to compensate for the deception. As the deception was relatively harmless and the task did not involve undue stress, we might judge this study to be ethically acceptable.

star**STUDY** Minority influence

(MOSCOVICI *ET AL*., 1969)

Aims

This study aimed to investigate the process of innovation – the view that social influence occurs not just through conformity (or dependence on the views of others) but through a change to the previously held opinions of a group. In order for this to occur, Moscovici *et al*. proposed that the minority must be consistent in its views and that this consistency will create conflict in the others, leading them to question and possibly change their views. A previous study by Moscovici looked at innovation in an ambiguous situation. The current study aimed to test the effects of consistency where the stimulus was explicit (unambiguous).

Procedures

All participants were female because Moscovici *et al*. thought that they would be more interested in a task that involved identifying colour! Altogether there were 32 groups of 6. Of the 6 participants in each group, 2 were **confederates**. The group was shown 36 blue-coloured slides. The use of filters varied the colour intensity of each slide. Participants were told that the experiment was about colour perception and that they would be asked to report the colour aloud. The two confederates consistently said that the slides were green.

In a second experiment, participants did the same task and then, later, were asked to do a similar task individually, writing down their answers. In a third experiment, the confederates answered 'green' 24 times and 'blue' 12 times, i.e. they were not consistent. In each experiment there were also control groups with no confederates.

Findings

Overall the participants agreed with the minority on 8.42% of the trials (i.e. they said the slides were coloured green). Most impressively, 32% gave the same answer as the minority at least once.

In the second experiment there was a greater private agreement with the confederates than in public. In the third experiment, when the confederates were inconsistent, agreement with the minority was reduced to 1.25%.

Conclusion

These findings show that minorities can influence majority opinion – not much, but an influence was demonstrated. The third experiment showed that consistency is a key element in this minority influence because influence fell off sharply when confederates were not consistent. The consistent minority had an even greater influence on private opinion than publicly expressed opinion.

However, cautious interpretation is important because, even though minority influence was shown, *most* participants were not affected by it.

Why is it necessary to have a control group? Minority experiments generally use two individuals as the minority rather than one because an isolated individual might be perceived as eccentric rather than consistent or certain.

Criticisms

Biased and atypical sample

Since the study involved female undergraduates, we might question how far these results can be generalised. Females have been found to be more conformist than males (or at least have a greater desire to be oriented towards interpersonal goals); therefore it is reasonable to assume that there might be a gender difference in the way that males and females respond to minority influence.

The group size (majority of 4) is also significant because other studies (see Clark and Maass, on page 171) have found no minority effects when the majority is larger than 4. This means that the findings here may not apply to all minority–majority situations.

It may be 'patterning' rather than consistency

Nemeth *et al*. (1974) proposed that 'patterning' is more important than consistency in determining minority influence. To test this, Nemeth *et al*. compared one condition where confederates were highly consistent (they said 'green' to every slide) with another condition where confederates were inconsistent but this inconsistency was related to a property of the stimulus (they said 'green' to the brighter slides and 'green-blue' to the dimmer slides). Such patterned 'inconsistency' led to greater agreement than the unrealistic consistency of the former condition.

If confederates said 'green' half the time and 'green-blue' the other half (i.e. inconsistent and random), there was also no minority influence. Overall this suggests that lack of repetition rather than repetition (consistency) can cause minority influence provided it is patterned, and this may even be more effective than repetition.

Minority influence (continued)

Moscovici and others have continued to investigate the factors that contribute to minority influence. Other research has examined the link between minority and majority influence. As is often the case with psychological research, this is an ongoing area of research interest, and the conclusions that may be drawn from the areas detailed on these pages are necessarily tentative.

▲ In the film *Twelve Angry Men*, one jury member (Henry Fonda) changed the minds of the rest of the jury through his consistent and passionate arguments proclaiming innocence of the accused.

Was Asch's study majority or minority influence?

Moscovici and Faucheux (1972) suggest that the confederates in Asch's experiment are actually a minority group rather than a majority. The true participant recognises that the line judgements are wrong and eccentric – it is a minority view in comparison with what most people would say. Therefore, to follow this eccentric view is to be influenced by a minority – who are consistent and confident.

Explanations of why people yield to minority influence

Group identification

Maass *et al.* (1982) arranged for a group of 'straight' participants to hear arguments about gay rights. If the minority group was gay it had less influence on the participants than if it was straight – presumably because the participants were better able to identify with the straight minority and this led to greater influence. Influence occurs when the minority (or majority) are members of our **'ingroup'** – the people we identify with. This challenges Moscovici's view that deviant minorities (or **outgroups**) are fundamental in innovation. As ingroup minorities share the same group identity as the majority, they are more likely to succeed in their attempts at social influence. Outgroups, on the other hand, are more likely to be discriminated against and less likely to be influential in changing the minds of the majority (Pennington *et al.*, 1999).

Social cryptoamnesia

There is a point in any group where, after some members have started to agree with the minority, the minority then turns into a majority. Van Avermaet (1996) called this the **snowball effect**. The minority position gains power as more people express the same opinion. Eventually minority influence changes to majority influence. However, we should remember that minority influence generally shows itself in private rather than public, so how does this snowball effect take place?

The answer may lie in **social cryptoamnesia**. It has been observed that major attitude changes (conversion) take place only when the spirit of the times (called the 'zeitgeist') has changed. For example, at the start of the suffragette movement a few militant women campaigned for a change in voting legislation – one threw herself in front of the king's horse at the Epsom Derby and was killed, and several chained themselves to the railings of 10 Downing Street. It was only some years later that popular (majority) opinion actually changed. Thus, opinion change was not the direct effect of minority influence. What probably happened was that the minority influence changed private attitudes, and these views gradually became the 'zeitgeist'. When change occurred (women were given the vote), this was in accord with majority opinion. Perez *et al.* (1995) called this 'social cryptoamnesia' – by the time change occurs people have forgotten the original source of opinion change, but innovation was actually due to minority influence.

Other research into minority influence

Minority or majority influence?

There is evidence that minority and majority influence may work together. Clark (1994) looked at social influence in a jury setting. Student participants were asked to read a transcript of the arguments presented in the film *Twelve Angry Men*. In the film, all but one member of a jury initially believe that the defendant in a murder trial is guilty. Slowly the one juror (played by Henry Fonda) changes the minds of the others because of his consistent and unwavering conviction about the man's innocence. In the experiment some participants were just given Henry Fonda's arguments to read, whereas others were told how he gradually changed the minds of the other jury members. Social influence occurred in both groups but was strongest where the participants read the arguments (minority influence) and knew that others eventually conformed (majority influence).

Situational factors

In the star study by Moscovici *et al.* (on page 169) the *order* in which participants gave their responses did not matter to the size of the influence. However, Moscovici and Nemeth (1974) demonstrated that *seating* position can affect minority influence. In this study five people sat around a rectangular table; one was a confederate who expressed a minority opinion. When the confederate was assigned a seat, position did not matter, but if the confederate chose to sit at the head of the table he exerted more influence. In other words, where you sit may be as important as what you say, or how consistently/confidently you say it.

Non-situational factors

Moscovici *et al.* suggested that consistency was the key characteristic of successful minority influence. Nemeth *et al.* pointed to 'patterning' as a key factor and showed that unreasonable consistency was not effective. Mugny (1984) showed that unreasonable confidence was also counterproductive. In this experiment, participants were less influenced by minority opinion when it was expressed in slogan-like terms than when more moderate language was used.

Flexibility rather than consistency has also been found to be important. Nemeth and Brilmayer (1987) found that a minority of one who refused to change his position (when arguing in a mock-jury situation for the amount of compensation to be paid to someone in a ski accident) had no effect on others, whereas a minority member who changed his opinion and moved in the direction of the majority did exert an influence on majority opinion.

Factors that affect minority influence

Size of the minority

Moscovici and Nemeth (1974) argue that a minority of one may be more influential than a minority of two or more, because one person can be more consistent over time and will not divide the majority's attention. In contrast, more recent research (e.g. Arbuthnot and Wayner, 1982) has found that a minority of one is less effective than a minority of two. This suggests that the one-person minority's advantage in terms of consistency is overshadowed by the majority's tendency to dismiss that person's point of view on the grounds of 'person variables' (such as being a bit weird). A minority of two is less easy to dismiss as simply being the eccentric views of one person, particularly when the arguments of the two 'deviants' are complementary. This gives more credibility to the arguments presented by the minority, and hence creates more conflict within the majority and ultimately more likelihood of a move towards the minority position.

Martin Luther King was an important leader of the Civil Rights Movement in America. What characteristics was he likely to have possessed in order to exert his minority influence?

Size of the majority

The **social impact model** (Latané and Wolf, 1981) predicts that there would be a decrease of minority influence, both publicly and privately, as majority size increased. In a situation where both the minority and majority have equal strength (power, status, etc.) and immediacy (proximity in space and time), as the majority increases in size the influence of the minority should decline. In support of this, Clark and Maass (1990) looked at the interaction between minority influence and groups of varying sizes. In other words, they varied the size of the majority in experimental groups – the majority was either 4, 8 or 12. There was a minority effect with a majority of 4, but not when this increased to 8 or 12. It is noteworthy that in the 'blue-green' experiment by Moscovici *et al.* (page 169), the size of the majority group was 4 – the limit of minority effect. If there had been a larger majority, Moscovici *et al.* might not have found evidence of minority influence.

Behavioural style

Moscovici and Nemeth (1974) have argued that a *majority* is influential because it is consistent in its position, both among its members and over time. In other words, its position must be right because everyone always goes along with it! Without this consistency, a majority would lose its credibility. We saw from Asch's research on majority influence that the introduction of a fellow dissenter lowered the degree of conformity dramatically. The majority was no longer speaking with one voice. Without majority consistency, the 'dissenter' experiences less conflict and his or her position appears less deviant. Moscovici suggests that if the minority can practise the same 'tactics', i.e. *consistently* maintaining a differing position, this will arouse conflict among majority group members and establish the minority position as viable. To be effective, the minority must be consistent within itself (inter-individual consistency) and also over time. However, consistency alone may be insufficient to bring the majority around to the minority point of view (see 'Non-situational factors').

To what extent has minority influence been shown to be a significant form of social influence?

We have met this form of 'challenging' question elsewhere in this book. Imagine you were Serge Moscovici or Charlan Nemeth (or even Henry Fonda!). How would you put together a justification of the power of the minority as a form of social influence? What research would you quote, and what observations would you make about minority influence? How would you respond to criticisms or alternative explanations? Over the previous four pages, we have outlined some of the major research findings relating to minority influence and shown how this phenomenon might be explained. Some possible inclusions for your 'minority influence manifesto' are as follows (remember one-third **AO1**/two-thirds **AO2**):

AO1

- What *is* minority influence?

- How can it be explained?

- What factors are important in minority influence?

- Description of research conclusions concerning minority influence.

AO2

- In what ways has minority influence been shown to be different to majority influence?

- Criticisms of research purporting to demonstrate the importance of minority influence.

- Research evidence that supports, challenges, refines or extends our understanding of minority influence.

- Is minority influence more or less powerful than majority influence?

The social psychology of experiments

If you put a group of people together, they are influenced by the others in the group. For example, they want to be liked or to please the others. The experimental situation is no different from any other social situation. Remember how in Asch's conformity study one explanation was that participants conformed because they wanted to be liked and didn't want to be an 'oddball' (normative social influence).

Furthermore, participants aren't just interested in social relations with other participants. They also interact with the investigator. In many studies, participants are paid for taking part, not enough to get rich but enough to make them feel they have agreed to a kind of social contract.

Finally, we should consider the fact that an investigator has expectations about what will take place in the study and may communicate these expectations to the participants, influencing their behaviour.

This means that there are many aspects of the research situation that influence the behaviour of the participants – aside from the key influence, the independent variable. The importance of all this is that the behaviour observed in a study may be explained by the social situation rather than by the independent variable. In order to produce more reliable findings from psychological research, we need to know about these effects and know how to control them.

Participant reactivity

There is an important distinction between an experimenter and an investigator. Many studies are designed by an experimenter but conducted by an investigator, such as one of the experimenter's research students. An investigator is the person who conducts the study – this may or may not be the experimenter.

A participant is not a passive automaton. In the past psychologists used the term 'subject' to describe a person taking part in a study, but more recently the active role of the participant has been recognised and the term 'participant' has replaced 'subject'. How do participants react to investigators? We will look at a few examples of **participant reactivity**.

The Hawthorne effect

Roethlisberger and Dickson (1962) were asked to investigate whether lighting had any effect on production levels at the Hawthorne Western Electric factory in Chicago. They found that increased lighting led to increased production – but they also found that *decreased* lighting led to increased production. Such contradictory findings perplexed them – until they recognised that increased production was *not* caused by the independent variable (lighting levels) – it was caused by the *increased attention* the workers were getting through being part of a study. The increased attention acted as a **confounding variable**. This **Hawthorne effect**, as it came to be known, is an issue in many studies.

Demand characteristics

We might explain the results of Asch's study in terms of demand characteristics. Participants sought for clues about how to behave in what was otherwise a rather simple task. Participants were not conforming as such but responding to the demand characteristics of the situation.

Orne (1962) observed that people behave in quite unusual ways if they think they are taking part in a psychology experiment. For example, in one experiment he asked participants to add up columns of numbers on a sheet of paper and then tear the paper up and repeat the task. If people believed this was part of a psychology experiment, some were willing to continue the task for over 6 hours! This led Orne to develop the idea of **demand characteristics**. People taking part in an experiment want to please an investigator and want their performance to be helpful. This results in people sometimes being over-cooperative and behaving in quite a different way from how they would usually. This means that such an experiment tells us little or nothing about behaviour in real life. A demand characteristic acts as a confounding variable.

Social desirability bias

We have come across **social desirability bias** already (see page 61). Participants' answers on questionnaires may not reflect their true opinion because they prefer to present themselves in a good light. The same is true in experiments.

Investigator effects

An **investigator effect** is anything the investigator does which has an effect on a participant's performance in a study *other than what was intended*. In many of the studies we have looked at a confederate acted in a way that was intended to affect the participant's behaviour (such as describing a blue slide as green). This behaviour was the independent variable in the study. If the participant is affected by some uncontrolled behaviour, such as unconscious cues from the investigator, this *confounds* the experiment.

Investigator (experimenter) bias

Rosenthal and Fode (1963) conducted a classic experiment that showed how even rats could be affected by subtle cues from an experimenter. Psychology students were asked to conduct a maze learning experiment with rats. The students were told that there were two groups of rats: one group was 'maze-bright', having been bred for this characteristic, whilst the other group was maze-dull. In fact there were no differences between the rats, who were randomly assigned to students. Despite this, the findings of the study showed that the supposedly brighter rats actually did better. The only explanation can be that the students' expectations affected the rats' performance.

Interviewer bias

Interviewers may affect an interviewee's behaviour by using **leading questions** (see page 30). Another way that interviewees' behaviour may be subtly affected by the interviewer is described by the **Greenspoon effect**. Greenspoon (1955) found that he could alter participant's behaviour by saying 'mm-hmm' (an example of **operant conditioning**) after certain responses. Both of these may affect behaviour in an experiment.

(see page 30)

Research methods *Experimental control: dealing with investigator effects*

Having recognised that the relationship between investigator and participants may act as a confounding variable in research, we need to find ways to control this.

Using single and double blind

One way to control some of these effects is to prevent the participants knowing the aims of the study (**single blind**). And, even better, tell them that the study is actually about something else. This means that the participants form innocuous expectations (but they are deceived).

Investigator bias can be prevented by using **double blind**, where neither the participant nor the investigator is aware of the true aims of the study.

Using placebo conditions

We can control for the effects of attention (the Hawthorne effect) by using a **placebo** condition. This is where some participants *think* they are receiving the experimental treatment but they aren't. In every other way they are treated the same as the true participants. For example, if we want to study the effects of anti-depressants on individuals with eating disorders, then all participants are given tablets to take – but some tablets are not the real thing. No one except the experimenter knows who is getting the real thing, not even the investigator.

Standardised instructions

If a participant is given a set of **standardised instructions** (as distinct from **standardised procedures**), there is less possibility that the investigator can communicate expectations.

Research methods *Experimental control*

Using blind conditions and placebos are methods of **experimental control**. The aim of experimental control is to ensure that no **extraneous variables** influence the dependent variable. Ways to control extraneous variables include the following.

Random allocation

In an **independent groups** study, one group of participants is given one IV and another group is given a different IV (or nothing). For example, in a study to investigate the effects of noise on test performance, group A would be given noise and group B would have less noise (or no noise). The IV is noise level. What happens if group A comprises all the people sitting at the front of the class? They may be more keen than those sitting at the back of the class. Keener people may do better on a test, and this would act as a confounding variable. In order to control for this we use **random allocation** to experimental conditions when using independent groups. In a repeated measures design, we might randomly allocate the various tasks to avoid confounding variables.

Counterbalancing

In a repeated measures study, participants may do worse on condition A (noise) than condition B (no noise) because of a **practice effect**, an example of an **order effect**. The practice effect would act as a confounding variable because better performance on condition B would be due to order rather than noise. To control for this we use **counterbalancing**. Half of the participants do condition A followed by condition B, while the other half do B followed by A. We can get even more clever and give each participant the following: ABBA.

ABBA is also a method of counterbalancing order effects

Standardised procedures

It is important that many situational variables are controlled, such as making sure that all participants are tested in a similar environment and at a similar time of day. In module 1 we looked at a study by Jenkins and Dallenbach (page 18). When the participants' memory was tested in the sleep condition it was tested in the morning, whereas when it was tested in the awake-for-8-hours condition it was tested late in the day. This introduced a **confounding variable**.

(page 18)

An **extraneous variable** is a variable that might *potentially* affect the dependent variable, thus acting as an additional independent variable (it is 'extra' to the experiment). Any extraneous variable that does this is called a **confounding variable** because it *confounds the results* of the experiment.

Obedience to authority

specification breakdown

> The Nazi extermination of European Jews is the most extreme instance of abhorrent immoral acts carried out by thousands of people in the name of obedience.
>
> Milgram, 1974

> 'It would have been comforting indeed to believe that Eichmann was a monster...The trouble with Eichmann was precisely that so many were like him, and that the many were neither perverted nor sadistic, that they were, and still are, terribly and terrifyingly normal.'
>
> Arendt, 1963

> Unable to defy the authority of the experimenter, [participants] attribute all responsibility to him. It is the old story of "just doing one's duty" that was heard time and again in the defence statement of the accused at Nuremberg...a fundamental mode of thinking for a great many people once they are locked into a subordinate position in a structure of authority.
>
> Milgram, 1967

Specification content	Comment
Research studies into obedience to authority.	Here you are expected to know about **obedience to authority** as a form of social influence. It is necessary to know the aims, procedures, findings, conclusions and criticisms of one study of obedience – the ones given here are examples.
Explanations of why people obey and how people might resist obedience.	You are specifically required to know about explanations of the processes involved in obedience (i.e. what causes people to obey and how they might **resist** obedience).
Issues of internal and external validity associated with such research.	You are also required to know about **internal** and **external validity** in the context of obedience research. It is, therefore, worth finding out what critics of Milgram's research said about validity issues, and how Milgram responded to such claims.

▲ Inmates of a concentration camp.

The 'Final Solution'

The Nazi extermination policy towards the Jews (known euphemistically as 'the Final Solution') began in 1941 when special mobile killing units operating along the eastern front started lining up and shooting Jews in mass graves. In 1942, battalions of German Order Police were added to the extermination force and carried out more mass shootings and deportations in Poland.

To increase the efficiency with which this annihilation of Jews could be achieved, Jews were forced into freight trains that ferried them without food or water to labour-death camps such as Majdanek, Treblinka and Auschwitz-Birkenau. Some camps were specifically equipped for mass killing by means of gas chambers and crematoria for disposing of the remains. Several methods were utilised. In the earlier camps, exhaust fumes from truck engines, or tank engines, were pumped into sealed gassing vans or specially constructed gas chambers. In some of the later camps, Zyklon-B (prussic acid) pellets were used. Those who were not gassed immediately were forced to live on a starvation diet and to endure harsh physical labour and unending brutality.

Rudolf Hoess, SS Kommandant of Auschwitz-Birkenau, described at his trial how he had gradually stepped up executions, beginning with a few hundred a day and then, as methods were perfected, rising to 1,200. By mid-1942, facilities had been sufficiently enlarged to dispatch 1,500 people over a 24-hour period for the smaller ovens, and up to 2,500 for the larger ones. By 1943, a new daily peak of 12,000 was achieved. (Hoess was tried in Warsaw in March 1947 and condemned to death. He was hanged on 16 April 1947 at Auschwitz.)

Auschwitz was the most efficient camp established by the Nazi regime for carrying out the 'Final Solution'. The total number of Jewish dead in Auschwitz-Birkenau will never be known for certain, for most were not registered. Estimates vary between 1 and 2.5 million. As well as those murdered at Auschwitz-Birkenau, others were subjected to horrific 'medical' experiments. One group, mostly twins and dwarfs, underwent experiments at the hands of doctors such as Josef Mengele, the 'Angel of Death'. Mengele subjected his victims to clinical examinations, blood tests, X-rays and various forms of measurement. He then killed them himself by injecting chloroform into their hearts, so as to carry out comparative pathological examinations of their internal organs. The purpose of these 'experiments' was to establish the genetic cause for the birth of twins, in order to develop a programme for doubling the birth rate of the 'Aryan' race. One survivor of Mengele's twin studies, Eva Moses Kor, remarked: 'I was not on Schindler's list; however, I was on Mengele's list. And it was better to be on Mengele's list than on no list at all.'

▲ *(top)* Socialisation of evil? Hitler meets members of the Hitlerjugend (Hitler Youth).

(above) The Nuremburg war trials, where many Nazis were convicted of crimes against humanity.

Was such brutality simply a product of evil and sadistic minds, or was this extraordinary behaviour performed by ordinary people? In 1960, just as Stanley Milgram was beginning his studies at Yale University, Adolf Eichmann, who had been in charge of implementing the 'Final Solution', was captured in Argentina by the Israeli secret service. His demeanour during the ensuing trial held in Nuremburg was hardly that of the vicious war criminal many had expected, as documented by Hannah Arendt in her book, *Eichmann in Jerusalem: A Report on the Banality of Evil*.

The disturbing implication was that 'in certain circumstances the most ordinary decent person can become a criminal' (Arendt, 1963), and it is exactly this proposition that Milgram's studies attempt to address. Eichmann's own excuse for his crimes was the familiar claim that he was acting on orders. Milgram's studies provided, at least in part, a test of the viability of such an explanation.

Source: Adapted from M. Cardwell (2000), 'Milgram – the legacy'. Psychology Review, 7:4.

What is meant by obedience to authority?

So far in this module we have looked at types of indirect social influence where people can choose whether or not they will yield to the perceived pressure of the majority or the minority. A more direct form of social influence, where the individual may have less choice in whether he or she gives way or not, is **obedience to authority**. In this form of social influence, the individual is faced with the choice of whether to *comply* with a direct order from a person of higher status (for example, a soldier obeying an order from his superior officer), or whether to *defy* the order. Because of the hierarchical superiority of the authority figure, the individual must also consider the *consequences* of his or her disobedience.

Much of the impetus for research in this area came from the need to understand the situational conditions under which people would suspend their own moral judgements in order to carry out an order from a malevolent authority figure. The underlying motivation for this, of course, was far more than simple idle curiosity. It was an attempt to explain the atrocities committed during the Holocaust, and defended during the Nuremberg war trials as 'simply obeying orders'.

KEY TERM

Obedience to authority: Obedience refers to a type of social influence whereby someone acts in response to a direct order from a figure with perceived authority. There is also the implication that the person receiving the order is made to respond in a way that he or she would not otherwise have done without the order.

http://www.stanleymilgram.com/references.html
A website with everything you ever wanted to know about Stanley Milgram.

---

starSTUDY — Obedience to authority
(MILGRAM, 1963)

Of all the experiments in this book, this is probably the one you will find most memorable – and most shocking. We have saved the best star study to last.

Aims

It makes sense to be obedient in some situations; obedience is a healthy and necessary social behaviour. But why do people obey when the action required is inhumane? Stanley Milgram set out to investigate whether ordinary people will obey a legitimate authority even when required to injure another person – i.e. obedience to unjust authority.

Procedures

Milgram recruited 40 male participants by advertising for volunteers to take part in a study of how punishment affects learning, to take place at Yale University. Everyone was paid $4.50 and told that they would receive this even if they quit during the study.

There were two confederates: an experimenter and a 'learner' (a 47-year-old accountant). The participant drew lots with the confederate and always ended up as the 'teacher'. He was told that he must administer increasingly strong electric shocks to the participant each time he got a question wrong. The machine was tested on the participant to show him that it worked.

The learner, sitting in another room, gave mainly wrong answers and received his (fake) shocks in silence until they reached 300 volts (very strong shock). At this point he pounded on the wall and then gave no response to the next question. He repeated this at 315 volts and from then on said/did nothing. If the 'teacher' asked to stop, the experimenter had a set of 'prods' to repeat, such as saying: 'It is absolutely essential that you continue' or 'You have no other choice, you must go on'.

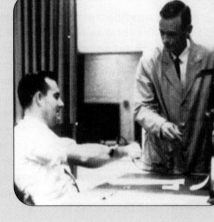

▶ The experimenter (in the lab coat) exerts his authority over the subordinate participant.

Ethical issues raised in this study

Lack of informed consent, deception and debriefing

The participants were deceived about the nature of the study, which denied them the right to provide informed consent. At the end of the study they were debriefed about its true purpose and introduced to the confederate to be reassured that all was well. We will discuss these issues more thoroughly in the next section on ethical issues.

The right to withdraw

The participants were told that they could leave at any time. However, the 'prods' from the experimenter made this quite difficult for some. Some participants did stop but, as we know, most continued.

Psychological harm

Baumrind (1964) attacked Milgram's study for the severe distress it created. Milgram defended himself in several ways. First, he did not know, prior to the study, that such high levels of distress would be caused (this did not stop him carrying out various replications). Second, he asked participants afterwards if they had found the experience distressing and interviewed them again a year later; 84% felt glad to have participated, and 74% felt they had learned something of personal importance. However, Freudians would predict that this is the response we would get. Participants are likely to find some way of explaining their behaviour, such as saying they were glad to have taken part. Third, Milgram suggested that it may be the findings of his study that are objectionable and cause discomfort more than the ethics of the study itself.

Findings and conclusions

Even the best of us sometimes get confused about what counts as a finding, and what is a conclusion. Milgram's study provides a good example of the distinction. He found that 65% of the participants fully obeyed the experimenter. This is a high percentage. But, if you make any statement about what these findings *show* us, you are dealing with conclusions. You might *conclude* that this result *shows* a very high level of obedience. Someone else might conclude that it *shows* a moderate level of obedience, particularly given the fact that participants were strongly advised to continue. We cannot argue over findings. They are facts. We can quibble about conclusions. They are interpretations.

Findings

Prior to the actual study Milgram asked psychology students to say how far they thought participants would go. They estimated that fewer than 3% would go to the maximum level.

The main finding was that 65% of the participants continued to the maximum voltage, far beyond what was marked 'Danger: severe shock'. Only 5 participants (12.5%) stopped at 300 volts, the point when the learner first objected.

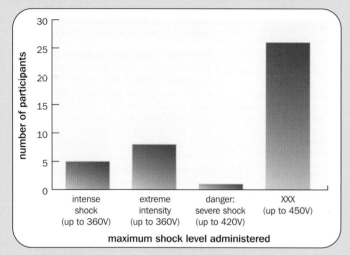

Conclusions

The findings suggest that ordinary people are astonishingly obedient to authority when asked to behave in an inhumane manner. This suggests that it is not evil people who commit evil crimes but ordinary people who are just obeying orders. In other words, crimes against humanity may be the outcome of **situational** rather than **dispositional factors**. It appears that an individual's capacity for making independent decisions is suspended under certain situational constraints – namely, being given an order by an authority figure.

A **situational factor** is anything in the environment, including the behaviour of other people.

A **dispositional factor** is an enduring aspect of an individual's behaviour – his or her disposition or personality.

Research methods
Bar charts and histograms

You might think that the graph immediately below left is a **bar chart**, a graphical representation of frequency data (data that illustrate frequency). It is a bar chart but it is also a **histogram**. The difference between the two is that a histogram represents continuous data starting from a true zero. Not all bar charts are histograms, as is the case for the bar chart at the bottom of the page. This bar chart does not represent continuous data (one category does not logically follow the next one even though the columns are in order – the categories are not continuous, and there is no zero).

Criticisms

Demand characteristics

It is possible to explain the unexpectedly high level of obedience in terms of demand characteristics. These are features of the experiment (prestigious university environment, scientific experimenter) that provide cues about how to behave. Most people found these hard to resist, but this does not mean they would always be so obedient to unjust authority. Subsequent replications showed that obedience rates drop when these demand characteristics are changed. This means that the baseline study only tells us about obedience in one particular setting. The findings may not generalise to real life (an issue considered later in this section).

Individual differences

Interviews with participants after the experiment showed considerably different attitudes about what they were doing. Some of the participants showed no emotion and were 'happy' to go along with what they were told to do. Others showed clear signs of being very uncomfortable. Some participants stopped relatively early on whereas, as we know, a number went all the way. When the experiment was repeated with different people it was found that educated participants were less obedient, and military participants were more obedient.

What all of this tells us is that the simple conclusion that situational factors cause obedience is wrong. Dispositional factors are important as well because not everyone obeys.

Star study extra: Variations on Milgram's baseline experiment

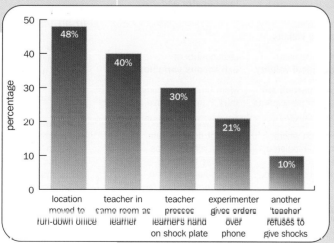

Milgram (1974) conducted various follow-up studies, following the same basic procedure. The findings are shown in the graph on the left. They support the view that situational factors affect obedience – such factors may either increase obedience or increase resistance to obedience.

In another replication Zimbardo (1969) found increased obedience if the 'learner' had to wear a name tag and hood (called **deindividuation** – removing the person's individual identity).

Cultural differences

Smith and Bond (1993) reviewed a number of studies that replicated Milgram's baseline experiment in different countries. Rates of obedience varied from 85% in Germany to 16% for female Australians. However, it's impossible to be sure how equivalent the studies are to each other, for example the conditions were often slightly different.

Other research on obedience to authority

M ilgram's studies have overshadowed research into obedience, but many other studies have contributed to our further understanding of obedience to unjust authority. You might wonder why all studies explore the issue of obedience to 'unjust' authority. This is because it is difficult to investigate 'just' authority (such as a lollipop lady telling you when to cross the road) as there would be no reason to disobey!

Research methods
Field experiments and other experiments

Many of the studies examined in this book are **laboratory experiments**. The essence of the 'laboratory' is that it is an environment that can be controlled by the experimenter. Studies conducted in more natural surroundings are called **field studies** (e.g. **naturalistic observations**) and **field experiments**. Field experiments have an IV and a DV, like all experiments. In most (but not all) field experiments the participants do not know that they are part of an experiment at all. When this happens all sorts of problems are reduced, such as demand characteristics, because participants aren't looking for cues about how to respond – they aren't even aware they are responding!

There is a third kind of experiment, called a **natural experiment**, in which the experimenter cannot manipulate the IV because it varies *naturally* (that is why it is called a natural experiment). Furthermore, in a natural experiment participants cannot be randomly allocated to conditions, which means that there may be biases in the different groups of participants (as was a possible problem with the Hodges and Tizard study described on page 64).

Were the nurses in Hofling *et al.*'s study obeying orders, or were they *complying* (conformity) to a social norm (the norm of what is expected for nurses)? This illustrates the difficulties inherent in making distinctions between things – it doesn't always work in practice! If you wish to use Hofling *et al.*'s study to illustrate conformity, make sure you are explicit about why it does illustrate conformity.

	Nature and use	Advantages	Disadvantages
Laboratory experiment e.g. Craik and Tulving's study of levels of processing	To investigate causal relationships under controlled conditions.	Can draw causal conclusions about relationship between IV and DV. Well controlled, confounding variables are minimised. Can be replicated, demonstrating **validity**.	Artificial, a contrived situation where participants may not behave naturally. **Investigator** and **participant effects**.
Field experiment e.g. Bickman's study of obedience	To investigate causal relationships in more natural surroundings.	Less artificial, usually higher **ecological validity**. Avoids some **participant effects** (when participants not aware of study).	Less control of **extraneous variables**. More time-consuming and thus more expensive.
Natural experiment e.g. Hodges and Tizard's study of institutionalisation	To investigate causal relationships in situations where the IV cannot be directly manipulated.	Allows research where IV can't be manipulated, e.g. studies of gender difference or of privation. Enables psychologists to study 'real' problems such as the effects of disaster on health.	Cannot demonstrate causal relationships because IV not manipulated and no random allocation to conditions. Inevitably many **confounding variables**.

Field studies of obedience to authority

Doctors and nurses

Hofling *et al.* (1966) conducted a study in a hospital. Nurses were telephoned by a 'Dr Smith', who asked them to give 20mg of a drug called Astroten to a patient. This order contravened hospital regulations in several ways: nurses were not to take instructions over the phone from an unknown doctor and the dosage was twice that advised on the bottle. Nevertheless, 21 out of 22 (95%) of the nurses did as requested. As in Milgram's study, when nurses were asked beforehand whether nurses would obey under these circumstances, they all said no nurse would. When the nurses involved in the study were interviewed afterwards they said, in their defence, that they had obeyed because that's what doctors expect nurses to do.

This study shows that obedience does occur in real-life settings – or does it? Rank and Jacobsen (1975) also asked nurses to carry out an irregular order. This time 16 out of 18 (89%) *refused*. The difference was that on this occasion the drug was familiar (Valium) and the nurses were allowed to consult with peers. Again we find that obedience rates changed with different circumstances, suggesting that situational factors are important.

In the street

Bickman (1974) also tested obedience in a more real-life situation, and examined the effects of perceived authority on obedience. Confederates dressed in a sports jacket and tie, a milkman's uniform or as a guard, and made requests to passers-by, for example asking them to pick up litter or to give someone a coin for the parking meter. Participants obeyed most when the confederate was dressed as a guard. This study shows what most of us know – we obey someone who looks like they have authority more than someone who does not.

In an interview

Meeus and Raajmakers (1995) asked participants to conduct job interviews in a manner that would create stress for an interviewee. The interviewees were in fact confederates who were told to begin the interview confidently but become more distressed as the interview progressed. The participants were given negative statements to use to increase the pressure, such as 'this job is too difficult for you'. The interviewee got to the point where he begged to stop; nevertheless, 22 out of 24 (92%) of the participants delivered all 15 of their negative remarks. This demonstrates, in a real-life and face-to-face setting, the willingness of a participant to obey an unjust command – unjust because the interviewers were clearly causing distress to the interviewees.

Factors that influence obedience to authority

Each of the factors below has arisen from Milgram's studies of obedience, outlined earlier (pages 176–7). When we consider the issue of validity (pages 182–5), we will examine whether these conclusions can actually be taken *beyond* the laboratory.

Proximity of victim

In Milgram's proximity study, both teacher and learner stayed in the same room, and in the touch-proximity study, teachers had to hold the learner's hand on a plate in order to deliver the shocks once the learner had refused to cooperate. Obedience rates dropped, suggesting that physical presence and contact made teachers empathise more strongly with the learner's suffering and made the suffering harder to deny or ignore.

Proximity of authority

In another variation, the experimenter left the room before the 'learning' session and continued to give instructions by telephone. Here, only 9 out of 40 participants (23%) went to the maximum shock level, showing that the authority's direct surveillance is a crucial factor in determining obedience in this setting.

Presence of allies

A further study gave the responsibility for shock delivery to three supposed participants (two accomplices and the real participant) acting as a team. When the two bogus teachers expressed reservations and refused to carry on, almost all 'real' participants also withdrew their cooperation. Only 4 out of 40 (10%) proceeded to 450 volts. This finding suggests that it may be difficult to confront authority alone, but that the presence of other rebels may help the person to see resistance as legitimate, and formulate strategies for disobedience.

Explanations of why people obey

Gradual commitment

As participants have already given lower-level shocks, it becomes hard to resist the experimenter's requirement to increase the shocks as the experiment continues. In actuality, no shock level is ever administered that is more than 15 volts from the previous level. Having committed themselves to a particular course of action (i.e. giving shocks), it became difficult for Milgram's participants to subsequently change their mind. This is similar to the **foot-in-the-door** method of persuasion.

Agentic shift

Central to Milgram's explanation of obedience is what he termed the **agentic state**, by which he meant 'the condition a person is in when he sees himself as an agent for carrying out another person's wishes' (Milgram, 1974). Milgram argued that people shift back and forth between an agentic state and an **autonomous state**, the latter referring to the state a person is in when he 'sees himself acting on his own'. Upon entering an authority system, Milgram claimed, the individual no longer views himself as acting out of his own purposes but rather comes to see himself as an agent for executing the wishes of another.

The role of buffers

In Milgram's original study the teacher and learner were in different rooms, with the teacher protected (i.e. *buffered*) from having to see his 'victim', and also from the consequences of his electric shocks. When the learner was in the same room this buffering effect was reduced, as was the tendency to obey the commands of the experimenter, and therefore the overall levels of obedience. This 'buffering' effect is similarly used to explain the apparent willingness of people to dispatch weapons of mass destruction. A cruise missile does not, after all, have the same immediacy of consequence as a rifle.

▲ The 'touch-proximity condition', where the 'teacher' holds the hand of the 'learner' on the shock plate. Obedience rates dropped in this condition, but some participants were still very obedient.

'Foot-in-the-door' is a tactic designed to maximise the likelihood of compliance. A trivial initial request, once accepted, is followed by larger requests that the individual then feels obliged to agree to.

CORNER

COMMENTARY

Why was Milgram's research subjected to so much hostile criticism?

Milgram's research changed the way we view the nature of destructive obedience. Prior to this research, it was traditional for social scientists to explain such behaviour as the Nazi war crimes in terms of the actions of deviant personalities. Milgram's research, however, suggested that destructive obedience may be evoked in the majority of people by purely situational factors. In other words, claimed Milgram, his research was criticised because of the *findings* rather than the procedures used. Milgram's findings appeared all the more shocking because they challenged Western assumptions about freedom and personal responsibility. The capacity for moral decision making, it appeared, is suspended when an individual is embedded within a powerful social hierarchy. This has led some to comment on the 'ordinariness' of such evil acts rather than seeing them as the product of pathological personalities (Arendt, 1963). Milgram's research effectively 'opened our eyes' to the possibility that each of us was capable of performing in the same way as had his research participants, and by implication, the same as SS guards in the Nazi death camps.

RESISTANCE TO OBEDIENCE

What is meant by resistance to obedience?

In Milgram's study of obedience, a high proportion of participants gave the maximum 450 volts, yet others defied the experimenter's instructions and withdrew before this point. Milgram was keen to investigate the situational conditions under which people felt able to defy the orders of an authority figure. Although there has been some interest in individual differences in this respect (e.g. gender differences, age differences, differences in moral reasoning), the research findings in these areas have been somewhat inconclusive. Far more productive has been the investigation of the situational constraints on obedience, and it is to those that we now turn.

KEY TERM

Resistance to obedience: The act of defying an order from an authority figure despite pressures to obey. The same factors that reduce obedience can be used to explain increased resistance, for example the proximity of the victim.

Ethical issues raised in these studies

Deception

We have discussed the ethical issues in Milgram's studies. In the study by Gamson *et al.* the participants were also deceived but in an interesting way. Volunteers were told that they could take part in studies on brand recognition of commercial products, product safety, topics in which they would be misled about the purpose until afterwards, or group standards. When the participants had agreed to being involved in all of the studies, they were told that only the last kind was in progress currently – but they had agreed to be deceived!

Psychological harm

You might think that the participants in the study by Gamson *et al.* would not be as distressed as those in some of the other studies. However, during debriefing many participants reported that they found the experience quite stressful. One participant reported that it was 'the most stressful experience I've had in the past year'. It is noteworthy that the researchers did stop the study prematurely, ending half-way through the number of groups they intended to test.

Research into resistance to obedience to authority

Studies of obedience

The studies by Milgram described on pages 176–7, and the other studies of obedience on page 178, tell us as much about resistance to authority as they do about obedience. This is especially true of those studies where fewer than 50% obeyed the experimenter. For example, when Milgram's study was moved to a downtown office more people felt able to resist authority. This tells us that status is a key factor in obedience/resistance. Resistance was also increased when the victim could be seen or when other confederates were present. This shows us that being made aware of the effects of our actions and having social support are means of increasing resistance.

What enabled some participants to resist obedience in Milgram's studies?

Milgram (1974) provided transcripts of the interviews with some of the participants in his various studies. These transcripts can illustrate some of the reasons why and how people resist orders. One participant, Gretchen Brandt, was a 31-year-old medical technician involved in the female-only experiment. When the shock level reached 210 volts she said: 'Well, I'm sorry, I don't think we should continue'. In response to the various prods she said: 'I think we are here of our own free will' and refused to go further. It transpired that she had spent her youth in Nazi Germany and said: 'Perhaps we have seen too much pain'.

Jan Rensaleer, an industrial engineer, stopped at 225 volts, saying: 'I know what shocks do to you. I'm an electrical engineer'. When asked who was responsible for the shocks he said: 'I would put it on myself entirely'. His ability to resist might be put down to a sense of knowledge and a sense of responsibility. Karen Dontz, a nurse who administered the full 450 volts, said: 'in hospital I know what rights I have, here I didn't know'. In hospital she would have felt in a position to question authority because of the knowledge she had, but she didn't feel able to do it here.

A minister refused to go further than 150 volts, saying: 'I don't understand why this experiment is placed above this person's life...If he doesn't want to continue, I'm taking orders from him'. In the post-experiment interview he said: 'If one has as one's ultimate authority God, it trivialises human authority'. The minister's ability to resist is due to a strong sense of moral responsibility.

The role of conformity in disobedience

Gamson *et al*. (1982) conducted an interesting study to show that people, under certain conditions, will not obey orders from authority – individuals who are members of groups are more likely to disobey because of the possibility of collective action.

In this study, paid volunteers worked in groups of 9. A (fictitious) public relations firm, MHRC, wanted the group to say what it thought about a Mr C. who ran a petrol station for an oil company. He had been fired because of immoral behaviour and was now suing the oil company. The coordinator instructed individuals to argue as if they were offended by Mr C.'s behaviour. The groups soon realised that they were being manipulated to produce a tape of evidence supporting the oil company's position. All of the groups expressed dissent, but 24% of the groups nevertheless signed an affidavit giving MHRC permission to their opinions in a trial, i.e. they obeyed. This means that 76% of the groups disobeyed. It was observed that, in any group, once sufficient individuals had taken a rebellious stance, the whole group conformed to it. This may be an example of **minority influence**.

The concepts considered on this page can be applied to the modern problem of terrorism, resisting the forces of terror and evil.

How people might resist obedience

Factors that influence resistance to obedience

There are several ways in which people resist obedience. These are determined by changes in the circumstances in which they deal with authority. We have already considered how such circumstances may change, when viewing Milgram's variations to his original study (page 176). Each of these variations was designed to test a particular **situational factor**. We can look at them again to consider the insights they provide into *resistance* to obedience.

Proximity of victim – In variations to his original baseline study, Milgram moved the learner progressively closer to the teacher. As a result obedience rates dropped, suggesting that physical presence and contact made teachers empathise more strongly with the learner's suffering and therefore made it harder to deny or ignore.

Proximity of authority – In another variation, the experimenter gave instructions by telephone. Here, only 9 out of 40 participants went to the maximum shock level. This shows that, in the laboratory setting at least, people find it easier to resist obedience in the absence of direct surveillance by the authority figure.

Presence of allies – When the two bogus teachers refused to carry on, almost all 'real' participants also withdrew their cooperation. Only 4 out of 40 proceeded to 450 volts. This finding suggests that it may be difficult to confront authority alone, but that the presence of other rebels may help the person to see resistance as legitimate, and formulate strategies for disobedience.

Resisting destructive obedience is not simply a theoretical concept or an academic exercise. It is a vital aspect of human existence. Gretchen Brandt's experience of growing up in Nazi Germany made her all too aware of the destructive nature of blind obedience. Within our own time there are many examples where the human capacity for evil has had profound consequences for others (e.g. Vietnam, Rwanda, Bosnia). In the following passage, Philip Zimbardo focuses on the psychological consequences of the terrorist attack on the US in September 2001 and the importance of resisting mindless compliance.

Opposing terrorism by understanding the human capacity for evil

Sept. 11, 2001 may change forever the way Americans live their lives. A small band of men armed only with box cutters did what no other global superpower has been able to do to the United States. They struck terror in our hearts by demolishing in a single hour an icon of American enterprise, the World Trade Center.

They are the new breed of 'terrorists', faceless people carefully programmed to destroy their enemy at all costs. They are likely to be educated, well-trained, blindly obedient to authority, totally dedicated to a religious-cultural ideology, with few possessions and nothing to lose except sacrificing their lives for a higher cause.

Evil has always existed in many forms and will continue to flourish in different ways in different places. Surely, there are individuals we acknowledge as embodying evil, Hitler, Stalin, Pol Pot and other national tyrants. But it is well for us now to go beyond our tendency to focus on **dispositional** evil as a peculiar property of particular individuals. Instead, we might focus on the **situational** determinants of evil that can seduce even good people to become perpetrators of evil.

Much psychological research reveals the ease with which ordinary people can be recruited to engage in harmful behaviours against their fellows. In one classic study by Stanley Milgram, the majority of ordinary American citizens who participated in it blindly obeyed an authority figure and administered what they believed were painful, even lethal shocks to a stranger. Research by John Steiner (an Auschwitz survivor) indicates that most Nazi concentration camp guards were 'ordinary men' before and following their years of perpetrating evil.

Heroism is to be defined not only as the sacrifice of life for others, but broadened to include the opening of ourselves to the needs of others. Heroes rise above the pressures toward mindless compliance and situationally induced conformity. They are both uniquely individual and uniquely socially focused. Heroic deeds reinforce the bonds of the human condition in ways that resist the forces of terror and evil.

Source: Adapted from Zimbardo, 2001

What is meant by internal validity?

'Validity' concerns the legitimacy of a study and its conclusions. First of all, the study may lack **internal validity**. This is the extent to which the study is 'legitimate' or valid within itself. Participants may have been acting according to what they thought was expected of them rather than following their true inclinations. In other words, they were responding to **demand characteristics** in the experiment. This would mean that the findings were due to something other than was intended (i.e. the experimental manipulation) and that the study therefore lacked internal validity. **Confounding variables** are also a threat to the internal validity of an experiment.

Another criticism that has been made of Milgram's study is that the findings apply to a specific setting (a laboratory-like environment) and it is not reasonable to generalise these findings to explain all situations of obedience in the real world. In other words, the study also lacks **external validity**, which will we consider on the next spread.

So, any psychological study involves both internal and external validity. In any study of behaviour we hold the theoretical idea that there is a *real* way that people behave and psychologists are trying to demonstrate/discover/ uncover what this is. But they may not succeed because there is something wrong *within* the study – such as demand characteristics or confounding variables – or because in some way we are unable to generalise from this experiment to the rest of the world.

Anything that challenges the legitimacy of a finding is a threat to the validity of the findings.

A study that is high in believability (e.g. Bickman's study of obedience) may be low in **experimental control**. This results in both high and low internal validity!

KEY TERMS

Validity: Refers to the legitimacy of a study, the extent to which the findings can be applied to real life as a consequence of either internal or external validity.

Internal validity: An experiment is internally valid if the observed effect can be attributed to the experimental manipulation rather than some other factor (in which case the wrong conclusion might have been drawn).

External validity: An experiment is externally valid if the findings can be generalised beyond the specific situation of the experiment (i.e. to other people, other settings and over time).

Examples of internal validity that have arisen in obedience research

Milgram intended to measure how obedient people were to unjust orders from an authority figure. But did the participants really believe they were delivering shocks, or did they see through the deception and realise that really there were no painful shocks? If the latter is true, then the experiment lacked internal validity – the findings were not a result of obedience but of pretending to obey.

It was Orne and Holland (1968) who launched this attack on Milgram's research, criticisms to which Milgram (1972) responded. We will look at both sides of the argument.

Orne and Holland's criticisms

Orne and Holland point out that the participant 'knows' that people in psychology experiments don't come to harm, in the same way that anyone volunteering to take part in a magician's act involving a guillotine knows that no harm will come to him or anyone else. Experimenters and magicians know the bounds of what is permissible. Therefore a participant will obey an experimenter's orders, whereas he would not obey the same orders given by someone else. This means that Milgram's study did not investigate what it intended to investigate, i.e. it lacked internal validity.

Orne and Holland also claim that Milgram's participants knew the shocks were not real. They must have otherwise wondered why such severe shocks were used in such a relatively trivial learning experiment. Why also was the experimenter so unperturbed by the distressed participant? Why was the participant required at all; why didn't the experimenter simply deliver the shocks himself?

In support of this, Holland (1967) replicated Milgram's experiment and found that, when questioned afterwards, 75% of the participants said they did not believe the deception. On the other hand, Rosenhan (1969) replicated Milgram's experiment and nearly 70% of the participants reported that they *did* believe in the experimental set-up.

Examples of internal validity from other research

Conformity research

Asch (see page 164) also used deception. Did participants realise that the other 'participants' were actually confederates? In order to prevent participants from guessing the true nature of the experiment, Asch arranged for the confederates to give the right answer much of the time to make the experiment seem more plausible. The fact that so many of the majority gave a 'wrong' answer, coupled with the fact that the role of the confederates was difficult (they were not trained actors), leads us to suspect that at least some of Asch's participants realised the experiment was a fake.

Memory research

Most of the studies of memory looked at earlier in this book were experiments with a high level of experimental control. Thus they are generally examples of good internal validity insofar as extraneous variables are concerned.

However, the study by Jenkins and Dallenbach (see page 18) involved a confounding variable (the time of day when testing took place). This led to low internal validity.

Developmental research

It is possible, in studies of children, that an investigator might communicate expectations to the children studied, so affecting their behaviour. For example, in studies of day care an investigator who believes that day care is detrimental to development may treat these participants in an unconsciously different manner to those children looked after at home. Performance on target measures may be affected by such differential treatment, thus invalidating the findings.

Internal validity and non-experimental studies

It would be a mistake to consider that internal validity was an issue only in experiments (though we started this spread considering *experimental* validity). Non-experimental studies, such as those involving a correlational analysis or observational studies, must also be concerned with the extent to which what happens inside the study produces meaningful findings. In a questionnaire there is something called the **questionnaire fallacy** – this is the erroneous belief that a questionnaire actually produces a true picture of what people do and think. Questions should be relevant, unambiguous and clear (i.e. well designed in order to elicit 'real' behaviour) (see page 99 for a discussion).

Milgram's response to the critics

According to Orne and Holland's claim, participants had not believed that they were giving electric shocks and pretended to be distressed as part of their 'role' in the experiment. Milgram defended his original conclusions through film evidence where participants appeared to be in considerable distress when delivering the shocks. After scrutinising responses to a follow-up questionnaire, distributed to participants a year after the study, Milgram reported that only a small minority indicated having any serious doubts about the nature of the shocks during the study. It would have been easy at this stage to have claimed that they *had* detected the hoax during their participation, and had therefore continued under the full knowledge that they were not actually shocking the learner. The fact that so few took this opportunity is testimony to the fact that they *did* believe they were administering real electric shocks.

Milgram also pointed to a number of other studies where participants demonstrated even higher levels of obedience. For example, Sheridan and King (1972) asked participants to give a puppy electric shocks increasing in strength. The shocks were genuine and participants could see and hear the puppy howling in distress. Nevertheless the participants obeyed the experimenter and all the female participants gave the maximum shock. This shows that disbelief is not an explanation for obedience because the participants in the Sheridan and King study knowingly gave shocks.

Milgram's conclusion was that the participants did believe in the deception and therefore the study did investigate what it set out to investigate.

Internal validity and confounding variables

Another aspect of internal validity is the extent to which **confounding variables** (such as investigator bias and order effects) may threaten the validity of the findings. Confounding variables act as an alternative IV and reduce internal validity (because the confounding variable rather than the experimental manipulation is responsible for the finding). Milgram's studies were carefully controlled, thus reducing confounding variables and increasing internal validity. Field studies, such as the study by Bickman (page 178), have less control. So, in this sense, Milgram's studies have good internal validity.

On the other hand, Orne and Holland claim that Milgram's participants may have been affected by **demand characteristics**. If the participant believes that the shocks are not real, then he will look for cues about how to behave. Thus other features of the experimental situation may account for the participants' behaviour rather than the independent variable (experimenter's instructions).

What is meant by external validity?

External validity concerns what goes on *outside* the experiment. If we are confident that an experimental effect has good *internal* validity, we might then ask how far we can generalise this *beyond* the immediate experimental setting. This involves a consideration of ecological validity, population validity and validity over time. We have already met this last category of validity in our discussion of the 'Asch effect' (a 'child of its time' – page 165), but we can consider the other two here. Any of these categories may pose a potential threat to the external validity of an experiment, and therefore the legitimacy of any conclusions drawn.

KEY TERMS

Ecological validity
This is one aspect of external validity. Refers to the ability to generalise an experimental effect beyond the particular setting in which it is demonstrated.

Population validity
This is another aspect of external validity. An experiment has population validity if the findings can be generalised to other groups of people besides those who took part in that study.

Examples of ecological validity in obedience research

Ecological validity refers to the extent to which the findings of a study relate to other settings beyond the experimental setting, most particularly real-life settings. Laboratory experiments are conducted in artificial, contrived surroundings and therefore *often* do not represent real life very well, whereas field experiments are conducted in more natural settings that may better reflect real life. There is a trade-off between the artificial nature of the laboratory experiment (greater experimental control, thus high internal validity but low ecological validity) and greater naturalness of the field experiment (less control, thus low internal validity but higher ecological validity). However, this is not always true.

Ecological validity in Milgram's research

Orne and Holland (1968) claimed that Milgram's research lacked ecological validity as well as lacking internal validity. If the experiment was actually measuring the experimenter–participant relationship rather than other authority–subject relationships, then it is not reasonable to generalise the findings beyond this specific setting to obedience behaviour generally. Milgram's response was that real life was no different. Experiments are like social situations, the experiment (being a social situation) is a reflection of life. The relationship between an experimenter and participant is no different to that between any authority figure and someone in a subservient position.

One way to assess ecological validity is to consider the extent to which Milgram's findings have been replicated in *other settings*. His own replications showed differences in rates of obedience; nevertheless, there was continuing obedience. Field studies of obedience (such as the study by Meeus and Raajmakers, page 178) also found high levels of obedience, and cross-cultural research lends further support to the idea that Milgram's findings have good ecological validity, i.e. they apply to a variety of settings.

Ecological validity in Hofling et al.'s study

You might think that the study of nurses by Hofling *et al.* (page 178) had greater ecological validity than Milgram's work because it was conducted in a more naturalistic setting. Coolican (2001) says that the key question is, 'to what extent might the findings of this study be likely to occur elsewhere?'. He then argues that this cannot be claimed for the study of nurses. First of all, the doctor–nurse authority relationship is a special one and therefore it is not reasonable to generalise from this to all other kinds of obedience. It is part of a nurse's job to obey the orders of doctors, as the nurses in Hofling *et al.*'s study argued in their defence.

In addition, one subsequent attempt to replicate this study (Rank and Jacobsen) found a complete reversal of findings. Almost no nurses obeyed. Admittedly the circumstances had changed (nurses were dealing with a known drug and allowed to discuss their actions with colleagues). Nevertheless, unlike the Milgram variations, the Hofling *et al.* findings are not supported so we can conclude that the latter study *lacks* ecological validity (the findings cannot be generalised beyond that one particular setting).

Examples of external validity in other research

Conformity research

Asch's study was criticised for concerning a rather trivial example of conformity – conforming to erroneous judgements of line lengths may not be equivalent to conforming to the opinions of others on nuclear power. This reduces the relevance of these findings to real life (i.e. it doesn't generalise to other settings).

Memory research

Memory research is generally high in internal validity because such research is mainly laboratory-based, well controlled and highly operationalised. This tends to make the conditions artificial, thus reducing the ecological validity of such studies. For example, the research on interference (page 19) focuses on one particular aspect of memory.

Physiological research

In the module on stress we noted that many studies involved male participants only. We also noted that males respond differently to stress than females for biological, social and cognitive reasons. The restricted samples mean that the studies lack population validity.

What is the difference between external and ecological validity?

Although these terms are often used interchangeably, *ecological* validity is just one aspect of external validity. Ecological validity is a measure of whether findings can be generalised across different settings. Together with measures of the degree to which the results can be generalised to different people and over time, this makes up the *external* validity of a piece of research.

What is the difference between experimental and ecological validity?

Experimental validity concerns the legitimacy of experiments – the way they are carried out, the conclusions drawn, and the implications for understanding related aspects of real life. The experimental validity of an experiment may be threatened by problems relating to both *internal* and *external* validity. So, experimental validity is an all-inclusive term, which *includes* both internal and external validity (see above). However, the term 'experimental' validity is sometimes treated as if it were synonymous with 'internal' validity.

Population validity in obedience research

The other most common threat to external validity is **population validity**. Ecological validity concerns the extent that one can generalise from the experimental *setting* to other settings. Population validity concerns the extent that one can generalise from the *population* studied in the experiment to other populations. Milgram's baseline experiment involved US males only. Clearly we cannot make generalisations to other groups of people because men may be more obedient than women and Americans may be more obedient than, say, Italians – they may also be less obedient than, say, the Japanese.

Research methods *Internal and external (ecological) validity*

In the research methods part of your examination you may be asked the following question: 'Name one feature of this study that might affect the validity of the data being collected'. In such a case you are permitted to identify and describe *anything* that would threaten either internal or external validity. You might also be asked specifically about how it can be improved. The methods of control were discussed on page 173.

Research methods *Internal and external reliability*

Reliability refers to whether something is consistent. A friend you can rely on is consistent. The same is true of a psychological test, or observation, or experiment. They each should be the same on every occasion, i.e. consistent.

Internal reliability is a measure of the extent to which something is consistent within itself. For example, all the questions on a psychological test should be measuring the same thing. This can be assessed using the **split-half method**. The test items are randomly split into two halves and the scores on both halves compared. The scores should be similar if the test is reliable.

External reliability is a measure of the extent to which a measure varies from another measure of the same thing. Two rulers should give the same measure. Two observers should provide the same observations. This is called **inter-observer reliability**.

	Ways of assessing	Ways of improving
Internal reliability, e.g. psychological test	Split-half method	Select test items that produce greatest similarity
External reliability, e.g. in an observational study	Compare observations of different observers (**inter-observer reliability**)	Use **behavioural checklist** Standardise procedures by training observers (e.g. in **pilot study**) Discuss problems and unusual cases

The external validity of obedience research: Is Milgram's research a valid representation of the crimes of the Holocaust?

Milgram provided a situational explanation for the atrocities carried out during the Holocaust. Dicks (1972) found further support for this in a series of interviews with former SS and Gestapo personnel. He claimed that these men displayed the same psychological mechanisms of obedience as shown by participants in laboratory-based obedience research. Indeed, Milgram's study was referred to in some psychological circles as 'the Eichmann experiment', an allusion to the Nazi bureaucrat who, in the course of just 'doing his duty', sent millions of people to their deaths. More recently, however, an analysis of Milgram's studies compared them to actual events in the Holocaust (Mandel, 1998) and cast doubts on the relationship between these events. To Mandel, Milgram offered little more than an 'obedience alibi' for the behaviour of Holocaust perpetrators.

Milgram found...	Equivalent event in the Holocaust: Reserve Police Battalion 101
The greater the proximity of the victim, the more the defiance of the 'teacher'.	On 13 July 1942, in Józefów, Poland, Major Wilhelm Trapp, Reserve Police Battalion 101 commander, announced that he had received orders to carry out a mass killing of Jews. His men were to 'concentrate' the Jews in the market square and then take them in smaller groups to the village outskirts and shoot them. Unlike Milgram's impassive experimenter, Trapp gave his men a way out by making a remarkable offer: those who did not 'feel up to the task of killing Jews' could be assigned to other duties. Despite this offer and the presence of all of the factors shown by Milgram to increase defiance (e.g. close physical proximity and use of physical force against the victims), only a dozen men out of roughly 500 stepped forward to be reassigned. This fact runs entirely counter to what may be reasonably inferred on the basis of Milgram's findings.
Absence of authority figure produced less obedience.	Holocaust perpetrators, too, were often faced with conditions of minimal supervision. Among Reserve Police Battalion 101 (and other units charged with the killing of Jews), obedience was very high. At the Józefów massacre, the killers were alone with their victims as they walked them to a killing site and then shot them. Not only were they not in the physical presence of their superiors, but also each killer had a personalised, face-to-face relationship to his victim, a fact which most social psychologists would agree should have produced empathy for the victim.
Disobedient peers produced greater defiance in 'teacher'.	Although the battalion's men were aware that several of their peers successfully extricated themselves from killing Jews, and that doing so was not seen as a violation of duty, the vast majority of those directly involved in the killing continued to do so until the massacre was completed. In stark contrast, the overwhelming majority of Milgram's participants seized the opportunity to extricate themselves from harming the victim and defy authority.

Overview of social influence research

We have now looked at a variety of examples of social influences – majority and minority effects, and obedience and resistance. We have considered various studies that provide insights into why and how people are influenced by others. There is one classic study that we haven't mentioned, a study that involves conformity and obedience.

This study is usually assumed to be an example of conformity (to social roles). If you use it in a discussion of obedience, make sure you are explicit about its relevance to obedience, e.g. in terms of prisoners obeying the guards.

Are prison officers evil? The prison simulation experiment

(ZIMBARDO ET AL., 1973)

This study explores how we conform to social roles. Each of us has a number of roles: sister, student, girl, brunette and so on. For each role in our society there is a set of norms that tell us how a sister or a student should behave and which we tend to follow. In some cases we can understand obedience as a form of conformity to social roles. People obey in the experimental situation and nurses obey doctors because that is what is regarded as 'normal' in those situations – this behaviour is an established social norm.

Philip Zimbardo was concerned about the growing unrest in US prisons in the 1960s, which led to some violent riots. Some people believed that the reason for such violence was that both prisoners and guards have personalities that make conflict inevitable. Prisoners lack respect for law and order, and guards are domineering and aggressive. This is a **dispositional** explanation – explaining behaviour because of the individual's personality or disposition.

The alternative explanation is that prisoners and guards behave as they do because of the situation they are placed in. Both display lack of respect because of the social role expected in the prison situation. This is a **situational** explanation. (Remember that we looked at both dispositional and situational explanations for obedience on page 177.)

Aim

The aim of this study was to explore the validity of the dispositional explanation. If 'ordinary' people were placed in a prison environment and some of them were designated as guards and others as prisoners, how would they behave? If the guards and prisoners in this mock prison behaved in a non-aggressive manner, this would support the dispositional hypothesis. On the other hand, if these ordinary people came to behave in the same way that we see in real prisons, then we must conclude that the environment plays a major role in influencing behaviour, the situational explanation.

Procedures

Male students volunteered for a psychological study of 'prison life', and were to be paid $15 a day. The 24 most stable (physically and mentally) men were selected and randomly assigned to being a prisoner or a guard. There were 2 reserves and 1 dropped out, finally leaving 10 prisoners and 11 guards.

The 'prisoners' were unexpectedly 'arrested' at home. On entry to 'prison' they were put through a delousing procedure, searched, given a prison uniform with ID number, nylon stocking caps (to make their hair look short) and an ankle chain. They were in prison 24 hours a day. The guards referred to the prisoners only by number. The prisoners were allowed certain 'rights' – for example, 3 supervised toilet trips and 2 hours for reading or letter-writing.

The guards had uniforms, clubs, whistles, handcuffs and reflective sunglasses. **Deindividuation** was an important part of the process, encouraged for example by wearing uniforms.

Findings

The guards grew increasingly tyrannical. They woke prisoners in the night and got them to clean the toilet with their bare hands. Some guards volunteered to do extra hours without pay. The participants appeared to forget that they were only acting. Even when they were unaware of being watched they played their roles. Five prisoners had to be released early because of extreme depression (crying and acute anxiety). In fact, the whole experiment was ended after 6 days, despite the intention to continue for 2 weeks.

▲ Students at Stanford University, California, were randomly assigned the roles of prisoners and guards in a mock prison. Their behaviour showed an alarming conformity to social roles.

Deindividuation is the consequence of wearing uniforms or anything else that removes an individual's sense of individuality. It also means that others treat you less like an individual. This may make people more conformist because they conform to the social role of the uniform (as with nurses or prison guards). Or it can result in greater obedience to unjust authority because you feel less concerned about an individual's feelings (as when the 'learner' wears a hood in a variation of the Milgram experiment, see page 177).

Ethical issues raised in this study

Distress (psychological harm)

Participation in this study must have caused all participants emotional distress. One defence is that the extremes of behaviour could not have been anticipated at the outset. In addition, Zimbardo did conduct debriefing sessions for several years afterwards and concluded that there were no lasting negative effects.

Deception

The 'prisoners' were arrested unexpectedly in their own homes, though otherwise they were not deceived in this experiment. The guards were under the impression that the study was primarily about the behaviour of prisoners; Zimbardo did not correct this false impression. Such 'deceptions' may be regarded as acceptable.

Issues of validity raised in this study

Internal validity

The fact that 'prisoners' may have been responding to demand characteristics means that this, rather than conformity, may explain their behaviour. This is a threat to **internal validity** because the findings are not necessarily due to the experimental treatment (IV).

External validity

The low internal validity also means that we cannot reasonably generalise these findings to real life (**external validity**). The prisoners and guards were playing the roles and their behaviour was not influenced by the same factors that influence behaviour in real life (e.g. personal motivation). This means that it is not reasonable to generalise from this setting to the real-life prison setting, i.e. the study has low **ecological validity**.

From the point of view of **population validity** this study involved US men only. Since it is possible that men are less conformist and probable that individuals from an individualist culture are less conformist, we should feel wary about generalising this beyond the population studied.

http://www.prisonexp.org/ *is a website devoted to the Stanford Prison study, with a slide show, discussion questions and links to other sites.*

Conclusions

This study appears to demonstrate that both guards and prisoners conformed to their social roles. Participants' behaviour was the result of normative social influence. In terms of the original aims of the experiment, we can conclude that situational explanations of the behaviour of prison guards appear to be more appropriate rather than dispositional ones, because 'ordinary' students all too easily became brutal prison guards when placed in the right setting.

Note that it is probably more accurate to say that the participants complied rather than showed 'true' conformity (internalisation) since they probably did not change their personal beliefs.

Zimbardo et al. suggested that two processes can explain the prisoners' final 'submission'. First, the process of **deindividuation**. The prisoners lost their sense of individuality because of what they wore. The guards also wore uniforms and, in this case, it freed them from the normal constraints to behave humanely. They followed the perceived role of a prison guard. Both conformed to social roles.

Second, the process of **learned helplessness** may explain the behaviour of the 'prisoners'. In certain situations individuals recognise that whatever they do has little effect on what happens to them. This lack of rewards leads to reduced efforts. In the mock prison the unpredictable decisions of the guards led the prisoners to give up responding. The fact that the prisoners depended on the guards for everything emasculated the men and increased their sense of helplessness.

Criticisms

Demand characteristics and artificiality

As you know, a **demand characteristic** is a feature of an experiment that in some way 'invites' a participant to behave in a particular way. Participants in this study took on very specific role behaviours because that is what they were asked to do (a demand characteristic). In real life a prison guard (or a prisoner) might be less likely to act as the social role dictates. Instead they would adapt the role to suit their personal beliefs and the requirements of the situation. Most of the guards later claimed that they had simply been acting. This means the experiment may tell us very little about people's behaviour in real life. (Though we do have to ask why some of the prisoners became so stressed.)

Usefulness

Savin (1973) believed that 'the ends did not justify the means' in this study. Although it is claimed that the study was influential in radically altering the way that American prisons are run, in truth the American prison system has become *more* impersonal rather than less so in the days since Zimbardo's study.

COMMENTARY CORNER

AO2 concerns evaluation. To 'evaluate' means to determine the value of something. What was the *value* of Zimbardo *et al.*'s research? As a result of this study, Zimbardo has testified before bodies concerned with prisons and prison reform. His testimony about the research influenced US Congress to change one law so that juveniles accused of federal crimes would no longer be housed before trial with adult prisoners, because of the likelihood of violence against them.

Quiet Rage, a video that he and his Stanford undergraduate students produced from footage of the experiment, continues to be used in college classes and by civil, judicial, military and law enforcement groups to enlighten and arouse concern about prison life.

The experiment has not, however, brought about the changes in prisons or even in guard training programmes that he would have liked.

In fact, prisons have been radically transformed in the United States in the last 25 years to make them less humane. Voters have increasingly elected politicians who take a tough public stance in favour of prisons as places for punishment, rather than for reforming social deviants.

In Zimbardo's view, prisons are 'failed social-political experiments' that continue to bring out the worst in relations between people. They are as bad for the guards as the prisoners in terms of their destructive impact on self-esteem, sense of justice and human compassion.

Haney (one of Zimbardo's fellow researchers) listed a number of lessons from the study that he said are largely ignored in American prisons as well as in other institutions of power today. The study demonstrated, for example, that 'good people are not enough' to prevent abusive excess. 'Individual differences matter very little in the face of an extreme situation. Institutional settings develop a life of their own independent of the wishes and intentions and purposes of those who run them' (O'Toole, 1997).

Critical issue:

Ethical issues in psychological research

specification breakdown

Specification content	Comment
Ethical issues surrounding the use of deception, informed consent and the protection of participants from psychological harm, including the relevance of these issues in the context of social influence research.	You are expected to know about **deception**, **informed consent** and **protection from psychological harm** as **ethical issues**, i.e. *why* these issues are so crucial in psychological research. These particular ethical issues have been chosen because they are important in social influence research, especially in the work of Milgram and Zimbardo. You should, therefore, be able to demonstrate exactly how these issues surfaced in this research, and whether, in the light of such ethical concerns, such research can be justified.
Ways in which psychologists deal with these issues (e.g. through the use of ethical guidelines, ethical committees).	Psychologists deal with ethical issues in various ways, but the most obvious way is through the development of **ethical guidelines**. You should know in general terms how the ethical guidelines are constructed and applied, and specifically how each of the three ethical issues mentioned above is handled by these guidelines. Remember to treat this area *critically*, as you may be asked to give criticisms of the particular way of dealing with ethical issues.

FOR 40 YEARS, from 1932 to 1972, 399 African-American males were denied treatment for syphilis and deceived by officials of the United States Public Health Service. As part of a study conducted in Macon County, Alabama, poor sharecroppers were told that they were being treated for 'bad blood'. In fact, the physicians in charge of the study ensured that these men were untreated. In the 25 years since the details were first revealed, the study has become a powerful symbol of racism in medicine, ethical misconduct in human research, and government abuse of the vulnerable.

The 1990s was a time of reflection upon the Tuskegee Study and its troubling implications. In February 1994, the issue was addressed in a symposium entitled 'Doing bad in the name of good?: The Tuskegee Syphilis Study and its legacy', convened at the Claude Moore Health Services Library. The discussion at this gathering led to the creation of the Tuskegee Syphilis Study Legacy Committee, which met in Tuskegee in January 1996. In its final report the following May, the Committee urged President Clinton to apologise for the wrongs of the Tuskegee Study. The Committee's work bore fruit on 16 May 1997, when the President apologised on behalf of the United States government to the surviving participants of the study. These men and members of the Legacy Committee were invited to the White House to witness the apology.

◀ President Clinton, on behalf of the US government, apologised to survivors of the Tuskegee experiment and descendents of those who participated in the study.

UNIVERSAL ETHICAL PRINCIPLES

Non-maleficence: Do not harm other people.

Beneficence: Help or benefit other people.

Autonomy: Allow people to make their own decisions and act on them.

The harm principle: Autonomy may be limited in order to prevent people from harming each other.

Utility: Maximise good consequences and minimise bad consequences for all people.

Honesty: Do not lie or deceive other people. Do not manipulate the truth.

Privacy: Respect personal privacy and confidentiality.

Fidelity: Keep your promises; be trustworthy.

Integrity: Make your actions reflect your moral commitments, principles, beliefs and virtues.

Justice: Treat people justly, fairly; promote just or fair social institutions; fight injustice.

The report on the left refers to one of the most infamous episodes in the history of science, the Tuskegee Syphilis Study – 'the longest non-therapeutic experiment on human beings in medical history' (Jones, 1993). In the years since the details of this study were disclosed, it has moved from a singular historical event to a powerful statement about the ethics of scientific research. It has come to symbolise 'racism in medicine, ethical misconduct in human research, and government abuse of the vulnerable'.

When the Tuskegee Study began, the standard treatment for syphilis (recommended by every standard textbook of the time) consisted of injections of arsenical compounds, supplemented by applications of mercury or bismuth ointments. After penicillin became available in the 1950s, the researchers withheld its use as well. Medical reports have estimated that between 28 and 100 men died as a result of their untreated syphilis. It is also entirely possible that the infected men passed syphilis to their sexual partners and to their children in utero (Hammonds, 1994). As a result, the physical harm may not have been limited just to the men enrolled in the study.

On 16 May 1997, the surviving participants of the Tuskegee Syphilis Study and the members of the Tuskegee Syphilis Study Legacy Committee gathered at the White House and witnessed the President's apology on behalf of the United States government. President Clinton recounted the injustice done to the study participants and concluded: 'What was done cannot be undone but we can end the silence. We can stop turning our heads away. We can look at you in the eye, and finally say, on behalf of the American people, what the United States government did was shameful and I am sorry'.

The Tuskegee Study will be instantly recognisable as an unethical study, obvious perhaps because of its blatant abuse of vulnerable people and the eventual harm that befell them. In fact, history is littered with examples of human abuse in the name of 'science'. At the Auschwitz-Birkenau death camp during the Second World War, prisoners were frequently subjected to horrific 'medical' experiments at the hands of doctors such as Josef Mengele, the 'Angel of Death'.

By what standards do we judge a study 'unethical'? We most probably examine it in the light of some generally accepted morals or values that we (and others) hold concerning our interactions with our fellow human beings. This may not be as straightforward as it at first seems, although most people would subscribe to some version of the moral principles outlined on the left.

What is meant by an ethical issue?

Ethics are standards of conduct that distinguish between right and wrong, good and bad, justice and injustice. Some ethical standards are highly general and apply to all situations (e.g. being honest, helping others). Other standards apply within the context of professional roles, such as medical ethics, academic ethics and so on. The existence of a multiplicity of ethical standards inevitably gives rise to ethical dilemmas. These are situations where the researcher can choose between at least two different courses of action that appear to be equally justified (or unjustified) from an ethical point of view. Different choices may be supported by different principles, and the conflict of these principles gives rise to the dilemma.

An ethical *issue*, therefore, is any situation that repeatedly gives rise to an ethical dilemma. Whether or not to deceive a research participant in a psychological study in order to gain more worthwhile findings is an ethical issue because it creates an ethical dilemma for the researcher. One of the main reasons why psychological bodies such as the British Psychological Society have developed ethical guidelines is that it removes the need for researchers to resolve these dilemmas on their own.

What is meant by deception?

In order to understand why deception is such a fundamentally important issue in psychological research, we need to examine its impact from the participants' point of view. There are many potential consequences of deception in research. Deception may, for example, make participants suspicious about a research investigation, or they may develop negative feelings about any future research participation. Diana Baumrind (1985) argued that deception is morally wrong on the basis of three generally accepted ethical rules in Western society: the right of informed consent, the obligation of researchers to protect the welfare of the participant, and the responsibility of researchers to be trustworthy.

Examples of deception in the context of social influence research

Asch told his participants that the study was about visual perception. Milgram told his participants that they were involved in a study of the effects of punishment on learning. Hofling *et al*. did not tell the participants anything. They all used deception, arguing that the experiment would be meaningless otherwise.

Was the deception necessary?

An interesting point to note about social influence research is that *almost all of the studies we have covered involved at least some form of deception*. Why? Because of the nature of social influence. As soon as you know that the other participant is a confederate or that he or she is trying to influence you, this is likely to alter your behaviour. For example, if you took part in Asch's study and knew the others were confederates but were asked to pretend they weren't, would you be as likely to conform? In fact, a study by Gallo *et al*. (1973) suggests that you might. In one study of conformity they found participants behaved the same whether they were deceived or

not. However, they found the opposite in a second study. Perhaps deception is not always necessary.

When is deception acceptable?

A second point to make in relation to social influence research is that, when deception is used in other psychological research, it is less important. Why? Think about memory research. In many memory studies participants were not told they would have to recall the information at the end of the study (for example in Craik and Tulving's study on the levels of processing, see page 12). Such deception is less damaging than when it occurs in social influence studies where personal distress may be involved (such as Milgram's study). What this tells us is that deception is not necessarily objectionable, but it becomes an issue in a study that creates psychological distress because the participant does not have the right to give informed consent.

However, there is evidence that participants don't actually object to being deceived, even when they have been distressed in an

experiment. Milgram's participants said afterwards that they did not object to the deception. Christiansen (1988) reviewed studies using deception and reported that participants do not seem to object to deception as long as it is not extreme. In fact, many say they enjoy taking part in studies involving deception, and have admired the skill of the experimenter.

Field studies and deception

In field studies there is no opportunity beforehand to ask participants to give their consent. Experimenters pretend to be ordinary pedestrians or doctors and thus are deceiving the participants. Furthermore, it is often difficult to tell them about the study afterwards. This is either because they cannot be found or, if they are told, it may alert other potential participants to the purpose of the study. In fact, Hofling *et al*. did tell the participants (nurses) afterwards. Does this excuse the deception? We will consider ways of dealing with deception, as well as dealing with other ethical issues, on page 195.

What is meant by informed consent?

The essence of the principle of informed consent is that the human participants of research should be allowed to agree or refuse to participate in the light of comprehensive information concerning the nature and purpose of the research (Homan, 1991). The more potentially serious the risks, the more participants need to know before agreeing to take part. More contentious still is the use of *implicit* coercion, either by use of unreasonable inducements (e.g. money) or by implied punishments (e.g. loss of parole). These may compromise the potential participant's ability to consent without undue pressure to do so.

Even if researchers have sought and obtained informed consent, it does not guarantee that participants really do understand what they have let themselves in for. As Schuler (1982) points out, many designs are unintelligible to other research psychologists, let alone potential participants! Indeed, Epstein and Lasagna (1969) found that only a third of participants volunteering for an experiment really understood what it was about.

Another problem is the requirement for the researcher to point out any likely benefits and risks of participation. However, researchers are not always able to accurately predict the risks of taking part in a study.

What is meant by protection of participants from psychological harm?

Investigators have a primary responsibility to protect participants from all forms of harm during an investigation. Normally the risk of harm must be no greater than in ordinary life. There are many ways harm may be caused to participants, some physical (e.g. getting them to smoke or drink alcohol or coffee excessively), some psychological (e.g. making them feel inadequate or embarrassing them). Protecting participants from *psychological* harm, therefore, means avoiding any situation that may cause them to experience negative feelings or emotions.

KEY TERMS

Ethical issues: An ethical issue arises in research where there are conflicting sets of values concerning the goals, procedures or outcomes of a research study.

Deception: Some forms of deception involve lying to participants about the nature of a study, others involve the unfolding of important information that may affect participant's willingness to take part in a study.

Informed consent: Research participants should be allowed to agree or refuse to participate in a research investigation based on comprehensive information concerning the nature and purpose of the research and their role in it.

Protection of participants from psychological harm: Research participants should be protected from undue risk during an investigation. This might include embarrassment, loss of dignity, or threats to a person's self-esteem as a result of participation.

Examples of lack of informed consent in the context of social influence research

There was no informed consent in most of the studies examined in this module. Gamson *et al.* did offer informed consent of a kind. Participants were asked if they would take part in various studies, including one where they would be deceived. The fact that they agreed to all of the studies was taken to be informed consent to participate in a study where they were deceived.

In Zimbardo *et al.*'s study the participants did give a limited degree of informed consent, yet this did not provide a full understanding of what was to happen next. This illustrates how informed consent does not guarantee true understanding, nor does it protect participants from harm.

Milgram described his experiment to students, who predicted very low levels of shocks. This suggests that any prospective participant might have agreed, not anticipating what would happen.

Examples of psychological harm in the context of social influence research

One of the main criticisms of Milgram's obedience study was that participants would have suffered a considerable loss of self-esteem as a result of their apparent willingness to deliver electric shocks to their helpless victim. Loss of self-esteem is also an important consideration when the experimental manipulation means that some participants are likely to fail a task, or experience unexpected difficulties in executing their role (e.g. as in Asch's study).

The possibility of long-lasting effects

If a study has damaged an individual's self-esteem, this may have a serious effect on the individual's life. Participants in Asch's study may have felt disappointed with themselves because of the way that they appeared to conform so mindlessly, and this may have reduced self-esteem. Participants in Moscovici *et al.*'s study, once they knew about the deception, may have never trusted a psychologist again. Participants in the study by Hofling *et al.* certainly may have ended up with little regard for psychology and participation in the study may also have altered their willingness to obey doctors in the future – which may not be a good thing.

Darley (1992) proposes a chilling effect of participation in Milgram's study. He suggests that the experience of administering shocks (even though they were not real) may activate a previously dormant aspect of an individual's personality such that he or she feels more able and more motivated to repeat the actions. Lifton (1986) reported that physicians in the Nazi death camps started out as ordinary people but became killing machines. In other words, their personalities altered as a consequence of the activities they were asked to perform.

Do participants suffer lasting effects?

Milgram arranged for a psychiatrist to interview the participants a year after the initial study. He reported that there was no evidence of emotional harm arising from participation in the study. Zimbardo re-interviewed his participants in the weeks and months after the prison study and found no lasting negative effects. In both cases participants claimed to have learned important lessons from the studies about how social influence can affect behaviour, and about how to resist such influences.

Ethical issues in *all* psychological research

You might think that ethical issues only occur in social influence research. What is special about social influence research? We have already suggested one problem: in order to investigate social influence, it is impossible to tell a participant what is going to be done without changing the nature of the study. Therefore deception is almost inevitable. The second problem is that many studies of social influence caused psychological distress. Such problems are less common in other areas of psychological research but by no means unknown, especially in sensitive areas such as research involving children.

Examples of ethical issues in other psychological research

- The use of the Strange Situation with very young children (page 48) may well lead to psychological distress, especially as the specific intention was to create mild stress in the infant.

- Asking cardiovascular patients to engage in tasks that create mild stress (page 90) or artificially inducing stress to observe effects on the immune system (page 92) creates psychological harm. In this case the effects may be more than psychological harm – the experiment may result in physical harm.

- Watson and Raynor caused Little Albert severe psychological distress (page 138). They considered that the loud noise was no more severe than he would experience in normal life and was therefore acceptable. A further issue, in this study, is that Albert was not returned to the state he was in prior to the study. We don't know if he remained scared of men in white beards for life because he was removed from the hospital, thus preventing attempts to countercondition him.

Other ethical issues in psychological research

The specification highlights the three ethical issues discussed on the previous page: deception, informed consent and psychological harm. There are many others, some of which we consider here.

The right to withdraw

Giving informed consent allows participants the right to withdraw if they decide during the study that they no longer wish to participate. However, sometimes the right to withdraw is not truly an option. For example, many psychological studies are conducted by university staff using their students as participants. The students are required to be participants as part of their course. In such cases participants' informed consent is negated because they do not truly have the right to withdraw.

In Milgram's study it was not clear to what extent participants felt that they had the right to withdraw. Milgram claimed that participants knew they were free to leave at any time, as demonstrated by the fact that some people did leave. Others argue that the 'prods' from the experimenter made it very difficult for some participants who felt they had to continue.

Confidentiality

Confidentiality is a legal right under the Data Protection Act. In all studies the identity of individual participants is protected, unless informed consent is provided. Psychologists generally do not record the names of participants. Instead they use numbers. When case studies of individuals are reported, psychologists use false names or initials. For example, we considered the case of Genie (page 66) and of HM, who suffered partial amnesia (page 9).

Confidentiality also applies to where a study takes place. It is usually the practice not to name particular institutions or geographical locations in sufficient detail that the population studied could be identified.

In Rosenhan's study of the sane in insane places (page 127), the pseudopatients attended 12 hospitals in 5 different states, thus protecting the hospitals' identity. In the study of Fijian adolescents and eating disorders (page 148), the actual township was identified. Sometimes, even though particular details are omitted, it is relatively easy to work out from other clues the details of what school or what day-care centre was studied.

Invasion of privacy

Individuals have a right to privacy. It is considered acceptable to observe anyone, without their informed consent, in a public place, where they would normally anticipate their behaviour to be observed by others. However, there is a need to be especially sensitive when observing 'personal' behaviour such as lovers on a park bench. In this book we have considered several field studies (observations and experiments) where privacy is an issue, such as the field studies of obedience (page 178). Informed consent is sought wherever possible, such as in field studies of day care.

Research with non-human animals

We have considered a few studies where non-human animals were involved: Harlow's study of attachment in monkeys (page 54), Lorenz's study of goslings (page 45), and Riley's study of stress in mice (page 93). Both psychological and physical harm are important in relation to such research, as is the question of interfering with an animal's natural life patterns.

It is regarded as acceptable to observe anyone in a public place – though lovers on a park bench might feel that their privacy was invaded by a psychologist taking notes about their behaviour.

'Research such as that carried out by Milgram and Zimbardo is seen by many as ethically indefensible, yet for others it is seen as work of great significance.' In the light of the ethical issues raised by social influence research, to what extent can such research be justified?

Questions such as this can at first sight be extremely daunting, particularly as there is also a quotation. It pays to think clearly about the demands of this question before diving in to answer it. As this is one of our last Commentary Corners, we might pause here to examine some of the points we have raised throughout this book.

First, the presence of a quotation should not put you off – it is there to *help* you construct a response. This quotation suggests that the psychological world is divided in its response to social influence research. This gives you an opportunity for a debate in your answer. Although Milgram (see page 176) and Zimbardo (see page 186) are mentioned by name, there is no explicit requirement to focus on their research (although you probably would do anyway).

Second, the question drops a helpful hint about the structure of your response. 'In the light of the ethical issues involved' tells you that your **AO1** content should be a description of the ethical issues raised by social influence research. Your **AO2** content can then be an assessment of whether these issues are sufficiently evident, proven or even significant to warrant the claim of 'ethically indefensible'.

Third, you need to be clear in your own mind where you are going, as an uncoordinated response will surely take you down a blind alley (e.g. describing aspects of Milgram's research or detailing particular procedures that would be considered unethical). From there you will lose track of time and miss many of the more significant points that *might* have been made in response to this question.

To help detail your thoughts and structure your response, making a plan is always worth the few minutes that it will take to construct. The time spent planning will pay off because you are doing most (if not all) of the real thinking up front rather than having to stop regularly throughout the answer and think where you should go next. Some of the points below might be included in your response to this question.

AO1 Description of ethical issues relating to Milgram and Zimbardo's research

- **Deception and informed consent.** Milgram told his participants that they were involved in a study of the effects of punishment on learning. This denied them the right to provide informed consent. Zimbardo's 'prisoners' were arrested unexpectedly in their own homes, though otherwise they were not deceived in this study. The guards were under the impression that the study was primarily about the behaviour of prisoners, and Zimbardo did not correct this false impression.

- **The right to withdraw.** Milgram's participants were told that they could leave at any time, although 'prods' from the experimenter made this quite difficult for some participants. Zimbardo's fiancée, Christina Maslach, is seen as the heroine who persuaded him to call a halt to the experiment. He had previously been obliged to release 5 of his 10 prisoners because of their extreme psychological reaction to the study.

- **Psychological harm.** Baumrind (1964) attacked Milgram's study for the severe distress it created. Participation in Zimbardo's study must have caused all participants emotional distress. Five of the prisoners had to be released because of 'depression, crying, rage and acute anxiety' as well as one who had developed a 'psychosomatic rash'.

AO2 Commentary on specific ethical issues relating to Milgram and Zimbardo's research

- **Deception and informed consent.** Milgram argued that the experiment would be meaningless without some degree of deception. Deception was vital for the internal validity of the study. Zimbardo's participants each signed an informed consent certificate, which specified that there would be an invasion of privacy, loss of some civil rights and harassment. He felt that full disclosure of procedural details (such as the home arrests) was justifiable given the nature of the study.

- **The right to withdraw.** Milgram argued that all participants were free to leave, and the fact that approximately one-third did leave before the final stages of the experiment bore this out. Zimbardo agrees that he was 'trapped' in his role as prison superintendent during the study, which made him impervious to the suffering of his research participants.

- **Psychological harm.** Milgram claimed he did not know, prior to the study, that such high levels of distress would be caused. A follow-up study found that many of the participants were glad to have participated, and felt they had learned something of personal importance. One defence of Zimbardo's study is that the extremes of behaviour could not have been anticipated at the outset. In addition Zimbardo did conduct debriefing sessions for several years afterwards and concluded that there were no lasting negative effects.

AO2 Other commentary on the ethics of Milgram's and Zimbardo's research

- **Why was Milgram's research subjected to so much hostile criticism? (page 179).** Milgram claimed that his research was criticised because of the *findings* rather than the procedures used. Milgram's research effectively 'opened our eyes' to the possibility that each of us was capable of performing in the same way as had his research participants, and by implication, the same as SS guards in the Nazi death camps.

- **Milgram and the 'obedience alibi' (page 185).** To Mandel (1998), Milgram offered little more than an 'obedience alibi' for the behaviour of Holocaust perpetrators. The 'only obeying orders' conclusion effectively exonerates Nazi war criminals of their role in the atrocities of the Holocaust and insults survivors of the Holocaust even further. This demonstrates how the misapplication of research findings can have an ethical impact far beyond their immediate research setting.

- **What was the value of Zimbardo et al.'s research? (page 187).** As a result of this study, Zimbardo has testified before bodies concerned with prisons and prison reform, although the experiment has not brought about the changes in prisons or even in guard training programmes that he would have liked. However, prisons have been radically transformed in the US in the last 25 years to make them less humane.

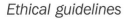

How do psychologists deal with ethical issues?

'Professionals' are people who monitor the behaviour of their group. All professionals (e.g. police officers, doctors, teachers) have a professional body whose job it is, among other things, to ensure that certain standards are maintained. In the UK psychologists have the British Psychological Society (BPS), in the US there is the American Psychological Association (APA), in Canada the Canadian Psychological Association (CPA), and so on.

Ethical guidelines

All professions draw up rules which 'guide' the behaviour of their members. Within psychology, different professional bodies have their own guidelines that apply to their own members, although there are many similarities between guidelines. These tend to present minimal information for what is considered acceptable and unacceptable behaviour when carrying out research with human participants. Each guideline is matched to an underlying ethical issue (e.g. advice about avoiding deception, maintaining confidentiality). This 'rules and sanctions' approach is inevitably rather general because of the virtual impossibility of covering every conceivable situation that a researcher may encounter.

Ethical committees

An **ethical committee** decides whether any piece of research is ethically acceptable. All institutions where research takes place have an ethical committee which must approve any study before it begins. They look at all possible ethical issues and at how they have been dealt with, weighing up the value of the research against the possible costs in ethical terms. In some cases the balance is seen to be reasonable, in other cases it is decided that the costs are simply too great or the research is simply not of sufficient value.

What is meant by ethical guidelines?

The 'role' of **ethical guidelines** in psychology is summarised in the BPS Code of Conduct: 'To preserve an overriding high regard for the well-being and dignity of research participants' (BPS, 1993). This recognises that psychologists owe a debt to the individuals who participate in research, and that in return those 'participants' should expect to be treated with the highest standards of consideration and respect. Ethical guidelines tend to be based on a 'cost–benefit' approach in that scientific ends (the benefits) are sometimes seen as justifying the use of methods that sacrifice individual participants' welfare (the costs), particularly when the research promises 'the greatest good for the greatest number'.

Each section of the BPS guidelines consists of a series of statements clarifying appropriate conduct relating to specific ethical issues (e.g. consent, confidentiality). Many of the social influence studies we have covered in the previous pages were conducted at a time when psychologists were not as sensitive to ethical issues. Therefore we are imposing our current standards on an earlier time and are critical of their behaviour. Milgram's research, for example, was instrumental in leading to the establishment of ethical guidelines in order to avoid such harm in the future. Ethical guidelines are regularly updated in order to reflect newly emergent issues in the discipline or inadequacies in earlier versions.

Socialisation

A third method of dealing with ethical issues is the process of socialisation within any professional group. This is where you come in. Part of learning about psychology is learning to take on psychologists' ethical attitudes. Just as carpenters learn how to look after their tools, research psychologists learn how to preserve the integrity and well-being of their research participants. All psychologists, no matter what their level, learn about research ethics. Psychologists operating under the auspices of the BPS are also required to undertake 'continuing professional development'. This enables psychologists who work in certain sensitive areas to attain new skills and keep up to date with developments relevant to their profession as well as helping to provide an assurance to the public.

Punishment

Finally, there is punishment. A psychologist who transgresses the ethical code for his or her profession appears before a special committee which judges the severity of the offence. The psychologist (or other professional) may be disbarred from the profession and thus prevented from working in it. Professional bodies cannot impose more severe sentences (though it is a severe 'sentence' for professionals). In some cases, however, an ethical infringement may amount to a criminal act and this is dealt with by the courts. This was the case for the doctor Harold Shipman, who was found guilty of murder, and it would also be the case if a psychologist were accused of sexual offences against a patient. Research with non-human animals is covered by legislation such as the Home Office Act (1986).

KEY TERM

Ethical guidelines: These are concrete, quasi-legal documents that help to guide conduct within psychology by establishing principles for standard practice and competence.

CRITICAL ISSUE: ETHICAL ISSUES IN PSYCHOLOGICAL RESEARCH

Dealing with the issue of deception

BPS guidelines: *Intentional deception of the participants over the purpose and general nature of the investigation should be avoided whenever possible. Participants should never be deliberately misled without extremely strong scientific or medical justification. Even then there should be strict controls and the disinterested approval of independent advisers.*

Debriefing

A way to compensate for deception is to inform participants, after the research has taken place, of the true nature of the study. This is called **debriefing**. In general the aim of debriefing is to restore the participant to the state he or she was in at the start of the experiment. Participants may be given the opportunity to discuss their feelings, as was the case in Milgram's study. Milgram also arranged for the participants to meet the confederate and see that he was unharmed.

Right to withhold information

During debriefing participants should be offered the right to withhold their data from the study. This is a form of retrospective informed consent.

Costs and benefits

Deception is not acceptable when a study has little value and/or when the costs (e.g. distress) are too great. Thus, the task for an ethical committee is usually to decide whether the value of a study is sufficient to justify the costs. We noted earlier that Savin concluded, with regard to Zimbardo's prison study (page 187), that the benefits to society were insufficient to justify the methods used. In contrast Erikson (1968), commenting on Milgram's research, said that it had made 'a momentous and meaningful contribution to our knowledge of human behaviour'. When the benefits justify the cost, or the costs are not too great, then deception may be acceptable.

Dealing with the issue of informed consent

BPS guidelines: *Wherever possible, the investigator should inform all participants of the objectives of the investigation. The investigator should inform the participants of all aspects of the research or intervention that might reasonably be expected to influence their willingness to participate. The investigator should, normally, explain all other aspects of the research or intervention about which the participants enquire. Failure to make full disclosure prior to obtaining informed consent requires additional safeguards to protect the welfare and dignity of the participants.*

Presumptive consent

An alternative to gaining informed consent from the participants themselves is to gain informed consent from others. This can be done, for example, by asking a group of people whether they feel the study is acceptable. We then *presume* that the participants themselves would have felt the same, if they had been given the opportunity to say so. In a sense Milgram did obtain this form of consent from a group of students because he showed that most people would not expect to cause harm, therefore it would be presumed that they wouldn't mind taking part.

Prior general consent

A second alternative is to seek prior general consent from the participants. Gamson *et al.* (page 181) asked participants to provide consent for a variety of studies, including a study that would involve deception. By agreeing to take part in all the studies participants were generally giving consent to being deceived.

Dealing with the issue of protection of participants

BPS guidelines: *Investigators have a primary responsibility to protect participants from physical and mental harm during the investigation. Normally the risk of harm must be no greater than in ordinary life, i.e. participants should not be exposed to risks greater than or additional to those encountered in their normal lifestyles.*

Anticipating harm and stopping the study

Some psychologists have attempted to excuse the distress caused in an experiment on the grounds that it was unexpected. This was Milgram's defence, though he did not stop the experiment after observing the effects on some participants. Both Gamson *et al.* and Zimbardo *et al.* did stop their studies soon after the extent of distress became apparent.

Using role play

Psychological harm may be excused if participants have had the opportunity to provide informed consent and know their rights about withdrawing. This can be achieved if role play is used, as in Zimbardo's study. However, even with informed consent and the right to withdraw, participants suffered severe psychological distress in Zimbardo's study.

Use of questionnaires

It might be possible simply to ask people how they might behave in the situation to be studied, rather than asking them to be part of a study. However, Milgram did ask people how they would behave and their answers were not remotely the same as the actual behaviour.

Debriefing

Milgram claimed that debriefing was an important part of protecting participants. As we know he did this, fully reassuring participants that their behaviour had been normal, even socially desirable, and therefore they should not feel bad or guilty about the way that they had responded.

http://www.bps.org.uk/documents/Code.pdf
Includes the full BPS guidelines.

Assessing ways of dealing with ethical issues

T he use of ethical guidelines for research is generally seen as the way that psychologists *deal* with the problems posed by the ethical issues previously discussed. But does the existence of ethical guidelines such as those published by the BPS mean that all psychological research is ethically sound? In this spread we examine the problems associated with the use of ethical guidelines in research with human participants (research with non-humans raises different concerns, which will not be discussed here).

Criticisms of ways in which psychologists deal with ethical issues

Although it may appear that the mere existence of ethical guidelines has resolved the problem of ethical issues in psychological research, these are not without their own problems. After all, we have laws but we still have crime, we have speed limits but we still have traffic accidents. Many of the problems associated with the use of ethical guidelines and their implementation through ethical committees relate to the analysis of costs and benefits.

Weighing up costs versus benefits

It is difficult, if not impossible, to predict both costs and benefits prior to conducting a study

Researchers frequently have an investment in the potential benefits of a study, and therefore focus more on those. These may make them oblivious to all the potential ways in which the participants may be harmed as a result of participation in the study.

It is difficult to quantify costs and benefits even after the study

How can costs and benefits be quantified? How much does personal distress cost? If the findings of a study demonstrate that people are more likely to obey someone in uniform, how much is that benefit? In Milgram's study some participants said the experience was personally beneficial in helping them cope better with this kind of inhumane authority in the future. Ethical guidelines may protect the immediate needs of research participants, but may not deal with all the possible ways in which research may inflict harm on a group of people or section of society.

Should costs and benefits be considered in terms of the individual or of society?

If we judge the costs and benefits from a participant's point of view, we might list distress and loss of time versus financial rewards and a feeling of having contributed to scientific research. If we judge costs and benefits in terms of society at large, we can consider the value in improving people's lives versus the possibility that individuals may be less trusting in future or be desensitised. You could also judge costs/benefits in terms of the *group* to which an individual belongs. When research is done to investigate cultural differences, the research may not harm the individual but the findings may lead to biased treatment of the individual's cultural group (for good or bad). The Canadian Psychological Association advises its members to 'analyse likely short-term, ongoing, and long-term risks and benefits of each course of action on the individual(s)/group(s) involved or likely to be affected'.

The cost–benefit calculation raises as many ethical issues as it is meant to resolve

Diana Baumrind (1975) argued that the cost–benefit approach solves nothing. The intention is to develop a means of solving ethical dilemmas but, in fact, we are left with another set of dilemmas (i.e. weighing up the potential costs against the potential benefits). Baumrind also argued that the cost–benefit approach in a way legitimises unethical practices. For example, it suggests that deception and harm *are* acceptable in many situations *provided* the benefits are worthwhile.

Problems with ethical guidelines

Paying lip service to the rules

The guidelines may be used in such a way as to serve the needs of the researcher rather than those of the participant. What passes for 'informed' consent may be aimed more at allaying the fears of potential participants (and so encouraging them to participate) than informing them of all potential hazards and risks. The voluntary nature of participation may be compromised when researchers use techniques that erode the participant's ability to resist or decline (e.g. by offering them money for participation or threatening punishment for non-participation).

The power of censure

Although professional bodies provide guidelines for acceptable conduct in research, their regulatory powers are limited. Unlike other professions (such as the medical profession), there is no obligation to take up membership and the sanctions of exclusion (e.g. from the BPS) are fairly weak. As a result, although ethical guidelines *threaten* sanctions for ethical infringements, in reality they have no teeth.

Absolves the researcher of responsibility

By putting guidelines into place the individual researcher is absolved of any need to consider the ethical issues arising in a study. The researcher need only focus on obeying the guidelines and receiving approval from an ethical committee.

There are particular issues that arise with particular research methods. You need to be aware of these and also how you might deal with them in an actual study.

Remember that in all cases the answer to 'how would you deal with this?' is also to refer to appropriate ethical guidelines, discuss ideas with colleagues and seek approval of an ethical committee.

Research method	Possible ethical issue	How you might deal with it
Laboratory experiment	Deception	Offer the right to withdraw.
	Informed consent (is it truly voluntary, do participants understand?)	Try role play or use questionnaires. Debrief participants after the study.
	Psychological harm (applies to all research methods)	Use presumptive consent or prior general consent. Debrief participants.
Field experiment and naturalistic observations	Informed consent	Debrief where possible.
	Difficulty debriefing	Use presumptive consent.
	Privacy	Only observe in public places.
Natural experiment	Confidentiality (such experiments often deal with sensitive issues)	Protect individual identities and that of the institution.
Investigations using correlational analysis	Misunderstanding of findings (the public perception is often that a cause has been identified and this may lead to erroneous understanding of important social issues)	Be clear about what the findings show, and what they don't show.
Questionnaire surveys and interviews	Confidentiality	Protect individual identities.
	Privacy	Do not ask unnecessarily personal questions.
Research with non-human animals	Psychological or physical harm	Avoid the use of non-human animals where possible. Reduce numbers involved. Consult Home Office legislation.

CORNER

COMMENTARY

Ethical issues and the problems posed by Internet research

Ethical guidelines may prepare the researcher for traditional research situations, where the researcher and participant are face to face, but more recently the Internet has become an increasingly popular research medium for psychologists. Researchers can potentially collect data from all over the world at relatively low cost and in less time than it takes in the physical world. As a result, there has been a steady increase in the number of Internet-based studies, ranging from surveys to 'naturalistic' observation.

Certain features of on-line research introduce concerns about the adequacy of traditional ethical guidelines and other practices governing psychological research. There is, for example, growing concern about the potential harm to on-line users who are completely unaware they have become research participants when they discuss diseases, marital problems or drug abuse. Ethical guidelines generally prohibit experiments on humans without consent, though some observations in public settings are acceptable. Many discussion groups are open to the public, and therefore might be considered a 'public setting', but participants generally assume that fellow members join because they have similar interests or concerns. That makes such forums less like a public square and more like someone's living room. The format of the on-line discussion group makes this an ideal place for researchers to engage in covert observation. After all, it is much easier for a researcher to lurk in a chat room undetected than it is to stand in a room full of people and take notes.

To gain *informed* consent from a participant requires the researcher to divulge all potential risks of participation. Whether the risks of on-line participation are greater or less than traditional research remains to be seen, but the risks are certainly *different*. On-line survey research, for example, may increase participants' risk of identity exposure *because* they are transmitting their responses via the Internet. The risk of exposure can surface at different stages of the research, from data gathering, data processing to data storage. As an example, let us suppose that someone sends an e-mail to a researcher regarding a particularly sensitive issue. A member of the sender's family may (inadvertently or not) retrieve the sent file and view its contents. Likewise, a researcher's response may be (inadvertently or not) opened by someone who shares the same computer or the same e-mail account, thus compromising the principle of confidentiality. Even the humble informed consent form, usually involving the participant reading a full account of the possible risks of a study then signing their agreement to take part, is replaced by an 'I agree' button and a single click of the mouse. How often do *you* read everything on-line before clicking the 'I agree' button?

Another feature of on-line research that complicates the application of existing guidelines is the existence of anonymous and pseudonymous (the participant adopts an on-line 'identity' or pseudonym) communications. In particular, the 'faceless' nature of on-line interactions poses problems for the researcher when it comes to debriefing the participants at the end of the study. In the physical world the researcher can *see* participants as they leave, and can offer appropriate debriefing. The faceless nature of on-line interactions does not, however, allow for this. Ethical guidelines also oblige researchers to protect the privacy of research participants (easy enough in the real world), yet many on-line users have pseudonyms (e.g. Maverick, Ann-on-a-mouse) that, despite their comparative anonymity in the physical world, are effectively a *real* identity in the on-line world.

In conclusion, the ability of a researcher to record interactions on a site without the knowledge of the participants, the complexities of obtaining informed consent, the illusion of privacy in cyberspace, and the blurred distinction between public and private domains highlight the inadequacies of current ethical guidelines.

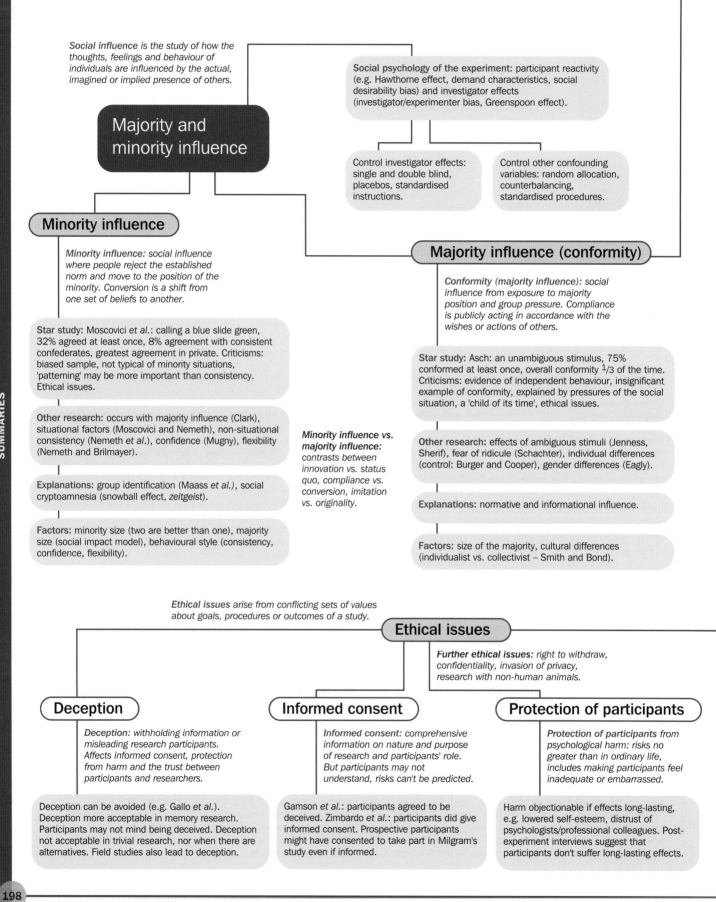

Social influence is the study of how the thoughts, feelings and behaviour of individuals are influenced by the actual, imagined or implied presence of others.

Majority and minority influence

Social psychology of the experiment: participant reactivity (e.g. Hawthorne effect, demand characteristics, social desirability bias) and investigator effects (investigator/experimenter bias, Greenspoon effect).

Control investigator effects: single and double blind, placebos, standardised instructions.

Control other confounding variables: random allocation, counterbalancing, standardised procedures.

Minority influence

Minority influence: social influence where people reject the established norm and move to the position of the minority. Conversion is a shift from one set of beliefs to another.

Star study: Moscovici *et al.*: calling a blue slide green, 32% agreed at least once, 8% agreement with consistent confederates, greatest agreement in private. Criticisms: biased sample, not typical of minority situations, 'patterning' may be more important than consistency. Ethical issues.

Other research: occurs with majority influence (Clark), situational factors (Moscovici and Nemeth), non-situational consistency (Nemeth *et al.*), confidence (Mugny), flexibility (Nemeth and Brilmayer).

Explanations: group identification (Maass *et al.*), social cryptoamnesia (snowball effect, *zeitgeist*).

Factors: minority size (two are better than one), majority size (social impact model), behavioural style (consistency, confidence, flexibility).

Minority influence vs. majority influence: contrasts between innovation vs. status quo, compliance vs. conversion, imitation vs. originality.

Majority influence (conformity)

Conformity (majority influence): social influence from exposure to majority position and group pressure. Compliance is publicly acting in accordance with the wishes or actions of others.

Star study: Asch: an unambiguous stimulus, 75% conformed at least once, overall conformity 1/3 of the time. Criticisms: evidence of independent behaviour, insignificant example of conformity, explained by pressures of the social situation, a 'child of its time', ethical issues.

Other research: effects of ambiguous stimuli (Jenness, Sherif), fear of ridicule (Schachter), individual differences (control: Burger and Cooper), gender differences (Eagly).

Explanations: normative and informational influence.

Factors: size of the majority, cultural differences (individualist vs. collectivist – Smith and Bond).

Ethical issues arise from conflicting sets of values about goals, procedures or outcomes of a study.

Ethical issues

Further ethical issues: right to withdraw, confidentiality, invasion of privacy, research with non-human animals.

Deception

Deception: withholding information or misleading research participants. Affects informed consent, protection from harm and the trust between participants and researchers.

Deception can be avoided (e.g. Gallo *et al.*). Deception more acceptable in memory research. Participants may not mind being deceived. Deception not acceptable in trivial research, nor when there are alternatives. Field studies also lead to deception.

Informed consent

Informed consent: comprehensive information on nature and purpose of research and participants' role. But participants may not understand, risks can't be predicted.

Gamson *et al.*: participants agreed to be deceived. Zimbardo *et al.*: participants did give informed consent. Prospective participants might have consented to take part in Milgram's study even if informed.

Protection of participants

Protection of participants from psychological harm: risks no greater than in ordinary life, includes making participants feel inadequate or embarrassed.

Harm objectionable if effects long-lasting, e.g. lowered self-esteem, distrust of psychologists/professional colleagues. Post-experiment interviews suggest that participants don't suffer long-lasting effects.

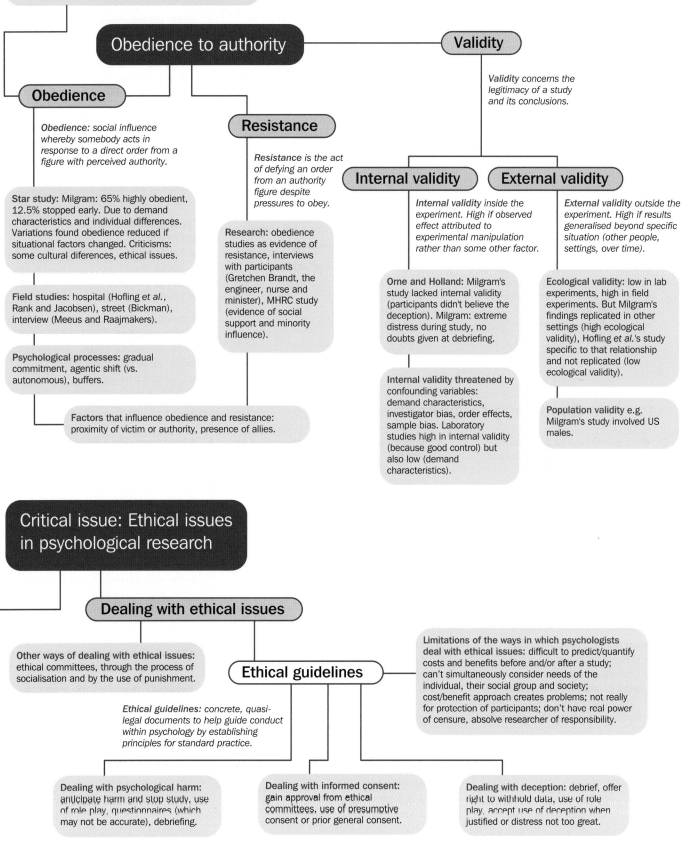

Zimbardo *et al.*: obedience and conformity. Situational explanations explain prisoner-guard behaviours. Criticisms: ethical issues, may lack internal and external validity.

Obedience to authority

Validity

Validity concerns the legitimacy of a study and its conclusions.

Obedience

Obedience: social influence whereby somebody acts in response to a direct order from a figure with perceived authority.

Resistance

Resistance is the act of defying an order from an authority figure despite pressures to obey.

Internal validity

Internal validity inside the experiment. High if observed effect attributed to experimental manipulation rather than some other factor.

External validity

External validity outside the experiment. High if results generalised beyond specific situation (other people, settings, over time).

Star study: Milgram: 65% highly obedient, 12.5% stopped early. Due to demand characteristics and individual differences. Variations found obedience reduced if situational factors changed. Criticisms: some cultural diferences, ethical issues.

Field studies: hospital (Hofling *et al.*, Rank and Jacobsen), street (Bickman), interview (Meeus and Raajmakers).

Psychological processes: gradual commitment, agentic shift (vs. autonomous), buffers.

Factors that influence obedience and resistance: proximity of victim or authority, presence of allies.

Research: obedience studies as evidence of resistance, interviews with participants (Gretchen Brandt, the engineer, nurse and minister), MHRC study (evidence of social support and minority influence).

Orne and Holland: Milgram's study lacked internal validity (participants didn't believe the deception). Milgram: extreme distress during study, no doubts given at debriefing.

Internal validity threatened by confounding variables: demand characteristics, investigator bias, order effects, sample bias. Laboratory studies high in internal validity (because good control) but also low (demand characteristics).

Ecological validity: low in lab experiments, high in field experiments. But Milgram's findings replicated in other settings (high ecological validity), Hofling *et al.*'s study specific to that relationship and not replicated (low ecological validity).

Population validity e.g. Milgram's study involved US males.

Critical issue: Ethical issues in psychological research

Dealing with ethical issues

Other ways of dealing with ethical issues: ethical committees, through the process of socialisation and by the use of punishment.

Ethical guidelines

Limitations of the ways in which psychologists deal with ethical issues: difficult to predict/quantify costs and benefits before and/or after a study; can't simultaneously consider needs of the individual, their social group and society; cost/benefit approach creates problems; not really for protection of participants; don't have real power of censure, absolve researcher of responsibility.

Ethical guidelines: concrete, quasi-legal documents to help guide conduct within psychology by establishing principles for standard practice.

Dealing with psychological harm: anticipate harm and stop study, use of role play, questionnaires (which may not be accurate), debriefing.

Dealing with informed consent: gain approval from ethical committees, use of presumptive consent or prior general consent.

Dealing with deception: debrief, offer right to withhold data, use of role play, accept use of deception when justified or distress not too great.

MULTIPLE-CHOICE QUESTIONS

Section 1 Majority and minority influence

1 Majority influence mainly affects
a Public behaviour
b Private beliefs
c Both (a) and (b)
d Neither (a) nor (b)

2 Asch's study looked at majority influence in
a An ambiguous situation
b An unambiguous situation
c A situation which was both ambiguous and unambiguous
d None of the above

3 The phrase 'child of its time' refers to the fact that
a Children are more conformist than adults
b Time of day is a potential extraneous variable in conformity experiments
c The findings relate to a particular historical period
d The research methods used are outdated

4 Normative social influence refers to situations where a person goes along with the majority
a Because the person wants to be accepted by the majority
b Because the person genuinely believes the majority to be right
c Because there is no clear answer
d Because the majority told the person to

5 Moscovici et al. found that minority influence was greatest when
a Opinions were expressed in public
b Opinions were expressed in private
c Only single-sex groups were involved
d Confederates answered first

6 Minority influence is affected by
a Consistency
b Patterning
c Flexibility
d All of the above

7 Social cryptoamnesia refers to
a A form of mental illness, where the individual fears the minority
b Stealing things from someone else
c Forgetting the source of innovation
d None of the above

8 Investigator bias occurs because
a Investigators unconsciously produce cues about how to behave
b Investigators have expectations about the study
c Both of the above
d Neither of the above

9 Investigator bias can be controlled by
a Single blind
b Double blind
c Use of placebos
d Counterbalancing

10 A practice effect is an example of
a An order effect
b The Hawthorne effect
c The social desirability effect
d Counterbalancing

Section 2 Obedience to authority

1 What percentage of participants delivered the maximum shocks in Milgram's baseline study?
a 50%   b 55%
c 60%   d 65%

2 In which of the following conditions did obedience increase?
a In a run-down office
b When another teacher delivered the shocks
c When a second teacher was present
d When the teacher had to put the learner's hand on the shock plate

3 What is the 'obedience alibi'?
a Offering an excuse for leaving a study
b Offering an excuse for why you don't want to take part in the study
c Offering an excuse for 'evil' behaviour in terms of simply obeying orders
d All of the above

4 Internal validity refers to the extent to which
a An experiment shows the relationship between the IV and DV
b An experiment is well controlled
c A questionnaire produces a true picture of what people do and think
d All of the above

5 External validity is
a The same as ecological validity
b A form of experimental validity
c A form of internal validity
d All of the above

6 Which of the following are factors that increase resistance to authority?
a Social support
b A sense of personal responsibility
c High self-esteem
d All of the above

7 In the study by Zimbardo et al. ethical objections were raised because the participants
a Did not provide consent
b Were arrested at home
c Were deindividuated
d Did not have the right to withdraw

8 A histogram differs from a bar chart because
a A histogram has a true zero and a continuous scale
b A histogram does not have a true zero but has a continuous scale
c A histogram shows frequencies
d A histogram has more information

9 In a field experiment
a The experimenter manipulates the independent variable
b Does not directly manipulate the independent variable
c There is no independent variable
d Manipulates both the independent variable and dependent variable

10 'Reliability' describes the extent to which something is
a Relevant
b Consistent
c Certain
d True

Section 3 Critical issue: Ethical issues in psychological research

1 Deception is
a Never acceptable
b Acceptable in social influence research
c Acceptable if the participants say they don't mind
d Acceptable if there are no alternatives

2 Informed consent involves
a Knowing about the aims of an investigation
b Letting participants know their rights
c Being informed about anything that may influence your decision to participate
d All of the above

3 Milgram claimed that the participants in his study had or were given
a The right to withdraw
b Informed consent
c Confidentiality
d Protection from harm

4 Ethical guidelines focus most on
a The concerns of the participant
b The concerns of the participant's social group
c The concerns of society in general
d All of the above

5 Costs and benefits
a Should relate to participants
b Should relate to society in general
c Both (a) and (b)
d Neither (a) nor (b)

6 One way to deal with the issue of deception is to
a Ask for prior general consent
b Use debriefing
c Give the right to withhold information
d All of the above

7 Gamson et al. got round the problem of informed consent by offering participants
a Presumptive consent
b Prior general consent
c The right to withdraw from the study
d Payment

8 The use of role play is a way of dealing with
a Deception
b Lack of informed consent
c Protection of participants from harm
d All of the above

9 Which ethical issue is most likely to arise in a laboratory experiment?
a Deception
b Psychological harm
c Privacy
d Confidentiality

10 Studies that use a correlational analysis may mistakenly be interpreted as demonstrating a cause. This could create
a Erroneous understanding of important social issues
b Low marks on a psychology examination
c Experimenter bias
d None of the above

Section 3 answers
1d 2d 3a 4a 5c
6d 7b 8d 9a 10a

Section 2 answers
1d 2b 3c 4d 5b
6d 7b 8a 9a 10b

Section 1 answers
1a 2b 3c 4a 5b
6d 7c 8c 9b 10a

RESEARCH METHODS
terms covered

- Bar chart
- Confounding variable
- Counter-balancing
- Debriefing
- Deception
- Demand characteristics
- Double blind

- Ecological validity
- Ethical guidelines
- Ethical issues
- Experimental control
- Experimenter bias
- External reliability
- External validity
- Extraneous variable
- Field experiment

- Field study
- Greenspoon effect
- Hawthorne effect
- Histogram
- Informed consent
- Internal reliability
- Internal validity
- Inter-observer reliability
- Investigator bias

- Investigator effect
- Laboratory experiment
- Leading questions
- Natural experiment
- Order effects
- Participant reactivity
- Placebo

- Population validity
- Practice effect
- Protection from harm
- Questionnaire fallacy
- Random allocation
- Replication
- Sample bias
- Single blind

- Social desirability bias
- Split-half method
- Standardised instructions
- Standardised procedures
- Validity

Revision list

Key terms

You may be asked to 'Explain what is meant by' any of the following. Each explanation may be for 2, 3 or 6 marks. Make sure that what you write is related to the number of marks. Use examples to amplify your explanations where appropriate.

✓

☐ Control of variables	p. 172
☐ Deception	p. 191
☐ Demand characteristics	p. 172
☐ Ecological validity	p. 184
☐ Ethical guidelines	p. 194
☐ Ethical issues	p. 191
☐ External validity	p. 182
☐ Informed consent	p. 191
☐ Internal validity	p. 182
☐ Investigator effects	p. 172
☐ Majority influence (conformity)	p. 164
☐ Minority influence	p. 168
☐ Obedience to authority	p. 176
☐ Population validity	p. 185
☐ Protection of participants from psychological harm	p. 191
☐ Resistance to obedience	p. 180
☐ Social influence	p. 164
☐ Validity	p. 182

Factors that influence

You should be able to write about at least two factors of the following:

✓

☐ Majority influence	p. 167
☐ Minority influence	p. 171
☐ Obedience	p. 179
☐ Resistance to obedience	p. 181

Star studies

This is the 'apfcc' question. You need 3 minutes' worth of writing on aims, procedures, findings and conclusions for each of these. You may also be asked for one or two criticisms of these studies. Criticisms can be positive or negative.

✓

☐ Majority influence (conformity) (Asch, 1956)	pp. 164–5
☐ Minority influence (Moscovici et al., 1969)	p. 169
☐ Into obedience to authority	pp. 176–7

Research

You need to be able to outline the *findings* and *conclusions* of research (theories and/or studies) into the following:

✓

☐ Majority influence (conformity)	p. 166
☐ Minority influence	p. 170
☐ Obedience to authority	p. 178
☐ Resistance to obedience	pp. 180–1

Ways that...

You should be able to write about several ways that ...

✓

☐ Psychologists have dealt with participant reactivity	p. 172
☐ Psychologists have dealt with investigator effects	p. 173
☐ Psychologists have dealt with ethical issues	p. 194
☐ Psychologists have dealt with deception	p. 195
☐ Psychologists have dealt with informed consent	p. 195
☐ Psychologists have dealt with protection of participants	p. 195

Examples of...

You should be able to describe several examples of

✓

☐ Internal validity in obedience research	pp. 182–3
☐ Ecological validity in obedience research	p. 184
☐ Deception in social influence research	p. 190
☐ Informed consent in social influence research	p. 191
☐ Psychological harm in social influence research	p. 191
☐ Ethical issues in all psychological research	p. 192

Theories/explanations

You may be asked to describe or outline a theory/explanation for 6 marks. You are also likely to be asked an AO2 question about theories/explanations and to discuss their strengths and limitations. When discussing a theory, it is useful to refer to other research (theories and/or studies) as a means of evaluation.

✓

☐ Why people yield to majority influence	p. 167
☐ Why people yield to minority influence	p. 170
☐ Psychological processes in why people obey	p. 179
☐ How people might resist obedience	p. 181

Sample social influence question with students' answers and examiner's comments

1 (a) Explain what is meant by the terms 'majority influence' and 'obedience', and give **one** difference between them.

(2 + 2 + 2 marks)

Alison's answer: Majority influence is where people are in a group and most of them believe they have the correct answer and they influence the rest of the group.

Obedience is when people feel they have to obey.

One difference between them is that people don't have any choice whether they obey (because they might get punished), but they do have a choice whether they conform.

Nigel's answer: Majority influence is when a minority's (or one person's) opinions are publicly changed by a majority – this can be for normative reasons for example.

Obedience is where a person complies with a direct order from someone with more authority than them.

A person is more likely to conform because they want to be accepted by the rest of the group, but they are more likely to obey because they have been socialised to obey orders given by legitimate authority figures.

Examiner's comments: Alison's definition of majority influence is partially right, but the description of *how* 'most' of the group influence the other members is too vague and imprecise for full marks. Her definition of obedience is circular, as she has simply recycled the term in a different form. In order to understand what goes on in obedience, we would need more information. The difference between these is also partially right. It is not really true to say a person has 'no' choice whether to obey, but certainly the individual is under more pressure because of the possible threat of punishment for disobedience. This is worth **1 + 1 + 1 mark**.

Nigel has produced two clear and accurate definitions. The extra information given (e.g. 'publicly changed', 'normative reasons', 'direct order', 'authority figure') ensures maximum marks. The difference between these is also accurate and sufficiently detailed. This is worth **2 + 2 + 2 marks**.

---

1 (b) Explain **two** ways in which people might resist obedience.

(3 + 3 marks)

Alison's answer: Feeling accountable for hurting somebody in the process of a research study. Participants who may never have seen themselves as the type to physically or mentally hurt another person may not feel that they are able to go through with carrying out a procedure which affects the well-being of another person.

Another reason may be due to an educated background. For example, Gamson *et al.* found that those participants with the most education were more likely to question orders and challenge their legitimacy.

Nigel's answer: When we feel our freedom is threatened, we may try to resist. A person may try to assert their independence by creating a 'boomerang effect' to the order given and therefore purposely disobeys.

A second way to resist obedience is by the presence of others who act as models of defiance. Milgram found that participants who were in the presence of stooges who refused to carry on shocking the learner found it easier to defy the experimenter than when they were on their own.

Examiner's comment: Alison's first example is clearly better than 'muddled and flawed', but perhaps not detailed enough to be 'accurate and detailed'. There is clearly something missing that tells us how the individual converts this concern for others into clear resistance of a direct order from an authority figure. Her second example is concise yet appropriately well detailed. The use of an appropriate example (i.e. Gamson *et al.*'s findings) ensures that all 3 marks are gained. This is worth **2 + 3 marks**.

Nigel's first 'way' is accurate and concise but also sufficiently well detailed for the full 3 marks. We are not told what the 'boomerang effect' actually entails (a person will move in the opposite direction to the order given), but it is appropriate in this context. Nigel's second 'way' is also very well explained and illustrated by appropriate elaboration and research context. It is not *necessary* to place answers within a research context as here, but this is a good way of elaborating an answer in order to gain maximum marks. An alternative approach would be to use appropriate real-life examples. This is worth **3 + 3 marks**.

---

1 (c) To what extent has obedience research been shown to be valid?

(18 marks)

Alison's answer: Ecological validity is the extent to which the researcher's findings can be generalised to the findings and research of others. Experimental validity is the extent to which the experiment carried out was able to do what it set out to do.

We obey the orders given by authority figures in real life. When we accept and listen to our parents and do as we are told, we are obeying orders given by them. Hofling *et al.* carried out a valid study on how nurses (when asked in a survey) were 100% sure that they wouldn't ever obey orders given by a doctor over the phone. In reality, 21 out of the 22 nurses questioned did obey orders given over the phone by a man saying that he was a doctor (when actually he was not). This was valid because it was carried out in a hospital. Milgram also carried out an experiment to see how far participants were willing to go in electrocuting others when they were told to do so by an authority figure. Milgram found that many of the participants were willing to do what the researchers told them to do if the pressure upon the participant was high enough. He found that participants were willing to carry on because they thought that if they did not, the experiment would be ruined.

The participants were deceived as Milgram did not mention the fact that participants would be asked to electrocute others in the advert published in the newspaper. One of the participants did come to visit Milgram after the experiment saying that they were suffering from psychological harm, but were glad to have done the experiment as it made them a better person. This means that Milgram's research, although unethical, was valid because the participants had gained something from taking part.

Examiner's comments: Alison's answer is a classic example of someone who appears to be answering a completely different question. In this case she appears to have been misled by the word 'validity' and has set about justifying the methods used in the study of obedience (i.e. are they *legitimate*?) rather than discussing whether this research faces threats to its internal and external validity. She does get *some* credit for this approach, although only at a very basic level. Alison is obviously aware of the need to address issues of validity in the question (she makes reference to this from time to time), but any attempt to do so is at the descriptive level only. Alison's answer is surprisingly rather typical. Students frequently fail to think sufficiently about the *specific* requirements of a question (the lesson throughout this book), and use a particular word as a trigger for material that may (but frequently does not) have some relevance to the question set. She would pick up some marks for AO1, but nothing for AO2, as her commentary is either misplaced or simply inappropriate – **3 + 0 marks** means only **3 marks** in total.

Nigel's answer: Milgram set out to discover whether the events of the Second World War (particularly the behaviour of Nazi guards in the death camps) could be explained by the psychological processes of obedience to authority. His conclusions, based on the findings of his laboratory studies of obedience, suggest that they could be. However, his critics, most notably Orne and Holland, claim that his studies do no such thing. They base their criticisms on a number of points. They claim that Milgram's participants were not taken in by the deception. This is crucial to the argument about whether his conclusions were valid. If the participants did not actually believe that they were giving shocks, this would be a threat to the internal validity of the experiment. It is possible, claim Orne and Holland, that the participants were simply acting as they had been paid to do, and this said more about the nature of the role of a research participant than it did about behaviour in real life. Also supporting this claim is the fact that the experimenter himself appeared apparently unconcerned about the distress of the learner. This, and other cues during the experiment, may have given a hint to the participants that all was not as it seemed. Milgram claimed that this was not so, and quoted evidence from the debriefing sessions where participants claimed that they did believe they were really shocking the learner.

Orne and Holland also claim that the study lacks external validity in that the findings could not be applied beyond the laboratory setting. This can also be challenged by the findings of numerous other studies. These were carried out throughout the world in the wake of Milgram's discoveries. Each of these varied in different ways, but each found significant levels of obedience, far greater than predicted prior to Milgram's initial study. More recently, critics of Milgram, such as Mandel, have claimed that there are too many inconsistencies between what Milgram found in his studies and what happened in the death camps for these to be a useful explanation of Nazi behaviour in the death camps. For example, Mandel points out that the 'buffering' effect claimed by Milgram to be responsible for the behaviour of his participants could not explain many of the killings in the death camps where the killer was face to face with his victim.

Examiner's comments (cont'd): Nigel's answer is clearly well informed. He engages with the question in an appropriately critical way. Nigel could have gone further than simply describing claims of misplaced validity, but has offered counter-criticisms to balance the discussion. The answer begins with what might be seen as an inappropriate statement of the aims of Milgram's research, but this ties in well with Mandel's criticisms towards the end of the answer. This is a good example of an answer that is informed and thorough and where material has been used highly effectively. There is sufficient AO1 material (e.g. the nature of Orne and Holland's claims) for the full **6 marks** available, and the informed and thorough critical commentary would earn the full **12 marks** for AO2. It would be worth **18 marks** in total.

Total marks: Alison 11/30 (approximately equivalent to a Grade D) and Nigel 30/30 (a resounding Grade A).

Research methods question with students' answers and examiner's comments

A university psychologist decides to study the effects of physical appearance (the independent variable) on people's compliance with a charitable request. She recruits a male final year student who, in one condition, wears two conspicuous facial studs, one through his lower lip and the other through one eyebrow. In the other condition, he wears no such adornments. Apart from these studs, there are no other differences in clothing or behaviour between the two conditions. In each condition he carries a collecting can and wears an 'official' badge for a fictional charity.

The student goes to a busy shopping centre on a Saturday morning and asks passers-by to make a donation to the charity. For the first hour he does not wear the studs and for the second hour he does. Each passer-by is subsequently stopped and interviewed by the psychologist, who has been standing out of sight around the corner recording the interactions. She asks each person *why* they had agreed or not agreed to the student's request, thanks them for their help and refunds them their money. The findings are shown in Figure 1 on the right.

	Student's appearance	
	With studs	Without studs
Gave money	26	38
Did not give money	33	22

▲ Figure 1: Quantitative data from the study

Although there were a number of reasons given why people had or hadn't given money, the following were representative of each condition.

◀ Figure 2: Examples of qualitative data from the study

	Student's appearance	
	With studs	Without studs
Gave money	'It was a worthwhile cause and I could afford it, so I thought why not?'	'I thought if he can be bothered to give up his Saturday to collect, then I can at least help by giving.'
Did not give money	'I don't like to give money in public – after all, you can't actually be sure it's a legitimate charity, can you?'	'I just didn't have any change on me – I did feel sorry for not being able to help though.'

(a) Identify the research method used in this part of the study explain one advantage and one weakness of the research method you identified. (1 mark + 2 marks + 2 marks)

Alison's answer: This is a field experiment. One advantage is because people aren't aware they are taking part in an experiment, they are more likely to behave naturally, and less likely to display demand characteristics.

One disadvantage is because the experimenter doesn't have the same control over extraneous variables, it is harder to determine cause and effect in the study.

Nigel's answer: A natural experiment. An advantage is that there are no ethical problems. A disadvantage is that there lots more variables to control.

Examiner's comments:

Alison's answer is correct, so 1 mark. Both the advantage and the disadvantage are accurate and well detailed by Alison. Mentioning demand characteristics is a nice touch, and shows that she knows what she's talking about. There is no requirement in this part of the question to set the answer in the context of the study, so **0 + 2 + 2 marks**.

Although this takes place in a naturalistic setting, it is not a 'natural experiment'. A tricky situation, as Nigel is actually evaluating the *natural* experiment. However, the advantage is wrong (there are potential ethical problems in all methods), and the disadvantage (which is not very specific) could apply equally to both the field and natural experiment, so **0 + 0 + 1 mark**.

(b) Describe one aspect of this study that might have raised ethical concerns, and explain how this might have been overcome. (2 marks + 2 marks)

Alison's answer: By posing as a charity collector, the student was deceiving the participants. This probably could not be overcome as some degree of deception is needed to gain worthwhile findings, but its impact can be lessened by full debriefing by the psychologist.

Nigel's answer: It is wrong to invade people's privacy by asking them for money, and this is probably considered unethical behaviour by legitimate charities anyway. This could be overcome by waiting for people to give money.

Examiner's comments: Alison loses no marks for failing to come up with a way of overcoming this ethical problem, as she cleverly turns the question around in order to introduce the idea of debriefing. She is accurate in her assessment of this ethical problem and its resolution, so **2 + 2 marks**.

Nigel's description of an ethical concern in this study is accurate and well detailed. The bit about legitimate charities is not necessary, but it is a nice touch. The resolution of the problem requires elaboration, especially as this would no longer be *compliance*. This is worth **2 + 1 marks**.

(c) Explain two features of the study that might affect the validity of the data being collected. (3 marks + 3 marks)

Alison's answer: Although we are told that his behaviour is the same in each condition, it is possible that he does act slightly differently when wearing the studs, and as this is now his second hour of asking he could be getting fed up, and this might be picked up by the people he asks.

Some people might have given money just because they were with someone (to impress them).

Nigel's answer: Because this study took place in a shopping centre, it may be that the people being asked were pretty selfish anyway (only being there to spend money on themselves); therefore it wouldn't be representative of other people in other settings.

We don't know anything about the ages of the people asked, and it's possible that younger people wouldn't have been affected by his studs, but older people would have had him down as a bit of a weirdo, so would be less likely to give him money.

Examiner's comments: The first feature is well expressed by Alison, and although a little speculative, is a logical conclusion from the information given in the stimulus material. The second feature is also appropriate but requires more detail. Alison needs to add something about how the presence of a friend might affect the internal validity of the study, as the person's decision to give money may have nothing to do with either the collector's appearance *or* the charity, but some other reason. This would receive **2 + 1 marks**.

Nigel's comment about selfish shoppers may be a bit cynical, but it is still appropriate. Being in a natural setting like this doesn't guarantee that the same findings could be found in other settings, with different people. Likewise, the age problem is a good point (as would be the gender interaction), so Nigel receives the full **2 + 2 marks**.

(d) Using the data collected by the psychologist in her interviews with the passers-by, suggest one way to analyse these data in a qualitative manner. (3 marks)

Alison's answer: It is likely that the psychologist will analyse the responses by drawing out quotations that are typical of the people interviewed. This then gives the reader a good sense of what people thought without having to read all the interviews.

Nigel's answer: One way to analyse qualitative data is to look for themes that recur in different people's responses. These themes can be listed and example quotations used to give a richer sense of what people were saying.

Examiner's comments: Alison's answer is appropriate and contains sufficient detail to be clear. However, she has not fully explained how the psychologist would select quotations, so **2 marks**.

Nigel's answer provides the bit of detail that is lacking in Alison's answer. Even though he has not used the 'proper' terms (e.g. 'thematic analysis'), he has indicated how he would conduct his analysis, so **3 marks**.

(e) Describe one advantage of using qualitative analysis. *(2 marks)*

Alison's answer: Using qualitative analysis enables the researcher to understand why a person behaved the way they did, rather than just finding out how they behaved, in other words it offers much richer data.

Nigel's answer: The researcher can get a lot more out of the participants than they could with just quantitative analysis.

Examiner's comments: Alison has given an appropriate, accurate and sufficiently well-detailed advantage, so **2 marks**.

The difference between Alison's and Nigel's answer is not just the complexity of the language used, it is the amount of information that these answers convey. In Nigel's answer, we are not told exactly what is the 'more' that researchers get out of qualitative data, so it is just worth **1 mark**.

(f) Give one conclusion that might be drawn from Figure 1, and one conclusion that might be drawn from Figure 2. *(2 + 2 marks)*

Alison's answer: Figure 1 shows that people were less likely to give money when the person was wearing studs than when he wasn't, showing that physical appearance did make a difference to compliance.

When the student was wearing the studs, people who gave money appeared to explain their actions in terms of the charity ('It was a worthwhile cause'). For those who didn't give money, they seemed to associate the appearance of the collector with the legitimacy of the charity ('you can't actually be sure it's a legitimate charity').

Nigel's answer: More people gave money when he wasn't wearing studs.

One conclusion from Figure 2 is that people look for excuses not to give money to charity collectors.

Examiner's comments: Two good answers. Alison has carefully woven in the information from Figure 1 with the original aims of the study. Her explanation of a conclusion that might be drawn from the qualitative data is very full, and shows a good ability to draw inferences from the data given. This would receive **2 + 2 marks**.

Nigel's short, undeveloped answers are fairly typical of the 1 mark response to questions such as this. The Figure 1 conclusion is stated more as a finding than a conclusion. Nigel might have then gone on to think about what this finding actually *tells us* for the full 2 marks. The qualitative conclusion, although again a little cynical, is possibly true when we look at the data in Figure 2, but perhaps Nigel should have explained *how* he had come to that conclusion. This would be worth **1 + 1 mark**.

(g) The psychologist then decides to go on to carry out a questionnaire survey on people's attitudes towards body adornments (such as the facial studs used in this study). Outline the procedures for carrying out such an investigation. *(6 marks)*

Alison's answer: The psychologist could use four age groups (0–20, 21–40, 40–60 and 60+) and a suitable location for her study (such as a city centre). She could use a questionnaire that had a mixture of closed and open questions. The closed questions (e.g. 'Do you wear any of the following – nose stud yes/no, tongue stud yes/no' etc.) would help her to get data that might be useful for data analysis later on. The open questions (e.g. 'how would you feel if your mother decided to have her tongue pierced?') would give her more detailed information about underlying attitudes or prejudices. She should be careful to avoid any leading or ambiguous questions, or any that would produce a social desirability bias. She could use an opportunity sample of 100 respondents in each age group, being sure to get their informed consent and debrief them properly after their participation.

Nigel's answer: I would ask for volunteers from the students in the university to take part in a study. It is best to ask for volunteers because ethical limitations would prevent the psychologist from insisting that students take part. I would then construct a questionnaire that had questions about body adornments and their attitudes to them. This could be given to a number of students of both sexes (because there may be gender differences in attitudes to body adornments), and the data could then be analysed.

Examiner's comments: Alison has made excellent use of the time available for this answer. She could have gone into far too much detail about any one of these different aspects of the study (e.g. the nature of the questions, the sampling procedure etc.), but was restrained enough to offer *enough* information about each important procedural stage in this study. This would be worth the full **6 marks**.

There are a number of relevant procedural details given here, and Nigel has designed a study that is clearly focused on the suggested area of study. However, there is some material that doesn't really need to be here (such as the reasons why students were not conscripted into the study) and some important details that are missing (such as the nature of the questions to be used). This isn't a bad answer, but it does need developing. It would be worth **3 marks**.

Total marks: Alison 26/30 (a resounding Grade A) and Nigel 18/30 (also equivalent to a Grade A).

Social influence question to try

1 (a) Outline **one** reason why people obey, and **one** way in which people might resist obedience. *(3 + 3 marks)*

(b) Outline findings of research into conformity. *(6 marks)*

(c) Outline and evaluate ways in which psychologists deal with ethical issues in research. *(18 marks)*

Research methods are the techniques that scientists use in order to conduct systematic studies and produce facts about the world. The research methods used by psychologists have been discussed throughout this book. In this section we offer a summary of the key points and a collation of all you need to know to answer the compulsory research methods question!

Research methods

Section 1

Quantitative and qualitative research methods

Section 2

Experimental design and implementation

Section 3

Data analysis

QUANTITATIVE AND QUALITATIVE RESEARCH METHODS

Specification content	Comment

The nature and usage of the following research methods, their advantages and weaknesses, and how they relate to the scientific nature of psychology. The nature and usage of ethical guidelines in psychology.

- Experiments (including laboratory, field and natural experiments)
- Investigations using correlational analysis
- Naturalistic observations
- Questionnaires
- Interviews

You are expected to be familiar with the main **research methods** used in psychology. This includes being able to describe the essence of each method, and knowing how it differs from the other methods.

It also includes familiarity with how to **conduct studies** using each method.

Further, you should have an awareness of at least **two advantages** and **two weaknesses** of each method.

An appreciation of how research methods 'relate to the scientific nature of psychology' refers to the need for **objectivity** in research. This is what distinguishes psychological knowledge from **common sense**. You should base all knowledge on scientific research rather than common sense.

Finally, an understanding of **ethical guidelines** is relevant to each method studied.

Comment

You should use the number of marks allocated to each question to guide you in how much detail to provide and how long your answer should be. The last question is worth 6 marks and therefore requires quite a lot of detail. Think of all the different aspects of designing an investigation: selection of participants, controls that could be used, and design decisions appropriate to your new method (e.g. behaviour checklists, writing good questions, etc.).

Sample questions

To be answered with the stimulus examples below.

1 What is the research method that has been used in this study? (*1 mark*) [You could also explain the reasons for your answer.]
2 Explain **one** advantage and **one** weakness of this method in the context of this study. (*2 marks + 2 marks*)
3 Identify **one** ethical issue that might arise in this study and suggest how you would deal with it. (*1 mark + 2 marks*)
4 What are the aims of this study? (*2 marks*)
5 How else could you conduct an investigation with similar aims using a different research method? Describe the procedures of another study which has the same aims as the original study but uses a different research method. (*6 marks*).

For each of the studies below, state the research method used and explain why it is an example of that method. Then try to answer as many questions on the left as are relevant to the study.

Study A A researcher investigating eating disorders wishes to assess the success of different therapies. In a clinic that treats individuals with eating disorders there are two therapists. One is a psychodynamic therapist and the other is behavioural. The researcher is given details of the patients from each therapist and compares their weight gain after 3 months as a measure of the therapy's success.

Study B A group of psychology students wish to test some aspects of Freud's psychoanalytic theory. They decide to look at 'orality' (the extent to which a person is an oral personality) and see if this is linked to smoking. 'Orality' is measured by watching a person for 10 minutes and counting how many mouth movements occur. To assess smoking they ask each individual if they smoke, and if so how many cigarettes on average they smoke a day.

Study C The research department of a beauty product company wishes to find out which features of the female face are perceived as most appealing by other women. They compose a set of questions to find out more about what women think about female attractiveness.

Study D A study was conducted to investigate the effects of anxiety on performance. Participants were given a puzzle to complete in a set time and told that the study was investigating problem-solving behaviour. One set of the participants was mildly stressed during the task. This was achieved by arranging for the experimenter to watch their performance closely. The other set of participants was not stressed – they were watched but in a friendly manner.

Study E A psychologist interested in memory decides to conduct some research about what kinds of things people find memorable. She plans to ask people a set of predetermined questions to begin with and then decide on further questions depending on what respondents say. She will present her questions in a face-to-face setting.

Study F A group of psychology students were studying social influence. As part of their studies they decided to investigate the extent to which drivers were influenced by the clothing a person wore. Would drivers be more likely to stop if a person on a pedestrian crossing were smartly dressed rather than being scruffily dressed? To test this, they counted how many drivers stopped when a smartly dressed person approached a pedestrian crossing. The next day a scruffily dressed person was used to repeat the study.

Study G A school decides to investigate pupil behaviours at break time to see how much anti-social behaviour is going on. They ask the school psychology department to organise a study which will record student behaviours during the break time.

Revision notes: Research methods

Research method *A way of doing things in a systematic manner.*	Nature and use	Advantages and weaknesses	Ethical issues	Page
Laboratory experiment	IV manipulated to observe effect on DV, under controlled conditions.	+ Can draw causal conclusions. + Confounding variables minimised. + Can be replicated. − Artificial. − Investigator and participant effects.	Deception Informed consent Psychological harm	▶ pp. 7, 178, 197
Field experiment	Investigate causal relationships in more natural surroundings.	+ Can draw causal conclusions. + Usually higher ecological validity. + Avoids some participant effects. − Less control. − More time-consuming.	Informed consent Difficulty debriefing Privacy	▶ pp. 178, 197
Natural experiment	IV not directly manipulated, participants not randomly allocated. Quasi-experiment.	+ Allows research where IV can't be manipulated. + Enables psychologists to study 'real' problems. − Cannot demonstrate causal relationships. − Inevitably many confounding variables.	Confidentiality	▶ pp. 7, 178, 197
Investigations using correlational analysis	Co-variables examined for positive, negative or zero association.	+ Can be used when not possible to manipulate variables. + Can rule out a causal relationship. − People often misinterpret correlations. − There may be other, unknown variables.	Misunderstanding of findings	▶ pp. 72, 97, 197
Naturalistic observations	Everything left as normal, all variables free to vary.	+ Can study behaviour where can't manipulate variables. + High ecological validity. − Poor control of extraneous variables. − Observer bias, low observer reliability.	Informed consent Difficulty debriefing Privacy	▶ pp. 49, 63, 197
Questionnaires	Set of questions.	+ A lot of data can be collected. + Does not require specialist administrators. − Leading questions, social desirability bias. − Biased samples.	Confidentiality Privacy	▶ pp. 102, 197
Interviews	Questions can be predetermined, or created in response to answers.	+ Lots of 'rich' data. + Telephone interviews. − Social desirability bias, interviewer bias. − Requires skilled personnel.	Confidentiality Privacy	▶ pp. 105, 197

A very shy guy goes into a pub and sees a beautiful woman sitting at the bar. After an hour of gathering up his courage, he finally goes over to her and asks, tentatively, 'Um, would you mind if I chatted with you for a little while?'

She responds by yelling, at the top of her voice, 'NO! I won't sleep with you tonight!' Everyone in the bar is now staring at them. Naturally, the guy is hopelessly embarrassed and slinks back to his table.

After a few minutes, the woman walks over to him and apologises. She smiles and says, 'I'm sorry if I embarrassed you. You see, I'm a psychology student, and I'm studying how people respond to embarrassing situations.'

To which he responds, at the top of his voice, 'What do you mean £200?!'

Specification content	Sample questions
In the research methods part of the examination you may be expected to *define* terms, but are most likely to be required to *use* the terms.	*To be answered with the stimulus examples on the opposite page (or you could try some of the questions with the star studies throughout this book).*
Aims and hypotheses (including the generation of appropriate aims; the formulation of different types of experimental/alternative hypotheses (directional/non-directional).	**1 a** Describe the aims of this study. **b** Suggest a suitable experimental (alternative) hypothesis. **c** Identify whether your hypothesis is directional or non-directional. **d** Explain why you used a directional (or a non-directional) hypothesis. **e** Suggest a suitable non-directional hypothesis for this study. **f** Suggest a suitable directional hypothesis for this study. **g** Identify the independent variable in this study. **h** Identify the dependent variable in this study. **i** Describe how you might measure the dependent variable. **j** Identify the co-variables in this study.
Experimental designs: including independent groups, repeated measures and matched participants. The design of naturalistic observations, questionnaires and interviews.	**2 a** What kind of experimental design has been used in this study? **b** Give **one** advantage and **one** disadvantage of the experimental design in the context of this study. **c** In an observational study, how would you sample behaviour? **d** Describe **one** way you could minimise the intrusive nature of your observations. **e** Describe **two** factors in good questionnaire design. **f** Describe **one** way you could minimise the effects the interviewer's behaviour might have on an interviewee.
Factors associated with research design, including the operationalisation of the IV/DV; conducting pilot studies; control of extraneous variables; ways of assessing and improving reliability and internal and external validity. Ethical issues associated with research design.	**3 a** Identify ways that you might operationalise a named variable. **b** Suggest **two** reasons for using a pilot study in this investigation. **c** Identify **two** variables that might need to be controlled in this study. Explain how you would control these variables. **d** Identify **one** way to ensure reliability among observers, and explain how you would do this. **e** Describe **two** features of the study that might affect the validity of the data being collected. **f** Describe **two** features of the study that might affect the internal validity of the investigation. **g** Describe **two** features of the study that might affect the external (ecological) validity of the investigation. **h** Describe **two** features of the study that might affect the reliability of the data being collected. **i** Describe **one** ethical issue that might arise in this study and suggest **one** way of dealing with it.
The selection of participants including random, opportunity and volunteer sampling.	**4 a** Explain how the investigator might have selected a random/opportunity/volunteer sample of participants. **b** How would you select participants to take part in your study? **c** Give **one** advantage and **one** disadvantage of your chosen sampling technique.
The relationship between researchers and participants (including demand characteristics and investigator effects).	**5 a** Explain **one** way in which the relationship between researcher and participant (e.g. an investigator effect) might have influenced the results obtained in this study. **b** How might you overcome this problem? **c** Name **one** possible investigator effect. **d** Suggest how demand characteristics might have been a problem in this study.

For each of the studies below, state the research method used and explain why it is an example of that method. Then try to answer as many questions on the left as are relevant to the study.

Study A   A psychologist chose to investigate the kinds of tasks which created stress for teachers. He asked for teachers from several schools to volunteer to take part in the study, and selected 20 male teachers. Each volunteer was asked to perform two tasks. One task involved presenting a prepared speech to a group of 200 students. The second task involved marking a set of books that were full of mistakes. At the end of each task the experimenter recorded the participants' blood pressure.

Study B   A group of psychology students conducted a study of obedience to see how much 'authority' affected obedient behaviour. They selected a random sample of pupils from the school register and asked them to come to a certain classroom in the lunch hour. Some were assigned to a condition where they were greeted by an 'experimenter' wearing a white coat. Others were greeted by the same person, dressed in ordinary clothes. The 'experimenter' told the pupil to sit down and spend 30 minutes writing the word 'psychology' on a paper.

Study C   In order to investigate the effects of early privation on popularity at school, a team of psychologists used the records of a local children's home. They identified babies who were placed in care under the age of 3 months and who were not adopted until after their first birthday. They were then able to locate 20 children raised entirely in their natural homes. Both groups were assessed in terms of their ability to get on with peers.

Study D   A study involved the investigation of a link between age and conformity. They expected to find that conformity increased with age. They tested conformity by giving participants a set of questions to answer. Some answers were already written on the questionnaire by previous participants. Some questions were ambiguous and others were not ambiguous. Each participant was given a conformity score at the end of the test and a scattergraph drawn to show the relationship between age and conformity. The study found a positive correlation.

Study E   As part of their AS studies, a group of students conducted a project to look at the differences between children in day care and those at home. Students worked in pairs and either observed a child in day care or a child at home. They spent 1 hour observing their target child and repeated this 5 times. Before beginning the study the class decided on a set of behavioural categories.

Study F   A research project into eating problems sought to find out about adolescent and pre-adolescent dieting practices. The study involved the use of a questionnaire, including both quantitative and qualitative questions. The questinnaire was piloted with a small group of university students.

Study G   A research project on memory aimed to find out about individuals' earliest memories. In order to do this the research team conducted unstructured interviews with people aged 10 to 50 years. The interviewers started with a set of standard questions but then adapted their questions in response to the answers given by the interviewees.

Revision notes: Aims and hypotheses

	Definition	Reasons for using	
Research	The process of gaining knowledge through the examination of data derived empirically or theoretically.	To produce objective facts.	▶ p. 5
Aims	The stated intentions of a study.	To be clear about the purpose of a study.	▶ p. 21
Hypothesis (or **research hypothesis**)	A clear statement, made at the beginning of an investigation, that aims to predict or explain events.	To make sense of the findings.	▶ p. 21
Experimental (alternative) hypothesis	A statement of the relationship between the IV and DV.	An alternative to the null hypothesis.	▶ p. 21
Directional hypothesis	States which set of scores will be better/faster, positively/negatively correlated.	Previous research suggests the direction.	▶ p. 21
Non-directional hypothesis	Proposes that there will be a difference or relationship but does not state the direction.	Allows for a difference/relationship occurring in either direction, or previous research has been inconclusive.	▶ p. 21

Revision notes: Research designs

Experimental design	**Repeated measures** Same participants in each condition.	+ Good control for participant variables. + Fewer participants. – Order effect (e.g. boredom, practice). – Participants guess the purpose.	▶ p. 13
	Independent groups Two (or more) groups of participants, one for each condition.	+ Avoids order effects and participants guessing the purpose of the experiment. – Needs more participants. – Lacks control of participant variables.	▶ p. 13
	Matched participants Participants matched on key participant variables.	+ No order effects. + Participant variables partly controlled. – Matching is difficult.	▶ p. 13
Design of naturalistic observations	**Behavioural categories** (checklists). **Sampling techniques** (time and event sampling). *Avoid* observer bias, *ensure* inter-observer reliability.		▶ pp. 49, 185
Design of questionnaires	Writing good questions (issues include: clarity, bias, analysis). Kinds of questions (open/closed, fixed-choice, Likert scale, semantic differential). Writing good questionnaires (sampling, order of questions, use of filler questions, pilot study).		▶ pp. 99, 183
Design of interviews	Structured, semi-structured (**clinical method**) and unstructured.		▶ p. 105

Revision notes: Factors associated with research designs

Variables	**Operationalisation**	Variables in a form that can be tested (operations).	▶ p. 76
	Independent variable	Manipulated by the experimenter.	▶ pp. 7, 18
	Dependent variable	The DV *depends* in some way on the IV.	▶ pp. 7, 18
	Extraneous variable	Variable that might affect the DV.	▶ pp. 7, 18
	Confounding variable	Variable, apart from the IV, that does affect the DV.	▶ p. 18
Pilot study	A small-scale trial run of a study to test the design, with a view to making improvements.		▶ p. 98
Control of investigator effects *Anything the investigator does which has an effect on a participant's performance other than what was intended.*	**Single blind**	Deception to prevent the participant knowing the experimental aim.	▶ p. 173
	Double blind	The investigator does not know the purpose of the experiment, to prevent expectations influencing the participant's behaviour.	▶ p. 173
	Placebo conditions	Control group thinks it is receiving the experimental treatment.	▶ p. 173
	Standardised instructions	A set of instructions that are the same for all participants. To avoid investigator effects.	▶ p. 5
Experimental control *Using techniques to ensure that confounding variables are eliminated.*	**Extraneous variables**	Hold constant or eliminate.	▶ p. 17, 18
	Random allocation	Participants to experimental groups; allocate items on a test.	▶ p. 173
	Counterbalancing	Order effects balanced to make sure each condition comes first or second in equal amounts.	▶ p. 173
	Standardised procedures	A set of procedures that are the same for all participants. To enable replication.	▶ p. 173
Reliability *Consistency.*	**Internal reliability**	Split-half method.	▶ p. 185
	External reliability	Inter-observer reliability (use training, pilot study, behavioural checklists).	▶ p. 185
Validity *The legitimacy of a study.*	**Experimental validity**	Internal and external validity of an experiment. The way an experiment is carried out and the implications for real life.	▶ pp. 182–5
	Internal validity *Observed effect due to IV rather than some other factor.*	**Demand characteristics**: Features of an experiment that elicit a particular response from participants.	▶ pp. 182–5
		Confounding variable affects the outcome of an investigation because it acts as an additional IV.	▶ pp. 182–5
	External validity *Ability to generalise to the real world.*	**Ecological validity** (generalise from one setting to another).	▶ pp. 182–5
		Population validity (generalise from one group of people to everyone).	▶ pp. 182–5

Revision notes: The selection of participants

Sample	Selected to be representative of the population.	May be biased, therefore can't generalise.	▸ p. 108
Population	The group of people from whom the sample is drawn.	May be biased.	▸ p. 108
Random sampling	Every member of the population has an equal chance of being selected.	+ Potentially unbiased. – Needs to be drawn from a large population to be unbiased.	▸ p. 108
Opportunity sampling	Selecting people who are most easily available.	+ Easy. – Very biased.	▸ p. 108
Volunteer sampling	Participants become part of a study by volunteering.	+ Access to a variety of participants. – Volunteer bias.	▸ p. 108
Generalisability	The findings of any particular study should apply to the whole population.		▸ p. 63

Revision notes: The relationship between researchers and participants

Participant reactivity *The fact that participants react to cues in an experimental situation.*	**Hawthorne effect**	Increased attention becomes a confounding variable.	▸ p. 172
	Demand characteristic	Features of an experiment that a participant, unconsciously, responds to when searching for clues about how to behave. A confounding variable.	▸ p. 172
	Social desirability bias	The desire to appear favourably.	▸ p. 99
Investigator effect *Anything the investigator does which has an effect on a participant's performance in a study other than what was intended.*	**Experimenter bias**	The effect of an experimenter's expectations, communicated unconsciously, on a participant's behaviour.	▸ p. 173
	Interviewer bias	The same in an interview situation through, for example, leading questions and the Greenspoon effect.	▸ p. 173

Revision notes: Terms to remember

Case study	Provides rich record of human experience, but it is hard to generalise from.	▸ p. 66
Confederate	An ally of the experimenter. Often acts as an IV and therefore an important part of the design.	▸ p. 22
Control condition	In repeated measures design, the condition that provides a baseline measure of behaviour before the experimental treatment.	▸ p. 31
Control group	In independent groups design, a group of participants who receive no treatment. Their behaviour acts as a baseline.	▸ pp. 19, 31
Cross-cultural research	A kind of natural experiment. Limitations include use of tests or procedures that were developed in one culture (**imposed etic**) and are not valid in another culture; may make generalisations on basis of a possibly biased sample. Strengths: insights into behaviour derived from making comparisons.	▸ p. 52
Cross-sectional design	An alternative to longitudinal design, individuals of different ages compared at same point in time (IV = age).	▸ p. 65
Debriefing	Post-experimental interview to compensate for any deception, check whether participants did believe in the set-up, and to elicit feedback from participant about aspects of the study.	▸ p. 165
Experimental condition	In repeated measures design, the condition containing the IV.	▸ p. 31
Experimental group	In independent groups design, a group of participants who receive the experimental treatment (the IV). An experiment may have more than one experimental group/condition.	▸ p. 31
Longitudinal design	A study conducted over a long period of time, to compare the same individual at different points in time (IV = age). Contrast with cross-sectional design.	▸ p. 65
Order effect	In a repeated measures design, a confounding variable arising from the order in which conditions are presented, e.g. a practice or boredom effect.	▸ p. 173
Significance	A 'significant result' is one where we can accept the research hypothesis.	▸ p. 97

DATA ANALYSIS

Specification content	Sample questions
	Refer to the data and illustrations below.
The nature of qualitative data including strengths and weaknesses.	**1 a** Give **one** advantage and **one** disadvantage using qualitative/quantative data. **b** Write **one** qualitative question. **c** Write **one** quantitative question.
Measures of central tendency and dispersion (including the appropriate use and interpretation of medians, means, modes; range and standard deviations).	**2 a** What method would be most suitable to use as a measure of central tendency with the values below? Explain your answer.

Set 1	2	4	5	7	9	9	10	11	11	11	14	18

Set 2	2	5	5	7	7	9	9	11	12	14	22	

Set 3	3	5	6	7	9	10	12	14	15	17	20	21

	b What method would be most suitable to use as a measure of dispersion? Explain your answer. **c** State the mode, median and mean for the data shown above. **d** State the range for the data shown above.
The nature of positive and negative correlations and the interpretation of correlation coefficients.	**3 a** A correlation coefficient of +0.63 was calculated in a study (N=20). What does this tell you about the data? **b** A correlation coefficient of −0.63 was calculated in a study (N=20). What does this tell you about the data? **c** A correlation coefficient of +0.43 was calculated in a study (N=20). What does this tell you about the data?
Graphs and charts (including the appropriate use and interpretation of histograms, bar charts and scattergraphs).	**4 a** Using the data in the table on the right, outline one finding and one conclusion that could be drawn from this investigation.

Stress score after speaking to class	No. of Males	No. of Females
0–9	2	5
10–19	6	11
20–29	14	9
30–39	11	4
40–49	4	0
Total	37	29

c Suggest a suitable method of representing these data graphically. Explain your choice.

d Using the information from the bar chart below, outline two findings from this study.

e Using the information from the scattergraph below, describe the relationship between the two co-variables.

f What conclusions can you draw from each graph?

Graphs showing findings of a study investigating conformity and age
Bar chart   *Scattergraph*

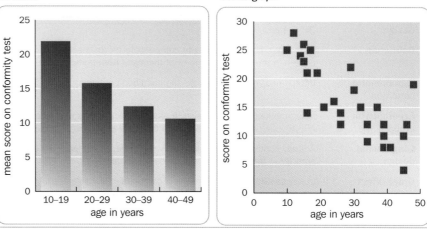

Revision notes: Analysis of qualitative data

Quantitative data	+ Easy to analyse. + Produces neat conclusions. – Oversimplifies reality.	▸ p. 99
Qualitative data	+ Represents the complexity of human behaviour. + Provides rich detail. – More difficult to detect patterns and reach conclusions. – Subjective, affected by personal expectations and beliefs.	▸ p. 99

Revision notes: Measures of central tendency and dispersion

Measures of central tendency	Mean	Add values, divide by number of values.	+ Makes use of all the data. – Can be misrepresentative if there are extreme values.	▸ p. 31
	Median	Middle value in an ordered list.	+ Not affected by extreme scores. – Not as 'sensitive' as the mean.	▸ p. 31
	Mode	The most common value(s)	+ Useful when data in categories. – Not useful when there are several modes.	▸ p. 31
Measures of dispersion	Range	Highest to lowest.	+ Easy to calculate. – Affected by extreme values.	▸ p. 129
	Standard deviation	Mathematical calculation.	+ Precise, all values taken into account. – Harder to calculate.	▸ p. 129

Revision notes: The nature of correlations

The nature of correlations	Positive	Co-variables increase together.	▸ pp. 73, 97
	Negative	One increases while other decreases.	▸ pp. 73, 97
	Zero	No relationship.	▸ pp. 73, 97
	Correlation coefficient	A number that tells us how closely the co-variables in a correlational analysis are related.	▸ p. 97

Revision notes: Graphs and charts

Graphs and charts	Histogram	Graph showing continuous frequency data with a true zero.	▸ p. 177
	Bar charts	Graph showing frequency data; data need not be continuous.	▸ p. 177
	Scattergraph	For correlations. Scatter of dots; each dot represents one case.	▸ p. 73

Appendix: How your answers are marked

There are three assessment objectives in the AQA specification A, AS examination. Assessment objective 1 (**AO1**) is concerned with *description* – assessing your *knowledge and understanding* of psychological theories, concepts, studies and methods. Assessment objective 2 (**AO2**) is concerned with *evaluation* of psychological theories, terminology, concepts, studies and methods. Assessment object 3 (**AO3**) is used only when assessing research methods questions. It is concerned with assessing your ability to *design, conduct and report* psychological investigation(s) choosing from a range of methods, and taking into account the issues of reliability, validity and ethics, and collect and draw conclusions from the data.

AO1 (assessment objective 1)

AO1 questions are worth 2, 3 or 6 marks. When examiners assess this assessment objective they use one of the mark schemes shown below. The 'partial performance' criterion is applied when you are asked to provide more than one of something (such as aims and conclusions of a study), but you only cover one. This is called 'partial performance'.

Examiners use grids like the ones shown below.

2 marks	Both **accurate** and **detailed**.
1 marks	**Basic, lacking detail, muddled** and/or **flawed**.
0 marks	**Inappropriate** or **incorrect**.

6–5 marks	3 marks	Both **accurate** and **detailed**.
4–3 marks	2 marks	**Limited**. It is **generally accurate** but **less detailed**. (Partial performance is **accurate** and **detailed**).
2–1 marks	1 marks	**Basic, lacking detail, muddled** and/or **flawed**. (Partial performance is **limited, generally accurate** but **less detailed**).
0 marks	0 marks	**Inappropriate** or **incorrect**.

AO2 (assessment objective 2)

This assessment objective is only applied in the part (c) questions, the ones that we have discussed throughout this book in the Commentary Corners. There are a few AO2 marks in the research methods question. There are three things the examiner looks for when deciding what mark to award: commentary, analysis and effective use of material, as shown in the table.

> **Analysis.** This means breaking your answer down into its constituent parts. Once you have read the question you need to analyse what you should put in your response. You might identify certain key arguments, studies, examples and so on.

> **Commentary.** You are 'invited' to make comments on any material you have described (AO1). Such comments might refer to the value of a study, the extent to which a particular theory is supported by research studies, the methodological flaws of a study, the limitations of a theory, possible applications and so on.

> **Effective use of material.** There is a crucial difference between describing theories, studies and so on and using these to make a point. The descriptive material must be used effectively – you must say what the study contributes to the topic being discussed or what a theory implies. These links are very important for gaining AO2 marks.

*The examiner is looking for your **opinion** but also looking to award marks to the extent to which you can demonstrate being 'psychologically informed'.*

	Commentary	Analysis	Effective use of material
12–11 marks	There is an **informed** commentary.	**Reasonably thorough analysis** of the relevant psychological studies/methods.	Material has been used in an **effective** manner.
10–9 marks	Reasonable	Slightly limited	Effective
8–7 marks	Reasonable	Limited	Reasonably effective
6–5 marks	Basic	Limited	Reasonably effective
4–3 marks	Superficial	Rudimentary	Minimal interpretation
2–1 marks	Just discernible	Weak and muddled	Mainly irrelevant
0 marks	Absent	Wholly irrelevant	

Glossary

acoustic coding involves coding information in terms of the way it sounds.

adaptive behaviours that are valuable in helping us adjust to the environment in which we live.

adrenaline *see* **epinephrine**

adrenocorticotropic hormone (ACTH) a hormone that is released by the pituitary gland and that stimulates the adrenal glands.

affectionless psychopaths individuals who experience little guilt or emotion, lack normal affection and are unable to form lasting relationships with others.

aims a statement of what the researcher(s) intend to find out.

alternative hypothesis a prediction about what is expected to happen with the samples being studied.

amok a mental disorder found in Southeast Asia where the individual behaves in a wild and aggressive manner for a limited period of time.

anaclitic depression a form of depression caused by separation from a caregiver.

analysis of dreams a psychoanalytic technique where the content of dreams is examined to detect any underlying motivation or disguised meanings.

androcentric bias a tendency within many explanations of human behaviour to see male behaviour as 'normal' and female behaviour as 'deviant'.

anorexia nervosa a type of eating disorder in which the person, despite being seriously underweight, fears that she or he might become obese and therefore engages in self-starvation to prevent this happening.

antigens substances (such as foreign bodies or viral toxins) that induce the formation of antibodies because they are recognised by the immune system as a threat.

arousal a state of readiness in which an organism is ready for 'fight or flight'.

atherosclerosis the narrowing of the coronary arteries owing to an accumulation of fatty substances.

attrition the loss of participants from a study over time.

autonomic nervous system (ANS) a division of the nervous system that controls the body's involuntary activities, such as breathing and digestion.

bar chart a graph used to represent the frequency of data; the categories on the x axis have no fixed order and there is no true zero.

behaviour checklist a list of the behaviours to be recorded during an observational study.

behavioural model a model that explains abnormality in terms of the development of behaviour patterns – established through classical and operant conditioning – that are considered maladaptive for the individual.

benzodiazepines (BZs) a class of drug used to treat anxiety. BZs act as an inhibitory transmitter to slow down the activity of the central nervous system.

biochemical an process in the body that is chemical in nature.

biofeedback a stress management technique that involves the individual's learning to control aspects of autonomic functioning possibly through operant conditioning.

biological model a model of abnormality that stresses the importance of organic processes in behaviour, and therefore sees abnormal behaviour as being caused by either anatomical or biochemical problems in the brain.

bond disruption the loss of emotional care that may accompany separation and lead to deprivation.

bulimia nervosa a type of eating disorder in which a person habitually engages in episodes of uncontrollable eating followed by self-induced vomiting or other compensatory behaviours.

capacity a measure of the amount that can be held in memory; measured in terms of bits of information such as number of digits.

cardiovascular disorder any disorder of the heart (e.g. coronary heart disease) and circulatory system (e.g. hypertension).

caregiver sensitivity hypothesis the belief that sensitive caregiving is more crucial than the amount of time a person spends with a child.

case study a research investigation that involves a detailed study of a single individual, institution or event. Case studies provide a rich record of human experience but are hard to generalise from.

central executive the part of working memory that directs our attentional resources.

challenge an aspect of the hardy personality in which life events are seen as opportunities for development rather than threats or stressors.

chunking short-term memory is thought to have a capacity of approximately seven items, although this can be increased by grouping items into 'chunks' of two or more items.

classical conditioning learning occurs through association; a neutral stimulus is paired with an unconditioned stimulus, resulting in a new stimulus-response (S-R) link.

clinical characteristics aspects of experience or functioning that are symptomatic of a physical or psychological disorder.

clinical method a semi-structured interview approach used by doctors and clinicians when interviewing patients.

clinical psychologist a person who is trained to diagnose and treat mental disorders.

clinician *see* **clinical psychologist**

closed questions in a questionnaire, questions that have a range of answers from which respondents select one.

cognitive any mental 'behaviour' connected with thinking, reasoning, etc.

cognitive development this refers to the changes in a person's mental structures, abilities and processes that occur over their lifespan.

cognitive model a model of abnormality that emphasises that cognitive distortions in thinking may be at the root of many psychological disorders.

cognitive therapy an attempt, through therapeutic intervention, to change a person's irrational thoughts and beliefs and so make them better able to cope with the world around them.

collectivist any culture that places more value on interdependence than on independence (see also **individualist**).

commitment an aspect of the hardy personality; hardy people are involved with the world around them and have a strong sense of purpose.

compliance publicly acting in accordance with the wishes or actions of others.

concordance rate a measure of similarity (usually expressed as a percentage) between two individuals or sets of individuals on a given trait.

confederates individuals in an experiment who are not real participants and are instructed how to behave by the experimenter.

confirmatory bias a form of selective memory that facilitates recall of material that supports a particular stereotype.

conformity *see* **majority influence**

confounding variable a variable that is not the independent variable under study but may nevertheless be found to have an effect on the dependent variable, thus confounding the findings of the study.

continuity hypothesis the idea that emotionally secure infants go on to be emotionally secure, trusting and socially confident adults.

control the extent to which an individual feels able to direct or regulate his or her behaviour.

control condition in an experiment, the condition that provides a baseline measure of behaviour without the experimental treatment, so that the effect of the experimental treatment may be assessed.

control group in an experiment, a group of participants who receive no treatment. Their behaviour acts as a baseline against which the effect of the independent variable may be measured.

controlled observation a form of investigation where behaviour is observed but under controlled conditions.

conversion a shift from one set of beliefs to another.

correlation in a study of the relationship between two variables, co variables may not be linked at all (zero correlation), they may both increase together, (positive correlation), or as one co-variable increases, the other decreases (negative correlation).

correlation coefficient a number between −1 and +1 that tells us how closely the co-variables in a correlational analysis are related.

cortisol a hormone, produced by the adrenal glands, whose function is to maintain a steady supply of blood sugar for continued energy in response to stress.

counterbalancing an experimental technique designed to overcome order and practice effects; ensures that each condition is tested first or second in equal amounts.

co-variables when one conducts a correlational analysis there is no IV or DV – the variables are called co-variables.

critical period hypothesis the belief that, for some behaviours, there is likely to be a limited window of development. Bowlby claimed that the years up until about 2½ were critical in the child's development.

cross-cultural research research that compares specific cultures in terms of a particular practice or behaviour. A form of natural experiment.

cross-sectional study any investigation that compares individuals of different ages at the same point in time, with a view to find out the influence of age on the behaviour in question.

cue-dependent forgetting occurs when information may be stored in memory but is inaccessible unless there is a specific cue to help retrieve it.

cultural some aspect of behaviour or way of thinking that we associate with a particular culture.

cultural relativism the view that behaviour cannot be judged properly unless it is viewed in the context of the culture in which it originates.

culture refers to all the rules, customs, morals and ways of interacting that bind together members of a society or some other collection of people.

culture-bound syndromes abnormal conditions that appear only in certain cultures, and are meaningful only within those cultures.

day care a form of temporary care (i.e. not all day and all night long), not given by family members or someone well known to the child, and usually outside the home.

debriefing a post-research interview designed to inform the participant of the true nature of the study, and to restore them to the same state they were in at the start of the experiment.

decay a gradual deterioration or fading away. There is an assumption that a memory trace in our brain disintegrates over time and so is lost.

deindividuation the loss of personal identity that may occur when a person is part of a large crowd or similar situation.

demand characteristics features of an experiment that a participant unconsciously responds to when searching for clues about how to behave. These may act as a confounding variable.

dependent variable (DV) a measurable outcome of the action of the independent variable in an experiment.

deprivation to be deprived is to lose something. In the context of child development, deprivation refers to the loss of emotional care.

despair a stage of separation anxiety characterised by signs of increasing hopelessness and decreased activity.

detachment a stage of separation anxiety characterised by an apparent state of well-being upon being re-united with the caregiver. However the child remains remote and apathetic and has become emotionally detached.

dhat a culture-bound syndrome, found in some Indian males, characterised by physical and mental exhaustion that is blamed on the presence of semen in the urine.

diathesis-stress model a belief that, in the case of certain disorders, individuals inherit a susceptibility for the disorder (diathesis), which develops only if the individual is exposed to intolerable stress conditions (stress).

directional hypothesis predicts the kind of difference (e.g. more or less) or relationship (positive or negative) between two groups of participants or between different conditions.

discrimination (in reference to conditioning theory) an animal's learned ability to distinguish between two stimuli and their consequences.

displacement refers to existing information being displaced out of memory by new information.

dispositional explanation see **dispositional factor**

dispositional factor some enduring underlying characteristic of a person (e.g. their personality) that is thought to cause them to behave in a certain way.

double blind a research design where neither the participant nor the experimenter is aware of the condition that an individual participant is receiving.

DSM (Diagnostic and Statistical Manual) a system for classification of psychological and psychiatric disorders published by the American Psychiatric Association. This changes regularly to reflect changes in the nature and understanding of these disorders. The present system (at the time of writing) is known as DSM-IVR.

dual-process model a belief that majority influence and minority influence operate in different ways, with the former representing the need for social approval and the latter the need for information about reality.

duration a measure of how long a memory lasts before it is no longer available.

ecological validity refers to the ability to generalise a research effect beyond the particular setting in which it is demonstrated.

ECT (electro-convulsive therapy) used as a treatment for depression, ECT involves the administration of an electric shock to the non-dominant hemisphere of a patient's brain, causing a seizure.

EEA (environment of evolutionary adaptiveness) a period in our ancestral past when many of the adaptive changes associated with the evolution of human behaviour took place, about 35,000 to 3 million years ago.

ego part of Freud's conception of the structure of the personality, the ego is driven by the reality principle, which makes the child accommodate to the demands of the environment.

encoding the way information is changed so it can be stored in memory.

environment of evolutionary adaptiveness (EEA) see **EEA**

epinephrine a hormone secreted by the adrenal medulla whose effects are similar to those of sympathetic arousal.

episodic memory that part of our long-term memory that deals with the memory of events in our past.

ethical committee a group of people within a research institution that must approve a study before it begins.

ethical guidelines concrete, quasi-legal documents that help to guide conduct within psychology by establishing principles for standard practice and competence.

ethical issues an ethical issue arises in research where there are conflicting sets of values concerning the goals, procedures or outcomes of a research study.

event sampling where a list of behaviours is drawn up prior to an observational period; a count is kept of every time each behaviour occurs.

evolution Darwin's theory of evolution claimed that some behaviours are naturally selected; any behaviour that promotes successful reproduction (including survival) is likely to be passed on to the next generation.

experiment a broad term that usually involves the direct manipulation of an independent variable (IV) in order to test its possible causal relationship with a dependent variable (DV).

experimental (alternative) hypothesis see **hypothesis**

experimental condition in a repeated measures design, the condition containing the independent variable.

experimental control the use of techniques designed to eliminate the effects of extraneous variables in an experiment.

experimental design a procedure used to control the influence of participant variables in an experiment (repeated measure, independent groups or matched participants).

experimental group in an independent groups design, a group of participants who receive the experimental treatment (the IV).

experimental validity concerns the legitimacy of an experiment – the way it is carried out, the conclusion drawn and its implications for understanding related aspects of real life.

experimenter bias see **investigator bias**

external reliability a calculation of the extent to which a measure varies from another measure of the same thing.

external validity the degree to which an experimental effect can be generalised to other settings (ecological validity), other people (population validity) and over time.

extinction in conditioning, the loss of a learned behaviour when the stimulus that maintained that behaviour is no longer present.

extraneous variable in an experiment, any variable other than the independent variable that might potentially affect the dependent variable and thereby confound the results. If this happens then it is called a confounding variable.

eyewitness testimony the evidence provided in court by a person who witnessed a crime, with a view to identifying the perpetrator.

field experiment the investigator studies the relationship between an independent and dependent variable within the context in which the behaviour normally occurs without (usually) the participant knowing they are part of a study.

field study any study that takes place away from the laboratory and within the context in which the behaviour normally occurs.

flashbulb memory a memory where an individual has a detailed and enduring recollection of the context in which they first heard about a personally important event.

'foot-in-the-door' a technique used in persuasion where a person's compliance with a small request is followed by larger and larger requests.

forced choice the participant must choose one item or alternative from (usually) the two offered.

forgetting the inability to recall or recognise something that has previously been learned. This may be due to a lack of availability (as in the case of decay when the information has disappeared), or may be due to a lack of accessibility (as in the case of cue-dependent forgetting when the memory is stored somewhere but can't be found at that time).

free association a technique used in psychoanalysis whereby the therapist introduces a topic and the patient talks freely about anything that comes into his or her mind.

frequency polygon the graph produced when a dot is placed in the centre of the top of each column in a histogram and the dots are joined.

galvanic skin response (GSR) when the ANS is active one of the effects is increased sweating. This can be detected if electrodes are placed on the skin because water conducts electricity and the electrodes detect greater electrical conductivity in the skin.

General Adaptation Syndrome (GAS) Seyle's GAS model describes how, through physiological changes in the body, an organism copes with stress in an adaptive way. The model is characterised by three progressive stages that are part of this adaptive process: alarm, resistance and exhaustion.

generalisability the degree to which the findings of a particular study can be applied to the whole population.

generalisation following learning of a conditioned association, the tendency for an animal to respond in the same way to similar stimuli.

graph a pictorial representation of the relationship between variables.

Greenspoon effect the tendency for an interviewee's responses to be affected by the reaction (e.g. saying 'mm-hmm' or 'uh-huh') of the interviewer (an example of operant conditioning).

grounded theory an emergent research process, where theoretical explanations 'emerge' during the course of the investigation.

Hawthorne effect the tendency for participants to alter their behaviour merely as a result of knowing that they are being studied.

histogram a type of frequency distribution where the number of scores in each category of continuous data is represented by vertical columns. In contrast to a bar chart, the data in a histogram have a true zero and a logical sequence.

hormone a general term for any substance produced in a gland or organ of the body which in turn has an effect on specific target cells in the body.

hypothalamic-pituitary-adrenal axis if stress becomes chronic, the hypothalamus stimulates the pituitary gland to secrete ACTH (adrenocorticotropic hormone). This stimulates the adrenal glands to produce cortisol.

hypothalamus an area within the brain that functions as a master control system for all autonomic and endocrine systems within the body.

hypothesis a form of predictive statement that can be tested against reality such that it can be supported or rejected.

id part of Freud's tripartite conception of the personality, the id is driven by the pleasure principle, an innate drive to seek immediate satisfaction.

immune system a system of cells within the body that is concerned with fighting intruders such as viruses and bacteria. White blood cells identify and kill foreign bodies (antigens).

imposed etic an attempt to explain behaviour in one culture using theories or other measures of behaviour developed within a completely different culture.

imprinting an innate readiness to develop a strong bond with the mother, and which takes place during a critical or sensitive period.

independent groups an experimental design where participants are randomly allocated to two (or more) groups representing different conditions.

independent variable (IV) some event that is directly manipulated by an experimenter in order to test its effect on another variable (the dependent variable).

individual differences important differences between people that may modify the effect of particular events. For example, there are many ways that differences between individuals might moderate the effects of stress, including gender, cultural background and personality.

individualist any culture that places more value on independence than on interdependence (see also collectivist).

informational influence a form of social influence whereby we look to others for the right answer or for appropriate behaviour.

informed consent an ethical requirement in psychological research whereby participants must be fully informed about their role in the study before giving their consent to take part.

ingroup members of a social group with whom we identify ourselves.

innate that which is inborn, as distinct from that which is acquired.

insecure attachment a form of attachment between infant and caregiver that develops as a result of the caregiver's lack of sensitive responding to the infant's needs.

insecure/ambivalent see insecure/resistant

insecure/avoidant an insecure style of attachment characterised by children who tend to avoid social interaction and intimacy with others.

insecure/resistant an insecure style of attachment characterised by those who both seek and reject intimacy and social interaction.

institutional care an 'institution' is a place dedicated to a particular task, such as looking after children awaiting adoption, or caring for the mentally ill. The term 'institutional care' therefore implies some form of regimentation and lack of individual care.

interference (in the study of forgetting) refers to the tendency for one memory to 'interfere with' the accurate retrieval of another (similar) memory.

internal reliability a measure of the extent to which something is consistent within itself. For a psychological test to have high internal reliability, all test items should be measuring the same thing.

internal validity an experiment is internally valid if the observed effect can be attributed to the experimental manipulation rather than to some other factor.

internal working model a schema that represents some aspect of the world, such as expectations about interpersonal relationships, that enables the individual to predict and control their environment.

inter-observer reliability: the extent to which there is agreement between two or more observers involved in observations of a behaviour.

interview an investigative method that involves a face-to-face interaction with another individual and results in the collection of data.

interviewer bias the effect of an interviewer's expectations, communicated unconsciously, on a respondent's behaviour.

investigator effect anything that the investigator does that has an effect on a participant's performance in a study other than what was intended.

koro a form of culture-bound syndrome, confined almost entirely to Asia, where a man believes that his penis or nipples will retract into his abdomen, resulting in death.

laboratory a very general term indicating a controlled environment where the experimenter can exercise considerable control over the variables under study.

laboratory experiment an experiment carried out in the controlled setting of a laboratory, and which enables the experimenter to draw conclusions about the causal relationship between the IV and DV.

leading questions questions that are phrased in such a way that it makes one response more likely than another (e.g. 'Don't you agree that…').

learned helplessness learned helplessness occurs as a consequence of lack of perceived control in situations of extreme frustration. Individuals may simply cease trying to deal with a situation and accept the suffering it entails.

leucocytes white blood cells; part of the body's immune system.

levels of processing theory this theory emphasises the importance of depth of initial processing (e.g. through meaning, organisation, distinctiveness, elaboration and effort) for the memorability of information.

life changes events in a person's life that necessitate a significant adjustment in various aspects of a person's life. As such, they can be seen as significant sources of stress.

Likert scale on a questionnaire, respondents can indicate the extent to which they agree or disagree with a statement.

longitudinal design *see* **longitudinal study**

longitudinal study a study conducted over a long period of time, to compare the same individual(s) at different ages.

long-term memory memory for events that have happened in the past. This lasts anywhere from 2 minutes to 100 years. The long-term memory store has potentially unlimited duration and capacity.

lymphocyte a type of white blood cell (leucocyte) that has an important role in the body's immune system.

majority influence a form of social influence that results from exposure to the majority position. It is the tendency for people to adopt the behaviour, attitudes and values of the majority members of a reference group.

matched participants design an experimental design where pairs of participants are matched in terms of key variables, such as age and IQ. One member of each pair is placed in the experimental group and the other member placed in the control group, so that participant variables are better controlled than is usually the case in an independent design experiment.

maternal deprivation hypothesis this stated that a break in the mother–child relationship before the age of 2½ will lead to more or less permanent impairment of the ability to make relationships later in life.

mean the arithmetic average of a group of scores, calculated by dividing the sum of the scores by the number of scores.

measures of central tendency a descriptive statistic that provides information about a 'typical' response for a set of scores (see also mean, median, mode).

measures of dispersion a descriptive statistic that provides information about how spread out a set of scores are (see also range, standard deviation).

median the middle value in a set of scores when they are placed in rank order.

memory the process by which we retain information about events that have happened in the past. This includes fleeting memories as well as memories that last for a few hours or days, and those memories that last a lifetime.

memory for faces refers to the processes involved in the recall or recognition of facial stimuli. This includes the recall and recognition of familiar and unfamiliar faces. It may involve identifying individual features or may involve a match with a more global configuration.

meta-analysis the researcher looks at the findings from a number of different studies in order to reach a general conclusion.

minority influence a form of social influence where people reject the established norm of the majority of group members and move to the position of the minority.

mode the most frequently occurring score in a set of data.

monotropy the idea that the one relationship that the infant has with his or her primary caregiver is of special significance in emotional development.

multi-store model explains memory in terms of three stores (sensory, short-term and long-term). The transfer of data can be explained in terms of attention (SM to STM) and rehearsal (STM to LTM).

natural experiment a type of investigation where the experimenter cannot manipulate the independent variable directly, but where it varies naturally.

naturalistic observation a type of investigation carried out in a naturalistic setting, where the investigator does not interfere in any way but merely observes the behaviour in question.

naturally selected the major process that explains evolution whereby inherited traits that enhance an animal's reproductive success are passed on to the next generation and thus 'selected', whereas animals without such traits are less successful at reproduction and their traits are not selected.

negative correlation a relationship between two variables such that, as the value of one co-variable increases, the value of the other decreases.

negative reinforcement if a behaviour results in an individual's escape from an unpleasant situation, that behaviour is more likely to reoccur in similar situations in the future.

nervous system that system in the body responsible for transmitting nerve impulses.

neuroendocrine the term that describes the controlling action of parts of the brain, especially the hypothalamus on the release of hormones.

neuron a specialised cell in the nervous system for transmission of information.

neurotransmitter a substance released from the axon terminal into the synapse. Neurotransmitters cause excitation or inhibition of the adjacent neuron.

non-directional hypothesis a form of hypothesis which proposes a difference, correlation or association between two variables, but does not specify the direction (e.g. more or less, positive or negative) of such a relationship.

normal distribution a symmetrical, bell-shaped curve that might be produced when a set of scores is represented on a frequency distribution.

normative influence a form of social influence resulting from an individual wanting to 'fit in' with the majority members of a group.

null hypothesis an assumption that there is no relationship (difference, association, etc.) in the population from which a sample is taken with respect to the variables being studied.

obedience to authority a type of social influence whereby someone acts in response to a direct order from a figure with perceived authority.

observer bias in observational studies, there is the danger that an observer might 'see' what they expect to see.

oestrogen a generic name for a range of hormones produced chiefly by the ovaries. Oestrogen is responsible for the development of female secondary sexual characteristics, and is thought to influence some aspects of stress-related behaviour.

open questions in an interview or questionnaire, questions that invite the respondent to provide their own answer rather than select one of those provided.

operant conditioning learning occurs when we are reinforced for doing something. It then becomes more probable that the behaviour in question will be repeated in the future. Conversely, if we are punished for behaving in a certain way, the probability of that behaviour reoccurring decreases.

operationalisation ensuring that variables are in a form that can be easily tested.

opportunity sampling selecting people who are most easily available at the time of the study.

order effect in a repeated measures design, a confounding variable arising from the order in which conditions are presented, e.g. a practice or boredom effect.

outgroup a group of people comprised of those who are not members of our ingroup.

oxytocin one of two hormones secreted from the posterior pituitary and thought to play an important role in stress-related behaviour.

paired-associate technique a way of testing the influence of interference on forgetting. Participants are shown a list of word pairs and are subsequently given the first word and asked to recall its partner.

parasympathetic nervous system part of the autonomic nervous system involved in the restoration of the body's relaxed state following sympathetic nervous system excitation.

participant effects a general term used to acknowledge the fact that participants react to cues in an experimental situation and that this may affect the validity of any conclusions drawn from the investigation.

participant reactivity *see* **participant effects**

participant variables characteristics of individual participants (such as age, intelligence, etc.) that might influence the outcome of a study.

peer relationships relationships with children of the same age.

phonological loop deals with auditory information and preserves the order of information. It is called a loop because information goes round and round in a loop.

physiological an explanation, process, etc., based on the biological or neurological functioning of the body.

pilot study a small-scale trial run of a study to test any aspects of the design, with a view to making improvements.

pituitary gland known as the 'master gland', the pituitary releases a variety of hormones that act on other glands throughout the body.

placebo a condition that should have no effect on the behaviour being studied, so can be used to separate out the effects of the IV from any effects caused merely by receiving any treatment.

pleasure principle (an aspect of Freudian psychology) reflects the id's primitive desire to seek instant gratification and avoid pain at all costs.

population the group of people from whom a sample is drawn.

population validity when the findings of a study can be generalised to other groups of people besides those who took part in the study.

positive correlation a relationship between two variables such that, as the value of one co-variable increases, there is a corresponding increase in the value of the other co-variable.

post-event information information you are given after a crime or 'event' that may alter your memory for the event, such as being asked leading questions.

practice effect in a repeated measures design, participants may do better on one condition rather than another because they have completed it first and are therefore more 'practised'.

précis a shortened version of a piece of text that retains the main gist of the information in the original text.

primacy effect the tendency to remember words from the start of a list (see also recency effect).

primary caregiver the person (usually the mother) who provides continuous emotional care for the child.

primary reinforcer a type of reinforcer (such as food to a hungry child) that satisfies a specific drive directly.

private acceptance the fact that an individual goes along with the majority in public does not indicate that they have changed their private attitudes or beliefs. Private acceptance of a position is more associated with informational influence.

privation a term originally introduced to distinguish children who had never managed to develop an attachment bond (privation) from those who had developed a bond but the bond had been broken (deprivation).

procedural memory a division of long-term memory that deals with our memory of how to perform specific actions.

prosopagnosia a form of neurological disorder characterised by an inability to recognise faces.

protest the initial distress when an infant is separated from his or her caregiver.

psychiatrist a person who is trained as a doctor and then specialises in the prevention, diagnosis and treatment of mental disorders.

psychoanalysis a theory of personality and development associated with Sigmund Freud; also a form of psychodynamic therapy based on the principles of this theory.

psychodynamic model a model of abnormality that sees abnormal behaviour as being caused by underlying unconscious conflicts of which the individual is largely unaware.

psychological model psychological models focus on the psychological dimensions of human behaviour rather than physiological dimensions.

psychosurgery a form of treatment for abnormal behaviour that involves cutting or removing parts of the brain thought to be implicated in that condition.

public compliance see compliance

punishment the application of an unpleasant stimulus such that the likelihood of the behaviour that led to it reoccurring is decreased.

qualitative analysis any form of analysis that focuses more on words (i.e. what participants say) than on other forms of numerical data. Qualitative analyses interpret the meaning of an experience to the individual(s) concerned.

qualitative data data that express what people think or feel. Qualitative data cannot be counted or quantified.

quantitative analysis any form of analysis (e.g. descriptive statistics) that uses numerical data as the basis for investigation and interpretation.

quantitative data data that represent how much or how long, or how many, etc., there are of something, i.e. a behaviour is measured in numbers or quantities.

quasi-experiment not truly an experiment because the IV is not directly manipulated and therefore we cannot claim to investigate cause-and-effect relationships.

questionnaire fallacy the erroneous belief that a questionnaire actually produces a true picture of what people do and think.

random allocation allocating participants to experimental groups or conditions randomly.

random sampling a technique for selecting participants such that every member of the population being tested has an equal chance of being selected.

randomly any technique where there is no systematic attempt to influence the selection or distribution of items or participants that form part of the investigation.

range a measure of dispersion that measures the difference between the highest and lowest score in a set of data.

recency effect the tendency to remember words from the end of a list (see also primacy effect).

reconstructive memory fragments of stored information are reassembled during recall, and the gaps are filled in by our expectations and beliefs to produce a coherent narrative.

reinforcement if a behaviour results in a pleasant state of affairs, the behaviour is 'stamped in' or reinforced. It then becomes more probable that the behaviour will be repeated in the future.

re-learning savings the tendency to forget less and less with each subsequent attempt to learn material.

reliability a measure of consistency within a set of scores or items, and over time such that it is possible to obtain the same results on subsequent occasions when the measure is used.

repeated measures design a type of experimental design where each participant takes part in every condition under test.

replication the opportunity to repeat an investigation under the same conditions in order to test the reliability of its findings.

representative sample a sample selected so that it accurately stands for or represents the population being studied.

repression a way of dealing with memories for traumatic events so that the anxiety created by the memory does not have to be experienced; the memory for the event is placed beyond conscious awareness.

research the process of gaining knowledge through the examination of data derived empirically or theoretically.

research design the overall plan of action to maximise meaningful results and minimise ambiguity using research techniques.

research technique the specific techniques used in a variety of research methods, such as control of variables and sampling methods.

retrieval failure when a person fails to successfully recover from memory something that was previously learned. These data may not be lost completely but cannot be retrieved at that particular time.

rich interpretation an aspect of psychoanalytic therapy whereby the therapist explains the patient's thoughts and feelings using Freud's ideas about personality development.

sample a selection of participants taken from the population being studied, and intended to be representative of that population.

sample bias a particular problem with questionnaire studies as certain types of people are likely to complete and return the questionnaire.

sampling the process of taking a sample.

scattergraph a graphical representation of the relationship (i.e. the correlation) between two sets of scores.

schema a schema is a packet of information about a thing. It is a cluster of related facts based on previous experiences which is used to generate future expectations.

secondary reinforcer something that is associated with a primary reinforcer, and eventually becomes a reinforcer in its own right.

secure attachment refers to those who seek and are comfortable with social interaction and intimacy. The securely attached infant is able to function independently because its caregiver acts as a secure base.

secure base the emotional stability provided by the primary caregiver, from which the child feels able to explore the world around him or her.

semantic coding this involves coding information in terms of its meaning.

semantic differential a way of measuring attitudes by using bipolar adjectives (e.g. 'good' or 'bad').

semantic memory our memory for words or other similar information.

sensitive period a period of time during which the child is particularly sensitive to a specific form of stimulation, resulting in the development of a specific response or characteristic.

separation refers to the physical disruption of the caregiver–child bond. The child may or may not receive suitable replacement care during the separation experience.

separation protest the distress shown when an infant is separated from his or her caregiver.

serial digit span used when testing the capacity of STM, it involves presenting a list of items and then checking how many are recalled in order.

serotonin a neurotransmitter found in the central nervous system and implicated in many different behaviours and physiological processes, including aggression, sleep and depression.

shaping a process whereby a desired behaviour is gradually conditioned by reinforcing behaviours that progressively move closer and closer to the behaviour in question.

short-term memory our memory for immediate events. Short-term memories last for a very short time and disappear unless they are rehearsed. The short-term memory store has limited duration and limited capacity.

significance a statistical term indicating that the research findings are sufficiently strong to enable us to reject the null hypothesis and accept the research hypothesis under test.

single blind a type of research design where the participant is not aware of the research aims nor of which condition of the experiment they are receiving.

situational factors aspects of an individual's environment that may be responsible for their behaviour at any given time.

snowball effect once a certain number of the majority in a group has shifted to the position advocated by the minority, the rest of the majority soon follow, making the previously 'deviant' minority position the new norm.

sociability the tendency to seek and enjoy the company of others.

social cryptoamnesia a tendency, over time, to forget the source of a particular position, thus making it less likely that conversion will be impeded by the association between a deviant minority and a particular attitude or belief.

social desirability bias a tendency for respondents to answer questions in such a way that presents themselves in a better light.

social development development of those behaviours associated with our relationships with others.

social learning theory (SLT) an explanation of learning based on our observation and imitation of the behaviour of others.

socialisation the process by which an individual learns all the customs, norms and other behaviours that characterise their culture.

socio-economic status (SES) an indication of a person's status in a stratified society determined by a variety of factors including background, education and income.

sociopath someone who has a sociopathic personality that prevents them from making and maintaining normal social relationships.

somatic therapies any type of treatment that involves a physical intervention (e.g. through the use of drugs) in the treatment of abnormal behaviour.

sources of stress those aspects of a person's environment or lifestyle that act as stressors.

split-half method a method of determining the internal reliability of a test. Test items are randomly split into two halves and the scores on both halves are compared. Scores should be similar if the test is reliable.

standard deviation a statistical measure of the amount of variation in a set of scores.

standardised conditions see **standardised procedures**

standardised instructions a set of instructions that are the same for all participants so as to avoid investigator effects caused by different instructions.

standardised procedures a set of procedures that are the same for all participants so as to enable replication of the study to take place.

stereotype a way of judging someone in terms of some readily available feature (e.g. race or gender) rather than their personal characteristics.

Strange Situation an investigative method designed to see how an infant behaves under conditions of mild stress and also novelty. Stress is created in the Strange Situation by the presence of a stranger and by separation from a caregiver. This tests stranger anxiety and separation anxiety respectively.

stranger anxiety the distress experienced by an infant when picked up or approached by someone who is unfamiliar.

stress although this term may be used interchangeably with 'stressor' and 'stress response', it may also be seen as the subjective experience of a lack of fit between a person and their environment (i.e. where the perceived demands of a situation are greater than a person's perceived ability to cope).

stress management the different ways in which people try to cope with the negative effects of stress. We may attempt to change the way our body responds to stress (the physiological approach) or change our relationship with the stressful situation (the psychological approach).

stressor any event that causes a stress reaction in the body. Stressors include environmental stressors (such as the workplace) and life events (such as illness or divorce).

structured interview any interview where the questions are decided in advance.

subcultures subgroups that exist within the same culture yet may have different norms for acceptable behaviour or differ in their experience of mental disorders.

superego part of Freud's conception of the structure of the personality, the superego embodies our conscience and sense of right and wrong.

sympathetic nervous system part of the autonomic nervous system involved in arousal during emergency or 'fight or flight' situations.

symptom substitution by treating only the symptoms of a disorder rather than the underlying cause, the symptoms may re-appear in a different guise.

synapse the 'communication point' between the axon terminal of one neuron and the dendrite or cell body of an adjacent neuron.

synoptic topics overarching issues and debates in psychology that represent a more global view of the subject.

target population a population (e.g. 16–18-year-old male adolescents) that is the subject of an investigation.

temperament an aspect of an individual's innate makeup that predisposes them to particular patterns of emotional reaction, mood and general sensitivity.

temperament hypothesis the belief that children form more secure relationships simply because they have an 'easy' temperament whereas difficult children are likely to form insecure relationships.

The Social Readjustment Rating Scale (SRRS) a way of measuring the relationship between life changes and stress, based on participants' experience of 43 life events.

thematic analysis themes or concepts are identified before starting a piece of research, then responses from an interview or questionnaire are organised according to these themes.

time sampling an observational technique where the observer makes a note of the target person's behaviour at predetermined time intervals.

trait any enduring characteristic of a person that might serve as an explanation for some consistency in their behaviour.

Type A the Type A individual is aggressive and ambitious with a competitive drive and a chronic sense of time urgency. These characteristics lead to both raised blood pressure and raised levels of hormones, both linked to ill health.

validity refers to the legitimacy of a study, the extent to which the findings can be applied to real life as a consequence of either internal or external validity.

variables anything the value of which can vary or change (see also independent variable and dependent variable).

vicarious conditioning behaviours are learned by seeing others rewarded or punished for their actions.

visuo-spatial sketchpad visual and/or spatial information is temporarily stored here. Visual information is what things look like. Spatial information is the relationship between things.

volunteer an individual who, acting on their own volition, applies to take part in an investigation.

volunteer bias a form of sampling bias because volunteer participants are usually more highly motivated than randomly selected participants.

volunteer sampling a sampling technique which relies solely on volunteers to make up the sample.

weapon focus a weapon in a crime may distract an eyewitnesses' attention from the main events and might explain why eyewitnesses sometimes have poor recall for certain details of a crime.

weapons effect in violent crimes, arousal may focus the witness on more central details (e.g. the nature of the weapon used) than more peripheral details of the crime.

word association a task where participants are asked to respond by saying any word that comes into their head.

word-length effect people cope better with short words in working memory than long words.

working memory model explains immediate memory in terms of a central executive, phonological loop (for verbal information) and a visuo-spatial sketchpad (for visual and spatial data).

workplace stressor some aspect of our working environment (such as work overload or impending deadlines) that we experience as stressful, and which causes a stress reaction in our body.

zero correlation see **correlation**

References

Abernethy, E.M. (1940) 'The effect of changed environmental conditions upon the results of college examinations', *Journal of Psychology,* vol. 10, pp. 293–301. ▶page 20

Aggleton, J.O. and Waskett, L. (1999) 'The ability of odours to serve as state-dependent cues for real-world memories: Can Viking smells aid the recall of Viking experiences?', *British Journal of Psychology,* vol. 90(1), pp. 1–7. ▶page 20

Ainsworth, M.D.S. (1964) 'Patterns of attachment behaviour shown by the infant in interaction with his mother', *Merrill-Palmer Quarterly,* vol. 10, pp. 51–8. ▶page 47

Ainsworth, M.D.S. (1967) *Infancy in Uganda: Child care and the growth of love,* John Hopkins University Press, Baltimore. ▶pages 47, 49

Ainsworth, M.D.S. and Bell, S.M. (1970) 'Attachment, exploration and separation: illustrated by the behaviour of two-year-olds in a Strange Situation', *Child Development,* vol. 41, pp. 49–65. ▶page 46

Ainsworth, M.D.S., Blehar, M.C., Waters, E. and Wall, S. (1978) *Patterns of attachment: A psychological study of the strange situation,* Lawrence Erlbaum, Hillsdale NJ. ▶pages 48–9, 57

Allport, G.W. (1968) 'The historical background of modern psychology', in G. Lindzey and E. Aronson (eds) *Handbook of Social Psychology,* 2nd edition, vol. 1, pp. 1–80, Addison-Wesley, Reading MA. ▶page 164

Allport, G.W. and Postman, L. (1947) 'The basic psychology of rumour', in E. Maccoby *et al.* (eds) *Readings in social psychology,* Holt. ▶page 29

Andersson, B.E. (1992) 'Effects of daycare on cognitive and socio-emotional competence of thirteen-year-old Swedish schoolchildren', *Child Development,* vol. 63, pp. 20–36. ▶pages 71, 75

Arbuthnot, J. and Wayner, M. (1982) 'Minority influence: Effects of size, conversion and sex', *Journal of Psychology,* vol. 111(2), pp. 285–95. ▶page 171

Arendt, H. (1963) *Eichmann in Jerusalem. A Report on the Banality of Evil,* The Viking Press, New York. ▶pages 174, 175, 179

Asch, S.E. (1956) 'Studies of independence and conformity: A minority of one against a unanimous majority', *Psychological Monographs,* vol. 70 (whole no. 416). ▶pages 164–5, 183

Ashton, H. (1997) 'Benzodiazepine dependency', in A. Baum, S. Newman, J. Weinman, R. West and C. McManus (eds), *Cambridge handbook of psychology, health and medicine,* Cambridge University Press, Cambridge. ▶page 109

Atkinson, R.C. and Shiffrin, R.M. (1968) 'Human memory: A proposed system and its control processes', in K.W. Spence and J.T. Spence (eds) *The Psychology of Learning and Motivation,* volume 2, Academic Press, London. ▶page 8–9

Attanasio, V., Andrasik, F., Burke, E.J., Blake, D.D., Kabela, E. and McCarran, M.S. (1985) 'Clinical issues in utilizing biofeedback with children', *Clinical Biofeedback and Health,* vol. 8, pp. 134–41. ▶page 111

Azar, B. (2000) 'The debate over child care isn't over yet...', *APA Monitor,* vol. 31(3). ▶page 75

Baddeley, A.D. (1986) *Working memory,* Clarendon Press, Oxford. ▶page 6–7 overmatter

Baddeley, A.D. and Hitch, G.J. (1974) 'Working memory', in G. H. Bower (ed.), *The psychology of learning and motivation,* vol. 8, Academic Press, London. ▶page 10

Baddeley, A.D. and Hitch, G.J. (1977) 'Recency re-examined', in S. Dornic (ed.) *Attention and performance,* Erlbaum, New Jersey. ▶page 18

Baddeley, A.D., Thomson, N. and Buchanan, M. (1975a) 'Word length and the structure of short-term memory', *Journal of Verbal Learning and Verbal Behavior,* vol. 14, pp. 575–89. ▶page 11

Baddeley, A.D., Grant, S., Wright, E. and Thomson, N. (1975b) 'Imagery and visual working memory', in P.M.A. Rabbitt and S. Dornic (eds) *Attention and performance,* vol. V, Academic Press, London. ▶page 11

Bahrick, H.P., Bahrick, P.O. and Wittinger, R.P. (1975) 'Fifty years of memory for names and faces: A cross-sectional approach', *Journal of Experimental Psychology: General,* vol. 104, pp. 54–75. ▶pages 6–7 overmatter, 17, 18

Bartlett, F.C. (1932) *Remembering,* Cambridge University Press, Cambridge. ▶page 26–27

Baumrind, D. (1964) 'Some thoughts on ethics of research: After reading Milgram's behavioural study of obedience', *American Psychologist,* vol. 19, pp. 421–3. ▶pages 176, 193

Baumrind, D. (1975) 'Metaethical and normative considerations governing the treatment of human subjects in the behavioural sciences', in E.C. Kennedy (ed.) *Human rights and psychological research: A debate on Psychology and ethics,* Thomas E. Crowell, New York. ▶page 196

Baumrind, D. (1985). 'Research using intentional deception: Ethical issues revisited', *American Psychologist,* vol. 40(2), pp. 165–74. ▶page 190

Beardsley, T. (1997) 'The machinery of thought', *Scientific American,* August, pp. 58–63. ▶page 9

Becker, A.E. (1999) *Acculturation and disordered eating in Fiji,* American Psychiatric Press, Washington DC. ▶pages 148, 158

Bekerian, D.A. and Bowers, J.M. (1983) 'Eye-witness testimony: Were we misled?' *Journal of Experimental Psychology, Learning, Memory and Cognition,* vol. 9, pp. 139–45. ▶page 33

Belsky, J. and Rovine, M. (1987) 'Temperament and attachment security in the Strange Situation: A rapprochement', *Child Development,* vol. 58, pp. 787–95. ▶pages 51, 77

Belsky, J. and Rovine, M.J. (1988) 'Non-maternal care in the first year of life and the security of parent-infant attachment', *Child Development,* vol. 59, pp. 157–67. ▶page 77

Bemis-Vitousek, K. and Orimoto, L. (1993) 'Cognitive-behavioural models of anorexia-nervosa, bulimia nervosa and obesity', in K.S. Dobson and P.C. Kendall (eds) *Psychopathology and Cognition,* Academic Press, San Diego. ▶page 149

Bickman, L. (1974) 'Clothes make the person', *Psychology Today,* vol. 8(4), pp. 48–51. ▶pages 178, 183

Bogdonoff, M.D., Klein, E.J., Shaw, D.M. and Back, K.W. (1961) 'The modifying effect of conforming behaviour upon lipi responses accompanying CNS arousal', *Clinical Research,* vol. 9, p. 135. ▶page 165

Bohman, M. and Sigvardsson, S. (1979) 'Long-term effects of early institutional care: A prospective longitudinal study', *Annual Progress in Child Psychiatry and Child Development,* pp. 148–56. ▶page 62–3

Boskind-Lodahl, M. (1976). 'Cinderella's stepsisters: A feminist perspective on anorexia and bulimia', *Signs, the Journal of Women in Culture and Society,* vol. 2, pp. 324–56. ▶page 145

Bowlby, J. (1944) 'Forty-four juvenile thieves: their characters and their home life', *International Journal of Psychoanalysis,* vol. 25, pp. 1–57, 207–20. ▶pages 55, 56

Bowlby, J. (1953) *Child care and the growth of love,* Penguin, Harmondsworth. ▶pages 61, 63

Bowlby, J. (1969) *Attachment and love, volume 1: Attachment,* Hogarth, London. ▶pages 60, 64

Bowlby, J., Ainsworth, M., Boston, M. and Rosenbluth, D. (1956) 'The effects of mother-child separation: A follow-up study', *British Journal of Medical Psychology,* vol. 29, p. 211. ▶page 62–3

Bradley, B.P. and Baddeley, A.D. (1990) 'Emotional factors in forgetting', *Psychological Medicine,* vol. 20, pp. 351–5. ▶page 23

Bradley, L.A. (1995) 'Chronic benign pain', in D. Wedding (ed.) *Behaviour and Medicine,* 2nd edition, Mosby-Year Book, St. Louis MO. ▶page 111

Brandimote, M.A., Hitch, G.J. and Bishop, D.V.M. (1992) 'Influence of short-term memory codes on visual processing: evidence from image transformation tasks', *Journal of Experimental Psychology: Learning, Memory and Cognition,* vol. 18, pp. 157–65. ▶page 7

Bransford, J.D. and Johnson, M.K. (1972) 'Contextual prerequisites for understanding: Some investigations of comprehension and recall', *Journal of Verbal Learning and Verbal Behaviour,* vol. 1, pp. 717–26. ▶page 28

Brewer, W.F. and Treyens, J.C. (1981) 'Role of schemata in memory for places', *Cognitive Psychology,* vol. 13, pp. 207–30. ▶page 28

Brown, G.W. and Harris, T. (1978) *Social origins of depression,* Tavistock, London. ▶page 71

Brown, R. and Kulik, J. (1977) 'Flashbulb memories', *Cognition,* vol. 5, pp. 73–99. ▶page 22

Bruch, H. (1980) 'Preconditions for the development of anorexia nervosa', *American Journal of Psychoanalysis,* vol. 40(2), pp. 169–72. ▶page 148

Bryant, B., Harris, M. and Newton, D. (1980) *Children and minders,* Grant McIntyre, London. ▶page 71

Buckhout, R. (1980) 'Nearly 2000 witnesses can be wrong', *Bulletin of the Psychonomic Society,* vol. 16, pp. 307–10. ▶page 32

Bulik C.M., Sullivan, P.F., Wade, T.D. and Kendler, K.S. (2000) 'Twin studies on eating disorders: A review', *International Journal of Eating Disorders,* vol. 27, pp. 1–20. ▶page 150

Burchinal, M. R., Roberts, J. E., Riggins, R., Zeisel, S. A., Neebe, E. and Bryant, D. (2000) 'Relating quality of center child care to early cognitive and language development longitudinally', *Child Development,* vol. 71(2), pp. 339–57. ▶page 75

Burger, J.M. and Cooper, H.M. (1979) 'The desirability of control', *Motivation and emotion,* vol. 3, pp. 381–93. ▶page 166

Burman, E. (1997) 'Developmental psychology and its discontents', in D. Fox and I. Prilleltensky (1997) *Critical Psychology: An Introduction,* Sage, London. ▶page 67

Burne, J. (1999) 'Don't worry, be happy', *The Guardian,* 24 August, pp. 8–9. ▶page 103

Campbell, F.A., Pungello, E.P., Miller-Johnson, S., Burchinal, M. and Ramey, C.T. (2001) 'The development of cognitive and academic abilities: Growth curves from an early childhood experiment', *Developmental Psychology,* vol. 37(2). ▶page 75

Caplan, R.D., Cobb, S., French, J.R.P., Van Harrison, R. and Pinneau, S.R. (1975) *Job demands and worker health,* National Institute for Occupational Safety and Health (publication no. 75–168), Cincinnati OH. ▶page 100

Cardwell, M. (2000) 'Milgram - the legacy', *Psychology Review,* vol. 7(4), pp. 14–17. ▶page 191

Carlson, M., Dragomir, C., and Earls, F. (1995) 'Effects of social deprivation on cortisol regulation in institutionalized Romanian infants', *Society of Neuroscience Abstracts,* vol. 21, p. 524.
▶page 93

Carmichael, L., Hogan, P. and Walter, A. (1932) 'An experimental study of the effect of language on the reproduction of visually perceived forms', *Journal of Experimental Psychology,* vol. 15, pp. 73–86 ▶page 28

Carroll, D. (1992) *Health psychology: Stress, behaviour and disease,* Falmer Press, London. ▶page 104

Chassler, Lynda (1998) '"Ox hunger": Psychoanalytic explorations of bulimia nervosa', *Clinical Social Work Journal,* vol. 26(4), pp. 397–412. ▶page 152

Christiansen, L. (1988) 'Deception in psychological research: When is its use justified?' *Personality and Social Psychology Bulletin,* vol. 14, pp. 664–75. ▶page 190

Christianson, S.A. and Hubinette, B. (1993) 'Hands up! A study of witnesses' emotional reactions and memories associated with bank robberies', *Applied Cognitive Psychology,* vol. 7, pp. 365–79. ▶page 31

Clark, R.D. III (1994) 'A few parallels between group polarisation and minority influence', in S. Moscovici, A. Mucchi-Faina and A, Maass (eds) *Minority influence,* Nelson Hall, Chicago. ▶page 170

Clarke-Stewart, K.A., Gruber, C.P. and Fitzgerald, L.M. (1994) *Children at home and in day care,* Erlbaum, Hillsdale NJ. ▶pages 72, 75, 77

Cohen, C.E. (1981) 'Person categories and social perception: Testing some boundaries of the processing effects of prior knowledge', *Journal of Personality and Social Psychology,* vol. 40, pp. 441–52. ▶page 28

Cohen, S., Tyrrell, D.A.J. and Smith, A.P. (1993) 'Negative life events, perceived stress, negative affect and susceptibility to the common cold', *Journal of Personality and Social Psychology,* vol. 64, pp. 131–40. ▶page 93

Comer, R.J. (1995) *Abnormal Psychology,* second edition, W.H. Freeman, New York. ▶page 133

Conrad, R. (1964) 'Acoustic confusions in immediate memory', *British Journal of Psychology,* vol. 55, pp. 75–84. ▶page 7

Conway, M.A., Anderson, S.J., Larsen, S.F., Donnelly, C.M., McDaniel, M.A., McClelland, A.G.R. and Rawles, R.E. (1994) 'The formation of flashbulb memories', *Memory and Cognition,* vol. 22, pp. 326–43. ▶page 22

Coolican, H. (2001) 'Experimental and ecological validity', *Psychology Review,* vol. 7(4), pp. 26–7. ▶page 184

Cooper, P.J. and Taylor, M.J. (1988) 'Body image disturbance in bulimia nervosa', *British Journal of Psychiatry,* vol. 153, pp. 32–6. ▶page 153

Craik, F.I.M. (1973) 'A "levels of analysis" view of memory', in P. Pliner, L. Krames and T.M. Alloway (eds) *Communication and affect: Language and thought,* Academic Press, London. ▶page 12

Craik, F.I.M. and Lockhart, R.S. (1972) 'Levels of processing: A framework for memory research', *Journal of Verbal Learning and Verbal Behavior,* vol. 11, pp. 671–84. ▶pages 12, 13

Craik, F.I.M. and Tulving, E. (1975) 'Depth of processing and the retention of words in episodic memory', *Journal of Experimental Psychology,* vol. 104, pp. 268–94. ▶pages 12, 13

Creps, C.L. and Vernon-Feagans, L. (1999) 'Preschoolers' social behavior in day care links with entering day care in the first year', *Journal of Applied Developmental Psychology,* vol. 20(3), pp. 461–79. ▶page 77

Curtiss, S. (1977) *Genie: A psycholinguistic study of a modern-day 'wild child',* Academic Press, London. ▶page 66

Cutts, T.F. and Barrios, B.A. (1986) 'Fear of weight gain among bulimic and non-disturbed females', *Behaviour Therapy,* vol. 17, pp. 626–36. ▶pages 152, 157, 158

Darley, J.M. (1992) 'Social organisation for the production of evil', *Psychological enquiry,* vol. 3(2), pp. 199–218. ▶page 191

Davison, G.C. and Neale, J.M. (2001) *Abnormal Psychology* (eighth edn) John Wiley, New York.
▶pages 95, 111, 127

DeLongis, A., Coyne, J.C., Dakof, G., Folkman, S. and Lazarus, R.S. (1982) 'The impact of daily hassles, uplifts and major life events to health status', *Health Psychology,* vol. 1, pp. 119–36. ▶page 98

DeLongis, A., Folkman, S. and Lazarus, R.S. (1988) 'The impact of daily stress on health and mood: Psychological and social resources as mediators', *Journal of Personality and Social Psychology,* vol. 54, pp. 486–95. ▶page 98

Denollet, J., Sys, S.U., Stroobant, N., Rombouts, H., Gillebert, T. and Brutsaert, D.L. (1996) 'Personality as independent predictor of long-term mortality in patients with coronary heart disease', *The Lancet,* vol. 347, pp. 417–21. ▶page 103

Dicks, H.V. (1972) *Licensed Mass Murder: A Socio-psychological Study of Some S.S. Killers,* Basic Books, New York. ▶page 185

DiLalla, L. F. (1998) 'Daycare, child and family influences on preschoolers' social behaviors in a peer play setting', *Child Study Journal,* vol. 28, pp. 223–4. ▶page 77

Dollard, J. and Miller, N.E. (1950) *Personality and psychotherapy,* McGraw-Hill, New York. ▶page 54

Eagly, A.H. (1978) 'Sex differences in influenceability', *Psychological Bulletin,* vol. 85, pp. 86–116. ▶page 105

Eagly, A.H. and Carli, L. (1981) 'Sex of researchers and sex-typed communications as determinants of sex differences in influenceability: A meta-analysis of social influence studies', *Psychological Bulletin,* vol. 90, pp. 1–20. ▶page 166

Eagly, A. H. and Wood, W. (1999) 'The origins of sex differences in human behavior: Evolved dispositions versus social roles', *American Psychologist,* vol. 54, pp. 408–23. ▶page 166

Ebbinghaus, H. (1885) *Memory,* Teacher's College Press, New York. ▶page 21

Egeland, B. and Hiester, M. (1995) 'The long-term consequences of infant day-care and mother-infant attachment', *Child Development,* vol. 66, pp. 474–85. ▶page 72

Eliot, L. (1999) *Early intelligence,* Penguin, Harmondsworth. ▶page 93

Epstein, L.C. and Lasagna, L. (1969) 'Obtaining informed consent', *Archives of Internal Medicine,* vol. 123, pp. 682–8. ▶page 191

Erikson, M. (1968) 'The inhumanity of ordinary people', *International Journal of Psychiatry,* vol. 6, pp. 278–79. ▶page 195

Ermisch, J. and Francesconi, M. (2000) 'Educational choice, families and young people's earnings', *Journal of Human Resources,* vol. 35(1), pp. 143–76. ▶page 74

Evans, P., Bristow, M., Hucklebridge, F., Clow, A. and Pang, F.-Y. (1994) 'Stress, arousal, cortisol and secretory immunoglobulin A in students undergoing assessment', *British Journal of Clinical Psychology,* vol. 33, pp. 575–6. ▶page 93

Evans, P., Clow, A. and Hucklebridge, F. (1997) 'Stress and the immune system', *The Psychologist,* vol. 10(7), pp. 303–7. ▶page 93

Eysenck, M.W. (1998) *Psychology: An integrated approach,* Longman, Harlow. ▶page 20

Eysenck, M.W. and Eysenck, M.C. (1980) 'Effects of processing depth, distinctiveness and word frequency on retention', *British Journal of Psychology,* vol. 71, pp. 263–74. ▶pages 12, 13

Farah, M.J., Peronnet, F., Gonon, M.A. and Giard, M.H. (1988) 'Electrophysiological evidence for a shared representational medium for visual images and visual percepts', *Journal of Experimental Psychology: General,* vol. 117, pp. 248–57. ▶page 11

Farley, F. (1990) 'The Type T personality, with some implications for practice', *The California Psychologist,* vol. 23, p. 29. ▶page 94

Fichter, M.M. and Pirke, K.M. (1995) Starvation models and eating disorders. In G. Szmukler, C. Dare and J. Treasure (eds) *Handbook of eating disorders: Theory, treatment and research.* Chichester: Wiley.
▶page 147

Fontana, A., Hyra, D., Godfrey, L. and Cermal, L. (1999) 'Impact of a peer-led stress inoculation training intervention on state anxiety and heart rate in college students', *Journal of Applied Behavioural Research,* vol. 4(1), pp. 45–63. ▶page 113

Foster, R.A., Libkuman, I.M., Schooler, J.W., and Loftus, E.F. (1994) 'Consequentiality and eyewitness person identification', *Applied Cognitive Psychology,* vol. 8, pp. 107–21. ▶page 31

Fox, N. (1977) 'Attachment of Kibbutz infants to mother and metapelet', *Child Development,* vol. 48, pp. 1228–39. ▶pages 53, 77

Frankenhauser, M. (1983) 'The sympathetic-adrenal and pituitary-adrenal response to challenge: Comparison between the sexes', in T.M. Dembroski, T.H. Schmidt and G. Blumchen (eds) *Biobehavioural biases in coronary heart disease,* Karger, Basel. ▶page 104

Freud, S. (1920) *Beyond the pleasure principle,* Norton, New York. ▶page 134

Friedman, M. and Rosenman, R.H. (1959) 'Association of specific overt behaviour pattern with blood and cardiovascular findings', *Journal of the American Medical Association,* vol. 169, pp. 1286–96. ▶page 102

Funk, S.C. (1992) 'Hardiness: A review of theory and research', *Health Psychology,* vol. 11, 335–45. ▶page 114

Galla, J.P. (1995) Paper presented on Thursday, April 6, 1995, at the National Social Science Association Conference, San Diego, CA (http://www.biopsych.net/bulimia%20papers/serotonin%20hypothesis.html). ▶page 151

Gallo, P.S., Smith, S. and Mumford, S. (1973) 'Effects of deceiving subjects upon experimental results',. *Journal of Social Psychology,* vol. 89, pp. 99–107. ▶page 190

Gamson, W.B., Fireman, B. and Rytina, S. (1982) *Encounters with unjust authority,* Dorsey Press, Homewood, IL. ▶pages 181, 191, 195

Garner, D.M. and Bemis, K.M. (1982) 'A cognitive-behavioural approach to anorexia nervosa', *Cognitive Therapy and Research,* vol. 6, pp. 123–50. ▶page 149

Gauld, A. and Stephenson, G.M. (1967) 'Some experiments relating to Bartlett's theory of remembering', *British Journal of Psychology,* vol. 58, pp. 39–50. ▶page 27

Geiselman, R.E., Fisher, R.P., MacKinnon, D.P. and Holland, H.L. (1985) 'Enhancement of eyewitness memory with the cognitive interview', *American Journal of Psychology,* vol. 99, pp. 385–401. ▶page 33

Glanzer, M. and Cunitz, A.R. (1966) 'Two storage mechanisms in free recall', *Journal of Verbal Learning and Verbal Behavior,* vol. 5, pp. 351–60. ▶pages 9, 17

Glass, D.C., Singer, J.E. and Friedman, L.W. (1969) 'Psychic cost of adaptation to an environmental stressor', *Journal of Personality and Social Psychology,* vol. 12, pp. 200–210. ▶page 101

Goldfarb, W. (1943) 'The effects of early institutional care on adolescent personality', *Journal of Experimental Education,* vol. 12, pp. 106–29. ▶page 66

Goodwin, D.W., Powell, B., Bremer, D., Hoine, H. and Stern, J. (1969) 'Alcohol and recall: State-dependent effects in man', *Science,* vol. 163, p. 1358. ▶page 20

Gorwood, R., Bouvard, M., Mouren-Simioni, M.C., Kipman, A. and Ades, J. (1998) 'Genetics and anorexia nervosa: A review of candidate genes', *Psychiatric Genetics,* vol. 8, pp. 1–12. ▶page 146

Greenough, W. T., Black, J. E. and Wallace, C. S. (1987) 'Experience and brain development', *Child Development,* vol. 58, pp. 539–59. ▶page 74

Greenspoon, J. (1955) 'The reinforcing effect of two spoken sounds on the frequency of two responses', *American Journal of Psychology,* vol. 68, pp. 409–16. ▶page 173

Greer, A., Morris, T. and Pettingdale, K.W. (1979) 'Psychological response to breast cancer: Effect on outcome', *The Lancet,* vol. 13, pp. 785–7. ▶page 103

Grossmann, K.E. and Grossmann, K. (1991) 'Attachment quality as an organizer of emotional and behavioural responses in a longitudinal perspective', in C.M. Parkes, J. Stevenson-Hinde and P. Marris (eds) *Attachment across the life cycle,* Tavistock/Routledge, London. ▶page 53

Gruber, B.L. and Taub, E. (1998) 'Thermal and EMG biofeedback learning in nonhuman primates', *Applied Psychophysiological Biofeedback,* vol. 23(1), pp. 1–12. ▶page 111

Guiton, P. (1966) 'Early experience and sexual object choice in the brown leghorn', *Animal Behaviour,* vol. 14, pp. 534–8. ▶page 45

Hammonds, E. M. (1994) 'Your silence will not protect you: Nurse Eunice Rivers and the Tuskegee Syphilis Study', in E. C. White (ed) *The Black Women's Health Book: Speaking for Ourselves,* second edition, pp. 323–31, Seal Press, Seattle. ▶page 189

Harlow, H.F (1959) 'Love in infant monkeys', *Scientific American,* vol. 200(6), pp. 68–74. ▶pages 54, 140, 192

Harvey, E. (1999) 'Short-term and long-term effects of early parental employment on children of the National Longitudinal Survey of Youth', *Developmental Psychology,* 35(2). ▶page 74

Hastrup, J.L., Light, K.C. and Obrist, P.A. (1980) 'Relationship of cardiovascular stress response to parental history of hypertension and to sex differences', *Psychophysiology,* vol. 17, pp. 317–18. ▶page 104

Hazan, C. and Shaver, P.R. (1987) 'Romantic love conceptualised as an attachment process', *Journal of Personality and Social Psychology,* vol. 52, pp. 511–24. ▶pages 50, 51, 56

Heinrichs, M., Baumgartner, T., Ehlert, U., Kirschbaum, C. and Hellhammer, D. H. (2001) 'Effects of oxytocin and social support on psychoendocrine stress responsiveness in healthy men', *Psychosomatic Medicine,* vol. 63, pp. 149–50. ▶page 105

Herman, C.P. and Mack, D. (1975) 'Restrained and unrestrained eating', *Journal of Personality,* vol. 43, 647–60. ▶page 153

Hitch, G. and Baddeley, A.D. (1976) 'Verbal reasoning and working memory', *Quarterly Journal of Experimental Psychology,* vol. 28, pp. 603–21. ▶page 11

Hockey, G.R.J., Davies, S. and Gray, M.M. (1972) 'Forgetting as a function of sleep at different times of day', *Quarterly Journal of Experimental Psychology,* vol. 24, pp. 386–93. ▶page 18

Hodges, J. and Tizard, B. (1989) 'Social and family relationships of ex-institutional adolescents', *Journal of Child Psychology and Psychiatry,* vol. 30, pp. 77–95. ▶pages 64–5, 178

Hoek, H.W., van Harten, P.N. and van Hoeken, S.E. (1998) 'Lack of relation between culture and anorexia nervosa - results of an incidence study on Curacao', *New England Journal of Medicine,* vol. 338, pp. 1231–2. ▶page 149

Hofling, K.C., Brontzman, E., Dalrymple, S., Graves, N. and Pierce, C.M. (1966) 'An experimental study in the nurse-physician relationship', *Journal of Mental and Nervous Disorders,* vol. 43, pp. 171–8. ▶pages 178, 184

Holland, A.J., Sicotte, N. and Treasure, J. (1988) 'Anorexia nervosa: Evidence for a genetic basis', *Journal of Psychosomatic Research,* vol. 32, pp. 561–72. ▶pages 146, 148, 158

Holland, C.H. (1967) 'Sources of variance in the experimental investigation of behavioural obedience', unpublished doctoral dissertation, University of Connecticut. ▶page 182

Holmes, D.S. (1990) 'The evidence for repression: An examination of sixty years of research', in J. Singer (ed.) *Repression and dissociation: Implications for personality theory, psychopathology and health,* University of Chicago Press, Chicago. ▶page 23

Holmes, T.H. and Rahe, R.H. (1967) 'The social readjustment rating scale', *Journal of Psychosomatic Research,* vol. 11, pp. 213–18. ▶page 96

Homan, R. (1991) *The Ethics of Social Research* Longman, London. ▶page 191

Howes, C. and Hamilton, C.E. (1992) 'Children's relationships with caregivers: Mothers and child care teachers', *Child Development,* vol. 63(4), pp. 859–66. ▶page 71

Jacobs, J. (1887) 'Experiments in prehension', *Mind,* vol. 12, pp. 75–9. ▶page 6

Jacobs, T.J. and Charles, E. (1980) 'Life events and the occurrence of cancer in children', *Psychosomatic Medicine,* vol. 42, pp. 11–24. ▶page 98

Jahoda, M. (1958) *Current concepts of positive mental health,* Basic Books, New York. ▶page 130

Jay, S. M. and Elliot, C. H. (1990) 'A stress inoculation program for parents whose children are undergoing medical procedures', *Journal of Consulting and Clinical Psychology,* vol. 58, pp. 799–804. ▶page 113

Jenkins, J.G. and Dallenbach, K.M. (1924) 'Oblivescence during sleep and waking', *American Journal of Psychology,* vol. 35, pp. 605–12. ▶pages 18, 173, 183

Jenness, A. (1932) 'The role of discussion in changing opinion regarding matter of fact', *Journal of Abnormal and Social Psychology,* vol. 27, pp. 279–96. ▶page 166

Johansson, G., Aronsson, G. and Lindstrom, B.O. (1978) 'Social psychological and neuroendocrine reactions in highly mechanised work', *Ergonomics,* vol. 21, pp. 583–99. ▶page 101

Jones, J. H. (1993) *Bad Blood: The Tuskegee Syphilis Experiment,* Free Press, New York. ▶page 189

Kagan, J. (1984) *The nature of the child,* Basic Books, New York. ▶page 51

Kahn, R.J., McNair, D.M., Lipman, R.S., et al. (1986) 'Imipramine and chlordiazepoxide in depressive and anxiety disorders. II. Efficacy in anxious outpatients', *Archives of General Psychiatry,* vol. 43, p. 79. ▶pages 109, 111

Kahn, R.L., Wolfe, D.M., Quinn, R.P., Snoek, J.D. and Rosenthal, R.A. (1964) *Organisational stress: Studies in role conflict and ambiguity,* John Wiley, New York. ▶page 101

Karon, B.P. and Widener, A. J. (1997) 'Repressed memories and World War II: Lest we forget!', *Professional Psychology: Research and Practice,* vol. 28(4), pp. 338–40. ▶page 23

Kaye, W.H., Klump, K.L., Frank, G.K.W. and Strober, M. (2000) 'Anorexia and bulimia nervosa', *Annual Review of Medicine,* vol. 51, pp. 299–313. ▶page 151

Kebbell, M.R. and Wagstaff, G.F. (1999) Face Value? Evaluating the accuracy of eyewitness information, Police research paper 102, Home Office (UK) Policing and Reducing Crime Unit. ▶page 32

Kendler, K.S., Maclean, C., Neale, M., Kessler, R., Heath, A. and Eaves, L. (1991) 'The genetic epidemiology of bulimia nervosa', *American Journal of Psychiatry,* vol. 148, pp. 1627–37. ▶pages 150, 158

Kiecolt-Glaser, J,K., Garner, W., Speicher, C.E., Penn, G.M., Holliday, J. and Glaser, R.(1984) 'Psychosocial modifiers of immunocompetence in medical students', *Psychosomatic Medicine,* vol. 46, pp. 7–14. ▶pages 93, 120

Kiecolt-Glaser, J,K., Marucha, P.T., Malarkey, W.B., Mercado, A.M. and Glaser, R. (1995) 'Slowing of wound healing by psychological stress', *The Lancet,* vol. 346, pp. 1194–96. ▶page 92–3

Kissileff, H.R., Wentzlaff, T.H., Guss, J.L., Walsh, B.T., Devlin, M.J. and Thornton, J.C. (1996) 'A direct measure of satiety disturbance in patients with bulimia nervosa', *Physiology and Behavior,* vol. 60, pp. 1077–85. ▶page 151

Klump, K., Bulik, C.M., Pollice, C., Halmi, K.A., Fichter, M.M., Berrettini, W.H., Devlin, B., Goldman, D., Strober, M., Kaplan, A., Woodside, B., Treasure, J., Shabbout, M., Lilenfeld, L.R., Plotnicov, K.H. and Kaye, W.H. (2000) 'Temperament and character in women with anorexia nervosa', *Journal of Nervous and Mental Diseases,* vol. 188, pp. 559–67. ▶page 146

Kobasa, S.C. (1979a) 'Personality and resistance to illness', *American Journal of Community Psychology,* vol. 7, pp. 413–23. ▶page 103

Kobasa, S.C. (1979b) 'Stressful life events, personality and health: An inquiry into hardiness', *Journal of Personality and Social Psychology,* vol. 37, pp. 1–11. ▶page 115

Koluchová, J.(1976) 'The further development of twins after severe and prolonged deprivation: A second report', *Journal of Child Psychology and Psychiatry,* vol. 17, pp. 181–8. ▶page 66

Koluchová, J. (1991) 'Severely deprived twins after twenty-two years' observation', *Studia Psychologica,* vol. 33, pp. 23–8. ▶page 66

Krantz D.S., Helmers, K.F., Bairey, C.N., Nebel, L.E., Hedges, S.M. and Rozanski, A. (1991) 'Cardiovascular reactivity and mental stress-induced myocardial ischemia in patients with coronary artery disease', *Psychosomatic Medicine,* vol. 53(1), pp. 1–12. ▶pages 90–1, 120

Lalancette, M-F and Standing, L.G (1990) 'Asch fails again', *Social Behavior and Personality,* vol. 18(1), pp. 7–12. ▶page 165

Lamb, M.E. (1981) 'The development of father-infant relationships', in M.E. Lamb (ed.) *The role of the father in child development,* Wiley, New York. ▶page 57

Larsen, K.S. (1974) 'Conformity and the Asch experiment', *Journal of Social Psychology,* vol. 94, pp. 303–4. ▶page 165

Lashley, K. (1931) 'Mass action in cerebral function', *Science,* vol. 73, pp. 245–54. ▶page 18

Latané, B. and Wolf, S. (1981) 'The social impact of majorities and minorities', *Psychological Review,* vol. 88, pp. 438 53. ▶page 171

Leach, P. (1994) *Children first,* Penguin, Harmondsworth. ▶page 76

Lee, S., Hsu, L.K.G. and Wing, Y.K. (1992) 'Bulimia nervosa in Hong Kong Chinese patients', *British Journal of Psychiatry,* vol. 161, pp. 545–51. ▶page 153

Lifton, R.J. (1986) *The Nazi Doctors: Medical killing and the Psychology of genocide,* Basic Books, New York. ▶page 191

Lilenfeld, L.R., Stein, D., Bulik, C.M., Strober, M., Plotnicov, K., Pollice, C., Rao, R., Merikangas, K.R., Nagy, L. and Kaye, W.H. (2000) 'Personality traits among current eating disordered, recovered and never-ill first-degree female relatives of bulimic and control women', *Psychological Medicine,* vol. 30, pp. 1399–1410. ▶page 151

Lindsay, D.S. (1990) 'Misleading suggestions can impair eyewitnesses' ability to remember event details', *Journal of Experimental Psychology: Learning, Memory and Cognition,* vol. 16, pp. 1077–83. ▶page 33

Lockhart, R.S. and Craik, F.I.M. (1990) 'Levels of processing: A retrospective commentary on a framework for memory research', *Canadian Journal of Psychology,* vol. 44, pp. 87–112. ▶page 12

Loftus, E.F. (1979a) *Eyewitness testimony,* Harvard University Press, Cambridge, MA. ▶page 32

Loftus, E.F. (1979b) 'Reactions to blatantly contradictory information', *Memory and Cognition,* vol. 7, pp. 368–74. ▶page 33

Loftus, E.F. and Palmer, J.C. (1974) 'Reconstruction of automobile destruction: An example of the interaction between language and memory', *Journal of Verbal Learning and Verbal Behavior,* vol. 13, pp. 585–89. ▶page 33

Loftus, E.F. and Zanni, G. (1975) 'Eyewitness testimony: The influence of the wording of a question', *Bulletin of the Psychonomic Society,* vol. 5, pp. 86–8. ▶page 30–31

Loftus, E.,F., Loftus, G.R. and Messo, J. (1987) 'Some facts about "weapon focus"', *Law and Human Behaviour,* vol. 11, pp. 55–62. ▶page 32

Loftus, E.F., Miller, D.G. and Burns, H.J. (1978) 'Semantic integration of verbal information into visual memory', *Journal of Experimental Psychology,* vol. 4(1), pp. 19–31. ▶page 33

Loftus, G. (1974) 'Reconstructing memory: The incredible eyewitness', *Psychology Today,* December, pp. 116–9. ▶page 33

Lorenz, K.Z. (1952) *King Solomon's Ring: New light on animal ways,* Thomas Y. Crowell, New York. ▶pages 45, 102

Maass, A., Clark, R.D. III and Haberkorn, G. (1982) 'The effects of differential ascribed category membership and norms on minority influence', *European Journal of Social Psychology*, vol. 12, pp. 89–104. ▶page 170

Maccoby, E.E. (1980) *Social development: Psychological growth and the parent-child relationship*, Harcourt Brace Jovanovich, San Diego. ▶page 47

Maddi, S.R. (1999) 'The personality construct of Hardiness: I. Effects on experiencing, coping and strain', *Consulting Psychology Journal: Practice and Research*, vol. 51(2). ▶page 114

Maddi, S.R., Kahn, S. and Maddi, L. K. (1998) 'The effectiveness of hardiness training', *Consulting Psychology Journal*, vol. 50, pp. 78–86. ▶page 115

Main, M. and Weston, D.R. (1981) 'The quality of the toddler's relationship to mother and father: Related to conflict behaviour and the readiness to establish new relationships', *Child Development*, vol. 52, pp. 932–40. ▶page 49

Mandel, D.R. (1998) 'The obedience alibi: Milgram's account of the Holocaust reconsidered', *Analyse & Krtik: Zeitschrift für Sozialwissenschaften*, vol. 20, pp. 74–94. ▶page 185

Mandler, G. (1967) 'Organisation and memory', in K.W. Spence and J.T. Spence (eds), *The psychology of learning and motivation: Advances in research and theory*, vol. 1, Academic Press, London. ▶page 12

Marmot, M., Bosma, H., Hemingway, H., Brunner, E. and Stansfield, S. (1997) 'Contribution of job control and other risk factors to social variation in health disease incidence', *The Lancet*, vol. 350, pp. 235–39. ▶pages 100, 120

Maurer D. and Maurer C. (1989) *The World of the Newborn*, Viking. ▶page 47

McLelland, L., Mynors-Wallis, L. and Treasure J. (1991) 'Sexual abuse, disordered personality and eating', *British Journal of Psychiatry*, vol. 158, pp. 63–8. ▶page 152

Meeus, W.H.J. and Raajmakers, Q.A.W. (1995) 'Obedience in modern society: The Utrecht studies', *Journal of Social Issues*, vol. 51(3), pp. 155–75. ▶pages 178, 184

Meichenbaum, D. (1977) *Cognitive-behaviour modification: An integrative approach*, Plenum Press, New York. ▶page 113

Meichenbaum, D. (1985) *Stress inoculation training*, Pergamon, New York. ▶page 112

Meichenbaum, D. (1996) 'Stress inoculation training for coping with stressors', *The Clinical Psychologist*, vol. 49, pp. 4–7. ▶page 113

Miles, C. and Hardman, E. (1998) 'State-dependent memory produced by aerobic exercise', *Ergonomics*, vol. 41(1), pp. 20–8. ▶page 20

Milgram, S. (1963) 'Behavioural study of obedience', *Journal of Abnormal and Social Psychology*, vol. 67, pp. 371–8. ▶pages 162, 176–7, 179, 180–1, 182–3, 184–5, 186, 19, 191, 192, 193, 195, 196

Milgram, S. (1972) 'Interpreting obedience: error and evidence', in A.G. Miller (ed.) *The social psychology of psychological research*, Free Press, New York. ▶page 182–183

Milgram, S. (1974) *Obedience to authority: An experimental view*, Harper and Row, New York. ▶pages 174, 179, 180

Miller, G.A. (1956) 'The magic number seven, plus or minus two: Some limits on our capacity for processing information', *Psychological Review*, vol. 63, pp. 81–93. ▶page 6

Miller, N. and DiCara, L. (1967) 'Instrumental learning of heart rate changes in curarised rats: shaping and specificity to discriminative stimulus', *Journal of Comparative and Physiological Psychology*, vol. 63, pp. 12–19. ▶page 110

Milner, B. (1966) 'Amnesia following operation on the temporal lobes', in C.W.M. Whitty and O.L. Zangwill (eds) *Amnesia*, Butterworth, London. ▶page 9

Moghaddam, F.M. (1998) *Social Psychology: Exploring universals across cultures*, W.H. Freeman, New York. ▶page 189

Moos, R.H. and Swindle, R.W. Jnr. (1990) 'Stressful life circumstances: concepts and measures', *Stress Medicine*, vol. 6, pp. 171–8. ▶page 98

Morris, C.D., Bransford, J.D. and Franks, J.J. (1977) 'Levels of processing versus transfer appropriate processing', *Journal of Verbal Learning and Verbal Behavior*, vol. 16, pp. 519–33. ▶page 12

Moscovici, S. (1976) *Social influence and social change*, Academic Press, London. ▶page 168

Moscovici, S. (1980) 'Toward a theory of conversion behaviour', in L. Berkowitz (ed.) *Advances in experimental social psychology*, vol. 13, Academic Press, New York. ▶page 168

Moscovici, S. and Faucheux, C. (1972) 'Social influence, conforming bias and the study of active minorities', in L. Berkowitz (ed.) *Advances in experimental social psychology*, vol. 6, pp. 149–202, Academic Books, New York. ▶page 170

Moscovici, S. and Nemeth, C. (1974) 'Social influence II: minority influence', in C. Nemeth (ed.) *Social psychology: Classic and contemporary integrations*, Rand McNally, Chicago. ▶pages 170, 171

Moscovici, S., Lage, E. and Naffrenchoux, M. (1969) 'Influence of a consistent minority on the responses of a majority in a colour perception task', *Sociometry*, vol. 32, pp. 365–80. ▶pages 169, 170, 171

Mugny, G. (1984) 'The influence of minorities', in H. Tajfel (ed.) *The social dimension*, vol. 2, Cambridge University Press, Cambridge. ▶page 170

Mumford, D.B., Whitehouse, A.M. and Plattes, M. (1991) 'Sociocultural correlates of eating disorders among Asian schoolgirls in Bradford', *British Journal of Psychiatry*, vol. 158, pp. 222–8. ▶page 153

Murray, B. (1993) 'Human Nature: Attitudes and Age', *Psychology Today*, vol. 26(2), p. 96. ▶page 133

Nasser, M. (1986) 'Comparative study of the prevalence of abnormal eating attitudes among Arab female students of both London and Cairo', *Psychological Medicine*, vol. 16, pp. 621–7. ▶page 153

Nemeroff, C.B. and Musselman, D.L. (2000) 'Are platelets the link between depression and ischemic heart disease?' *American Heart Journal*, vol. 140(4S), pp. 557–62. ▶page 103

Nemeth, C. (1995) 'Dissent as driving cognition, attitudes and judgements', *Social Cognition*, vol. 13, pp. 273–91. ▶page 168

Nemeth, C., Swedlund, M. and Kanki, G. (1974) 'Patterning of the minority's responses and their influence on the majority', *European Journal of Social Psychology*, vol. 4, pp. 53–64. ▶page 169

Nemeth, G.J. and Brilmayer, A.G. (1987) 'Negotiation versus influence', *European Journal of Social Psychology*, vol. 17, pp. 45–56. ▶page 170

NICHD Early Child Care Research Network (1997) 'The effects of infant child care on infant-mother attachment security: Results of the NICHD study of early child care', *Child Development*, vol. 68(5), pp. 860–79. ▶page 72

NICHD Early Child Care Research Network (1999) 'Child care and mother-child interactions in the first three years of life', *Developmental Psychology*, vol. 35, pp. 1399–1413. ▶pages 71, 77

NICHD Early Child Care Research Network (2001) 'Further explorations of the detected effects of quantity of early child care on socioemotional development', paper presented at the Biennial Meeting of the Society for Research in Child Development, Minneapolis MN. ▶pages 72, 77

O'Toole, K. (1997) *The Stanford Prison Experiment: Still powerful after all these years*, Stanford University News Service 8/1/97, Stanford News. ▶page 187

Oltmanns, T.F., Neale, J.M. and Davison, G.C. (1999) *Case studies in Abnormal Psychology*, John Wiley and Sons, New York. ▶page 131

Orne, M.T. (1962) 'On the social psychology of the psychological experiment: With particular reference to demand characteristics and their implications', *American Psychologist*, vol. 17, pp. 776–83. ▶page 172

Orne, M.T. and Holland, C.C. (1968) 'On the ecological validity of laboratory deceptions', *International Journal of Psychiatry*, vol. 6(4), pp. 282–93. ▶pages 182–3, 184

Palmer, S. and Strickland, L. (1995) *Stress Management: A Quick Guide*, Daniels Publishing, Cambridge. ▶page 87

Palmere, M., Benton, S.L., Glover, J.A. and Ronning, R. (1983) 'Elaboration and recall of main ideas in prose', *Journal of Educational Psychology*, vol. 75, pp. 898–907. ▶page 12

Pennebaker, J.W., Hendler, C.S., Durrett, M.E. and Richards, P. (1981) 'Social factors influencing absenteeism due to illness in nursery school children', *Child Development*, vol. 52, pp. 692–700. ▶page 72

Pennington, D.C., Gillen, K. and Hill, P. (1999) *Social Pscyhology*, Arnold, London. ▶page 170

Perez, J., Papastamou, S. and Mugny, G. (1995) 'Zeitgeist and minority influence - where is the causality? A comment on Clark (1990)', *European Journal of Social Psychology*, vol. 25, pp. 703–10. ▶page 170

Perrin, S. and Spencer, C. (1980) 'The Asch effect: A child of its time', *Bulletin of the British Psychological Society*, vol. 33, pp. 405–6. ▶page 165

Peterson , L.R. and Peterson, M.J. (1959) 'Short-term retention of individual verbal items', *Journal of Experimental Psychology*, vol. 58, pp. 193–8. ▶pages 4–5, 16

Quinton, D., Rutter, M. and Liddle, C. (1985) 'Institutional rearing, parenting difficulties and marital support', *Annual Progress in Child Psychiatry and Child Development*, pp. 173–206. (1985) ▶page 66

Rahe, R.H., Mahan, J. and Arthur, R. (1970) 'Prediction of near-future health-change from subjects' preceding life changes', *Journal of Psychosomatic Research*, vol. 14, pp. 401–6. ▶pages 96–97, 120

Rank, S.G. and Jacobsen, C.K. (1977) 'Hospital nurses' compliance with medication overdose orders: A failure to replicate', *Journal of Health and Social Behaviour*, vol. 18, pp. 188–193. ▶page 178

Reitman, J.S. (1974) 'Without surreptitious rehearsal, information in short-term memory decays', *Journal of Verbal Learning and Verbal Behaviour*, vol. 13, pp. 365–77. ▶page 16

Riley, V. (1981) 'Psychoneuroendocrine influence on immuno-competence and neoplasia', *Science*, vol. 212, pp. 1100–1109. ▶pages 93, 192

Robertson, J. and Bowlby, J. (1952) 'Responses of young children to separation from their mothers', *Courier Centre International de l'Enfance*, vol. 2, pp. 131–42. ▶pages 58, 59, 62

Robertson, J. and Robertson, J. (1967–73) *Young Children in Brief Separation Film Series*, Concord Video and Film Council, New York University Film Library. ▶page 62

Robertson, J. and Robertson, J. (1989) *Separation and the very young*, Free Association Books, London. ▶page 63

Rodin, J. (1991) 'Effects of pure sugar vs. mixed starch fructose loads on food intake', *Appetite*, vol. 17, pp. 213–19. ▶page 153

Roethlisberger, F.J. and Dickson, W.J. (1939) *Management and the worker*, Harvard University Press, Cambridge MA. ▶page 172

Rosenhan, D.L. (1969) 'Some origins of concern for others', in P. Mussen, J. Langer and M. Covington (eds) *Trends and Issues in Developmental Psychology*, Holt, Rhinehart and Winston, New York. ▶page 182

Rosenhan, D.L. (1973) 'On being sane in insane places', *Science*, vol. 179, pp. 250–8. ▶pages 126–127, 192

Rosenthal, R. and Fode, K.L. (1963) 'The effect of experimenter bias on the performance of the albino rat', *Behavioural Science*, vol. 8(3), pp. 183–9. ▶page 173

Rozanski, A., Blumental, J.A. and Kaplan, J. (1999) 'Impact of psychological factors on the pathogenisis of cardiovascular disease and implications for therapy', *Circulation*, vol. 99, pp. 2192–2217. ▶page 91

Ruderman, A.J. (1986) 'Dietary restraint: A theoretical and empirical review', *Psychological Bulletin*, vol. 99(2), pp. 247–62. ▶page 153

Ruhm, C.J. (2000) *Parental employment and child cognitive development*, National Bureau of Economic Research, NBER Working Paper no. 7666. ▶pages 74, 75

Russek, H. I. and Zohman, B. L. (1958) 'Relative significance of heredity, diet and occupational stress in CHD of young adults', *American Journal of Medical Sciences,* vol. 235, pp. 266–75. ▶page 91

Rutter, M. (1981) *Maternal deprivation reassessed,* second edition, Penguin, Harmondsworth. ▶page 66

Rutter, M. and The ERA Study Team (1998) 'Developmental catch-up and deficit following adoption after severe early privation', *Journal of Child Psychology and Psychiatry,* vol. 39, pp. 465–76. ▶pages 51, 61, 63, 64

Rymer, R. (1993) *Genie: Escape from a silent childhood,* Michael Joseph, London. ▶page 66

Savin, H.B. (1973) 'Professors and psychological researchers: Conflicting values in conflicting roles', *Cognition,* vol. 2, pp. 147–9. ▶page 187

Scarr. S. and Thompson, W. (1994) 'Effects of maternal employment and nonmaternal infant care on development at two and four years', *Early Development and Parenting,* vol. 3(2), pp. 113–23. ▶page 72

Schachter, S. (1951) 'Deviation, rejection and communication', *Journal of Abnormal and Social Psychology,* vol. 46, pp. 190–207. ▶page 166

Schafer, W. (1992) *Stress management for wellness,* second edition, Holt, Rinehart and Winston, Fort Worth TX. ▶page 98

Schaffer, H.R. (1998) *Making Decisions about Children,* Blackwell, Oxford. ▶page 77

Schaffer, H.R. and Emerson, P.E. (1964) 'The development of social attachments in infancy', *Monographs of the Society for Research in Child Development,* vol. 29(3), Serial No. 94. ▶pages 47, 57

Schaubroeck, J., Jones, J. R. and Xie, J. L. (2001) 'Individual differences in utilizing control to cope with job demands: Effects on susceptibility to infectious disease', *Journal of Applied Psychology,* vol. 86(2), pp. 265–78. ▶page 101

Schmolck, H., Buffalo, E. A. and Squire, L.R. (2000) 'Memory for serial order: A network model of the phonological loop and its timing', *Psychological Science,* vol. 11(1), pp. 39–45. ▶page 22

Schuler, H. (1982). *Ethical problems in psychological research,* Academic Press, New York. ▶page 191

Schweinhart, L.J., H.V. Barnes and D.P. Weikart. (1993) 'Significant Benefits: The High/Scope Perry Preschool Study through Age 27', *Monographs of the High/Scope Educational Research Foundation,* vol. 10, High/Scope Press, Ypsilanti MI. ▶page 77

Sebrechts, M.M., Marsh, R.L. and Seaman, J.G. (1989) 'Secondary memory and very rapid forgetting', *Memory and Cognition,* vol. 17, pp. 693–700. ▶page 6

Selye, H. (1936) 'A syndrome produced by diverse noucous agents', *Nature,* vol. 138, p. 32. ▶page 89

Selye, H. (1950) *Stress,* Acta, Montreal. ▶page 89

Shallice, T. (1967) 'Temporal summation and absolute brightness threshold', *British Journal of Mathematical and Statistical Psychology,* vol. 20, pp. 129–62. ▶page 17

Shepher, J. (1971) 'Mate selection among second generation Kibbutz adolescents and adults', *Archives of Sexual Behaviour,* vol. 1, pp. 293–307. ▶page 45

Sheridan, C.L. and King, K.G. (1972) 'Obedience to authority with an authentic victim', *Proceedings of the 80th Annual Convention of the American Psychological Association,* vol. 7, pp. 165–6. ▶page 183

Sheridan, C.L. and Radmacher, S.A. (1992) *Health Psychology,* Wiley. ▶page 89

Sherif, M. (1935) 'A study of some factors in perception', *Archives of Psychology,* vol. 27, no. 187. ▶page 166

Shirom, A. (1989) 'Burnout in work organisations', in C.L. Cooper and I. Robertson (eds) *International Review of Industrial and Organisational Psychology,* Wiley, Chichester. ▶page 101

Shrecker, E. (1994) *The Age of McCarthyism: A Brief History with Documents,* St. Martin's Press, Boston MA. ▶page 163

Simon, H.A. (1974) 'How big is a chunk?' *Science,* vol. 183, pp. 482–8. ▶page 7

Skeels, H. and Dye, H.B. (1939) 'A study of the effects of differential stimulation on mentally retarded children', *Proceedings and Addresses of the American Association on Mental Deficiency,* vol. 44, pp. 114–36. ▶pages 60, 62, 63

Skodak, M. and Skeels, H. (1949) 'A final follow-up study of 100 adopted children', *Journal of Genetic Psychology,* vol. 75, pp. 85–125. ▶pages 62–3, 66

Smith, P. and Bond, M.H. (1993) *Social psychology across cultures: Analysis and perspectives,* Harvester Wheatsheaf, New York. ▶pages 167, 177

Soverow, J. (1997) 'Thinking about disease', *Progressive Review,* November. ▶page 153

Sperling. G. (1960) 'The information available in brief visual presentations', *Psychological Monographs,* vol. 74 (whole no. 498), pp. 1–29. ▶page 9

Spitz, R.A. and Wolf, K.M. (1946) 'Anaclitic depression', *Psychoanalytic Study of the Child,* vol. 2, pp. 313–42. ▶pages 63, 66

Squire, L.R., Ojemann, J.G., Miezin, F.M., Petersen, S.E., Videen, T.O. and Raichle, M.E. (1992) 'Activation of the hippocampus in normal humans: A functional anatomical study of memory', in Milner (1966). ▶page 9

Sroufe, L. A., Carlson, E. A., Levy, A. K. and Egeland, B. (1999) 'Implications of attachment theory for developmental psychopathology', *Development and Psychopathology,* vol. 11, pp. 1–13. ▶page 56

Stone, S.V., Dembroski, T.M., Costa, P.T., Jr. and McDougall, J.M. (1990) 'Gender differences in cardiovascular reactivity', *Journal of Behavioural Medicine,* vol. 13, pp. 137–57. ▶page 104

Sui-Wah, L. (1989) 'Anorexia nervosa and Chinese food', *British Journal of Psychiatry,* vol. 155, p. 568. ▶page 149

Sulin, R.A. and Dooling, D.J. (1974) 'Intrusion of a thematic idea in retention of prose', *Journal of experimental psychology,* vol. 103, pp. 255–62. ▶page 28

Szasz, T.S. (1972) *The manufacture of madness,* Routledge and Kegan Paul, London. ▶page 136

Szasz, T.S. (1974) *Ideology and insanity,* Penguin, Harmondsworth. ▶page 129

Takahashi, K. (1990) 'Are the key assumptions of the "strange situation" universal?' *Human Development,* vol. 33, pp. 23–30. ▶page 53

Taylor, S.E., Klein, L.C., Lewis, B.P., Grunewald, T.L., Gurung, R.A.R. and Updegraff, J.A. (2000) 'Biobehavioral responses to stress in females: Tend-and-Befriend, Not Fight-or-Flight', *Psychological Review,* vol. 107(3). ▶pages 104, 105

Temoshok, L. (1987) 'Personality, coping style, emotions and cancer: Towards an integrative model', *Cancer Surveys,* vol. 6, pp. 545–67 (supplement). ▶page 103

Teti, D. M., Gelfand, D. M., Messinger, D. S. and Isabella, R. (1995) 'Maternal depression and the quality of early attachment: An examination of infants, preschoolers and their mothers', *Developmental Psychology,* vol. 31(3), pp. 364–76. ▶page 51

Thomas, A. and Chess, S.B. (1977) *Temperament and development,* Mazel, New York. ▶page 51

Tizard, B. (1979) 'Language at home and at school', in C.B. Cazden and D. Harvey (eds) *Language in early childhood education,* National Association for the Education of Young Children, Washington DC. ▶page 77

Topal, J., Miklosi, A., Csanyi, V. and Doka, A. (1998) 'Antal attachment behavior in dogs (*Canis familiaris*): A new application of Ainsworth's (1969) Strange Situation Test', *Journal of Comparative Psychology,* vol. 112(3), pp. 219–29. ▶page 51

Triseliotis, J. (1984) 'Identity and security in adoption and long-term fostering', *Early Child Development and Care,* vol. 15(2–3), pp. 149–70. ▶page 66

Trojano, L. and Grossi, D. (1995) 'Phonological and lexical coding in verbal short-term memory and learning', *Brain and Cognition,* vol. 21, pp. 336–54. ▶page 11

Tronick, E.Z., Morelli, G.A. and Ivey, P.K. (1992) 'The Efe forager infant and toddler's pattern of social relationships: Multiple and simultaneous', *Developmental Psychology,* vol. 28, pp. 568–77. ▶page 53

Tulving, E. and Psotka, J. (1971) 'Retroactive inhibition in free recall: Inaccessibility of information available in the memory store', *Journal of Experimental Psychology,* vol. 87, pp. 1–8. ▶page 19

Tyler, S.W., Hertel, P.T., McCallum, M.C. and Ellis, H.C. (1979) 'Cognitive effort and memory', *Journal of Experimental Psychology, Learning, Memory and Cognition,* vol. 5, pp. 607–17. ▶page 12

Underwood, J. (1957) 'Interference and forgetting', *Psychological Review,* vol. 64, pp. 49–60. ▶page 19

Van Avermaet, E. (1996) 'Social influence in small groups', in Hewstone, W. Stroebe and G.M. Stephenson (eds), *Introduction to social psychology: A European perspective,* second edition, Blackwell, Oxford. ▶page 170

Van IJzendoorn, M.H. and Kroonenberg, P.M. (1988) 'Cross-cultural patterns of attachment: A meta-analysis of the Strange Situation', *Child Development,* vol. 59, pp. 147–56. ▶page 52–53

Vandell, D.L., Henderson, V.K. and Wilson, K.S. (1988) 'A longitudinal study of children with day-care experiences of varying quality', *Child Development,* vol. 59(5), pp. 1286–92. ▶page 77

Vanderlinden, J., Norre, J. and Vandereycken, W. (1992) *A Practical Guide to the Treatment of Bulimia,* Brunner Mazel, New York. ▶page 153

Violata C.and Russell C. (1994) Effects of non-maternal care on child development: a meta-analysis of published research, paper presented at 55th annual convention of the Canadian Psychological Association, Penticon BC. ▶page 77

Vögele, C., Jarvis, A. and Cheeseman, K. (1997) 'Anger suppression, reactivity and hypertension risk: Gender makes a difference', *Annals of Behavioural Medicine,* vol. 19, pp. 61–9. ▶page 104

Waganaar, W.A. and Groeneweg, J. (1990) 'The memory of concentration camp survivors', *Applied Cognitive Psychology,* vol. 4, pp. 77–87. ▶pages 6–7 overmatter, 27

Wagstaff, G. (2002) 'Eyewitness Testimony', *Psychology Review,* vol. 9, p.1. ▶page 32

Walsh, B.T., Wilson, G.O. and Leob, K.L. (1997) 'Medication and psychotherapy in the treatment of bulimia nervosa', *American Journal of Psychiatry,* vol. 154, pp. 523–31. ▶page 151

Watson, J.B. and Rayner, R. (1920) 'Conditioned emotional reactions', *Journal of Experimental Psychology,* vol. 3, pp. 1–14. ▶page 192

Waugh, N.C. and Norman, D. (1965) 'Primary memory', *Psychological Review,* vol. 72, pp. 89–104. ▶page 17

Westermarck, E. (1891) *The history of human marriage,* Macmillan, London. ▶page 45

Wiebe, D.J. (1991) 'Hardiness and stress modification: A test of proposed mechanisms', *Journal of Personality and Social Psychology,* vol. 64, pp. 491–9. ▶page 115

Williams, J.E., Paton, C.C., Siegler, I.C., Eigenbrodt, M.L., Nieto, F.J. and Tyroler, H.A. (2000) 'Anger proneness predicts coronary heart disease risk: Prospective analysis from the atherosclerosis risk in communities (ARIC study)' *Circulation,* vol. 101(17), pp. 2034–9. ▶page 91

Williams, L.M. (1994) 'Recall of childhood tauma: A prospective study of women's memories of childhood abuse', *Journal of Consulting and Clinical Psychology,* vol. 62, pp. 1167–76. ▶page 23

Williams, T.P. and Sogon, S. (1984) 'Group composition and conforming behaviour in Japanese students', *Japanese Psychological Research,* vol. 26, pp. 231–34. ▶page 165

Wright, D.B. (1993) 'Recall of Hillsborough disaster over time: Systematic biases of 'flashbulb' memories' *Applied Cognitive Psychology,* vol. 7, pp. 129—38. ▶page 22

Wynn, V.E. and Logie, R.H. (1998) 'The veracity of long-term memories: Did Bartlett get it right?' *Applied Cognitive Psychology,* vol. 12, pp. 1–20. ▶pages 27, 29

Yuille, J.C. and Cutshall, J.L. (1986) 'A case study of eyewitness testimony of a crime', *Journal of Applied Psychology,* vol. 71, pp. 291–301. ▶page 33

Zigler, E. and Styfco, S.J. (1993) 'Using research and theory to justify and inform Head Start expansion', *Social Policy Report, Society for Research in Child Development,* vol. 7, pp. 1–21. ▶page 75

Zimbardo, P.G. (1969) 'The human choice: Individuation, reason and order versus deindividuation, impulse and chaos', *Nebraska Symposium on Motivation,* vol. 17, pp. 237–307. ▶page 177

Zimbardo, P.G. (2001) 'Opposing terrorism by understanding the human capacity for evil', *APA Monitor on Psychology,* vol. 32(10). ▶page 181

Zimbardo, P.G., Banks, P.G., Haney, C. and Jaffe, D. (1973) 'Pirandellian prison: The mind is a formidable jailor', *New York Times Magazine,* 8 April, pp. 38–60. ▶pages 186–7, 193, 195

Index

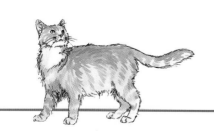